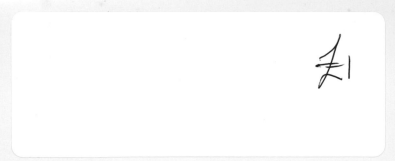

*1

THE
ILLUSTRATED ENCYCLOPEDIA
OF
WORLD
MOTOR RACING

WHSMITH

EXCLUSIVE
·BOOKS·

Foreword

To my mind there is no sport in the world that can equal motor racing for skill and excitement. One minute you're riding high — the most exhilarating feeling — and the next you might be cast down, justifiably or unjustifiably.

Loving racing as I do, it makes me sad, even angry, to see this marvellous sport suffer from a lack of coverage in the printed media. To me, it is the sport of the twentieth century. Millions of television viewers think so too, and they help account for its tremendous following as it approaches its centenary.

Many publications have emerged — numerous knowledgeable, many less so. But the amount of support by the national press in Britain, even at times of supreme performances by both British drivers and British machines, has been negligible. Why is this? How could the historic successes achieved by such persons as Tony Vandervell with the Vanwall, Jaguar, and subsequently companies such as Lotus, Tyrrell, McLaren and Williams, pass by with often just the odd by-line in the Press?

I think the answer is ignorance. Ignorance of a sport that shows the very best balance of all the attributes that a top sportsman requires — competitiveness, intelligence, sensitivity, complete coordination and fitness — coupled with a demonstration of the best of the latest technology within the automotive world. This technology, which ultimately benefits the man in the street, has in recent years reached levels that would have been unthought of just a few years ago, mainly through a close association with aerospace technology and the intense competition between rival manufacturers. They are spurred on, not only by the wonderful opportunities to inspire their engineers, but also by the publicity opportunities of worldwide television coverage. This coverage has also provided, with its attraction to sponsors, the vast financial resources needed to fund present-day motor racing.

I spent some of my racing years in an environment which was somewhat different — Italy, where a national fervour takes place should an Italian car succeed, or an Italian driver, or for that matter any nationality that they accept as being one of their own. You can do no wrong one moment and you can be subjected to quite vitriolic and unfair criticism the next, but the feeling is there, and I for one certainly do not believe there is anything wrong in showing a bit of patriotism.

It is therefore extremely pleasing to see (bearing in mind that the authors' opinons are their own) a book such as The Illustrated Encyclopedia of World Motor Racing *— a book which can be used as a further reference by the professionals or, perhaps more importantly, the beginner or casual acquaintance with motor racing who just occasionally sees it on television. With the aid of this book, they will be able to understand that much more about what they are seeing and so spark a deeper interest and create yet another real enthusiast — and, one never knows, perhaps a future World Champion.*

John Surtees

House Editor Joey Chapter
Editor Jeremy Coulter
Art Editor Gordon Robertson
Picture Research Moira McIlroy
Production Craig Chubb

Produced exclusively for WH Smith Limited
by Marshall Cavendish Books Limited
58 Old Compton Street
London W1V 5PA

Concept, design and production by
Marshall Cavendish Books Limited

First printing 1990
1 2 3 4 5 6 7 8 9   99 98 97 96 95 94 93 92 91 90

© Marshall Cavendish Limited 1990

Typeset by J&L Composition Ltd, Filey, North Yorkshire
Printed in Hong Kong

ISBN 1 85435 324 1

Contents

Motor Racing 1895–1990

Man is a competitive animal. No matter where and no matter when, one of a group has to prove that he is the best. Sometimes this is a personal contest but sometimes animals or machines are also involved. Just as soon as motor cars were invented, therefore, competitions followed on. The world's first recorded motoring competition was held in France in 1894. The *Concours des Voitures sans Chevaux* (literally, 'a test for horseless carriages') was promoted by a newspaper, *Le Petit Journal*, and ended with a reliability run from Paris to Rouen and back. According to the regulations it was meant to be a trial, but most competitors made a race of it. On that occasion the fastest time between two cities was set by Compte de Dion whose steam-powered device averaged 11.6mph (18.6km/h).

The start of the 1899 Tour de France as portrayed in a French journal of the times

In less than a century the world of motor racing has developed, from a standing start, into something whose technology is as advanced as anything found in space. The Victorian pioneers could have had no idea of the speeds, the forces and the commercial pressures which would develop in the future.

In the early days, of course, top speeds were around 20mph (32km/h), brakes and tyre grip were almost non-existent, and the 'cars' were crude in the extreme. Even so, man's competitive spirit was aroused, and everybody was trying just as hard as they do today.

Town to town races

In the beginning there were no special circuits, so motor racing events were held on public roads. It might have been anti-social, and it might have been dangerous, but no one worried at the time. Until the danger was realized, the classic motor race was a long-distance dash from one place to another — this was the period of the town-to-town race.

The world's first official motor race was staged in France, in July 1895, over the formidable distance of 732 miles, from Paris to Bordeaux and back. Conditions, of course, were indescribable, for the roads were still unsealed, which meant that every passing vehicle set up clouds of dust, pot-holes soon developed, and safety features were non-existent.

The hero of the first event, unquestionably, was Emile Levassor, who drove a 4hp Panhard et Levassor car, without rest *and* without a relief driver to help him. To win the race, he was at the wheel for 48¾ hours, of which only 22 minutes were spent in involuntary stops for repairs or wheel changes. The brave Frenchman covered the distance at 15mph (24km/h), and arrived back in Paris eight hours ahead of the next competitor!

This was only the start. In the next five years competition intensified, speeds rocketed — and the first serious accidents followed. The self-appointed governing body of world motor sport was set up in Paris, the result being that all early motor races were held in that country.

In 1896 the big test was Paris–Marseilles–Paris, in 1898 it was Paris–Amsterdam–Paris, and in 1900 it was Paris–Toulouse. Race distances were always 800 miles (1287km) and more, but average speeds rose to no less than 40mph (64km/h).

It was magnificent, it was heroic, but it was also incredibly dangerous. The miracle was that town-to-town races survived for eight years before public opinion turned against them. The crunch came in 1903, when the Paris–Madrid race was stopped at Bordeaux. On a hot and dusty summer's day, a series of accidents resulted in no fewer than 15 deaths to competitors and to spectators. The cars were ignominiously towed to the railway station behind horses, and the sport was in disgrace. The hero of that black day, however, was Gabriel, whose 60hp Mors averaged an incredible 65.3mph (105km/h).

Gordon Bennett — circuit racing

Even before 1903, the authorities had invented circuit racing, though these circuits were long loops of public highway, closed for the occasions. The spark came from James Gordon Bennett, who offered a trophy to the Automobile Club de France for a competition between teams nominated by various national clubs.

The first 'Gordon Bennett' race was held in 1900, between teams entered by France and the USA, and the last in 1905, when teams were entered from France, Italy, Germany, England and the USA. These were the precursors of Grand Prix racing as we know it, for on each occasion rigid rules were applied to the engines and weight of the cars, to make the sport as equal as possible.

In the meantime other countries, notably the USA, Italy and Great Britain, had started promoting motor races. Town-to-town races had disappeared, but long-distance trials (which eventually became rallies) were invented instead.

In the vibrant early years of the twentieth century, each country developed motor racing in its own way — the French staying faithful to races organized on long 'natural' circuits in the open countryside, the USA on closed tracks such as Indianapolis, the British first on 'natural' circuits like the Isle of Man, but soon on the new Brooklands banked circuit, the Italians on demanding circuits such as the Targa Florio in Sicily.

Grand Prix racing — the first years

By the 1980s Formula 1 Grand Prix racing was a world-wide sport, embracing 16 races and several continents. Before World War 1, however, there was only one Grand Prix — *the* Grand Prix — every year, this always being held in France. The Germans soon promoted their own race, the Kaiser Prize — but it was not until 1921 that another 'Grand Prix' — the Italian — was added to the list.

Grand Prix racing, therefore, was a very restricted business for some years, and the reason for this was straightforward enough. World motor racing was administered by the French, Grand Prix racing was invented by the French as a natural progression from the Gordon Bennett racing, and it seemed to be devised for the benefit of French manufacturers at first.

Only six true Grands Prix were held between 1906 and 1914, and the technical rules changed on every occasion. Administrators were constantly searching for a 'Formula' which would make it possible for more cars to be competitive, but this was applied in several different ways. The first race, in 1906, set a maximum car weight, the 1907 event a fuel economy limit, the 1908 race limited engine piston area and car minimum weight, the 1912 race set maximum dimensions for the car body, the 1913 race required fuel economy and minimum weight limits, while the 1914 race set a maximum engine size. Confused? So was everyone else.

As an annual event, however, the Grand Prix at least allowed the world's most ambitious manufacturers to compete on level terms, even though those terms changed so often, and so confusingly. It was an event where reliable speed *and* endurance counted for more than flashing acceleration and delicate technology.

The pre-Great War Grands Prix were utterly different from more modern events. Today we expect to see Nigel Mansell, Ayrton Senna and Alain Prost in tiny cars which can exceed 180mph (290km/h), performing with surgical precision for 90 minutes at a time — in 1906 the first-ever Grand Prix occupied two days, the cars looked big and were heavy to drive, and the winner was at the wheel for more than 12 hours.

Let us not forget that punctures and wheel-changing were accepted hazards, and that drivers like Renault's F. Szisz also had 'on board' riding mechanics who tackled running repairs and wheel changes as well as re-fuelling, pumping up the fuel pressure, and urging on the driver to better efforts. At the end of a Grand Prix, in those days, the driver

Above: Brooklands in the late Thirties with a good crowd watching the cars competing on the smaller road circuit, rather than the main oval banked track

was exhausted, so Szisz's first victory, at 63mph (101km/h) over a circuit near Le Mans, by 32 minutes from his nearest rival, was a stupendous achievement.

Although costs were high, the original Grand Prix attracted 32 starters (of whom only 11 finished), and in the following year no fewer than 38 cars, from six nations, appeared. This was the year in which 'national' colours were imposed — green for the British, red for the Italians, blue for the French, white for the Germans, yellow for the Belgians, white-and-red for American cars, and red-and-yellow for Swiss machines.

In the first three years the French won once, the Italians (Fiat) once, and the Germans (Mercedes) once, which may explain why Grand Prix racing then went into abeyance until 1912! That was the year in which Peugeot produced the world's first successful twin overhead camshaft engine (and won the Grand Prix, at 68.45mph/ 110.20km/h), but it was in 1914 that Mercedes chilled everyone by entering a massive team of 4½-litre cars at the Lyons

circuit, dominating practice, and taking a 1-2-3 result in the race itself.

This was the approach to motor racing which made Mercedes (later Mercedes-Benz) feared, and often hated, by rival teams. It was clinical, it was efficient, it was purposeful and, somehow, it was completely joyless. It was no wonder that, over the years, many came to respect the German approach to motor sport but few came to admire the way it was done.

Voiturette racing

Once Grand Prix racing, which was the summit of the motor racing pyramid, had become established, it was time to invent other formulae, and for some years there was a 'Division 2' for what became known as 'voiturettes'. Such cars invariably had smaller engines, and less performance, than the Grand Prix cars of the day, but they were cheaper to build, and the racing of these models attracted a lot of attention from sporting manufacturers.

Voiturette racing, in fact, was dominant in Europe for a few years, bringing fame and fortune to marques such as Delage, Hispano-Suiza, Peugeot, Vauxhall and Sunbeam. After World War 1 there always seemed to be a lot of 'junior formula' racing for such cars, and many well-known racing marques (notably Bugatti and ERA) came to prominence by this route.

Many years later, of course, the spirit and heritage of voiturette racing was passed on to the other junior formulae such as Formula 2 and Formula 3.

Brooklands — and the British scene

In Britain there was no lack of enthusiasm for motor racing, but there was always one major problem — a distinct lack of places to hold events. Unlike other European countries, mainland Britain's legal system did not allow roads to be closed for competitive motor sport, which meant that there was no way of matching French and Italian enterprise. Some early races — notably the TT and the Gordon Bennett events — got round this by being promoted in the Isle of Man and Ireland, where the law was different.

It was to eliminate this problem, and also to provide Britain's fledgling industry with somewhere to test its new model cars at speed, and in safety, that Hugh Locke-King built a large banked concrete circuit in the grounds of his home in Surrey, calling it Brooklands. His neighbours hated it at first, but soon came to terms, so from 1907, when it opened, until 1939, when World War 2 broke out, Brooklands was the home of British motor racing. It also doubled as an airfield, and by the end of its life the Vickers concern was building military aeroplanes in factories in the grounds.

Brooklands had, and still has, its supporters, but in many ways it ensured that British cars, and British drivers, lagged behind their European competitors for many years. Not only was the atmosphere extremely class conscious at all times ('The right crowd, and no crowding . . .' was one advertising slogan), but in almost every case the organizers attempted to provide close racing by imposing handicaps on every car.

Many cars were built at Brooklands, raced at Brooklands, repaired at Brooklands, and rarely visited another circuit during their competitive career. The result was that most cars which raced at Brooklands were 'specials', specifically designed to excel in the short sprints which made up most of the events. Because most had crude suspension, 'short-life' engines and lightweight construction, many were uncompetitive — usually ineligible too — for events in other countries.

On the other hand, some magnificent machines were built, purely to be the fastest cars of all, and a series of exciting lap record attempts were witnessed in the 1930s, the result being that John Cobb's Napier-Railton (a machine which also took many long-distance endurance records at other locations) lapped the high-speed concrete bowl at 143.44mph (230.83km/h), achieving up to 160mph (257km/h) on the straights.

For more than 30 years Brooklands hosted a multitude of races throughout the year, with various clubs using as many variations on the basic circuitry as possible. Only rarely were long events held — the 200 Miles race, the Double-Twelve endurance event and the flat-out 500 Miles race being the most famous — and on only two occasions was the British GP held there.

Well before 1939, when the last race was held on this track, the owners had built an extra 'road' circuit (called the Campbell circuit) to make the sport more realistic, but by the end of the decade all the facilities had started to crumble, and enthusiasts were turning to other British circuits, notably at Donington Park, in Derbyshire.

The great sports car events

By 1914 the world's fastest sports cars were very reliable, so it was inevitable that a number of long-distance races evolved to test their endurance. Even though the cars generally carried open styles at first, which made life cold and blustery for the drivers, some of these races lasted for 24 hours. Except for events later held at circuits like Brooklands and the Nürburgring, these were usually run on roads normally used by the public.

Open road races asked a lot of drivers, and cars. Not only were road races usually held on bumpier surfaces than tracks, but they were festooned with all manner of natural hazards. The very best not only featured potholes, ditches, bridges and tunnels, but towns and villages, railway level crossings and tramways. Added to that was the unpredictability of spectators and animals, and the sheer challenge of such races could be imagined. It was no wonder that the most successful sports cars were large, heavy and solidly engineered. Brute force, if not ignorance, was all important, it being thought more vital to have a lot of power than to have a light car with good wind-cheating properties.

The first major long-distance race was the Targa Florio, first run in 1906, which took place on a lengthy and sinuous open road circuit in Sicily. It was so demanding, and so difficult to learn, that average speeds rarely rose above 50mph (80km/h). The circuit was eventually adjudged too long, and too difficult, and was replaced by a shorter loop — but not that much shorter, for lap times took ages to get down to less than 60 minutes!

The most famous of all, no question, was the French Le Mans 24-Hour race, first held in 1923, and really a spiritual descendant of the early Grands Prix. Held on a closed circuit to the south of Le Mans itself, the 'Circuit of the Sarthe' was fast, and featured one very long straight where cars could reach their ultimate velocity, and hold that speed for well over two minutes.

Like other races of the day, the Le Mans event used public roads especially closed for the occasion, these roads often being gravel strewn, with crumbling edges, the sort which taxed drivers' skills, and a tyre company's endeavours, to the limit. At night, and particularly just before dawn, fog was a problem. Not only that, but the organizers seemed to change their regulations every year; at one stage the open cars had to spend an early period of the race with hoods erect.

It was at Le Mans that the British Bentley concern made its name as a great sports car in the Twenties, while in the Thirties Alfa Romeo and Bugatti made most of the headlines. Average speeds rose over 70mph (113 km/h) in the Twenties to well over 80mph (128km/h) in the Thirties, the first 'streamlined' bodies were introduced in the Thirties,

Below: The start of the first Le Mans 24 Hours race in 1923, won by a French Chenard & Walcker

and speeds along the great Mulsanne straight soon rose to 120mph (193km/h) and beyond.

The most charismatic long-distance race of all, however, was the Italian Mille Miglia event, a 1000-mile (1609km) dash around Italy's fastest roads, where the start and finish was located in Brescia and the half-way point was always Rome, but where the route changed in detail from year to year. This race catered for all types of car, large and small, super-sporting or merely brave touring. The slowest cars started first, but the fastest Alfa Romeos and Bugattis traditionally started at around dawn, to be faced with a day-long dash around the nation.

In the late Twenties and early Thirties, before speeds rose dangerously, the winner of the Mille Miglia took up to 14 hours to complete the race, usually driving the whole distance without rest, without food, and with no relief except for a quick stretch at refuelling points dotted around the route. No wonder this was the most *machismo* of events, where true Italan heros were made and confirmed, and no wonder Italy was the country which bred the best cars for this crazy sort of flat-out marathon.

All other major sports car races, even those held at the German Nürburgring, or the Belgian Spa circuits, paled into insignificance, and no British effort came close. The Tourist Trophy and the Irish Grand Prix were good races, and attracted fine entries, but they could not compete in charisma, scenery, length or character.

Brooklands, in its own way , tried its best, but not even the 'Double Twelve' events (24-hour races, held in two 12-hour sections on consecutive days) could make an impact. The problem with the Double Twelve, as with almost every other Brooklands event, was that handicaps were imposed on various cars, handicaps being based on engine size, power output and — sometimes — the reputation of an individual machine.

In the late Twenties, therefore, this meant that the fastest Bentleys were often obliged to start a long way behind the snarling hordes of MGs and Austin Sevens, and spent two days trying to catch up. In 1930, for instance, the winning Bentley averaged 86.68mph (139.49km/h) for 24 hours, though the third place (on handicap!) Riley Nine could only manage 69.96mph (112.58km/h). What with this, and the continual visits to the pits for fuel, new tyres and driver changes, it was no wonder that the poor spectator was confused.

Indianapolis, USA

Early in the twentieth century motor racing took hold in North America, with many events held on board circuits, or other temporary facilities. Promoters realized that American spectators wanted to see thrills and spills, lots of starts, finishes and close racing — and this was what was provided.

The American spectator, no matter what the sport, soon gets bored unless the action is varied, and continuous. This explains why long-distance events were few and far between, and why sports car racing never became popular.

It was as early as 1911 that a promotor hit on the right mixture of speed, spectacle and 'show business', and produced the original Indianapolis 500-mile race. The format was simple. At Indianapolis, Indiana, a permanent circuit, with a lap distance of 2½ miles (4km), was erected, and surrounded by spectator grandstands, most of which were open to the elements. There were two long, and two short, straights, linked by long and slightly banked 90-degree curves. The whole track, at first, was surfaced in bricks — the result being that it was nicknamed 'The Brickyard'.

Right from the start, Indianapolis stuck to its own rules, and soon set up its own traditions (the race was always held on Memorial Day, whatever day of the week that fell; no women were ever allowed in the pitlane, not even if they owned a car which was racing; the race was always stopped if it rained . . .). Cars needed to be strong, and specialized, if only because the 500 was a flat-out 200-lap affair, where the bravest drivers only needed to slow down for pit stops, where they took on fuel, and changed tyres.

The fact that the cars did not handle well, and that their advanced technology was almost entirely centred around the engine, was not thought to be important. Year after year the racing was fast, furious, close, and the high-speed accidents which followed were usually accepted as inevitable.

By 1919 the winning speed had risen to 87.95mph (141.53km/h), but the fastest lap had already exceeded 100mph (161km/h). Famous names like Offenhauser and Miller came to prominence at Indy; drivers like Tommy Milton, Louis Meyer, Wilbur Shaw and Mauri Rose became superstars. It was a race which the Americans kept to themselves, for there would be few successes by European-built cars until the Forties, while Jim Clark was the first European driver to win the event — in 1965.

Grand Prix racing in the Twenties

In the Twenties, racing cars of all types changed considerably. Inspired by changes to the rules, and by rapid advances in engine technology, engines became smaller but more efficient, cars became lighter and more nimble, yet speeds at every circuit continued to rise.

Some aspects of racing car design, however, were still crude and undeveloped. In particular there appeared to be little understanding of aerodynamics, no great advance in roadholding or chassis design, while tyres were durable but not at all sophisticated.

The governing body of world motor sport, the AIACR, which was based in Paris, seemed constantly to be worried about the way that racing cars became faster and faster, for in the Twenties each new Grand Prix

formula catered for smaller cars than before. For 1921, GP engines were restricted to 3 litres, for the 1922–1925 period they were reduced to 2 litres, and in 1926–1927 they were further reduced in size, to a mere 1.5 litres. Each year too, it seemed, other piffling restrictions were imposed — minimum weights one time, maximum dimensions another, the need to carry two occupants at all times — yet the most resourceful engineers always rose to the challenge, with costs and complications following suit.

In this period famous marques like Fiat set the standards, but new marques such as Bugatti, Alfa Romeo, Delage and Sunbeam rose to prominence and success. The most important technical development of the period (first tried in sports car racing by Mercedes), introduced to Grand Prix racing by Fiat in 1923, was the supercharger. This was so unexpected that the AIACR had never even considered it when defining the latest formulae!

Supercharging had originally been developed for aero-engines, to allow them to breathe more deeply in the thin air of high altitudes; when this forced-induction method was applied to motor racing engines on the ground it immediately helped produce a lot more power.

At a stroke, engine builders could produce units which were small, complex but extremely powerful, and it meant that speeds once again rocketed upwards. In Grand Prix racing, the takeover by supercharged engines was complete, and until 1939 almost every major event was won by a car of this type — unless, that is, the regulations specifically banned their use.

The same phenomenon, if not quite as abrupt, was observed with turbochargers in Formula 1 in the Eighties — once turbo engines had been made reliable, they rapidly elbowed normally-aspirated engines right out of the limelight until the regulations were changed.

Although the American Duesenberg 3-litre car came over to Europe in 1921, with Indianapolis hero Jimmy Murphy winning the Grand Prix against all the odds, early and mid-Twenties racing was henceforth dominated by French, Italian and British manufacturers. Fiat set all the standards in 1922 and 1923, though Britain's Sunbeam company (which had hired a Fiat designer to design its new car!) soon matched them, and by 1924 Alfa Romeo also had a winning car.

By the mid-Twenties there were several Grands Prix every year, which helped to make up a racing 'circus', with the French event eventually settling at Montlhery and the Italian at Monza, both being high-speed permanent circuits. A few years later Germany joined in, after thousands of labourers had helped to build the long and twisting Nürburgring circuit in the Eifel mountains to the west of the Rhine valley.

This was the period, too, in which the first

two British GPs were held, both of them at Brooklands, both of them with various artificial corners being built up to slow down the cars, and both of them conclusively won by Delage. Because events went on for hours, and because the racing was not at all close, the British spectators hated it all, so after two years the project was abandoned. There would be no more top-quality GP racing in the UK for another decade.

As engines became smaller, they also became more complex, and before long one needed at least an eight-cylinder unit, with supercharging, to achieve success. Alfa Romeo's P2, Bugatti's Type 35 and the 1926 Delage all used engines of this type. The 1924–1925 Delage, however, went one better, for it had an amazingly complex 2-litre V12 unit, which produced 195bhp in supercharged form in 1925, and helped Delage to become Champions of Europe.

The typical Grand Prix car of this period, therefore, had a simple ladder-style chassis frame, with a complex supercharged engine 'up front' driving the rear wheels, with a beam front axle and a solid rear axle. Suspension was by short and very stiff leaf springs, wheels were high and narrow, and there were large but relatively ineffective drum brakes all round.

Bodies were slim, elegant, but narrow '1½-seaters', but no attempt was made to cheat the wind. Behind the seats the tail, usually pointed, or at least very slim, was almost full of fuel tank.

Even in 1923, when Fiat's pioneering super-charged engine produced less than 140bhp, Salamano's car won the Italian GP, at Monza, at 91.06mph (146.54km/h), and top speeds were already back to 130mph (209km/h) and more. When the AIACR imposed smaller engines (1.5 litres instead of 2 litres) for 1926 and 1927, it reduced speeds for a while — but not for long. In 1927 the winning Fiat's race average speed at Monza was no less than 94.57mph (152.19km/h), helped along by an engine producing about 180bhp, this being one of the very first racing engines to develop more than 100bhp/litre. All this was achieved at high expense, mostly because the cars were becoming very complex indeed.

At the end of 1927, therefore, teams like Fiat withdrew from the sport. As that great self-styled doyen of Grand Prix racing, Laurence Pomeroy Junior, once wrote:

'Within two years, Grand Prix racing fell from one of its recurrent peaks to an absolute rock-bottom.'

The Land Speed Record

Almost as soon as motor sport had got started, there was an urge to see who, and what, could be fastest of all. Thus it was that in 1898 the Jeantaud car reached the staggering speed of 39.24mph (63.14km/h), that Jenatzy's special reached 65.79mph (105.87km/h) only a year later, and that Rigolly's Gobron-Brillie reached no less

than 103.55mph (166.64km/h) in 1904.

In a mere six years, what became known as the 'Land Speed Record' (the fastest straight line speed in the world) had already been pushed to unimaginable heights. But this was only the beginning. Once the sponsors — particularly the oil companies — realized that 'fastest' could mean good publicity for their wares, the rush to encourage larger, more powerful and ever faster machines began.

Today's Land Speed Record (held by Richard Noble's Thrust 2) stands at 633.648 mph (1019.729km/h), but in 1983 his valiant efforts were almost ignored by the world's press. In the Twenties and Thirties, by comparison, the efforts of personalities like Henry Segrave, Parry Thomas, Sir Malcolm Campbell and John Cobb were reported at great length.

Up to 1914, flat-out speeds could be achieved in a relatively confined space but by 1924, when Eldridge's massive Fiat achieved 146mph (235km/h) on a public road at Arpajon, the world's fastest men were looking for wide-open spaces. From 1924 to 1939, the ever-increasing speeds were achieved on stretches of sand or salt, with Daytona beach and the Bonneville Salt Flats (both in the USA) being chosen time and time again.

In fifteen years the Land Speed record was pushed up at a phenomenal rate. In 1924 the level stood at a mere 143.3mph (230.6km/h), which was not much more than a Grand Prix car could achieve, if suitably geared, but by 1939 it had been raised to a monumental 369.7mph (594.9km/h), which was almost as fast as could be achieved by a specially prepared aeroplane.

Such records, of course, could only be set by single-purpose machines, huge monsters usually powered by aero-engines, with tyres which needed renewing after every run, and on specially-prepared tracks of up to 15 miles (24km) in length. Even so, these were the cars which pushed aerodynamic knowledge and technique to its outer limits and which, as far as the public was concerned, brought great prestige to the country involved.

It was the right sort of sport for a particular period, but its popularity died away completely after World War 2. Like all such ultra-specialized sports it was only available to the wealthiest and most heavily-supported teams. After the war there was much less interest in raising a record which the British seemed to have made their own, and the Land Speed record was not to be attacked again properly until the Sixties.

The Depression hits motor racing

In the late Twenties the world's economies slid into depression, and at the same time the world of motor racing seemed to go into decline; there had to be a connection somewhere, this most probably being a shortage of 'optional' money, and sponsors, to back the ongoing improvement of the cars.

For the next few years the sport of Grand Prix racing seemed to go into suspended animation, for some factory teams withdrew from the sport, while the same makes and models of cars which had been winning in 1927 flogged on, with varied results, until the early Thirties. There seemed to be a different set of rules for every season (and then not always applied to all events), and the

factories gave up developing radically new cars. Sports car racing, too, was badly hit, though Mercedes-Benz and Alfa Romeo both developed new cars in the early Thirties which made a fast sport even faster.

From 1928 to 1933, Grand Prix racing was dominated by three makes — Bugatti, Alfa Romeo, and a new Italian company called Maserati. Although each marque produced powerful new engines (and Bugatti finally admitted that the twin overhead camshaft layout was an improvement on its original layout), each stayed faithful to old-style chassis and styles.

The 1928 GP formula imposed a minimum weight and a minimum race distance (but no limit to engine sizes or types), while in 1929 and 1930 minimum dimensions *and* fuel consumption limits were added. For the next three years, effectively, *Formula Libre* reigned supreme, though the AIACR tried to impose a minimum race duration of 10 hours in 1931, five to 10 hours in 1932, and a minimum race distance of 500 kilometres (310 miles) in 1933. Was it any wonder that interest fell away?

At that time a designer's philosophy was to provide super-stiff suspension, but a frame which was positively flimsy by later standards. The result was that cars leapt from bump to bump, skittered all over the road under braking or hard acceleration, and needed complicated brake linkages to ensure that chassis flexing did not unbalance the systems. The latest rules, at least, banned riding mechanics, so this was the time when the first true single-seater racing cars were produced.

In 1928 the only true regular 'works' team

Right: The start of the 1938 Donington GP with the Auto-Union and Mercedes teams dominant and British cars as makeweights at the end of the field

entries came from Bugatti of France, who financed his racing by selling similar racing cars to customers, at considerable profit. Alfa Romeo reappeared from time to time, and 'left-over' Talbots also started some races. 1929 was distinguished only by the promotion of the very first Monaco GP (using a town-centre circuit which is still essentially the same in 1990).

Early Thirties races featured the twin-cam Bugatti Type 51s, the sensational supercharged eight-cylinder Alfa Romeo 'Monza', and special machines such as the 12-cylinder 'twin-engined' Alfa Romeo, and the 16-cylinder 'twin-eight' Maserati. Bugatti produced the 4.9-litre Type 54, which was much quicker than the old 2-litre and 2.3-litre models.

Race speeds, naturally, continued to rise. At Monza, for instance, the 1930 GP was won at 93.55mph (150.55km/h), the 1931 race at 96.6mph (155.4km/h), the 1932 race at 110.8 mph (178.3km/h), while at the 1933 event a new lap record of 116.81mph (187.98 km/h) was set. Top speeds were now over 140mph (225km/h), way ahead of road-holding and braking capabilities. Drivers like Achille Varzi, Louis Chiron, Rudi Caracciola and Tazio Nuvolari became superstars, and deserved their daredevil reputations.

1934–1939 — Deutschland Über Alles

By 1932 the sport's administrators were alarmed by the way that speeds continued to rise, and (if the truth be told) they were also unhappy at the way motor racing — for Grand Prix *and* sports cars — was being dominated by Italian manufacturers. It was at this juncture that they decided to impose a new Grand Prix formula — in a decision which handed over supremacy, at a stroke, to the Germans!

The intention of the new formula was to reduce speeds and, by being flexible, to allow other makers to get back into the sport. The theory was that performance would be reduced by imposing a maximum (not a minimum) weight limit — this had not applied to Grand Prix racing since 1913 — and a minimum body width dimension. There would be no limit on the engines which could be used, though it was thought that the practical limit would be at about 3 litres. It was well meant, but it was also misguided.

The new regulations (which eventually ran from 1934 to 1937) were simple enough — cars had to weigh not more than 750kg (1653lb), discounting tyres, fuel and lubricants — and this was a laudable objective, but the outcome could not have been foreseen. Existing racing car manufacturers (such as Alfa Romeo, Maserati and Bugatti) merely refined their 1933 models, but two German manufacturers — Mercedes-Benz and Auto-Union — seized an opportunity to produce faster and better cars by spending a fortune on design, testing and new materials.

In Germany Adolf Hitler had recently come to power, and for the two German concerns there was an incentive to use hidden subsidies and to win massive success bonuses, all as part of Hitler's master plan to show the supremacy of the German nation,

and its people. If not immediately, then after the first year, it was clear that Grand Prix racing was to be a series of one-sided contests, between small traditional firms on the one hand, and between colossal new companies which were backed by the German state on the other.

Although Bugatti and Alfa Romeo won many GP races in 1934, the first Mercedes-Benz and Auto-Union victories came in the same year. In 1935 the old guard was swamped, and after that almost every Grand Prix race was a straight battle between the two German marques. At one and the same time it brought new colour — and less colour — to the sport, for both teams used silver-painted machines.

The Germans were only interested in Grand Prix racing and spent heavily to achieve success. This ensured that GP entries fell, and it was logical to predict that there would soon be a revival in voiturette racing, and that French and Italian makers would redouble their efforts to raise the profile of sports car racing.

Before the Germans burst upon the scene, racing car design had got into a deep rut, and their new approach helped to transform the sport. Not only were they well supported by the state (something not previously granted to traditional racing car companies), but they completely rethought the layout of racing cars.

Mercedes-Benz/Auto-Union domination

Both German teams used engines which were considerably larger than originally fore-

cast (the use of exotic light alloy materials helped to keep weights down), but the real advance came in general layouts. Both teams of designers chose tubular chassis frames, with independent suspension at front and rear (later cars had De Dion at the rear), while Auto-Union actually carried its engine *behind* the driver, a real break with tradition. Both the cars were larger but lower, and considerably more streamlined, than before.

There is no doubt that both these cars were real monsters, in almost every way, enormously fast, very thirsty, apt to chew up tyres faster than any previous racing car, and both were difficult to handle.

In both cases their engines grew, and grew, and grew. Mercedes-Benz used a super-charged straight-eight, which in 1934 was originally of 3.3 litres, with about 350bhp (what was that about reducing speeds?). By 1937 it had been replaced by a re-designed 5.6-litre unit which could produce up to 646bhp. Auto-Union chose a supercharged V16 originally of 4.4 litres/295bhp, and finally of 6 litres/520bhp.

The result was that Bugatti and Maserati soon dropped out, and although Alfa Romeo tried hard, it was outclassed. Year upon year the interest of other nations, and organizers, ebbed away, with the French turning to sports car racing, and with the Italians adding speed-slowing chicanes to the Monza circuit. Nothing, however, could stop the German teams, the result being that in 1937 they won every important event, including the Donington GP, their first appearance on British soil.

By this point top speeds had risen to a staggering 180 or 190mph (289–305km/h), more still if full-width streamlined bodies were used for circuits such as the banked Avus track in Berlin. Deeply humiliated, the authorities decided to try again.

For 1938 and 1939 a new Grand Prix formula was imposed, this having a sliding scale relating engine size to minimum weight. In practice, however, it resulted in 850kg (1873lb) cars, with 3-litre supercharged engines (or, in a few cases, with 4½-litre unsupercharged engines).

If the intention had been to bring back more variety to Grand Prix racing, it was a complete failure, as Mercedes-Benz and Auto-Union (but, most particularly, Mercedes-Benz) were completely in command. Each of the German teams stayed faithful to original layouts, though both had new supercharged V12 engines. Cars handled better, had better brakes, and had very advanced power units.

The result was that by 1939 the 3-litre Mercedes-Benz W163 model had 483bhp, a top speed of up to 190mph (305km/h), and it could lap circuits faster than its 5.6-litre predecessor. Only Alfa Romeo tried to face up to this might, but its 308 model was outclassed, even when equipped with a 350bhp V16 power unit.

If World War 2 had not intervened, it is

highly likely that Grand Prix racing would have died out, as no other concern was willing to fight the Germans, while several organizers were unwilling to promote races where there was no national interest. The last such GP, in fact, was the Yugoslavian race, actually held on the day that Britain declared war on Germany; five German cars started, but the rest were makeweights.

The heroes of this age, no doubt, would have won races in other cars, but Caracciola, Nuvolari, von Brauchitsch, Hans Stuck, Bernd Rosemeyer, Richard Seaman and Hermann Lang will always be remembered for their exploits in the monstrously powerful German machines.

Variety in the Thirties

The fact that the Germans drove every other marque away from Grand Prix events gave a welcome boost to many other forms of motor racing. In Europe, what we would now call 'Formula 2', or 'Division 2', racing (but officially called 'Voiturette' racing) was encouraged for 1½-litre cars.

This was very fertile ground for companies like ERA, Maserati and Alfa Romeo, so much so that the Italians abandoned their own famous Grand Prix for 1939, and promoted a 1½-litre championship instead. Unhappily for them, Mercedes-Benz took umbrage at this, designed a brand-new 1½-litre car (the W165) in great secrecy, brought it out for the Tripoli GP of that year, and took first and second places! Alfa Romeo, however, designed and refined a new car, the 158, which was to become even more famous in post-war years.

Post-war racing — a different world

Between 1939 and 1945, the world was at war, and all thoughts of motor racing had to be swept aside. When peace returned it was, quite literally, a different world.

In Europe, and especially in the UK, France, Italy and Germany, nations had been battered by the fighting, companies, men and machines had been wiped out, and at first the grim struggle to survive was more important than any frivolities.

This, at least, allowed the authorities the chance for a complete rethink of motor sport, its classes and its activities. No one questioned the fact that Grand Prix racing would resume, but where, for what cars, and for which teams? Should the regulations be changed? What about the lesser formulae? What about the circuits? Which of the drivers had survived? Were there any cars left over?

In Britain, neither the Brooklands nor the Donington circuits were available for motor racing, in France the Montlhery track was in a terrible shape, while road circuits such as Spa, Le Mans and Reims had all suffered badly at the hands of tanks, guns and marauding armies.

One thing, at least, was clear: Germany, as the defeated nation, was in no sort of shape to return to motor racing. In any case, as the defeated nation, it was summarily banned from returning to international motor sport. For the next few years, at least, the Nürburgring and Avus tracks would be 'off-limits'.

The French and the Italians were in better shape, so it was cars, drivers and teams from those nations which came back to prominence. The world's first post-war motor race was held near Paris in September 1945, a joyful, if unconventional, affair.

The United States had not suffered from bombing, or from fighting over its landscapes, so motor racing at Indianapolis could soon get under way again. Only nine months after the end of the war with Japan the first post-war 'Indy' race was promoted, in May 1946.

Post-war racing formulae

So that motor racing could get back on its feet with the minimum of heartache, motor racing's governing body (now called the Federation Internationale de l'Automobile — or FIA for short) took a pragmatic view.

The 1938–1939 GP formula was already dead on its feet when war intervened, but to encourage the use of existing cars, a new formula took account of supercharged 1½-litre cars (such as the Alfa Romeo 158 voiturettes, and the latest British ERAs), and of the big 4½-litre cars which had occasionally turned out against the German teams. The 1½-litre supercharged versus 4½-litre unsupercharged formula was a rather scratch affair, but between 1947 and 1951 it provided excellent racing, in good spirit, and it allowed one important new marque — Ferrari — to find its feet.

For the first time, it seemed, someone began to think about a progression — not only for drivers but for car builders as well — and two other formulae were eventually established, to run at the same time. GP racing was dubbed Formula 1 (F1), while under it there was to be a new Formula 2 (at first for unsupercharged 2-litre cars), and even a Formula 3, where the cars were limited to using 500cc engines.

As in the Thirties, sports car racing was a less rigidly controlled, less structured business, which meant that individual races, rather than championships, took the limelight. In the late Forties, as so famously in the Twenties and Thirties, Italy promoted its fabulous 1000-mile (1609km) Mille Miglia road race, the Sicilians ran the Targa Florio over the 'Little Madonie' circuit, and the Automobile Club de l'Ouest laid plans to revive the famous Le Mans race. Miraculously, the Belgians managed to repair the roads around Spa (which had been fought over, several times, in 1940, 1944 and 1945), and also promoted a 24-hour production car race.

Grand Prix racing revival

It was a miracle that F1 racing re-established itself so quickly, and so well, for in the beginning there were really only two

competitive marques — Alfa Romeo and Maserati — and even those manufacturers had to use cars which had been designed in the late Thirties.

Other enthusiasts and other designers, however, had ambitions to 'join the club', the result being the solid and ultimately successful rise of Ferrari, the abject failure of the heavily-promoted British BRM, and the unsuccessful preparation of the Cisitalia and CTA-Arsenal types. Talbot and OSCA both had a go, but were never really competitive.

This was the period when a proper World Championship series was established, when normally-aspirated engines came back into prominence and when a new generation of drivers (including Juan-Manuel Fangio, Alberto Ascari and Dr Giuseppe Farina) made their names. The racing gradually settled into a pattern, with a *Grande Epreuve* in most West European countries, with races lasting around three hours, or 300 miles (482km), but with race grids limited to fewer than a dozen competitive machines.

Until 1951, Alfa Romeo was much the most successful marque, even though its supercharged Alfettas were pre-war designs. Year on year the Italians found more power, and unimpaired reliability. The Alfas eventually had an enormous appetite for tyres and fuel, but it was not until 1951 that Ferrari's 4½-litre cars started to beat them. For the first time since the mid-Twenties, therefore, normally-aspirated cars were GP winners.

Even so, two factors — Alfa Romeo, and the cost of it all — killed off this particular Formula 1, for the number of starters plum-

meted, so for the next two years GP racing was organized for Formula 2 cars, where 2-litre Ferraris and Maseratis fought it out. Then, from 1954 to 1960, the FIA defined a replacement Formula, for 2.5-litre cars, which led to a complete change of emphasis.

Almost immediately Mercedes-Benz came back, to dominate F1 for two seasons; Lancia tried, failed, and handed over its cars to Ferrari; BRM made a tardy but eventually successful effort, but Britain's privately-financed Vanwall team finally burst into the lead in 1957 and 1958. Gradually, GP racing supremacy settled on the UK, and would stay there for at least the next decade.

By the end of the Fifties, however, the rules had changed again, the cars followed suit, and by the Sixties a technical revolution had occurred. The requirement to use conventional petrol, and the decision to cut race distances, led to much smaller cars being developed. In addition, the British Cooper concern started to use mid-engined cars (with the engine positioned behind the driver, rather than in front of his feet), which transformed the sport. Within three years the front-engined cars had been made obsolete, while Ferrari, BRM and Lotus all produced mid-engined machines.

Sports cars — the Golden Age

In many ways the Fifties and Sixties will be remembered as the 'Golden Age' of sports car racing, though it was also a time when open road racing was hounded out of existence by public opinion, while long and testing circuits such as the Targa Florio, the Nürburgring

Above: 1952 Champion Alberto Ascari in his Ferrari on his way to victory in the 1952 Belgian GP, held at Spa

Above: Fifties sports car racing at its best with a Ferrari Testa Rossa in full flight during the 1958 Nürburgring 1000km

methods, by using extremely powerful engines in simply-engineered chassis; and finally Aston Martin, whose DBR1s finally won the World Sports Car Championship in 1959.

In the Sixties, as in the Fifties, Ferrari changed over from front-engined to mid-engined two-seaters, from open to closed styles, but was ever-present, while other makes blossomed, then faded away. Maserati, whose finances had been hit hard by a succession of race car crashes and fires, slipped back, while Aston Martin pulled out of the sport when the DBR1 became obsolete. No matter — Porsche and Ford-USA, of all people, arrived to take up the challenge.

Porsche, of West Germany, having started modestly in the Fifties with air-cooled 1½-litre engines, made steady progress, and soon began beating Ferrari on circuits like the Nürburgring, and in Sicily, where agility was more important than straight-line performance. At the very end of the Sixties it launched the fabulous 917, a 5-litre flat-12-engined monster, still with air-cooling, which blasted sports car racing to an entirely different plane, where top speeds of 220/230mph (354/370km/h) at the Le Mans circuit were soon commonplace.

The most determined assault came from Ford of Detroit. Having tried, and failed, to buy Ferrari in 1962, Ford reacted by setting up its own racing programme, and trying to crush the Italian concern. At first with help from British designer Eric Broadley and from team chief (ex-Aston Martin) John Wyer, but soon with a great deal of its own efforts, Ford won the Le Mans 24-Hour race 'classic' on four successive occasions, and defeated Ferrari on race tracks all round the world. All the cars used big, heavy V8 engines, with closed coupé styles, relying on the old American adage of 'There's no substitute for cubic inches' for high performance. Even so, Ford was involved for only a few years, and by the time Porsche's 917 had been developed it had retreated to Detroit, its cars in museums, and its reputation unsullied.

Motor racing for everyone

The between-wars motor racing enthusiast would be astonished by the sheer number of different races being held in modern times. Many more people were racing than ever before, indeed many more people could afford to go racing; before 1939 the sport had been elitist in many ways, but now it was available to almost everyone.

The FIA started the process by formalizing Formula 3, for tiny 500cc cars, but the growth of saloon car racing, production sports car racing, and a whole variety of 'one-make' series was a natural progression. The administrators had to hurry to keep up with all the pressures, and to provide some form of motor sport for everyone.

Formula 3 gave way to Formula Junior, which was itself displaced by a new Formula 3 again. Formula 3 cars started out with 1-litre

and Spa hung on into the Seventies. The problem was that two-seater sports cars became so fast that they were dangerous unless raced in strictly-controlled conditions.

This was the category of motor sport where designers first began to take account of aerodynamics, and produced all-enveloping body styles. At the beginning of the period all standards were being set by Ferrari, whose brutally-styled machines had simple chassis, but immensely powerful V12 engines. A Ferrari could usually outrun *and* outlast its rivals, in almost every type of sports car race.

Year in and year out, Ferrari produced race-winning cars, though there was never a shortage of rivals: Mercedes-Benz, whose 1954–1955 300SLRs were not only technically advanced, but even faster and more sturdy than the Ferraris; Jaguar, whose C-types and D-types were ruggedly simple, but had better brakes and more aerodynamically efficient shapes; Maserati, which agreed with Ferrari's engines, but became 1.6-litre in the Seventies, and 2-litre in the Eighties. Along the way Formula 2 was relaunched as a 1.5-litre series for 1957, then became 1 litre in 1964, 1.6 litres in 1967, and 2 litres for the Seventies and beyond.

Ford invented Formula Ford single-seater racing in the Sixties, Renault followed with Formula Renault a few years later, VW was soon promoting Formula Vee. Then came production sports cars (Prod Sports), Group 5 (highly modified) saloon cars, Group 1 (near standard) saloon cars, Grand Touring Cars, Formula Atlantic, go-karts . . . to say nothing of what was happening in North America!

By the Eighties there was a completely structured framework, which allowed a driver to start simply, slowly and at the bottom, but to climb rapidly up the ladder and (if he was fortunate enough) to make it to Formula 1, or World Championship sports car, racing.

The USA scene in modern times

For many years North America ignored European motor racing trends, and developed its own race cars and its own formulae. It is, after all, the world's most prosperous continent, and its own people want to concentrate on their own sports.

Stateside motor racing, therefore, differs from that of the rest of the world, with much more glamour, much more obvious 'glitz' and 'show business' in the racing, and with several special categories. In all cases, close racing was encouraged — and if one type of car became dominant the rules would be changed to lessen its advantage!

The Indianapolis 500, despite its use of an absurdly fast and simple circuit, was always the most important American race, where the cars were rugged, specialized, and ferociously rapid. For the whole of May the teams tested, practised, and hopefully qualified, and the winner was a hero for years to follow. Lap speeds rose above 150mph (241km/h) in the Sixties, and above 200mph (322km/h) in the Seventies. It was only the ruthless application of engine limits which kept them in check in the Eighties.

At Indianapolis the mid-engined revolution was late arriving, but by the mid-Sixties the old front-engined roadsters were obsolete. Although there was a brief flirtation with gas-turbine cars in the Sixties, Indy racing (along with USAC and CART events, which were closely related) soon settled into the use of mid-engined machines, and turbocharged engines had also taken over by the end of that decade.

Once Bill France established the NASCAR series, touring car racing in the USA became big business. Mostly held on oval tracks, some as large as the massive Daytona facility, but some a mere half mile round, NASCAR events have always featured extremely close racing.

The category was, and is, so closely controlled that the NASCAR organizers always required current model-year cars to be used, and could even agree, with a manufacturer, as to which cars could be used, and which could not. Not fair and reasonable? Maybe not — but the sight of ten or twenty cars thundering around an oval track in close company, and the prospect of having different winners every weekend, has always appealed to the American public. McLaren domination, as in Eighties F1 racing, would bore them to tears.

Formula 1 in the Sixties and Seventies

The FIA made no friends, but plenty of enemies, by providing a new 1.5-litre GP formula for the 1961–1965 period, but if (according to legend) this was what Ferrari and Porsche had lobbied so hard to achieve, it soon backfired upon them. British manufacturers, notably Lotus, BRM, Brabham and Cooper, soon produced a series of neat, lightweight, efficient and agile mid-engined machines, and came to dominate motor sport, world-wide, as never before or since. Grands Prix were short, fast and exciting, most being well under two hours long.

There was one epoch-making technical advance at this time — the launch of the monocoque chassisless structure by Lotus — an improvement which was so dramatic that every other maker followed suit within three or four years. Pit stops for tyre changes and refuelling, of course, had disappeared years ago.

Even though engine outputs immediately fell from around 280bhp (the old 2.5-litre cars) to 170bhp, speeds fell very little. Later cars had up to 210bhp and lap speeds continued to rise. The new cars, however, were demonstrably safer, more nimble, and more efficient than any which had gone before.

For 1966 the FIA, to everyone's surprise, then announced a 3-litre formula for 1966, coupling this with a 1.5-litre formula for supercharged cars, though no one took any notice of the latter. It was the first time for many years that administrators, entrants and drivers had all agreed about a formula, and it provided a real boost for motor sport. It soon became the most successful, and most long-lived, GP racing formula of all time, for it ran without a break until the mid-Eighties.

At first there was a great deal of variety in cars and engines, with Ferrari setting the pace, and with BRM, Eagle (Dan Gurney's new team), Brabham-Repco, Maserati, Alfa Romeo, Honda and Ford-USA all providing new engines. Power outputs, at first, were in the 320–360bhp bracket. But from 1967 the establishment was turned on its head by the arrival of the Cosworth-Ford DFV V8 engine, which was the first true 400bhp-plus engine of its time. In 1967 the DFV engine was only available to Lotus, but it was eventually made available to all comers. Peak power was gradually pushed up from 420bhp to 490bhp; only Ferrari and Alfa Romeo, with their flat-12 units, could match it.

For the first time, this allowed tightly-financed teams to reach for Grand Prix stardom. By the early Seventies the scene had changed considerably. Ferrari — who else? — battled on, but every other engine faded away, and hordes of new 'kit car' manufacturers followed the 'own chassis+Cosworth engine+Hewland gearbox' route. Not only Lotus, but McLaren, Matra, Brabham, March and Tyrrell began winning World Championship events, and DFV-engined cars won almost all races from 1968 to 1978.

In the meantime the authorities had finally allowed F1 teams to display sponsorship liveries from 1968 and, almost at a stroke, this meant that 'national' colours disappeared as cars turned themselves into fast-moving billboards. Although Ferrari stuck it out — a Ferrari was *always* bright red, though latterly a few decals found a place on the flanks — eventually there were cigarette brands (JPS and Marlboro) chasing deodorants (Yardley), oil companies (Elf and Texaco) battling with finance companies (First National City), and fashion houses (Benetton) fighting it out with airlines (Saudia), food supply chains (Parmalat) and high-technology enterprises (TAG) — all exciting stuff, but not at all as 'pure' as the diehards would wish.

This was the period in which Grand Prix ceased to be pure motor sport, for it also began to take on the trappings of show business. Led by a thrusting entrepreneur, Brabham team-owner Bernie Ecclestone, the manufacturers formed the Formula One Constructors' Association (FOCA), and began to negotiate package deals with administrators and race organizers.

FOCA, on the one hand, guaranteed to produce a race package of cars, in exchange for a very large sum of money which would be distributed, following a secret formula, according to qualifying positions on the grid, finishing positions, and the previous year's record. Ecclestone was determined to get a good deal for his teams, this leading to a huge increase in costs to race organizers, sponsors and spectators alike. Even so, this was the most closely-contested, colourful and vigorously-promoted GP formula yet seen.

Sports cars — decline and rebirth

Once Ford-USA had withdrawn from motor racing, and after Porsche's 917 had been outlawed by rule changes, sports car racing was contested by two-seater 3-litre cars, and gradually went into decline. The great days of Le Mans, and of contests between the world's top drivers, had gone for ever.

One reason for this was that the watching public's taste had changed, and its attention span had been reduced. Most people were no longer willing to persist in watching a motor race which went on for hours, especially as the cars were now all closed, and the drivers could not be seen at work.

The most important reason, though, was that major manufacturers were no longer interested in bearing the expense, particularly when the publicity gained was now dwarfed by the explosion of interest in F1.

Ferrari stuck it out for a couple of years in the early Seventies, and won most of the races, then withdrew in favour of the Matra-Simca team. After Matra withdrew, Alfa Romeo enjoyed a season's supremacy, but by the late Seventies there was really no top-line competition any more.

The administrators almost ruined Eighties sports car racing by allowing only limited amounts of fuel for each car, for each race. The resulting 'fuel efficiency' contests pleased almost no one, and if Porsche had not produced the 956/962 series there might have been no cars to run at all. In the mid-Eighties Jaguar (through TWR) picked up the challenge (the V12-engined cars eventually winning the World Sports Car Championship *and* the Le Mans 24-Hour race), and when Mercedes-Benz officially began to support Sauber the recovery was nearly complete.

FISA almost torpedoed the remnants of sports car racing by promoting its idea of 'Silhouette' racing, but the big manufacturers would have nothing to do with this and it rapidly died away. For the Nineties, FISA

Right: Patrick Tambay in his turbocharged Renault during the 1984 French GP. Renault pioneered the change to turbocharged engines in the Seventies although ultimately theirs were not the most successful cars

tried again, proposing to impose the same engine regulations as for Formula 1; this made people a lot happier, and prospects were more rosy than for the previous 20 years.

Formula 1 — the turbo years

A new type of forced-induction engine layout, using exhaust-driven turbochargers, arrived on the motor racing scene in the Sixties and Seventies. Starting in the USA, in Indy racing, then crossing the Atlantic for use by BMW, Porsche and Renault in saloon and sports car formulae, it eventually arrived in F1 in 1977.

According to F1 regulations issued in 1966, 'supercharged' engines of 1.5 litres could be used, and it was Renault which first decided that a turbocharged engine was eligible, and could be made very powerful. Renault's reliability problems, in the late Seventies, caused traditionalists to scoff, but the derision was muted in 1979 when Renault began winning races, and it ceased altogether in 1981 when first Ferrari, then BMW, joined in the 'turbo' power race.

For the first time in 50 years a modern Grand Prix car was more powerful than the formidable Mercedes-Benz W125 of 1937. It was also a lot lighter, and had considerably better roadholding and braking. But this was only the beginning, for the next few years saw a dramatic increase in the number of turbo-powered F1 cars, and in the reliable power produced by such engines. To win races in 1978 one needed 500bhp, but by 1986 and 1987 a race-reliable 1000bhp was necessary, and at that time some cars qualified with up to 1200bhp.

The changeover from 'atmo' to 'turbo' engines was rapid, with the last normally-aspirated success (by a Cosworth-engined Tyrrell) being at Detroit in mid-1983. The cars, however, began to look dangerously fast, so FISA then performed one of its celebrated administrative somersaults, allowed 3.5-litre 'atmo' engines from 1987, trimmed the turbo engines' power for 1988, banned them at the end of that year, and introduced a brand-new formula, for normally-aspirated 3.5-litre-engined cars, in 1989.

If this was a move to reduce speeds, it failed completely. The new, less powerful, 3.5-litre 650bhp 'atmo' cars were faster round a circuit than the 1000bhp cars of 1986, and speeds look set to rise even further in the Nineties. But then, in the whole history of motor racing, that's progress, and enthusiasts wouldn't have it otherwise.

The Post-War Grand Prix Car

At the pinnacle of motor sport is the single-seater Grand Prix car. Generally, it is a finely-crafted machine designed to the limits of a given set of regulations to go as fast as possible for the duration of a race. The design of Grand Prix cars is a discipline which has attracted some of the most talented and intuitive engineering brains. In the early years of the sport, certain models dominated the grids for several seasons. Yet nowadays the pace of change is such that a front runner can slip to the back of the grid with astonishing rapidity if the pressure of development work is not maintained.

The organization of Grand Prix racing into a Championship for the first time in 1950 was the key to the general quickening of the pace of development in the sport. Inexorably a more professional approach than hitherto became an important factor in achieving success. The rewards became higher and the costs went through the roof. Today, GP racing is a slickly-run and tightly-controlled, multi-million-pound, multi-national enterprise tackled with ruthless professionalism by the leading teams.

But when the lights turn green the basic spine-tingling fascination of watching top-flight Grand Prix cars in action is much the same as it has always been right from the earliest days of motor sport.

The anatomy of a modern GP car. This was Nigel Mansell's Ferrari in undressed state during practice for the 1989 Monaco GP

Between 1934 and 1939 the world had witnessed a series of magnificent battles for Grand Prix supremacy, between two determined German manufacturers — Mercedes-Benz and Auto-Union. No other marques, not Alfa Romeo, nor Bugatti, nor Maserati, could match them. Until war intervened the struggle was set to intensify — but then six years of bitter fighting changed everything.

Even though nothing could dampen the spirit of motor racing enthusiasts in 1945, the Grand Prix scene would never be the same again. Not only was a defeated German nation partitioned, a political move which left most of the old Auto-Union combine behind the 'Iron Curtain', while the Mercedes-Benz business had been pounded into rubble, but there was one other immediate post-war decision: Germany was to be banned from competing in all international sport. On the other hand, because Italy had changed sides during the conflict, ending up on the side of the victorious Allies, the Italian racing teams were welcomed back just as soon as they could make themselves ready.

There was no lack of will. Just as soon as the debris was cleared away, the roofs could be got back on the workshops, and the long-hidden racing cars could be wheeled out of storage, drivers were anxious to start racing again.

Somehow or other, many of Europe's fastest racing cars had miraculously been preserved from damage — some had been stored in private garages and some in small workshops many miles from the factories — while most of the drivers, technicians and designers eventually filtered back to their peacetime occupations.

Because there was widespread civil and financial chaos in some countries (especially in France, Germany and Italy, where much of the fighting had taken place), it was remarkable that racing could take place at all in the first few years. There was a shortage of specialized equipment — in particular of

tyres and the best blends of fuel — and many well-known suppliers had severely-damaged factories which were in no sort of state to deal in frivolities for racing cars.

No matter. The flesh might indeed be weak, but there was no doubt that the spirit was willing. The mere fact that the world was at peace once again made everyone determined to enjoy themselves. The only thing necessary was to rewrite the scripts. Instead of Auto-Union and Mercedes-Benz, the new star names were to be Alfa Romeo, Maserati, Talbot and — an important new company — Ferrari.

There was no hope of welcoming Grand Prix cars to British circuits, simply because there was no longer a suitable circuit. Brooklands, the original 'home of British motor racing', had been knocked about during the war to allow its aircraft runway to be extended, buildings had sprung up on its bankings, the facilities had become badly run down, and the new owners were not at all interested in bringing racing cars back to its delapidated track.

The first post-war motor race was a joyous but rather informal affair, held on September 9, 1945 at a circuit in the Bois de Boulogne, just outside Paris. The rules were *Formula Libre* (free formula), with victory going to Jean-Pierre Wimille in an old Bugatti.

During 1946, and even though a new set of Formula 1 regulations had been announced, 19 races were held in Europe, with each country imposing its own regulations. The

Below: *A scene from one of the first post-war race meetings, held at the Bois de Boulogne just outside Paris. Racing quickly re-established itself and a World Championship was introduced in 1950*

dominant cars came from Maserati and from Alfa Romeo, both using modified and up-dated versions of machines designed and built for 1½-litre voiturette competition at the end of the Thirties.

A new Grand Prix Formula

The governing body of motor sport, the Federation Internationale de l'Automobile (FIA), could see that there was no point in resurrecting the Grand Prix regulations which had applied in 1938 and 1939, as there were no longer any competitive cars which could be used. In any case, that formula had rapidly been dying out, for most manufacturers were quite unable to compete with the German teams.

In a very pragmatic move, therefore, the administrators met in February 1946 and decided to bring together most of the existing racing cars in a new formula which would suit them all, and provide good racing, at least for the time being. On the one hand there were a number of unsupercharged 4½-litre cars which had raced in the 1938–1939 series, and on the other hand there were even more of the modern supercharged 1½-litre 'voiturettes' which had been so popular in the late Thirties.

Very well, the FIA decided. In the immediate post-war years a new Grand Prix Formula would be imposed — for cars either with supercharged 1½-litre engines, or with 4½-litre unsupercharged engines. In fact the two types of cars were surprisingly well matched, with power outputs expected to be in the 250–300bhp bracket at first.

A few races would be nominated as *Grandes Epreuves* (which translates as 'Major Tests'), but many other races would be run to the new rules. Without exception, a Grande Epreuve was the national Grand Prix of a particular country, and every year one of those events was also to be nominated as the Grand Prix of Europe — a meaningless title, but one which brought publicity, if nothing else, to the nation in question.

Initially the new rules were set up to run until the end of 1953. Any sort of fuel would be allowed, and it was expected that pit stops for new tyres, and for refuelling, would continue to be a part of the spectacle. Part of the intriguing prospect for this new formula was that 4½-litre unsupercharged cars would be more fuel efficient, and would have to make fewer pit stops, than the 1½-litre 'blown' machines. Which type, eventually, would come out on top?

Whereas German marques had made all the running in the late Thirties, it was Italian companies which were to be dominant in the post-war years. Although fortunes ebbed and flowed as the seasons passed by, it was Maserati which took many early wins, and the highly-developed Alfa Romeo Type 158/Type 159 cars which swept them aside; but finally it was the unsupercharged 4½-litre Ferrari which began to defeat the Alfa Romeos.

A few years later the FIA also decided on a

subsidiary formula — Formula 2, which was to be for cars with unsupercharged 2-litre engines. Races for these cars were popular, and in 1952 the existence of such machines was going to be very significant indeed. At this time, of course, Grand Prix racing cars were also retitled Formula 1 cars.

Alfa Romeo v Ferrari: 1947 to 1951

Right from the start, the eight-cylinder supercharged Alfa Romeo, the Type 158, became the car to beat. Even in 1946, when Grand Prix racing was still struggling back to its feet, the Alfa was a well-developed car, for it had originally been raced in 1938, and its engine was virtually one bank of the V16 used in an earlier Alfa Romeo GP car.

It set the technical standards for the next few years by using a tubular chassis frame, trailing link independent front suspension and swing-axle independent rear suspension, and it had its gearbox in unit with the rear axle/final drive. By 1947 the engine was producing 265bhp at 7500rpm, and with drivers like Jean-Pierre Wimille, Count Trossi and Achille Varzi it was almost invincible.

The main opposition came from the 4CL Maserati (with drivers like Luigi Villoresi, Giuseppe Farina and Alberto Ascari notching up several victories), while Louis Rosier and Louis Chiron tried hard in their heavy and underpowered French Talbots.

Ferrari was already planning to produce a GP car (which would first appear in 1948, with a V12 supercharged engine of 230bhp), while in the UK Raymond Mays, of ERA fame, set up the British Racing Motors (BRM) concern, persuading the British motor industry to help him with money and technical assistance, and promising them a world-beating car.

On paper the projected BRM was a very advanced car, for it was to feature a supercharged 1½-litre V16 engine for which 400–500bhp was forecast. The problem was that the design was laid down in 1946, the first car would not run until 1949, and the first (unsuccessful) appearances would not be made until 1950.

By the end of 1948 Alfa Romeo had improved its engine to produce 310bhp, and the cars could lap established race circuits almost as quickly as the fabulous 3-litre German cars of 1939. The cars won all the major events, including the European (Swiss), French, Italian (Turin) and Monza GPs. Maserati's latest car, the 4CLT/48, was nimble, but produced only 240bhp, so the only potential opposition to Alfa Romeo came from Ferrari. At that point, however, Alfa Romeo amazed everyone by withdrawing from Grand Prix racing, stating that there was too much production car design work to be done back in Milan. The truth, however, was that Alfa Romeo thought the Type 158 was at its limit, and as the company did not relish being beaten the car was withdrawn before it turned into a gallant loser.

This was the year, incidentally, in which the Silverstone circuit was first used for motor racing in the UK. Silverstone had originally been developed as a World War 2 bomber airfield base in the early Forties, and its wide perimeter tracks and runways looked ideal for motor sport.

The very first post-war British GP was held on October 2, 1948, and was won by Luigi Villoresi's Maserati at an average speed of 72.28mph (116.32km/h). In those early days the GP circuit used runways as well as perimeter tracks, and had many slow corners; the pits were on the approach to what is now known as the Woodcote complex, and spectator facilities were absolutely minimal. Things have come a long way since then, not least in speeds round the circuit, where a GP car can average up to 150mph (241km/h)!

In 1949 Grand Prix racing was dominated by Ferrari and Maserati — Ferrari with an improved version of its new 1½-litre car, and Maserati with the conventional, but old-fashioned, 4CLT/48. Ferrari won the Swiss, Dutch, European (Italian) and Silverstone International Trophy races, while Maserati won the British GP and several minor races. Surprisingly, Louis Chiron's Talbot won the French GP at Reims, though a Ferrari had been fastest in practice. One new, and very significant, name appeared in the winners' circle at San Remo, Pau and Albi — Juan-Manuel Fangio of Argentina.

For 1950 the FIA decided to introduce a

Right: Farina in flowing action in the Alfa 158 during the 1950 British GP at Silverstone. He took the car to the flag and went on to be the first World Champion

Left: The British challenger in GP racing was the 16-cylinder BRM which was years in the making and temperamental, although powerful. This shot was taken during a rare GP appearance

World Drivers' Championship. This, and the fact that the opposition had certainly not advanced as fast as feared, persuaded Alfa Romeo to come back to Grand Prix racing, only one year after pulling out of the scene. By improving the car (not least by pushing up the peak power to 350bhp at 8500rpm), it became the Type 159.

Maserati knew when it was beaten, but Ferrari was still improving. During 1950 it produced a new car, longer in the wheelbase

and easier to drive because it used De Dion instead of swing-axle rear suspension, but this time fitted with an unsupercharged V12 engine, at first of only 3.3 litres, then 4.1 litres and finally (from the Italian GP of that year) of 4.5 litres.

Alfa Romeo was dominant in 1950 — the cars won *every* Grande Epreuve, and Giuseppe Farina became the first official FIA World Champion, though his new team-mate Juan-Manuel Fangio ran him close — but by the end of the season the big Ferrari had started to win lesser events. By this time Talbot was outclassed, and the BRM was still an underdeveloped flop, for it only started two races and failed in both.

The highlight of the 1951 season, which followed, was the titanic struggle for supremacy between Alfa Romeo and Ferrari — old design versus new design, supercharged engine versus normally-aspirated engine, straight-eight versus V12, experience versus youthful zest. There was added piquancy to the battle because Enzo Ferrari, the founder of the car which bore his name, had run the Alfa Romeo 'works' racing effort for some years in the Thirties. Old scores, and old rivalries, had to be settled.

Faced with the deep-breathing Ferrari, whose 4½-litre engine was eventually persuaded to produce 380bhp, Alfa Romeo wrung the last ounce of development from its own machine. Progressing to Type 159A, the gallant old car ran in 1951 with De Dion rear suspension, and highly-boosted engines producing up to 400bhp, with a horrendous thirst for fuel.

The two-way fight should have been a stupendous three-way battle if BRM had been ready (as so often promised), but the lack of development, and the embarrassing failures, continued, so that the car was never competitive, and never capable of meeting the Italian cars in a straight fight. BRM would not become a major force in Formula

1 Grand Prix racing until the end of the Fifties, with an entirely different, and much simpler, type of car.

In 1951 honours were shared — with Alfa Romeo winning the Swiss, Belgian, French and Spanish GPs, and with Ferrari winning the British, German and Italian GPs. The two marques were never far apart, but it was clear to all that the Ferrari still had more development to come, whereas the Alfa Romeo was finally at its peak. The Alfa's fuel consumption had reached no less than 1.5mpg, which meant that the cars had to carry about 65 gallons (296 litres) of fuel in tanks dotted all round the chassis to be able to complete a race.

The battle was so intense that lap speeds finally began to beat those set by larger-engined machines in 1939, a trend which would persist in years to come. In the process Juan-Manuel Fangio won his first Drivers' World Championship: at the time no one realized just how much the quiet Argentinian was going to dominate GP racing in the next few years.

1952 and 1953 — Formula 2 GPs

At the end of 1951 Alfa Romeo realized that the Type 159A could not be improved further, so the team withdrew from Grand Prix racing. Since the British BRM was *still* not race ready, this meant that the Ferraris were the only competitive Formula 1 cars in existence.

European promoters got together with FISA, therefore, the result being that the old Formula 1 was effectively abandoned, and

that 1952 and 1953 Grand Prix racing was disputed by Formula 2 cars.

For two years the Formula 2 scene was dominated by two Italian makes, Ferrari and Maserati, the former having a four-cylinder engine, the latter a six-cylinder engine. Power outputs were about 180bhp at first, but had risen to 200bhp by the end of 1953. The cars were surprisingly fast, and much more reliable and fuel efficient than the obsolete F1 machines; pit stops became rare, and race-long average speeds were almost as high as in 1951.

Although Maserati was building fine cars, these two years belonged undoubtedly to Alberto Ascari, in his Ferraris, the swarthy Italian driver becoming World Champion in both years. Fangio was unquestionably the faster driver of the two, but never got his hands on the best car. The British Connaught and HWM marques tried hard, but never had powerful enough engines to be a serious threat, while promising young drivers like Stirling Moss, Mike Hawthorn and Jean Behra all came to prominence.

2½-litre F1 cars — 1954 to 1960

At the end of 1951 the FIA announced a new Formula 1, to come into force on January 1, 1954. Initially it was meant to last for four seasons, but in the end it was to stay in force for seven enormously successful years, from 1954 to 1960 inclusive.

The new Formula, very simply, catered for cars with unsupercharged engines of 2½ litres, or cars with supercharged engines of a mere 750cc (45.8cu in). The rule-makers had

Below: In the years that GPs were run to F2 regulations, Ascari's Ferrari dominated the sport. He was World Champion in 1952 and 1953

clearly decided that supercharged engines could still be further developed, and that they should fight on an even less equal basis than between 1947 and 1951.

Engine designers were not impressed, and no new 750cc 'blown' engine was ever produced. As a result, from 1954 to 1960 all Grand Prix cars used 2½-litre normally-aspirated engines, which made this the simplest formula which the world of motor racing had seen since the mid-Twenties. At first peak power ratings were around 240bhp, but by 1957 the best cars had more than 285bhp (using 'rocket' fuel), though the imposition of 'pump' fuel saw these figures reduced a little by the end of the Fifties.

Even so, a great deal of development, and real technical advance, took place in those seven years. Early cars were really no more than 1953-model Formula 2 cars with enlarged engines, but by the late Fifties the sport was in the realms of shorter races for much smaller cars, with mid-mounted engines running on normal pump fuel, multi-tubular chassis frames and disc brakes. Not only that, but a different generation of manufacturers and teams had sprung up, for Grand Prix racing was affordable by more people than ever before.

The most important development in the early days of the new Grand Prix formula was that two large motor manufacturers — Mercedes-Benz and Lancia — announced their intention to build and race new cars. This was excellent news for the sport, not only because the 'names' were fresh, but because it meant that Grand Prix racing was seen to be important both for publicity and technical reasons.

The ban on German participation in motor sport had been lifted a few years earlier, but Mercedes-Benz had made its comeback only gradually, most notably by building 300SL racing sports cars in 1952. In 1954, as in the Thirties, they were expected to produce remarkably advanced cars which were likely to set new standards.

Lancia, for its part, had never previously built Grand Prix cars, but its management had hired a famous old-stager, Vittorio Jano (who had designed many famous Alfa Romeo racing cars in the Twenties and Thirties), to make the jump into the big time.

BRM, for its part, was now under new management. Instead of trying to run an over-complex car like the old V16, it now proposed to run a simple four-cylinder-engined machine instead. It was typical of BRM, however, that the first car was not ready to race until the new Formula was two years old, and that it would not be reliable and competitive until 1957.

Much more encouraging for British enthusiasts, however, was the commitment of the 'thin wall' engine bearings tycoon Tony Vandervell who, in his own words, was determined to 'beat those bloody red cars'. Vandervell had started by supporting the BRM project then, frustrated by its slow progress, had bought a Ferrari GP car, refined it into what he called the 'Thinwall Special', and then decided to produce his own brand of GP car for the 2½-litre Formula. Tentatively at first, but with growing

Below: By 1960 the change to mid-engined GP car designs was well under way. Although the front-engined Ferraris were still fast they were beaten by more nimble cars from Cooper and Lotus. This is the start of the 1960 French GP at Reims showing the mixed field

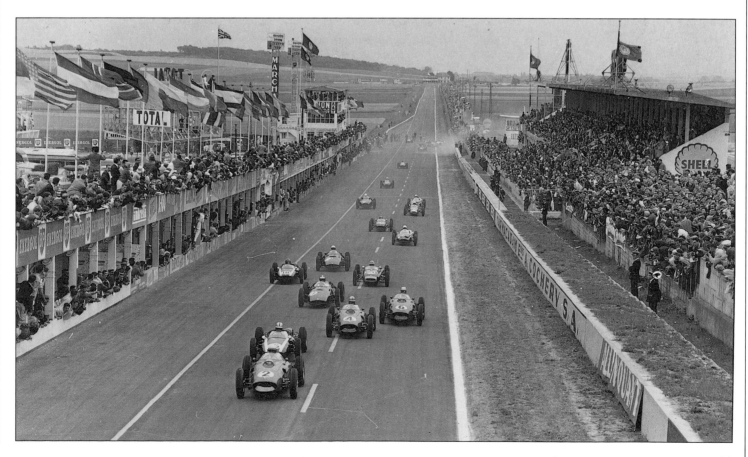

strength in the years which followed, the Vanwall team surged to the front.

Faced with this rush of new ideas and new projects, 'the establishment' — which meant Ferrari and Maserati, with Gordini and Connaught struggling on as best they could — carried on building conventional cars to familiar early-Fifties layouts. As one might expect, such cars won races in the early years, but were soon swamped by a new generation of Grand Prix cars.

In 1954 the big headlines were all made by Mercedes-Benz. The new W196 (W = *wagen*) model was technically impressive, not only because it used a complex 'space frame' chassis, but because its eight-cylinder engine was laid over almost horizontally (and featured what was known as desmodromic valve gear — which is to say that valves were opened *and* closed by cams); the new engines produced about 270bhp at first, and more than 280bhp in 1955.

In addition the original cars had full-width streamlined bodywork, though later in the season a more conventional exposed-wheel style was also adopted. The new-generation 'Silver Arrow' won its debut event, the French GP, and also went on to win in the German, Swiss, Italian and (non-championship) Berlin GPs of 1954.

Like Honda in the late Eighties, Mercedes-Benz in the Fifties seemed to have limitless money to spend to achieve supremacy. In 1954 they hired Juan-Manuel Fangio as star driver, the Argentinian repaying them by winning the Drivers' Championship.

In 1955 Mercedes-Benz not only signed Stirling Moss to back Fangio, and produced a closely related sports-racing version of the car (the 300SLR), but went on to produce a bewildering number of different versions of the car — short-, medium- and long-wheelbase, open-wheel or streamlined, in-board or outboard brakes — as well as designing a four-wheel-drive system for which the layout was always intended.

Fangio won the World Championship again in 1955, with Moss loyally finishing close behind him in many races, the W196s always winning unless they hit some form of mechanical trouble. To compete with them, Maserati produced the 250F, which handled like a dream, but which was out-gunned; Ferrari floundered, and Connaught's engine was underpowered. Then, at the end of the year, Mercedes-Benz suddenly withdrew from GP racing only a year and a half after rejoining the scene, and standards immediately fell back to an earlier level.

The Lancia D50 project looked promising, this car having a front-mounted V8 engine, and a unique style which featured petrol tanks mounted in sponsons which filled the gap between front and rear wheels. Alberto Ascari and Luigi Villoresi were signed up to drive the cars, but development took a long time. The first appearance, in the Spanish GP of 1954, was encouraging, but disaster

struck in 1955, first when Ascari crashed into the water at the Monaco GP, then a few days later when he was killed while testing a Ferrari sports car at Monza.

At this point Lancia lost heart, but a typically pragmatic Italian deal was then reached with Ferrari. Ferrari needed a new design, Lancia *had* a new design but needed money, so the entire team of cars, spares, drawings and expertise was handed over.

Without Mercedes-Benz and Lancia, the 1956 season was fought over by the old Italian rivals, Ferrari and Maserati — one team with updated versions of the Lancias, the other with refined versions of the 250F. Ferrari had Fangio and Peter Collins in its team, Maserati had Moss and Jean Behra. Between them, these teams won every important race, for the Gordinis were out-paced, the BRMs and the Connaughts were not competitive, and the latest Vanwalls were not yet reliable enough. Fangio won his third consecutive World Championship, though Stirling Moss was firmly established as the man most likely to take over from him in the next few years.

The British Vanwalls had made remarkable strides in less than two years. The 1954 and 1955 cars were effectively old-style chassis with an extremely powerful engine, but for 1956 they were given new multi-tube chassis, designed by Colin Chapman of Lotus, and aerodynamically-efficient bodies designed by Chapman's associate, Frank Costin.

The result was a car which won one non-Championship event, the 180-mile (289km) International Trophy at Silverstone, and which battled head-to-head against Ferrari and Maserati in several Grandes Epreuves. Driver Harry Schell's bravura performances at Reims and Monza both ended in car failure, but not before he had given the Italians a real fright.

1957–1960 — British domination

British enthusiasts had been waiting, impatiently, for a miracle since 1945, and it finally arrived in 1957. Not only did Vanwall begin to win Grands Prix, but it emphatically beat the Italian cars on their home ground. The four-cylinder BRM gradually achieved credibility, and began winning minor races, while the first mid-engined Coopers showed a lot of promise.

On the other hand, Gordini and Connaught both dropped out of Formula 1 — neither team could sustain the expense any longer — and the starting grids began to look rather sparse.

This was the year in which Fangio, the most astute of drivers, moved from Ferrari to Maserati, where the 250F was suddenly becoming competitive once again. The new V12 engine was a flop, but the latest light-weight cars, with low-line styles, were very effective on almost every circuit. Even so it was Fangio himself who added the final

Opposite: British domination in GP racing came partly from the success of the new Vanwall. This example was driven by Roy Salvadori in the 1957 French GP at Rouen, just two weeks before the make's maiden win in the British GP at Aintree

32

touch, for his stunning drives at Rouen, and at the Nürburgring, set the seal on a remarkable season. Naturally he became World Champion for the fifth time, remarkable for a seasoned campaigner who, by this time, was in his late forties.

Ferrari's Lancia-based cars, if anything, were slower than in 1956, which meant that British drivers Mike Hawthorn and Peter Collins struggled to stay on terms. Vanwall had made the greatest advance, using updated versions of the disc-braked 1956 cars, this time with coil spring suspension, and with a driving team which included Stirling Moss and Tony Brooks.

At the start of the season the Vanwalls were hit by irritating component failures. After a second place at Monaco, and a third in the French GP, Stirling Moss went on to win the British, Pescara and Italian GPs, while Stuart Lewis-Evans was second in Morocco. The same cars were expected to win most races in 1958 — and they did.

By 1958 Maserati had withdrawn from Grand Prix racing, its 250F now obsolete and its finances exhausted, while Ferrari's new front-engined Dino 246 model (complete with four-cam V6 engine of a type later to be redesigned for use in road cars) was not quite fast enough. Vanwall, able to choose from ten chassis, and backed by a great industrialist's capital, set all the standards, winning six Grands Prix, including the last four — Germany, Portugal, Italy and Morocco — in succession. Team owner Tony Vandervell then withdrew from the scene, and no other serious Vanwall entries were ever made in Formula 1 racing.

Although Stirling Moss and Tony Brooks each won three races for Vanwall it was Mike Hawthorn, with one victory and a host of second places in his Ferrari Dinos, who won the World Drivers' Championship. It was a lasting tragedy that the blond Englishman then retired to build up his garage business in Surrey, but was killed in a road accident in the first weeks of 1959.

For 1958 the ground rules of Grand Prix racing had changed considerably, for cars were obliged to run on pump fuel (which, in fact, tended to be aviation-based spirit), and minimum race distances were reduced from 300 to 200 miles (322km). This encouraged the building of smaller cars with small fuel tanks, one of which was the sleek and slim front-engined Lotus-Climax which became known as the 'mini-Vanwall'.

The Cooper ascendancy

It was in 1958, however, that the first mid-engined Coopers began to achieve results. Cooper had started in the Forties by building mid-engined 500cc Formula 3 cars, progressing to building 1½-litre Formula 2 cars in the Fifties, then making the jump to F1 by putting enlarged Coventry-Climax F2 engines into the tiny cars. Along the way, in the 1955 British GP, Jack Brabham had amused the

traditionalists by driving a fully-streamlined car which, on this occasion, was fitted with a six-cylinder Bristol engine.

Cooper racing cars had multi-tube chassis defying all engineering logic, for they featured curved tubes, with mounting brackets some way away from rigid junctions, but they were so small, so light, and (in a racing driver's jargon) so 'chuckable' that their agility made up for engineering difficulties.

In January 1958 Stirling Moss drove Rob Walker's 2-litre-engined Cooper-Climax to victory in the Argentine GP, while later that year Maurice Trintignant repeated the trick at Monaco. But in 1958 the Coventry-Climax engines could not be enlarged beyond 2.2 litres (and about 200bhp) and on fast circuits the Coopers were still outclassed.

The revolution in Grand Prix car design — from substantially engineered front-engined cars to smaller, simpler, mid-engined cars — came about quickly in 1959 and 1960. In 1959 GP racing was a straight fight between the compact mid-engined Coopers and 'the rest', but in 1960 Lotus and BRM joined in, the result being that the old-style front-engined cars from Ferrari, Aston Martin and (briefly) Scarab of the USA were outclassed.

Coventry-Climax provided 240bhp 2½-litre engines for Cooper and Lotus to use in 1959, the result being that Jack Brabham's Cooper won the Drivers' Championship, and Lotus finally became convinced that its front-

Left: Exciting action during the days of the small, 1.5-litre GP cars, with Phil Hill's Ferrari about to crash into Stirling Moss's Lotus during the 1961 French GP

engined F1 car design had to be abandoned forthwith. This was the year in which Ferrari's front-engined Dino 246 could only win the French and German GPs, and in which Jo Bonnier gave the front-engined BRM its only GP victory, in the Dutch GP.

By 1960 all the teams knew that their cars were entering their final season, as the authorities had now settled on a 1½-litre formula for the 1961–1965 period, but the competition for Grand Prix supremacy was as intense as ever. Cooper produced a new 'low-line' mid-engined car, Lotus produced its first mid-engined car (the Type 18), while BRM also built a new mid-engined machine which not only looked good, but was encouragingly fast.

By this time the front-engined Ferraris, which were still lineal descendants of the 1958 models, though with disc brakes, were completely outclassed, though the team won the Italian GP when other teams boycotted the race over a regulations dispute. Cooper won six of the other eight races, while Lotus won the other two. It was a year in which Stirling Moss (driving a Lotus 18) survived a high-speed crash in practice for the Belgian GP, but with broken limbs, then recovered remarkably quickly and won the USA GP to prove that neither his fitness nor his skill had been impaired.

The year, however, belonged to Cooper, and to Jack Brabham, for 'Black Jack'

won five GPs in succession — the Belgian, French, British, Portuguese and Italian (European) GPs — to become World Champion for the second year. Even though the Cooper was not as technically advanced as the Lotus Type 18, it was more reliable, and was backed by a resourceful little team.

1961–1965 — the 1½-litre years

At the end of 1958 the Commission Sportive Internationale (CSI) set about developing a new formula for Grand Prix cars, and ran into real difficulties from the very outset.

On the one hand the British teams wanted to maintain their new stranglehold on the business, but on the other hand Ferrari wanted to get back into the frame, while Porsche wanted to move up from Formula 2, and even Maserati was talking wistfully about returning to the sport.

In a very controversial move, the CSI therefore announced that the *next* Formula 1 would be for 1½-litre cars — which really meant that the old F1 was being killed off, and that the existing Formula 2 was being upgraded. At a stroke it meant that the GP cars for the 1961–1965 period were going to be much slower, less powerful, and even smaller than those of the late Fifties. Would the spectacle be maintained?

British constructors cried 'foul' (the fact that Ferrari and Porsche were strong in F2 was seen to be significant), for if anything they had wanted to see even larger engines for the early Sixties, and in the hope that a massive publicity campaign would move things their way they got together to suggest that they would have nothing to do with a new Formula. Instead, they announced, they would promote an 'Intercontinental' formula for 3-litre cars, and use developed versions of their 1960 models.

Ferrari, in the meantime, said very little, spent a lot of time getting ready for 1961, and was in a good position to win races when the British teams — Cooper, Lotus and BRM — realized that their campaign was doomed.

For 1961, therefore, Ferrari produced a brand-new mid-engined GP car, the famous 'shark-nosed' machine powered by one of two different V6 engines. With 170bhp on tap, and with a driving team including Phil Hill, Richie Ginther and Wolfgang von Trips, the Italian company was well set.

At the last moment the British teams realized that the war was lost and, for 1961 at least, all turned to Coventry-Climax for four-cylinder 1½-litre engines (which were, in fact, smaller versions of the famous FPF engine which had won so many 2½-litre races

Below: During the 1961 Dutch GP, Stirling Moss in the 1.5-litre Lotus Climax pursues the Ferrari of eventual winner Wolfgang von Trips

in 1959 and 1960). Although this was a reliable unit, it only produced about 150bhp, and not even the famed agility of the British cars could make up for the power deficit behind Ferrari.

Porsche arrived with a mid-engined car powered by the well-known flat-four air-cooled engine, but it was not until 1962, when the specially-designed flat-eight engine was ready, that the German constructor seemed likely to win races.

Except for two races — the Monaco and German GPs — where a combination of the Lotus 18/21's agility and Stirling Moss's genius made up for the power deficit, the 1961 season belonged to Ferrari. As on so many previous occasions, the fact that the cars were less powerful than before didn't seem to make them much slower, for improved handling, traction and braking made up for the 80bhp power losses.

Britain fights back

But it was not all bad news — Coventry-Climax and BRM both designed and built prototype V8 1½-litre engines, which raced briefly before the end of the season, while

Lotus found a remarkable young driver called Jim Clark.

So it was that in 1962 the British teams, now with V8 power, came back with a flourish, and Ferrari's one-year domination was killed off. As before, Lotus and Cooper produced 'customer cars' for sale, while Coventry-Climax and BRM V8 engines were allocated to several worthy teams and individuals. The real sensation came from Lotus, which not only produced the Type 24 for its 'customer' teams, but developed the trend-setting monocoque Type 25 for Jim Clark and Peter Arundell to drive. Not only was this even sleeker than earlier Lotus single-seaters, but its structure was very much stiffer than ever before, and the road-holding was improved accordingly.

The GP racing of 1962 was fairly evenly matched, for both British V8s produced about 175bhp, with BRM winning four races, Lotus three races, and Cooper and Porsche one each. Graham Hill won the Drivers' World Championship, but everyone was talking about the virtuosity and apparently effortless skill of Jim Clark in the Lotus team. While Porsche faded away, a new marque, Brabham (owned and driven by 'Black Jack' himself), appeared.

In the following season both the BRM and Coventry-Climax engines gained Lucas fuel injection, their peak power rising towards 190bhp, but the Lotus-Clark-Colin Chapman combination swept all before them, with Clark's Type 25 winning no fewer than seven of the ten races. Clark, naturally, was World Champion in his third full year in Formula 1.

Graham Hill's BRM won twice (Monaco and the USA), and John Surtees' new V6-engined Ferrari once (German GP). The Brabhams were improving all the time, but that vital first victory still eluded the team. Porsche, unable to match the high-revving British V8s, gracefully withdrew, to concentrate on sports car racing.

Speeds were almost back to late Fifties standards. At Silverstone in the British GP, for example, Jim Clark's race-winning average was no less than 107.75mph (173.40 km/h), just one mph slower than that achieved by Jack Brabham's 2½-litre Cooper-Climax in 1960.

Ferrari, too, was on the way back to the top. A mass defection of engineers from Ferrari (to found the unsuccessful ATS concern) had allowed young designers, including Mauro Forghieri, to have their say, and a new generation of nimble mid-engined cars was being developed. Not one, but two, new 1½-litre engines would appear in the near future — a V8 and a flat-12.

Swan-song of the 1½-litre GP

The racing in 1964 was closer than it had been for some years, for while Lotus suffered reliability problems, the Ferrari-Surtees combination prospered, BRM produced its first successful monocoque car, and

Brabham (with Jack himself and Dan Gurney behind the wheel) enjoyed more success. Only Cooper, whose star driver was still Bruce McLaren, seemed to be in decline.

The result was that ten race wins were shared between four different marques, with Ferrari and Lotus winning three races each, and BRM and Brabham twice each. It was the closest possible battle for the drivers' crown, which eventually went to John Surtees' Ferrari in the last race, in Mexico, after Jim Clark's Lotus engine packed in, and Graham Hill's BRM was punted out of contention by Lorenzo Bandini's Ferrari.

For the final year of 1½-litre racing, Coventry-Climax (which had recently been taken over by Jaguar Cars) heartened, then disappointed, everyone, at one and the same time. Not only did the resourceful Coventry-based company produce a couple of extra-powerful (210bhp) 32-valve V8 engines, but it also showed a flat-16 1½-litre engine that was projected to produce 220–230bhp.

In Jim Clark's brilliantly-driven Lotus 33s the 32-valve V8 engine was a great success, so much so that the flat-16 engine was never used in a car, even though it was at least as powerful as that final V8. Unhappily, Coventry-Climax (which had produced a total of 33 1½-litre V8s) decided that it would have to pull out of motor racing at the end of the current formula, which made the British constructors think very hard indeed.

For 1965, read 1963, but with minor changes. Once again it was to be the Jim Clark-Lotus combination which set every standard, for the peerlessly-talented Scot won six of the ten Grands Prix, four of them (Belgian, French, British, Dutch) in succession. Clark's Silverstone average rocketed to 112.02mph (180.27km/h), and naturally he won the World Championship.

Graham Hill's BRM won two races (Monaco and the USA), but there were two other important successes. Another talented young Scot, the beady-eyed Jackie Stewart, came straight into F1 from the 1-litre F3 scene, joined BRM, and won the Italian GP (and finished second in three other races), while the last 1½-litre GP race of all was won by Richie Ginther, driving a noisy but very powerful Honda. This was the first ever Japanese success in Grand Prix racing, and even at the time it was seen as an important event, with enormous implications for the future of the sport.

The Return to Power

At the end of 1963 the CSI was once again ready to announce a new Grand Prix formula, this time for the late Sixties, and this time they seemed to satisfy everyone. Nothing had been gained by cutting engine sizes to 1½ litres in the early Sixties, so the administrators decided to 'take the brave pill', and announced a real 'Return to Power'.

From January 1, 1966, it was revealed, Grand Prix racing would be for cars either

Above: Colin Chapman of Lotus was one of the pioneers of sponsorship on GP cars, with his Gold Leaf Lotuses, seen here at Monaco in 1968, the first to appear branded in the sponsor's colours

with normally-aspirated engines of up to 3 litres, for Wankel rotary engines, for gas-turbine engines, or for 'supercharged' engines of 1½ litres. The last provision was a surprise, but it was apparently done to allow 1½-litre engine builders to convert their engines for the new formula.

As a gesture it failed completely. Noted engine designers such as Walter Hassan of Coventry-Climax made it very clear that *they* would not be tackling such projects, and that if they *had* wanted to produce a 'blown' 1½-litre engine they would not have started on that basis!

Even so, it was an intriguing option for, according to the standards which existed in the 1947–1951 Grand Prix period, it should already have been possible to make a winning engine of this type. The motor-sport business, however, had changed a lot since then, no one wanted to tackle the expense of producing complex, high-revving, super-charged engines, and it was quietly forgotten.

Until, that is, Renault produced its first turbocharged engine in the mid Seventies, and sparked off an engine-design revolution which was to see Grand Prix car power outputs double in a matter of five or six years . . .

No one took the Wankel engine or gas-turbine options seriously at first though, as we shall see, Lotus went on to develop a turbine car, first for the specialized Indianapolis 500 race in the USA, and later adapted to F1 rules.

In the beginning, the new 3-litre Formula was only set to run for three years, to the end of 1968, but in the end it became the longest-running Grand Prix racing formula of all time. Formula 1 racing for 3-litre cars (and, from 1977, for turbocharged 1½-litre cars) ran, without a break, until 1985 — for 20 glorious years.

Even in the years after that, there was only a gradual changeover to something new, originally by banning the use of normally-aspirated engines, then by rejigging all the rules regarding fuel efficiency and car weight *and* allowing the use of 3½-litre normally-aspirated engines, and finally — for 1989 — by banning turbocharged engines and making 3½-litre 'atmo' engines compulsory.

It was a time when the whole face of Grand Prix racing changed completely, from a period in which the FIA/CSI bodies organized the Championship and the teams toed the line, to the period where a constructors' association, FOCA, organized everything in conjunction with FISA (a renamed CSI). In the same period the racing took on a true 'World' character, with GPs eventually being held in Japan, Australia, North America, Sweden, Hungary, Brazil and even Switzerland, all of which extended the season considerably, and expanded the series to 16 events.

Direct sponsorship was authorized from the start of 1968, which meant that 'national' car colours disappeared almost overnight, more and yet more safety regulations were imposed (and few disputed their worth), and technology increased by leaps and bounds.

The first 3-litre cars produced about 350bhp, but by the mid-Seventies the best figures had reached 500bhp. Turocharged engines produced 600bhp in the late Seventies,

800bhp by the early Eighties, and up to 1000bhp (1200 in qualifying tune) by 1986! Aluminium monocoques replaced tubular frames, then in the Eighties high-tech carbon-fibre monocoques replaced aluminium.

In the late Sixties various constructors tried four-wheel drive, but this was difficult to tame. Aerofoils and aerodynamic effects (external at first from 1968, then buried under the bodywork from 1977) became important, and all manner of engine layouts were tried before engines with more than 12 cylinders were banned from 1973.

It was a period in which the rules and regulations became more and more complicated. Take a deep breath before you read the next few lines, for by the Eighties not only were the engine sizes and configurations limited by definition, four-wheel drive was banned, and cars with more than four wheels were banned, but there were minimum weights and maximum dimensions to be observed, maximum heights and positions of aerofoil sections to be noted, the imposition of a 'flat bottom' rule for monocoques, the banning of bodywork which covered the wheels, the mandatory fitment of fire-extinguishing systems, mandatory provision for a pure oxygen feed to drivers' helmets, limits to the size of fuel tanks which could be used, limits to the octane rating of fuels which could be used, the requirement that *all* teams should enter *all* races ... it wasn't quite endless, but to a hard-pressed designer it must have felt like that at times.

Along the way, Bernard ('Bernie') Ecclestone bought the Brabham team, talked his way into the confidence of almost every other team, turned the constructors into a formidable negotiating body, forced up the prize fund for each race to unimaginable (and unannounced) heights, made sure that television coverage not only became all important but became very lucrative as well, and helped make Grand Prix racing into one of the biggest media circuses in the world.

1966 and 1967 — a changing scene

Even though the constructors had two full years to prepare the 'Return to Power', many teams were not ready in 1966. British teams, in particular, were thrown into confusion by Coventry-Climax's announcement that it would not design or build engines for the new formula. At a stroke this meant that Lotus, Brabham and Cooper had to begin all over again.

The change from small and delicate 1½-litre cars to bigger and more broad-shouldered 3-litre cars was so great that it needed a complete rethink from the constructors. At a stroke, designers had to get rid of their 200bhp engines and start to cater for 400bhp units instead.

The problem for almost everyone except Ferrari (who *always* seemed to be ready) was the choice of engine. Except that the CSI imposed a minimum weight of 500kg (1102lb), which was 50kg (110lb) higher than for the old 1½-litre cars, there were few limitations. So, should the new engines have four, six, eight, 12 or even 16 cylinders?

The majority opinion was that engines needed more cylinders, which meant more piston area, higher revs, and more peak power. Yet engines like this were more

Above: During 1968 many GP teams experimented with aerodynamic devices to improve grip, such as the wing sported by this Ferrari at the Nürburgring

heavy, were complex to design, expensive to build and difficult to maintain. Although most teams began to home in on eight-cylinder or 12-cylinder engines, it was obvious that a new generation of engines *and* cars would be needed.

The cars which appeared in 1966, therefore, were a mixed bag — some were new designs, some were new but with interim engines, and some were old 1½-litre cars with enlarged engines. A bookmaker trying to sort out sensible odds would have been hard pressed to read 'the form'.

There were several all-new cars — Ferrari with a version of its famous V12 engine, Cooper with a Maserati V12, Brabham with a Repco V8, and BRM with a monstrously complex and heavy H16 engine, which was really two flat-eight units on top of each other, geared together to a single outlet! The BRM would not be race-ready (and even then by no means reliable) until the end of the year. Honda decided to build a new V12-engined machine, but that was originally a heavy car, and was not to be reliable until 1967.

Dan Gurney, having left Brabham, produced the Eagle, for which a new Weslake V12 engine was being designed, but ran it with an ancient-design 2.7-litre Coventry-Climax engine at first. Bruce McLaren left Cooper to 'fly solo', deciding to use a Ford-USA V8 engine (and later trying an Alfa

Romeo V8), while Ferrari produced a grown-up F2 car, this one using a 2.4-litre 'Dino' V6 engine related to those used by the GP cars in the late Fifties. Lotus agreed to take H16 engines from BRM as soon as supplies were available.

In the short term BRM also used 1965-type cars with enlarged engines of 1.9 litres (later 2.1 litres), while Lotus also used 1965-type cars with enlarged (2-litre) Coventry-Climax V8s.

In 1966 the result was that no car had anything like 400bhp to use in the new formula. Several cars were competitive, for in the end BRM, Ferrari, Brabham, Lotus and Cooper all won World Championship races, using V8, V12, V8, H16 and V12 engines respectively! The year's simplest and most reliable car, no question, was the Brabham BT19, whose Repco V8 engine only had 310bhp, but which had impressive torque and drive-ability. Jack Brabham won four GPs in succession (French, British, Dutch and German), and consequently became the first driver-constructor to win the Drivers' title.

Although every team finally found full 3-litre engines to use in 1967, the big event of the year was the arrival, and astonishing success, of the Cosworth-designed Ford DFV V8 engine. Colin Chapman of Lotus had got together with Walter Hayes of Ford to hire Keith Duckworth of Cosworth to produce this squat, compact and rugged unit,

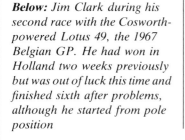

Below: Jim Clark during his second race with the Cosworth-powered Lotus 49, the 1967 Belgian GP. He had won in Holland two weeks previously but was out of luck this time and finished sixth after problems, although he started from pole position

which produced more than 400bhp on its first test runs.

Lotus built an entirely new team around this amazing new engine, building the new Type 49 car to accept it, and hiring Graham Hill away from BRM to join double World Champion Jim Clark to drive it. Although the Type 49 was a difficult car to drive at first, and the DFV was a very inflexible engine at first (the drivers use to say that there was one engine below 6000rpm, but *two* engines above 6000rpm!), it was much faster than all its rivals.

On its very first event, the Dutch GP of June 4, Graham Hill's car was fastest in practice, while Jim Clark's car won the 90-lap race at record speeds. On that important day the 'Cosworth era' was founded, for the 49-DFV combination went on to lead every race for the rest of the season, and won three more of them. The cars were so dominant that Hayes actually spun a coin before the USA GP to decide who should cross the line first; Graham Hill won the toss, but his car gave trouble, and Jim Clark took the flag instead.

Even though Lotus won only four races out of the eleven World Championship rounds, the Lotus 49-DFV was definitely 'class of the field'. When Ford announced that it would be supplying engines to other teams in 1968 the queue to buy formed at once.

In the meantime, in 1967, Lotus's four wins were matched by four wins for Brabham-Repco whose engines had been boosted to give about 330bhp, and single victories for Cooper-Maserati (in South Africa), Eagle-Weslake (Belgium) and Honda (Italy). Ferrari's glorious-sounding V12-engined cars were outclassed, the H16 BRM was neither reliable enough, powerful enough or light enough, and an alternative V12 engine was only fleetingly used in a one-off McLaren late in the year.

By winning two races (Monaco and Germany), and by scoring well on several other occasions, Denny Hulme took the World Drivers' Championship.

The Cosworth Years, 1968–1977

From 1968 the Cosworth DFV engine began to dominate top-line motor sport, not only in its purest form — as a Grand Prix engine — but in sports cars and (from the mid-Seventies) as a turbocharged unit in American Indy racing as well.

Not only was it an incredibly powerful and successful engine, but it was eventually built in large numbers, and supplied to any customer who could afford the prices. In almost every case it was linked to the ubiquitous Hewland five-speed gearbox/transaxle, this making it possible for any number of small constructors to gain entry into the 'kit car' F1 business.

The DFV's class is proven merely by quoting the number of Grand Prix wins in the next decade:

DATE	VICTORIES
1968	11 victories
1969	11 victories
1970	8 victories
1971	7 victories
1972	10 victories
1973	15 victories
1974	12 victories
1975	8 victories
1976	10 victories
1977	12 victories

The 50th GP win came at the Canadian GP in 1972, and the 100th at Monaco in 1977.

Although Cosworth produced a tiny number of extra-powerful development engines, almost every customer, and every driver, was offered the same race-winning package. If a team could produce a good chassis, and the driver had the talent, there was no reason why it should not win big events.

Using Cosworth DFV power Jackie Stewart, Jochen Rindt, Emerson Fittipaldi, Ronnie Peterson, Jody Scheckter and James Hunt dominated the victory list, while Lotus, McLaren, Matra, Brabham, March, Tyrrell, Hesketh, Penske, Wolf and Shadow all provided winning chassis. This was the period in which British constructors almost took over the business of Grand Prix racing, and when only Ferrari doggedly hung on to challenge their total supremacy. It was no wonder that Bernie Ecclestone and the F1CA (which became FOCA) organization grew so strong at the same time. The scene changed gradually, but persistently, from year to year. In 1968 DFV-engined cars won all but one of the season's big races — the exception being the French GP at Rouen, won by Jacky Ickx in a V12-engined Ferrari. Eagle's V12-engined programme collapsed, BRM ditched its H16 engine in favour of the V12 first seen in Bruce McLaren's car in 1967, while Brabham produced a new four-cam Repco V8 which suffered agonies of unreliability.

It was the year in which Jim Clark effortlessly broke Juan-Manuel Fangio's record for the number of Grand Prix victories, but it was the same tragic year that Clark was killed in a Formula 2 crash at Hockenheim, and when Jo Schlesser lost his life when he lost control of a new air-cooled V8-engined Honda at Rouen. This, too, was the year in which aerodynamic aids were taken up by many teams, with aerofoils (to give increased downforce on the tyres) first used by Ferrari in the Belgian GP, then with high-mounted aerofoils progressively being adopted by all front-running teams.

Jackie Stewart (Matra-Cosworth DFV) battled throughout the year with Graham Hill (Lotus 49-DFV) — three victories each — with the Championship finally going to Hill.

In the following year the script was re-written although principal personalities were almost the same. Brabham abandoned its Repco engine programme to become yet another user of DFVs, and Ferrari soldiered on, knowing that a new flat-12 engine design was on the way for 1970. BRM's V12 clearly produced a lot of power, but the team was no more successful than before — driver John Surtees stormed out of the team, and technical chief Tony Rudd was sacked; after that things could only get better for the Bourne-based team. Matra withdrew its temperamental V12, to think again. Cooper finally fell out of Grand Prix racing, unable to keep up with the increase in costs and technical advances, while Honda withdrew before the loss of face, by being defeated when British 'kit cars' became serious.

The Cosworth-powered cars were now so powerful (the 'going rate' was up to about 430bhp by this time), and so light, that wheel-spin was becoming a problem. At the beginning of the year, therefore, the technical talk was all about aerodynamic aids, and about four-wheel drive.

At first all cars sprouted high-mounted front *and* rear aerofoils, but their characteristics were not always clearly understood, and after both Lotus 49s suffered collapsed wings in the Spanish GP these were speedily

banned, in favour of aerofoils more securely mounted at body-height level.

Several different concerns — Lotus, Matra, McLaren and Cosworth itself — all built four-wheel-drive cars, but although the traction was excellent the handling was not, and all were speedily abandoned.

This time Stewart won six races, with Hill, Ickx (now with Brabham), Denny Hulme and the thrusting young Austrian Jochen Rindt sharing the other victories. DFV-powered cars won every Grand Prix, and no other engine got a look-in. Jackie, naturally, won the first of his three Drivers' Championships.

Just in time — for, in truth Grand Prix racing was beginning to look a bit boring — several 12-cylinder engines became competitive. Ferrari's flat-12 engine proved to be very reliable, BRM's V12 was finally matched to a great chassis (the P153), while Matra reintroduced its own shrill-sounding V12. March began building racing cars — and winning — on the back of an impressive programme of hype (the cruel joke of the year was that the March initials stood for 'Much Advertised Racing Car Hoax'!). Jack Brabham finally retired, and would soon sell his business. Jackie Stewart started the season in a March, but ended it in the original Tyrrell racing car.

Even though this was also the year in which Jochen Rindt won five consecutive GPs, in the radically-styled, wedge-nosed Lotus 72 (and became posthumous World Champion after being killed in a practice crash at Monza), various pundits began to write off the DFV. Even though it 'only' won eight races, and a further seven in 1971, the obituary was premature.

The Seventies scene

The next three years belonged to the Tyrrell-Ford-Jackie Stewart partnership. The cars were uncomplicated but workmanlike, the engines were supreme, and Stewart's driving and analytical approach to the business of Grand Prix racing was also unmatched. Jackie won six races in 1971, four in 1972 and a further five in 1973 — if it had not been for an enforced layoff due to a stomach ulcer in mid-1972 that record would certainly have been higher. The greatest raw talent of the period, though, was undoubtedly Ronnie Peterson, who drove Marches, then Lotus 72s, in an effortless and graceful manner.

The result was that Jackie won the Drivers' crown in 1971 and 1973, with Lotus-driver Emerson Fittipaldi (five wins) taking the title in 1972. These were the years in which Jackie crusaded for more and more safety, both of circuits and of cars. It made him unpopular with some diehards, but it bore fruit.

Tragically, this was the year in which his team-mate, François Cevert, was killed in a race crash, one result being that Jackie retired, having won 27 Grands Prix in only 99 starts — a record which was unbeaten until Alain Prost took it from him in the late Eighties.

Far right: Jackie Stewart in the Tyrrell at Silverstone in 1973. Peter Revson won that day but Stewart's results elsewhere were sufficient to secure him the Championship

Against such expertise, however, the BRMs and Ferraris were almost helpless. These teams won two races each in 1971, but only one each in 1972, and none at all in 1973. Lotus, which had produced four-wheel-drive gas-turbine-powered cars for the Indianapolis 500 race in 1968, even found time to build a modified version of this (the Type 56B) for Grand Prix racing in 1971, but it was not a success.

In the mid-Seventies, however, Ferrari (particularly when the Austrian Niki Lauda was driving) achieved a great revival. Bernie Ecclestone bought Brabham, American interests (in the shape of Penske and Vels Parnelli Jones) dabbled in Grand Prix racing, and all manner of 'kit car' builders produced low-budget one-offs.

In 1974 Ferrari won three races though Emerson Fittipaldi (McLaren) won the Drivers' title, but in 1975 Lauda's Ferrari won five races and there was no doubt who was driver of the year. The 1976 season started the same way, but Lauda was grievously burnt in a Nürburgring crash, missing races thereafter, while James Hunt (driving McLaren-DFVs) made a late charge to win the Drivers' Championship by a tiny margin. Then, just to prove that he not only had driving ability but real guts, the rejuvenated (it would even be reasonable to say 'back from the dead') Lauda won the Drivers' crown for the second time, then promptly left Ferrari to join Brabham!

By this time Tyrrell had shown, developed and raced its six-wheeler cars (four tiny front wheels instead of two rather larger ones in the quest for greater top speeds), but by far the most important development was in 'ground effect' aerodynamics, which was being pioneered by Lotus.

Ground effect and skirts

The Norfolk-based Lotus concern had been in the doldrums since 1974, for the long-running Type 72 had not successfully been replaced. Colin Chapman and Tony Rudd went back to basics, and a lot of fundamental research was carried out, especially in a wind-tunnel. It was here that Lotus discovered the phenomenon now usually

Above: Niki Lauda looked set to win the 1976 World Championship but for his terrible accident in his Ferrari soon after this photograph was taken at the Nürburgring

Above: Britain's James Hunt at Zandvoort in his McLaren M23 on the way to another win in his Championship year, 1976

described as 'ground effect' aerodynamics, and speedily capitalized on this in the Type 78 of 1977.

Lotus discovered that by carefully profiling the shape of side pods and (later) the full underbody of single-seater racing cars, they could use the rush of air-flow to suck the car harder into the ground without increasing the drag too much. This meant that the car's weight could be 'increased', which meant that the tyres could work harder and develop more cornering force.

To make the best of this, and to keep the air running along the sculpted channels, Lotus fitted ground-sweeping 'skirts' at the outer edges of the side pods. At first these were fixed, but it was not long before they were arranged to slide up and down, so that ground effect was never lost even though the car's structure moved up and down, or rolled in cornering.

In almost every way this was extra cornering power 'for free', and until other makes caught up with the trend Lotus was way out on its own. In 1977, with the Type 78, and especially in 1978, with the Type 79, the black-and-gold Lotuses were at the head of every field. 1978, indeed, was almost a walkover year for Lotus, which won eight Grands Prix. The American driver Mario Andretti became World Champion, but his team-mate Ronnie Peterson died after a multiple-car crash at the start of the Italian GP.

In the next few years the race to make more efficient 'wing cars' intensified. Lotus, in fact, slipped back in the early Eighties, but new designs from Ligier, Williams and Brabham all improved on the original.

Cornering speeds, and therefore lap speeds, increased considerably. At Silverstone, for instance, the 1969 GP was won at 127.25mph (204.78km/h); by 1977 this had only risen to 130.36mph (209.78km/h), but by 1981 (when 'skirt technology' had reached fever pitch) the winning average rose to 137.64mph (221.50km/h). All these wins were with Cosworth DFV-engined cars, the power of which only rose from about 440bhp to 490bhp in the same period.

Brabham's designer, Gordon Murray, thought up another way to tame the air, by building what became known as the 'fan car' in 1978. This used an engine-driven fan to suck air out of the underbody region, and exhaust it to the rear, thus creating an even more effective low-pressure zone. Niki Lauda won the car's first event — the Swedish GP — but the concept was speedily banned by the authorities, and the cars never raced again.

Enter the turbo

But if the taming of ground-effect aerodynamics was a minor upheaval, the arrival of turbocharged engines was a cataclysm. In the mid-Seventies peak power from 3-litre Grand Prix engines had stalled at around 500bhp. The first turbocharged engines to be raced produced about 550bhp, but by the mid-Eighties qualifying outputs had rocketed to 1200bhp, and race-long ratings of nearly 1000bhp were possible!

Way back in 1966, when the CSI had decreed a 3-litre formula, it had also allowed the option of 'supercharged' 1½-litre engines. No engine builder took any notice of this at the time, for it was widely agreed that the supercharged engine era had died out.

In the early Seventies, however, turbocharged engines were thoroughly established in 'Indy' racing in the USA, and had been developed for use in sports racing cars, these proving to be very effective indeed. Both types — supercharging and turbocharging — relied on pushing pressurized air into the engine, but used different methods.

A supercharged engine effectively used an engine-driven compressor for this job, which

meant that a lot of power was needed to drive it. On the turbocharged engine, however, the compressor was powered by an exhaust-gas-driven turbine. As the exhaust gas energy would otherwise have been expelled, this was another case of 'power for free', which made turbocharged engines much more efficient than their ancestors.

Renault, which had already produced turbocharged V6 engines in its sports racing cars, decided to enter Grand Prix racing with a special version of that unit, and on July 16, 1977, at the British GP, the first ever turbocharged Grand Prix car took the start. It was no dream debut though, for Jabouille's RS01 qualified 21st fastest and retired early on.

There was a great deal of cynicism about Renault's efforts, but the sneers turned to frowns when the car's straight-line speed was observed, and especially when Jabouille's car achieved its first grid 'pole position' — in the 1979 South African GP. The first victory was not long delayed, with Jabouille winning the French GP; Renault turbos were also 'on pole' in the German, Austrian, Dutch and Italian races.

By the end of the Seventies, therefore, there were two distinct trends — the British teams like Williams and Brabham using sophisticated aerodynamics, and European teams beginning to develop turbocharged cars. Ferrari's flat-12 'atmo' engine was good enough to give Jody Scheckter his Drivers' Championship in 1979, but it made underbody ground effect difficult to achieve. Alan Jones (Williams) won the Drivers' crown in 1980, to be succeeded by Nelson Piquet (Brabham) in 1981.

The Cosworth-DFV-powered cars kept on winning Grands Prix — nine in 1978, eight in 1979, and 11 in 1980, but it was beginning to

be a real struggle. Not only had Alfa Romeo produced powerful 12-cylinder units (for Brabham and for its own team), but Ferrari and BMW were designing turbocharged engines.

In 1981, however, the balance shifted decisively, for in an effort to reduce cornering speeds FISA banned sliding skirts. At a stroke this reduced the chances of cars using Cosworth DFV engines, and it brought the 'Cosworth era' to a rapid close. Not even Lotus's ingenious 'twin chassis' Type 88 could get round such regulations, and it, too, was speedily banned. By 1983, when the run of wins finally came to an end, DFV-powered cars had won no fewer than 155 World Championship Grands Prix, and countless other events.

It was at this time that FOCA (the constructors) squared up to FISA (the governing body), and threatened to organize its own World Championship, but after one 'pirate' event (the South African GP of 1981) had been held, the sides got back together, signed the 'Concorde Agreement', and settled their differences.

Turbo domination — 1981 to 1986

It was not long before Renault's turbocharged cars were faced with rivals — from Ferrari in 1981, and from Brabham-BMW in 1982. Ferrari's V6 was all-new, while BMW's engine was a much-changed version of the famous four-cylinder Formula 2 unit which had been so successful in the Seventies. Gilles Villeneuve's Ferrari 126C won its first race at Monaco in May 1981, Nelson Piquet's Brabham BT50-BMW its first race in Canada in June 1982. Renault's turbocharged cars won three races in 1981, and a further four in 1982; René Arnoux was the fast-qualifying

Left: The French Renault team were at last on the pace in 1979 with their innovative turbocharged cars. This is René Arnoux during the German GP at Hockenheim

45

hot-shot, but Alain 'The Professor' Prost was the smooth, refined, rising star.

Even though Keke Rosberg won the Drivers' Championship, using Cosworth-powered Williams cars, in 1982, this was a points-accumulating, rather than a dominating, performance. For the time being the 'atmo' engine era was over. McLaren, having sold out to Ron Dennis's organization, backed both horses, winning races in 1982 and 1983 with DFV-powered cars, but commissioning a brand-new V6 turbocharged engine from TAG-Porsche for future seasons.

Turbocharged engines then came quick and fast — Renault making more changes, and supplying engines to Ligier, Lotus and Tyrrell, Alfa Romeo, Cosworth-Ford, Hart and Zakspeed designing their own — but it was Honda who eventually overwhelmed the rest of the world. Not only that, but Brabham 'reinvented' the mid-race pit stop, where tyres could be changed, and more fuel could be added to thirsty turbocharged cars.

Especially as FISA imposed a 'flat-bottom' regulation for F1 monocoques in 1983, the season belonged to Nelson Piquet, Brabham, and the turbocharged BMW 'four', which developed about 650bhp in race trim, but 750bhp in qualifying; but by 1984 everything had changed again.

Not only did FISA ban refuelling in 1984, but it also cut the overall fuel tank size from 250 litres (54 gallons) to 220 litres (48 gallons). McLaren had mated the new TAG-Porsche to a fine chassis, hired Niki Lauda and Alain Prost to drive the cars, and went on to sweep the board. McLaren won 12 of the 16 races, with Lauda (five victories) pipping Prost (seven victories) by half a point to win the Drivers' crown. This was the year, though, when Keke Rosberg's Williams FW09-Honda won the USA (Dallas) GP, and set the F1 establishment by its ears . . .

There was more competition in 1985, with race victories going to McLaren-TAG-Porsche, Ferrari, Brabham-BMW, Lotus-Renault and Williams-Honda. Renault produced uncompetitive cars, and withdrew at the end of the season. McLaren was at the peak, Williams was charging fast, and the season's outstanding 'new talent' was undoubtedly that of Ayrton Senna at Lotus, and Nigel Mansell at Williams. Alain Prost won the Drivers' Championship, with five outright wins. It was about time, for he had so nearly lifted the same title in 1982, 1983 and 1984 as well. The last 3-litre 'atmo' car (a Tyrrell-Ford) raced in Germany in mid-year. For 1986, the turbocharged 1½-litre engines would be mandatory.

In 1986, two extremely powerful turbocharged V6 engine/car combinations — the McLaren-TAG and the Williams-Honda — swept all before them. Cars regularly raced with up to 1000bhp, the acceleration and overall performance of the cars was almost unbelievable, and the racing was exciting throughout the season.

In the end the Drivers' Championship was not settled until the final round, in Australia, when Nigel Mansell's Williams FW11 blew a tyre at high speed and Alain Prost won the event, and also won his second Championship. This was the year in which Ayrton Senna proved that he was probably the fastest *driver* in the F1 business, but his Lotus 98-Renault was not, in which Ferrari (usually strong on engine power) was completely outgunned, and where all other makes were outclassed. Renault withdrew their engines at the end of the year, and took a two-year 'sabbatical' from the sport.

Full circle — the banning of turbos

By this time officials of FISA were appalled by the way that speeds continued to rise (Silverstone's lap record was now up to 150mph/241km/h, and rising fast), and teams were also worried by the rapidly rising costs of it all. The result was a complete change of mind. In 1986 normally-aspirated engines had been banned, but for 1987 two major changes were announced — 3½-litre (not 3-litre) 'atmo' engines were to be allowed back in, and maximum turbo boost was to be limited to 4 Bar (57.6psi) with FISA supplying a series of blow-off valves to engine builders; at the same time turbo-car fuel capacities were cut to 195 litres (43 gallons).

To encourage the use of 'atmo' engines FISA invented a new Drivers' Championship for cars using these engines. As a result, Tyrrell, March and Lola all adopted Cosworth DFZ engines, these being enlarged DFVs — suddenly it was 1977 again, and at the end of the year it was Dr Jonathan Palmer (Tyrrell DGO16) who won the Jim Clark trophy.

At that moment FISA also gave notice that turbocharged engines would soon be banned completely, stating that in 1988 boost limits would be cut to 2.5 Bar, and fuel limits to 150 litres (33 gallons). In 1989, FISA stated, turbocharged cars would be completely banned. In three years, therefore, the emphasis in Grand Prix racing swung right back to its position in the Seventies, the only important difference being that 3½-litre, not 3-litre, engines, were mandatory.

There was still time for one last, glorious, ultra-powerful fling in 1987, for Honda was now supplying engines to Lotus, which meant that the Williams-Hondas, the McLaren-TAG-Porsches and the Lotus-Hondas could compete on more or less equal terms. Even though Ford-Cosworth's tiny 1000bhp V6 turbo came to maturity in 1987, in the Benetton car, it was not enough to defeat the established runners, and Ferrari continued to struggle, though it won two races at the end of the season. Though Nigel Mansell's Williams won six races it was his team-mate Nelson Piquet who won the World Championship.

1988 was an interim year, for TAG-Porsche abandoned the sport, and Honda switched its 2.5-Bar engine supplies from Williams to

McLaren, who had the formidable driving team of Alain Prost and Ayrton Senna, while continuing to supply Lotus; only Ferrari and Megatron-BMW bothered to develop their turbo engines for one final year. Everyone else was obliged to use 'customer' engines from Cosworth, or from Judd.

The result was 'Formula McLaren', a complete walkover for the Marlboro-sponsored team, who won 15 out of 16 Grands Prix; only at Monza, where Senna's leading car collided with Schlesser's Williams-Judd, did they fail. Ayrton Senna, not popular, but definitely a genius behind the wheel, beat Alain Prost to the World Championship.

Finally, in 1989, Grand Prix racing had a rebirth. All teams were obliged to run with 3½-litre normally-aspirated engines, and most teams had the benefit of newly-designed units — eights, 10s or 12s. Ferrari and Lamborghini produced glorious-sounding V12s, Honda provided high-revving V10 units to McLaren, Renault a new V10 to Williams, while Cosworth produced a brand-new 75-degree V8 for Benetton.

Grand Prix racing was becoming very secretive, so power outputs and other engine details were not divulged. Honda was reckoned to have 700bhp by the end of the season, with the other new engines exceeding 650bhp. Other teams had to make do with updated Judd and Cosworth V8s.

The result was that better-handling and more tractable cars were faster, not slower, than before — the Silverstone race average was no less than 143.694mph (231.246km/h) but, once again, McLaren-Honda led almost every race, and won many of them, though Ferrari and Williams were always close behind. As in 1988, the real battle was between Senna and Prost, who became bitter, non-speaking, rivals during the year. When Senna finished a race he usually won it, but engine and transmission failures ruined his chances of a back-to-back Championship. A much-publicized coming-together of the two McLarens in Japan resulted in Prost's retirement and Senna's disqualification from that race. As a result Alain Prost won his third World Championship, McLaren decided to sue FISA in the French courts to establish its rights, and Grand Prix racing ended the Eighties as something of a laughing stock in the world of the media.

Above: The combination of Alain Prost and a McLaren proved a formidable one in the late Eighties. He is seen here during the 1989 Portuguese GP in the MP4/5

The Grand Prix Races

The major races that have comprised the World Championship since 1950 are the meat of this chapter. Some races like the Hungarian GP or the Australian GP appear to be of recent origin. However they are typical of GPs that have a heritage that goes back many years to a time when Grand Prix racing wasn't organized into a World Championship and the sport was generally much less formal.

Grand Prix races have come and gone. The Swedish GP is no more; likewise the Swiss, Dutch and South African events. Others, like the Italian and British GPs, were on the Championship calendar in 1950 and haven't missed a year since. Of course there are other famous races besides Grand Prix — Le Mans, the Mille Miglia and Indianapolis to name but three. These and others are described in sufficient detail in other chapters for further words to be unnecessary here. Their year-by-year results are listed in the final section of the book.

The camera on board Alain Prost's Renault in 1982 captures an image that gives a vivid impression of the speed and power of a modern Grand Prix car

Argentine GP

The Argentine GP became a fixture on the F1 calendar in 1953. The first race, held in mid-January, was won by Alberto Ascari's Ferrari. It was an event marred by tragedy when Farina's Ferrari crashed into a section of the wildly enthusiastic crowd that pressed too closely against the sides of the Buenos Aires circuit. Nine spectators died in the accident.

With the return of the GP cars in 1954 so began a four-year period of domination by local ace Fangio, who won the race for Maserati (twice), Mercedes-Benz and Ferrari. In breaking Fangio's dominance in 1958, Stirling Moss also ushered in a new era in GP racing by winning in a rear-engined car for the first time.

As the Argentine racing heroes of the Fifties faded away, so did the Argentine GP until a local resurgence of interest in the early Seventies when for several seasons a partisan crowd hoped for victory by new local hero Carlos Reutemann.

The limitations of the Buenos Aires circuit, combined with political uncertainty in the country, conspired against the Argentine GP. The last race was staged in 1981 and was won by Nelson Piquet in a Brabham.

Below: Carnage for the midfield runners at the start of the 1987 Austrian GP, the last year the race was run

Australian GP

Australia first staged a GP in 1928 when A. C. R. Waite's Austin Seven took the honours in a loose-surface event held at Philip Island. However, that race was largely a domestic affair. It remained thus until the Fifties when visiting European stars travelled over to give the locals a run for their money. Notable among them was Stirling Moss, who drove his Maserati to victory in 1956.

Not until 1985 did the event become a round of the World Championship with the preparation of a new street circuit in Adelaide. Keke Rosberg won that first Championship race for Williams — his last race. Nigel Mansell's exploding rear tyre in the 1986 Australian GP robbed the Englishman of a likely win in the Championship.

The 1989 GP will be remembered as much for the terrible wet weather as for the result, which saw Thierry Boutsen take his second win of the year for Williams. Just eight cars finished this incident-filled race in which Ayrton Senna led decisively, only to crash into a slower car on lap 13, finally handing the Championship to his fellow McLaren driver, Alain Prost.

Left: *The Australian GP takes place on an attractive circuit conjured up from Adelaide's city streets*

Austrian GP

International F1 racing visited Austria for the first time in 1961 when Innes Ireland scored an early major win for Team Lotus at Zeltweg. F1 came back in 1963 for a non-Championship GP which was won by Jack Brabham in his own Brabham Climax.

In 1964 the Austrian GP became a Championship race for the first time and the result was the first and only win for Lorenzo Bandini, driving a Ferrari. However, the race was a hard one as the track surface was rough and the straw bales that lined the circuit provided inadequate protection for cars and drivers. The facilities at the makeshift circuit were poor and there would be no further GPs in Austria until the opening of a new track which was nearby, christened the Osterreichring.

The first Austrian GP of the new era was in 1970 when Jackie Ickx took over where Bandini had left off and won for Ferrari. The fast sweeping corners of the Osterreichring and its undulating terrain have thrown up odd winners over the years. Vittorio Brambilla won for March in 1975 and John Watson scored Penske's only win a year later. The home crowd had to wait until 1984 for an Austrian victory when Niki Lauda powered his McLaren to the chequered flag. The last winner of the Austrian GP was Nigel Mansell in 1987, for Williams. Thereafter the event was dropped from the international calendar pending the completion of improvements to the circuit.

Belgian GP

Grand Prix racing came to Belgium as long ago as 1925 with a victory for the Alfa Romeo of Ascari in a gruelling 503-mile (809.5km) race held over a challenging circuit at Spa Francorchamps. Under various formulae the GP continued throughout the Thirties with victories for such stars as Nuvolari, Caracciola and Lang.

With the instigation of the World Championship in 1950, the Belgian GP has taken place each year since with just the odd gap. Fangio won in 1950 and repeated the trick again in 1954 and 1955. Spa was a very fast and dangerous circuit and claimed more than its fair share of lives. Yet the circuit responded to driving skill, exemplified by Jim Clark's remarkable string of four wins, starting in 1962.

In 1970, that bravest of drivers, Pedro Rodriguez, won the last of the old-style Belgian GPs in his BRM before the problems of safety at the circuit became just too great. The Belgian GP then decamped to a temporary circuit at Nivelles for 1972 and subsequently moved to Zolder. While Nivelles would stage just two GPs, Zolder would hold the stage through to 1983 when a revamped Spa was opened. Alain Prost's Renault won the first race at the new Spa, while his sparring partner Ayrton Senna placed his stamp on the race in 1985, 1988 and 1989.

British GP

One of the Blue Riband events on the international GP calendar, the British GP was first held in 1948 to the 4.5-litre unsupercharged/1.5-litre supercharged formula. A race amounting to a British GP had been held pre-war as the RAC GP at Brooklands in 1926 and 1927 and as the Donington GP at Donington Park between 1935 and 1938. The events of 1937 and 1938 had seen the top-flight German teams come to Britain for the first time and emphasize just how backward were some aspects of the sport in Britain.

The first GP of the post-war era was held on the converted airfield circuit of Silverstone and saw a victory by Villoresi's Maserati. By 1950 the Championship had arrived and the British GP was the first event of the new

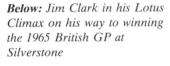

Below: *Jim Clark in his Lotus Climax on his way to winning the 1965 British GP at Silverstone*

year, held in May at Silverstone. Soon-to-be World Champion Farina opened his score card that day in his Alfa Romeo. For 1951 the GP moved to its now-traditional mid-summer slot. An exciting race saw Gonzales win in his unblown Ferrari, ending the dominance of the supercharged cars.

Silverstone retained the British GP until 1955 when it moved to a new venue at Aintree. Stirling Moss was the star that year, his Mercedes leading home team-mate Fangio. Fangio was back on top in 1956 but in 1957 had to give best to Brooks and Moss who shared a Vanwall to score a memorable win for British drivers in a British car.

Aintree and Silverstone alternated races through to 1962, after which date Brands Hatch in Kent replaced the northern circuit as the Silverstone alternative. Brands Hatch and Silverstone provided an excellent contrast in racing styles with the open fast corners of the Northamptonshire venue contrasting with the tight undulations of the purpose-built Kentish venue.

Jim Clark was the dominant force in British GPs of the Sixties, winning on no fewer than five occasions. In the Seventies, the British GP became a byword for controversy and incident as races were stopped with multiple pile-ups, such as in 1973 and 1976. In that latter year there were ugly scenes as the partisan crowd tried to hold up a restart to allow James Hunt time to appear in his spare car. He won on the track but was disqualified later.

Nigel Mansell was the local hero in 1986 and 1987, winning on both occasions. He starred again in 1988, eventually finishing second in an underpowered car. He was second again in 1989. By that year the GP was entrenched at Silverstone, having visited Brands Hatch for the last time in 1986.

Canadian GP

Having been run as a sports car race from 1961, the Canadian GP was adopted as a round of the F1 World Championship in 1967. The challenging Mosport circuit was the venue and Jack Brabham in his own Brabham Repco was the winner of the first Canadian GP. Until 1970 the race alternated between Mosport and St Jovite but Mosport became the sole venue between 1971 and 1977. Jody Scheckter scored one of his three victories in the Wolf Ford at the last Mosport event before the GP moved to a new circuit in Montreal.

The growing fame of Canadian driver Gilles Villeneuve was a key factor in the growth of domestic interest in the sport. Villeneuve played his part superbly and duly won the first Montreal Canadian GP in 1978. Villeneuve almost won again in 1982 but Alan Jones pipped him to the flag.

In the wake of a dispute over sponsorship and problems over safety features of the circuit, the 1987 Canadian GP was dropped from the calendar. However, it was back in 1988 and remains a popular North American round with the circuit now renamed after Gilles Villeneuve, who lost his life in 1982. The wet 1989 race marked one of McLaren's rare failures of the 1989 season, leaving Thierry Boutsen to pick up his first GP win for Williams.

Dutch GP

The Dutch GP lapsed from the international calendar in 1985 awaiting the redevelopment of Holland's only circuit, Zandvoort. Hitherto it had been a regular and popular round of the Championship. The race was added to the Championship calendar in 1952, having been run as a sports car event previously.

Ascari ran true to his 1952 and 1953 World Champion's form by winning the Dutch GP in both years. When it was next staged, in 1955, the all-conquering Fangio won in a Mercedes. BRM made their Championship GP breakthrough with Bonnier's win in 1959. Graham Hill would win again for the team in 1962, his first victory of many. Between 1963 and 1965 Jim Clark was unstoppable as he scored a Lotus hat trick. Equipped with the new Ford Cosworth engine he won again in 1967.

One other notable result from the record of the Dutch GP is James Hunt's win in 1975. He drove his Hesketh to the team's only success, beating Lauda's Ferrari fair and square in an exciting duel. Hunt would win again in his Championship year of 1976.

Niki Lauda's name is the last one in the record books, winning for McLaren in 1985 from his team-mate and 1984 (and 1981) winner, Alain Prost.

French GP

The French GP is the oldest of all the famous GP races, having first been staged in 1906. The gruelling event, held over two days and comprising laps of a massive 64-mile (103km) circuit of rough roads, was won by the Renault of Szisz who was at the wheel for more than 12 hours at an average speed of 62mph (100km/h).

Fiat, Mercedes, Peugeot and Duesenberg would variously share the victories in the next few years with Henry Segrave winning in a British Sunbeam in 1923. The French GP was held in various forms until the outbreak of war. The mighty German Mercedes team made the French GP their first overseas event in 1934 but returned home in disgrace after an Alfa Romeo 1–2–3. They did not repeat the failure the following year, clinching a 1–2 finish for Caracciola and von

Brauchitsch. Mercedes won again in 1938 and Auto-Union were first in the last pre-war running of the great race.

The first post-war French GP was run at a road circuit at Lyons and Frenchman Louis Chiron was the popular victor in his French Talbot. For the first French GP as a round of the new World Championship the race moved to Reims, a circuit it had visited in 1932. Fangio in an Alfa took his third victory of the year in an exciting race on the fast circuit where the average speed was over 100mph (161km/h).

In succeeding years the French GP was held at five other circuits: Rouen, Clermont Ferrand, Le Mans, Paul Ricard and Dijon. There were some fine races along the way and some notable results, such as Mike Hawthorn's hard-fought win in 1953 and Peter Collins' impressive victory in 1956. Dan Gurney won an isolated victory for Porsche in 1962 and, more recently, Renault chose their home race to stage their second win in the French GP, 73 years after the first. Jean-Pierre Jabouille was at the wheel that day. Renault would win three more times with a hat trick in 1981, 1982 and 1983.

German GP

The high-speed Avus circuit in Berlin staged the first German Grand Prix, a 1926 event for sports cars. The result was a success for a rising star, Rudolf Caracciola. Sports cars contested the race again in 1927 and 1928 before the single-seaters took over. Then in 1931 the GP moved to the circuit that would be its permanent home almost without a break through to 1976, the Nürburgring.

The years of the 750kg (1653lb) formula in the mid-Thirties witnessed some great races, none more so than Nuvolari's astonishing victory for Alfa Romeo in 1935 when he defeated both Mercedes and Auto-Union in perhaps his greatest race. Englishman Richard Seaman also scored a memorable victory, driving for Mercedes, in 1938.

In the post-war years, the German GP became something of a Ferrari speciality until the return of Mercedes in 1954. Ascari won for Ferrari in 1950/1951 and 1952, as did Farina in 1953. Then Fangio won for Mercedes and came back to do it again for Ferrari in 1956 and, even more impressively, for Maserati in 1957.

Apart from great races at a most challenging circuit, the German GP is clouded by tragedy. Peter Collins died at the 'Ring in 1958 while Jean Behra died in 1959 when the race paid a one-off return visit to Avus.

Stirling Moss scored one of his best wins in Rob Walker's Lotus in 1961. Since then the results of the race have tended to go with the trend of the season, especially after the move to Hockenheim, following Lauda's near-fatal accident at the Nürburgring in 1976.

Hungarian GP

Nuvolari (Alfa Romeo), Rosemeyer (Auto-Union) and Varzi (Auto-Union) were the illustrious 1–2–3 of the first Hungarian GP in a Budapest park, run to the 750kg (1653lb) formula in 1936. This visit to Hungary by GP cars remained a one-off until the construction of the new Hungaroring in 1985/6. Nelson Piquet's Williams-Honda won the reconstituted event in 1986 and 1987 and then came Ayrton Senna's turn to take the chequered flag in 1988. Senna looked a likely winner again in 1989 until Britain's Nigel Mansell produced one of his best ever performances to snatch the lead and take his second win of the year for Ferrari.

Italian GP

The Italian GP is pre-dated among European GPs only by the French, having been first staged in 1921. It was initially run on a road circuit at Brescia but it moved to its spiritual home at Monza in 1922. Missing just 1929, the GP took place every year through to the outbreak of war. The names of Nuvolari, Caracciola, Rosemeyer and Fagioli are

Left: Nigel Mansell, sixth on the grid, produced one of his best ever drives to win the 1989 Hungarian GP in his Ferrari

among those inscribed on the pre-war list of winners. The races were fast, exciting and dangerous, with many fatalities among crowds and competitors.

Post-war, the GP was run at alternative circuits in Milan and Turin respectively in 1947 and 1948, before Monza was restored and ready for competition use again in 1949. It was the closing round of the first World Championship in 1950 and has been staged every year since. Fangio dominated the race between 1953 and 1955 and Stirling Moss made it his own in 1956, 1957 and 1959. It was still, however, a dangerous race, claiming the lives of von Trips, Peterson and Rindt, to name but three.

The Italian GP has been won by many of the great drivers but a couple of unlikely names are also recorded as winners. In 1966 Ludovico Scarfiotti scored Ferrari's first win in the team's home GP for 14 years, his only Championship GP victory. Former World Champion John Surtees persevered with his unwieldy Honda in 1967 to bring it home to its only GP win of the season. Similarly, Ronnie Peterson brought his March home to a rare win in 1976. Peter Gethin scored his only GP win by dramatically forcing his BRM to the front of the nail-biting 1971 slipstreaming race. In 1988 Gerhard Berger assured himself of lasting glory in Italy by

winning the Italian GP for Ferrari, with team-mate Alboreto second.

Safety at Monza has been improved in recent seasons but the Italian GP remains the fastest GP in the Championship.

Japanese GP

The Japanese GP grew to F1 World Championship status via a series of sports car GPs in the mid-Sixties. The first GP as part of the international calendar came in 1976. The weather was terrible at Mount Fuji but it was a dramatic race, won by Mario Andretti. However, the real excitement was elsewhere when Niki Lauda refused to race on in view of the weather and James Hunt came home third to scrape the World Championship crown by the narrowest of margins. Hunt went two better in 1977 and won the GP.

There followed a 10-year break in the running of the race until the move to Suzuka in 1987. Gerhard Berger started a winning run for Ferrari while Nigel Mansell's failure to score points saw the beginning of the end of his Championship hopes. The 1989 race was in many ways the most extraordinary yet as team-mates Prost and Senna duelled for the lead and the Championship. Eventually they hit each other as Senna tried desperately to overtake. Prost retired but Senna recovered to win, only to be disqualified, effectively handing the title to Prost.

Mexican GP

The Mexican GP became legendary for lack of crowd control and this factor was a major element in the abandonment of the race between 1970 and 1986. The *Grand Premio de Mexico* was first run in 1962 and it became a Championship event in 1963. Jim Clark was the first winner, in a Lotus. The following year's Mexican GP was a thrilling end-of-season event which saw a Championship shoot-out between Jim Clark, John Surtees and Graham Hill. In fact, Dan Gurney won the race but John Surtees emerged as Champion.

Richie Ginther's only GP win came at Mexico City in 1965, the experienced American braving the crowds that lined the circuit and sometimes even ran across it.

By 1970 the event was considered just too dangerous, and the race was stopped short and Jackie Ickx declared the winner. Sixteen years later the track had been improved, as had the spectator control, and the GP cars came back. Gerhard Berger scored his first GP win in what was the penultimate event of the year. Thereafter the race has tended to go with form, with Mansell, Prost and Senna winning up to 1989.

Right: The McLarens lead the way around Casino Square during the 1989 Monaco GP

Monaco GP

Probably the best known of all the GPs, the Monaco round of the Championship is in many ways also the most unsatisfactory as the roads that wind round the Principality and make up the racing circuit are really too small for modern GP cars. The roads were tight even when the race was first run back in 1929. The great Mercedes and Auto-Unions of the Thirties made an astonishing spectacle as they threaded their way between the houses. Bugatti won the first three GPs at Monaco and Mercedes the last three before the war.

Farina beat modest opposition in his Maserati to win the first post-war event. The quality of the field improved for the first Championship GP in 1950 but a huge pile-up on the opening lap depleted the field, leaving Fangio, who had avoided trouble, to come home as victor in his Alfa. There was no F1 GP through to 1955 although there was a sports car GP in 1952. The 1955 Monaco GP was the only Championship race that year not won by Mercedes-Benz (apart from Indianapolis) and it was diminutive Maurice Trintignant who took the flag in his aged Ferrari. Just to prove that it was not a freak result, Trintignant would win again three years later.

Stirling Moss was the class of Monaco in 1956/60 and 1961 and his crown was assumed in 1963 by Graham Hill, sometimes known as 'Mr Monaco', who went on to win in 1963/64/65/68 and 1969 — a remarkable record. More recently Alain Prost has come close to equalling this feat with four wins, but in 1989 he had to give best to Senna and settle for second spot.

Monaco has been the scene of some terrible accidents and some cars have even ended up in the harbour, such as Alberto Ascari's Lancia in 1955. Jean-Pierre Beltoise scored BRM's last GP win in 1972. Ten years later there was an extraordinary race that looked like being open to just about anyone to win. Successive leaders crashed, broke down or ran out of petrol. It was Patrese's Brabham that eventually completed the 157 miles (257km) first!

Ayrton Senna chose Monaco to stage one of his displays of virtuoso wet-weather driving in 1984 when he would have won for Toleman but for the race being stopped by officialdom on the lap in which he would have taken the lead. He would gain his revenge, however, by winning in 1986 and again in 1989.

San Marino GP

The Italian appetite for motor racing is almost insatiable, so what better reason to find some way of running two GPs in that country? Imola staged the Italian GP in 1980 and held on to an F1 race by calling it the San Marino GP in 1981. It has been run each year since and has produced some excellent racing. Patrick Tambay scored a good win in 1983 in memory of his friend Gilles Villeneuve who had been killed just a year before and whose place he had taken at Ferrari. The 1985 race was marked by several of the likely winners running out of fuel in the closing stages. The record shows that the 1989 race was the expected McLaren 1–2, but possibly more noteworthy was Gerhard Berger's miraculous escape from a massive accident on a 160mph (257km/h) corner.

South African GP

Witney Straight in a Maserati won the first event to be called the South African Grand Prix, in 1934. The race was run for various formulae on seven further occasions before it became a Championship GP in 1962. That year's World Champion, Graham Hill, was the winner, but in the next two South African GPs the best he could do was finish third behind Jim Clark's Lotus.

In 1967 the event moved from the cramped

Below: Emerson Fittipaldi leads the way at the start of the 1972 South African GP at Kyalami. Hulme's McLaren would, however, beat him to the chequered flag

Portuguese GP

Castellotti, Gonzales, Behra and Fangio were among the great names to win the Portuguese GP when it was run for sports cars in the early Fifties. When it became an F1 race on Oporto's streets in 1958, it was Stirling Moss in the Vanwall who led the field home. He did it again at the Monsanto circuit the following year, that time driving a Cooper. The race lapsed after 1960 and was not revived until 1984, following the redevelopment of an existing circuit at Estoril.

Alain Prost has been the most consistent winner at Estoril with three victories to his credit, although Senna's win in 1985 is one of the best-remembered results, such was his skill in the wet.

Most dramatic among recent Portuguese GPs was 1989 when Nigel Mansell overshot his pit during a stop and reversed in the pit lane. He rejoined the race and resumed battle with Senna, the culmination of it all being a coming-together that left both the McLaren and the Ferrari in the sand. Mansell was subsequently confirmed as disqualified for reversing in the pit lane; his team-mate Berger won the race for Ferrari.

circuit at East London to Kyalami where it would remain until its demise in 1985. Familiar names appear in the winners' list, latterly drivers of turbocharged cars as the rarefied air of the high-altitude circuit favoured cars so powered. Nigel Mansell was the last winner of the GP before the race became too politically sensitive to continue.

Swedish GP

Sweden staged a Winter Grand Prix on four occasions, starting in 1932, plus a Summer Grand Prix in 1933, 1948 and 1949. It was from the latter event that a GP for sports cars developed in the mid-Fifties, attracting entries by many famous drivers. However, not until as recently as 1973 was a Championship Swedish GP arranged.

A Swede never won the GP although Peterson nearly managed it that first year but had to settle for second spot behind the McLaren of Denny Hulme. Jody Scheckter scored his first-ever GP win in a Tyrrell in 1974 and repeated the win again two years later, driving the remarkable Tyrrell six-wheeler — the car's only success. Niki Lauda was the other driver to win the Swedish GP twice, succeeding in 1975 and 1978, the latter victory coming in the controversial Brabham 'fan car' which was promptly banned. With the deaths of both Swedish racing stars Ronnie Peterson and Gunnar Nilsson the driving force behind the Swedish GP waned and the event faded away.

Spanish GP

Touring cars contested the first Spanish GP as far back as 1913. However, it wasn't until the construction of the ill-designed Sitges-Terramar circuit in 1923 that the race assumed international status and Frenchman Albert Divo remained on the dangerous banking long enough to score his first major victory, driving a Sunbeam.

The race then moved to the flatter environs of San Sebastian and ran to various formulae up to the war. The first Championship race was in 1951 on the Pedralbes street circuit in Barcelona. Fangio was the victor in the final winning appearance of the venerable 1.5-litre supercharged Alfa 159. Mike Hawthorn took his second GP win in the hotly-contested 1954 event before the Spanish GP lapsed from the international calendar.

The event re-emerged in 1967 as a non-Championship affair staged in Montjuich Park in Barcelona. This led to a fully-fledged GP in 1968, not staged at Montjuich, but at the new purpose-built facility at Jarama, near Madrid. Thereafter the GP would alter-

Right: Detroit, pictured here in 1988, is one of five US cities to stage the US GP on its streets in recent years

nate between the two venues with Jarama gradually gaining dominance as the bumps and dips of Montjuich became too much for modern GP cars and drivers. When in turn Jarama became outpaced, the GP circus moved to the new circuit out in the wilds at Jerez in the south of the country.

Swiss GP

Motor racing in Switzerland ended with the banning of the sport following the Le Mans tragedy of 1955 when a Mercedes crashed into the crowd killing many spectators. Hitherto, missing only the war-affected years of 1940 to 1946, the country had staged a major GP at the Bremgarten circuit in Berne every year from 1934 to 1954. Pre-war the winners all came from the Mercedes or Auto-Union teams. Caracciola won for Mercedes on no fewer than three occasions and the winners for Auto-Union were Stuck and Rosemeyer.

Jean-Pierre Wimille in an Alfa Romeo was the first post-war winner in 1947 and when the event became part of the Championship in 1950 it was the year's Champion, Farina, who took the spoils. Piero Taruffi took his sole Championship GP win in 1952 while his team-mate and likely winner Ascari was away practising for the Indianapolis 500 race

taking place two weeks later. The 1954 race was won by Fangio who swept all before him that season driving for Maserati and Mercedes-Benz. Then came the disaster of 1955 and the Bremgarten race was no more. However, a non-Championship race titled the Swiss GP was held at Dijon in France in 1975 and this became a Championship round for 1982 only.

United States GP

A GP described as a 'Grand Prize' rather than a Grand Prix took place in the USA as early as 1908 over a 402-mile (647km) circuit in Savannah and ran through to 1916 with most of the winners driving European cars, Benz, Fiat and Peugeot among them. Meanwhile, Indianapolis had opened for business in 1911 and it was the form of oval racing promoted there that diverted motor sport in the USA away from European-style road racing.

Not until 1958 was there another USA GP, this one for sports cars and held at Riverside where Chuck Daigh's home-grown Scarab had the legs of the rest of the field. The following year's USA GP was for single-seaters and became a Championship round, staged at Sebring in Florida. Bruce McLaren's Cooper won that first race. Then followed three years of Lotus domination as Moss, Ireland and Clark took it in turns to win. Ireland's win, his sole Championship victory, came when the race moved to Watkins Glen, near New York, which would become its home until 1980.

Graham Hill scored a memorable hat trick of wins for BRM starting in 1963 and then Jim Clark won again for Lotus in 1966 and 1967, making it nine straight years that British drivers won the USA GP.

1976 marked the introduction of a second GP in the USA, called the US GP (West). It was staged in March at the Long Beach street circuit in Los Angeles. Clay Regazzoni came out on top that day but it was James Hunt who won the traditional east-coast fixture later in the year.

Watkins Glen was last used for a GP in 1980 and thereafter one of the country's two races began a nomadic existence, taking in Las Vegas, Detroit, Dallas and Phoenix. Long Beach kept going until 1983 before turning to domestic racing, rather than F1. In 1982 the USA managed to stage no fewer than three GPs, with races at Long Beach, Detroit and Las Vegas. By 1985 the tally was back down to just one: Detroit, where Rosberg maintained his winning form of 1984. By 1986 Ayrton Senna was clearly the fastest driver on tight street circuits and he won in Detroit three years running through to 1988. He looked like winning from pole at Phoenix in 1989 too, but his car failed him and Alain Prost came through to win.

Circuit racing in the USA

The physical and cultural differences between the United States and Europe meant that motor sport was bound to develop differently in the two spheres. Historically the Indianapolis 500 on the 'Brickyard' oval has dominated the sport in the USA. Its influence is now reduced but its legacy is still a major influence on the sport. Although European technology is prominent and British drivers have won the race, this form of racing is still a mystery to many onlookers outside the USA.

The USA stages at least one F1 Championship GP each year (three in 1982), but domestic motor sport is dominated by outwardly similar forms of single-seater racing referred to as 'CART' and 'USAC' on both ovals and road circuits. Drivers known only to enthusiasts in Europe are household names in the States where the rewards are high and the competition intense.

The start of the 1988 Indianapolis 500, the major circuit race of the United States motor-sporting calendar

The early forms of motor sport had two main influences — horse racing and cycle racing. Most horse races were on grass, which worked well with hooves for traction, but proved almost farcical when wheels started spinning. It was more than obvious that cars were better suited to racing on the road, although this led to problems with crowd control and non-competing road users, such as horses and carts. A quick solution in Europe was to close a few roads in a rough circle or triangle so that they could be adequately policed. This did not work so well in the United States, however, because the centres of population tended to be further apart and better served by the railways. Interconnecting roads tended to be in an appalling state, not least because railway barons — with the notable exception of Willie K. Vanderbilt — discouraged anybody from improving them. The only roads suitable for racing tended to be in city centres, which attracted crowds of unmanageable proportions.

As it happened, horse trotting was popular in America. It was a form of racing in which the jockey was carried on a sulky hitched to the horse. In many ways the sulky resembled a two-wheeled version of the early cars, and

Below: Cars preparing for the start of the 24-hour race held on Brighton Beach, New York, in 1908

centred on beach racing as an alternative to the road races which had started it all at the same time as the Europeans.

Road racing, notably for the Vanderbilt Cup, carried on for several years in the United States, but crowd control caused so much trouble that the emphasis rapidly switched to track events. One of the earliest promoters, Carl Fisher, was also one of the most ambitious. He began planning a permanent speedway soon after seeing the number of spectators the Vanderbilt Cup attracted in 1904 and going over to France to watch the Gordon Bennett races the following year. Fisher, whose Indianapolis-based company was a major motor-industry supplier, could also see there was money to be made by creating a testing facility for car makers. A lot of capital was needed, however, so he talked engine-builder James Allison, Indianapolis's main car manufacturer Arthur Newby, and carburettor-maker Frank Wheeler into joining him in the venture.

The birth of the Brickyard

They bought the most attractive site near Indianapolis, a 320-acre parcel of land called Presley Farm, for $80,000. The four partners then found enough money to build a 2.5-mile

it did not take long for entrepreneurs to put the two together. Dirt tracks had been laid out at some of the bigger centres of population to provide a more durable surface than grass, which would be ideal for cars and motor cycles.

There were the additional attractions that crowd control was easier and money could be more readily extracted from spectators than by the roadside, so track racing got off to a flying start in the United States where land was relatively cheap. The sheer cost of building a track near a large centre of population put off all but the most determined promoters in Europe. Further variations in America

(4-kilometre) rectangular circuit with curved corners, surfaced throughout in a mixture of crushed rock and tar. By the time the speedway opened in August 1909 it had cost them $500,000. The surface proved less than adequate, however, and led to several fatal accidents, so Fisher talked the other three partners out of an additional $200,000 to completely repave the oval with 3,200,000 bricks four months later.

By the following year, several races were being held. But they seemed like an anticlimax after the first events and attracted only small crowds. So Allison had the idea of running just one race each year, of such a

Left: *The competitors had to contend with loose surface roads in the 1908 Vanderbilt Cup*

stature that it would attract large crowds without the problems of paying a full-time staff to keep the stadium open all year. Such an event would have to last all day, so they decided on a 500-mile (805km) race which would last around seven hours. The first of these events, in May 1911, won by Ray Harroun's Marmon, was such a success that the Indianapolis 500 soon became a permanent fixture. Newby's enthusiasm was maintained when the winner, Joe Dawson, drove one of his National cars in 1912, but interest began to wane when Europeans like Jules Goux, in his Peugeot, started to win the following year. Americans loved nothing better than to cheer home the local boy, having vanquished all the foreign opposition.

The spectators had become used to doing this in long-distance events on one-mile dirt tracks or beaches in which the racing was frequently fixed. These meetings had developed from 24-hour, or 1000-mile (1610km), record-breaking attempts by cyclists which had been taken up by cars on tracks around Detroit as early as 1904 and were popularly known as 'grinds'. By 1907, such events had taken on a distinctly commercial flavour. Posters and banners bearing trade names covered fencing rails all around the track. An impresario called Bill Pickens, well aware of the fascination generated by dramatic wheel-changing, refuelling and repairs, arranged for these activities to be centralized in front of the main grandstand in the first 'pits' at Point Breeze, Philadelphia. Arc lights lined the circuit and the bars stayed open all night.

Already track racing was becoming something of a circus.

Leading drivers to emerge from the grinds included Barney Oldfield, Louis Chevrolet and Ralph de Palma. Accidents were frequent as massive cars stormed through clouds of dust raised by deeply-rutted tracks. By 1910, strings of red lights were being used at Brighton Beach to signal that all runners should stop while the track was cleared of debris. It would be years before this safety warning system was adopted at Indianapolis and elsewhere. By the start of World War 1, however, dirt-track grinds were almost extinct. Race fans were beginning to prefer a programme of several shorter events, some for cars of unlimited power, some for cars of varying capacity. Local distributors of lesser-powered cars were also more likely to support such events rather than compete where they stood little chance of winning. Frequently there were fewer than a dozen entries for such demanding events, which — with inevitable non-finishers — made for less-than-spectacular racing.

Oldfield versus de Palma

Much of the publicity that attracted huge crowds to the dirt tracks was generated by showman Oldfield and his famous feud with former bike racer de Palma. The Italian-American motor mechanic from Brooklyn was one of the most naturally-gifted drivers and a perfect gentleman, in distinct contrast to the cigar-chewing Oldfield. Crowds everywhere poured out their hearts to de Palma, not only when he won dozens of races, but also when he lost. One of his most famous defeats had been at Indianapolis when the engine of his old grey Mercedes threw a connecting rod while he was two laps in the lead with three to go. As his speed dropped ever further, Dawson's big blue National began to catch him, until the Mercedes crawled and clattered on at an agonising 15mph (24km/h). Dawson was still behind when it ground to a halt, and de Palma refused to quit. With his Australian riding mechanic, Rupert Jeffkins, he began to push the 1½-ton car, only to be caught almost on the line by Dawson, happy to pick up a $20,000 first prize. The crowd could not care less who won; they would always come back to cheer on the gallant de Palma, especially when he was on the receiving end of Oldfield's villainy.

Oldfield, who had helped Henry Ford raise the capital to build cars by driving one to victory over America's first auto king, Alexander Winton, had billed himself as the World's Speed King at reaching 131mph (211km/h) with his 'Blitzen' Benz at Daytona in 1910. The combination became the greatest attraction at county fairs as Pickens stirred up publicity throughout the United States. Oldfield was always having a duel with somebody, especially his sidekick, Ben Kerscher, 'The Flying Dutchman'. Typically he would win the first heat in grand style. Then Kerscher would take the second, edging out the cigar-chewing King of Speed by a fraction. A nerve-shattering battle would follow in the final heat with Kerscher and Oldfield side by side in the last bend

before the Blitzen Benz slid through to win by the width of a cigar band.

In reality, Oldfield was a far better driver than he reckoned, but there were few people in the same class as de Palma. In 27 years' racing, in which he covered 30,000 miles (48,280km), he entered 2800 events and won more than 2000. Yet the only time he won at the Brickyard, as Indianapolis had become known, was in 1915, despite leading a record 613 laps. Although he was one of the favourites, the 'smart money' was on Dario Resta's Peugeot, a combination which had won the Vanderbilt Cup two months earlier. It looked as though the gamblers might be right as Resta powered past the leading Stutz after only 18 miles. But De Palma's Mercedes was a close second, taking the Peugeot when it ran into tyre trouble. Then, jinx of jinxes, a connecting rod went with only three laps to go as Resta charged back into contention. But this time, de Palma managed to nurse his car home first.

He was riding on the crest of a wave of success, having beaten his own jinx, as American motor racing entered a new phase with board tracks replacing the dirt ovals and open roads. All sorts of ingenious events were organized, such as a match race between de Palma in a 12-cylinder Sunbeam and Wild Bob Burman in his ex-Oldfield Blitzen Benz record-breaker at the Sheepshead Bay two-mile (3km) boardway. It was a needle match, the judges crediting victory to de Palma by .005 seconds. Then, as de Palma stepped up to the winner's podium, he raised a hand for silence, before declaring: 'As we

Below: *A scene from the very first Indianapolis 500-mile race, held in 1911. This photograph was taken by Henry Ford*

crossed the finishing line, I was watching our front wheels. Bob's were three inches in front of mine. He's your winner!'

As de Palma invariably played the white knight, Oldfield proved more innovative. As early as 1916, his cars were carrying advertising, proclaiming that Firestone Tires Are My Only Life Insurance! De Palma considered that most ungentlemanly, and refused to have anything to do with such rubberware. It cost him races, and his nephew, Peter de Paolo, told him: 'If you don't change to Barney's tyres, I'm going to leave you.' And leave he did, to become the first man to win at Indianapolis — in a Duesenberg in 1925 — averaging more than 100mph (161km/h).

The spread of track racing

At that time the track was only a mediocre commercial success. After 16 years, the original partners sold out for $700,000 to World War 1 flying ace Eddie Rickenbacker, who had driven in early events. The 1920s belonged to the far more spectacular 'rinky-dink' mile-and-a-quarter (2km) board tracks than to the wide-open spaces of the Brickyard.

Most of the tracks were built by promoter Jack Prince and engineer Art Pillsbury. Prince would search out a location, assess wealth by dividing the number of banks into the numbers of local population, raise the finance, then wire Pillsbury who would arrive to hire labour, design the track, get it going and await his next cable from Prince. The principle became: 'Get 'em up fast and collect the cash before the termites take over.'

The first board track was built at Playa del Rey, California, in 1910 and the last in the East just before World War 2. But they were at the height of their fame in the Roaring Twenties, as a special breed of driver took all manner of risks, from rotting boards flying through the air to splinters puncturing his cloth helmet. De Palma, Gaston and Louis Chevrolet, Wilbur Shaw, Billy Arnold, Lou Moore, Frank Lockhart, Jimmy Murphy and de Paolo were numbered among the top drivers, but Tommy Milton was the greatest. To quote Pillsbury: 'He had no peer. He was frightening, tenacious, intelligent, motivated and vicious. He won many times with a slower car and when he started his move, everybody knew it. He challenged the impossible and you shut your eyes.'

Altoona, in the Pennsylvania coal-producing area, had one of the longest-living tracks that carried the dubious honour of sounding the death-knell for such activities by running a 200-mile (322km) race on a surface so dangerous that popular Indianapolis winner Ray Keech lost his life in a multi-car pile-up. Even the coalminers — hardened to numerous deaths on such tracks — could not take that. Within three months, during the height of the Depression, Altoona died too.

The cars they drove doubled up for the Brickyard. Murphy started a trend by installing a Miller engine — based, like many others, on the 1913 twin-cam Peugeot — in the Duesenberg with which he won the 1921 French Grand Prix. The Duesenberg-Miller gave him victory at Indianapolis the following

Below: By 1919 the track had ben resurfaced at Indianapolis and the event had grown in stature and significance

year. Harry Miller, a self-taught Wisconsin machinist, had migrated to Indianapolis in time to see the first 500-mile (805km) race. The first engine he built under his own name was a rush job for Burman, who could not get Peugeot parts from France in 1914. By the time the American Automobile Association had reduced maximum capacities to 122 cu in (1999cc), Miller's straight-eights were dominating track racing, Milton winning at Indianapolis in 1923. Miller, who was aided considerably by designer Leo Goosens and foreman Fred Offenhauser, made both front-wheel-drive and rear-wheel-drive cars. They produced one of the most beautiful racing cars ever built, the Miller 91, when the AAA maximum capacity was further reduced to 91 cu in (1491cc) in 1926, when they filled the first 14 places. Only Lora Corum, de Paolo and George Souders could break up a tidal wave of Miller successes at Indianapolis before Shaw imported a Grand Prix Maserati.

Leon Duray took two Packard Cable Specials (Miller 91s) to Europe in 1929, breaking records at Monza and Montlhery. It was Duray's *traction avant* Millers that inspired Ettore Bugatti's twin-cam Type 50 and André Citroën's immortal 12CV. A four-cylinder version of the straight-eight would go on to dominate American track racing for more than 30 years, bearing the name Offenhauser after the foreman bought out Miller's factory in 1934. The 'Offy' ran in normally-aspirated, supercharged and turbocharged forms to provide winners as late as 1975, before a completely new engine was developed in 1977.

Just as the board tracks were costly to maintain, so was the Brickyard. It deteriorated during World War 2, and eventually Shaw, who had won in 1939 and 1940, persuaded Rickenbacker to sell it to Indiana businessman Tony Hulman Jnr. Hulman ploughed in more money, repairing the surface and building new concrete and steel grandstands. The speedway was fully refurbished in time for George Robson to win the 1946 race in a Thorn-Sparks Special.

Kurtis-Kraft

The board tracks might have died but the dirt tracks still lived. There were more than 1000 quarter- to half-mile ovals around the United States, running races for Midgets — scaled-down Indianapolis cars. As many as 60 cars and drivers would turn up for any event, making enough money for a meagre living if they raced every night. Two-thirds of the cars would be powered by Offenhauser engines, now made by Meyer and Drake Engineering, cheaper units being used in the rest. In the same way, the majority of chassis were the products of another specialist, Kurtis-Kraft.

Frank Kurtis was the self-taught engineer son of a Californian blacksmith, who rapidly gained a reputation before the war for building beautiful hot rods. He built his first racing car in 1932, but the early ones were only moderately successful because the drivers who commissioned them would not let Kurtis incorporate any radical features. It was not until 1938 that a young driver called Rex Mays let Kurtis incorporate some of his own ideas — notably an offset engine because these Midgets only turned left. The idea worked and soon there was a queue for Kurtis-Kraft cars. By the end of the war, a buyer could order a new Midget with torsion bars, half-elliptic or quarter-elliptic springs, any wheelbase between 66 inches (168cm) and 72 (183cm), with mounts to take Offenhauser, Ford V8 or two-cylinder Drake engines. By 1950, Kurtis had sold 550 Midgets, around 75 per cent of those running in the United States.

Naturally, he also produced Indianapolis cars, including the front-wheel-drive Novis for Goossen and Bud Winfield. The Blue Crown Spark Plug Special which won the

Right: In 1954 all the cars racing at Indianapolis had Offenhauser engines. This is the opening lap of the 500-mile race

Indy 500 three times from 1947 to 1949 was similar in concept. But, as ever, Kurtis had other ideas on how a car should be developed. His K2000 Indy-and-fairgrounds car of 1948 had independent front suspension and a De Dion rear axle that became all independent the following year. These cars went so well that by 1950 the grid at Indianapolis was packed with Kurtis cars and Johnnie Parsons won with the Wynn's Friction Proof Special. For the next 14 years every winning Indy roadster was either built by Kurtis or, like those constructed by A. J. Watson, followed a design strongly influenced by his cars. Drivers included Troy Ruttman, Bill Vukovich, Bob Sweikert, Pat Flaherty, Sam Hanks, Jimmy Bryan, Rodger Ward, Parnelli Jones and the greatest of them all, the Texan A. J. Foyt.

Meanwhile the bodies organizing racing in the United States were changing. Former saloon car driver Big Bill France started the National Association of Stock Car Auto Racing (NASCAR) in 1947 after being snubbed by the AAA, which preferred to concentrate on established Indianapolis cars. As NASCAR went from strength to strength, the SCCA and NHRA (National Hot Rods Association) broke away from the AAA, which disbanded its contest board in 1955 and left the United States Auto Club (USAC) to run its remaining events, including the Indianapolis 500.

The European influence

The days of the traditional Indy roadster were numbered, however, when World Champion Formula 1 driver Jack Brabham took a tiny, underpowered Cooper-Climax to the Brickyard to finish ninth in 1961. Before that the track still had strong elements of its original brick surface. The turns were coated in asphalt as early as 1936; only the front straightway was still exposed some 20 years later, but the rough brick surface was enough to keep down the speed of the

Right: Graham Hill in the Lola on the way to victory in the 1966 Indianapolis 500

Below: Pounding round the Brickyard in 1966. Graham Hill's winning average that year was more than 144mph (232km/h)

dirt-track specials which were ideal for such purposes. But when the front straight was finally paved in 1961, cars with small wheels like the Cooper-Climax were at no disadvantage. The 150mph (241km/h) barrier was finally broken in 1962, and British World Champion Jim Clark's Lotus powered by Ford was winning in 1965. Graham Hill was well on the way to becoming the only man to win motor sport's top three titles, the World Championship, Le Mans and the Indy 500, when he took the 1966 race with a Lola-Ford.

As the European mid-engined cars, with their far superior high-speed handling and tiny frontal areas, took over at Indianapolis, the Americans adapted the basic design to their own specialized needs. As early as 1968, Bobby Unser was winning in an Offenhauser-powered Eagle constructed by All-American Racers, run by former Grand Prix star Dan Gurney. Starting grids are limited to 33 cars on the basis that each needs 400 feet (122m) of track for safety reasons. By 1973, 22 of the cars were Eagles (although Mark Donohue's McLaren-Offenhauser won), a total that nearly equalled Kurtis's best — 23 — in 1952 (when Ruttman won in an Agajanian).

But already the USAC championship racing, which had thrived on the dirt tracks when the same cars could run in the Indy 500, was in trouble. The new brand of mid-engined racers were no use on a dirt track and presented a far less dramatic spectacle than the NASCAR saloons on the paved speedways. Banked tracks, which were ideal for the Indy cars, were few, which meant that they had to be visited frequently to make up a full championship calendar, again diluting the spectacle. The money was also beginning to run out: Indianapolis could justly claim to be the world's richest motor race with the first million-dollar purse in 1970, but the prize money was pegged after that. By the mid-Seventies, the USAC championship teams were feeling the pinch. Attempts were made to expand the championship by taking in 'road-racing' circuits — normal tracks like those used for CanAm with both right-hand and left-hand unbanked bends — but, with so many rival series, the Indycars failed to provide the major attraction. Foreign rounds — two races in Britain — during 1978 fared no better although Al Unser managed to win the only Triple Crown (Indianapolis, Ontario and Pocono 500-mile races) in Indycar history.

USAC versus CART

Much of the blame for the decline was laid at the doors of the conservative USAC, which tried to reduce the cost of competing by framing new regulations aimed at keeping the old Offenhauser engines competitive against the increasingly popular turbocharged Cosworths. Most of the teams objected, pointing out that the new regulations were ill conceived and would cost them all a lot more money. As a result, they lost faith with the USAC and formed their own organization, CART — Championship Auto Racing Teams — to run their own races, inspired by leading owners Roger Penske and Pat Patrick.

The USAC had their headquarters at Indianapolis and kept the famous 500-mile race within their fold as the two organizations both ran championships in 1979 — the same teams being allowed to compete in both following legal action by CART to prevent USAC from banning them. By the end of the season, CART had the initiative, having staged 10 races to the seven of USAC, including the Indy 500. More importantly, only four of the races were televised, one of them the Indy 500 and the other three CART events. Individual championships were won by Rick Mears' Penske (CART) and Foyt's Parnelli (USAC). The Texan veteran had set a record by winning at Indianapolis for the fourth time in 1977 and felt that he had to stay within the USAC orbit to stand a chance of winning for the fifth time.

CART and USAC tried to resolve their differences in 1980, briefly operating together as CRL (Championship Racing League) before falling out again, CART emerging with the only viable series. USAC held on to the Indy 500 and Pocono 500, at a track owned by Indianapolis. By November, CART was strong enough to post a million-dollar prize fund, leaving USAC with only the Indy 500. News that Porsche were developing an engine for the race, one of the few they had not won, proved alarming. The German manufacturers' plan was to use the power unit, based on the one that was dominating world sports car racing, in an Interscope car run by customer Ted Field. But the hierarchy at Indianapolis were fearful that it would result in a walkover like that which had helped kill the Canadian–American (CanAm) sports car series in 1973, and changed their rules to render the Porsche engine uncompetitive.

The CART fields, using mostly Cosworth power units, were generally deeper and stronger, attracting more new teams and drivers. American chassis continued to dominate the category. Indy 500 winner Johnny Rutherford took the CART title as well with a Chaparral, but various Penskes were the most numerous, although Tom Sneva achieved wonders in taking third place in the championship with an old McLaren.

By the end of 1981, CART prize money was up to $3.5 million with complete TV coverage, both track and 'road' races, and around 40 cars attempting to qualify for 24 places on a typical grid. Many of the new competitors came from the rapidly-declining CanAm championship run by the Sports Car Club of America (SCCA). This 'road-racing' series had been originated for sports cars, but switched to single-seaters with all-enveloping bodywork after the club's Formula 5000 — for

American V8-powered versions of Formula 1 cars — expired and Porsche began winning everything with their 917–30 sports car. The 1979 CART champion Rick Mears took the title again for Penske as a new threat emerged in the March driven by Sneva.

The rise of March

Until March began making new cars for anybody that could afford them, smaller teams were having to buy year-old cars from Penske or Patrick and try to keep them competitive. These modern Indy cars were essentially a kit with a variety of extra parts enabling them to be converted from one aerodynamic specification to another, depending on where they competed. They were produced in Britain — the centre of the world's motor-racing industry where development costs could be laid off over a variety of projects, including building sports racing cars for America's IMSA series — because it would have cost far more to set up such an operation, involving numerous small sub-contractors, in the United States. The American Penske team recognized as much by having their cars made in Britain, too.

By 1982, around 80 per cent of competitors were using either Penske or March chassis — in roughly equal proportions, with Mears taking a third title for the Penske from Rahal's March. The following season was the best to date for the CART series, with a steady influx of new teams and drivers to challenge the establishment. There were eight different race winners, including Teo Fabi (four), Mario Andretti (two), Sneva (two), with Al Unser Snr, John Paul Jnr, Mears, Rahal and Johncock winning one each. March provided seven winners as CanAm and Formula 1 refugee Fabi pulled up to second place behind champion Al Unser Snr, in his 19th season of Indycar racing and rated alongside Mario Andretti,

Below: Massive crowds turn out for Daytona Speed Week in Florida. This was the scene at the start of the 1988 500-mile race

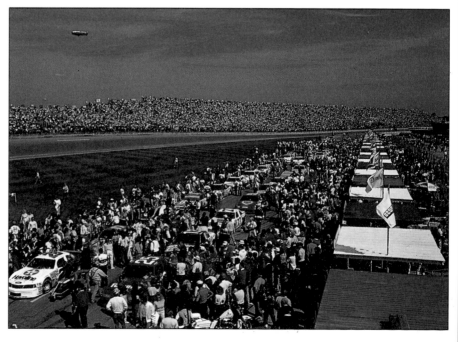

Above: Indianapolis is conceived with the spectator and TV viewers in mind. The crowds can get close to the action in safety as revealed here in 1988

Foyt and de Palma as one of America's greatest drivers.

Most Indycar competitors, including the Penske team, were equipped with March chassis in 1984, but it was Mario Andretti, in one of two works Lolas, that took the championship in the last few laps of the last race from second-placed Sneva, and Rahal, running third in Marches. The story might have been different, however, had Indy 500-winner Mears (March) not missed the last five races of the season with accident injuries, to tie for fourth place with Danny Sullivan in the other works Lola. Safety became a major issue with a number of spectacular accidents, especially as cars were now lapping at more than 200mph (322km/h) on the Indianapolis and Michigan speedways. Many drivers, including Andretti, asked for more power so that they did not have to run flat out all the time, but CART and USAC kept their limitations, opting for aerodynamic changes that would limit ever-increasing downforce.

Second-generation winners

1985 was similar to 1984, the vast majority of competitors using March chassis, with Lola providing almost all the remaining runners. A historic moment was recorded in the Indianapolis 500, when 30 out of the 33 starters, and all the finishers, drove a March. Cosworth DFX engines provided most of the power, save for two Buick V6-engined Marches in the Indy 500 and two normally-aspirated Chevrolet V8s that struggled to qualify. But the season still went down in the memories of Americans as one of the most dramatic with Al Unser Snr, in a March, holding on to win the championship by a

single point from his son, Al Unser Jnr, driving a Lola! Two-thirds of the way through the season, there were still six drivers in contention for the championship as the two Unsers began regularly to share the winners' rostrum. The unlucky Andretti, who won eight races, and the steady former double World Champion Emerson Fittipaldi, one race, chased in Rahal, three wins, and Indy 500-winner Danny Sullivan (one other victory).

Another son of a famous father, Michael Andretti, rose to stardom in 1986 with what amounted to the works March, leading 11 of the 17 Indycar races, although he won only three, partly through problems with engines. He had to concede first place in the championship to Indy 500-winner Rahal, driving a works Lola to the British firm's first CART championship. March and Lola then began to battle it out for orders with Penske hiring former Lola chief engineer Nigel Bennett to produce an updated version of the Lola chassis. It was a policy that Penske had followed before, earlier chassis having been inspired by the McLaren M24, because their production run was not sufficiently large to pay for extensive development.

Rahal's total of six wins — three on ovals, three on 'road' circuits — was the highest number for any champion since Mears in 1981 and the first time anybody had 'done the double' since 1980. Even though Rahal won six races, there were seven other winners, the title race lead alternating between Sneva, Kevin Cogan, Michael and Mario Andretti, and Al Unser Jnr. Although the spectacle of single-seaters running wheel to wheel at 200mph (322km/h) remained the essence of Indycar racing, the addition of more street circuits — such as Long Beach and Meadowlands — gave the series a far broader television appeal.

Rahal continued where he had left off in 1987 by being the master of consistency, putting his Lola on the front row of the grid seven times, on the way to three wins, five second places and two thirds. To put the whole championship into perspective, Rahal was on the victory rostrum in 10 races, which made him the winner of the end-of-season, big-buck Marlboro Challenge, as well as becoming the only Indycar driver to win more than $1 million two years in a row . . . But Al Unser Snr went into the history books alongside A. J. Foyt having won the Indy 500 for a fourth time.

Mears took his third win at Indianapolis in 1988, but team-mate Danny Sullivan took the championship. Their limited-production-run Penske chassis had become the best in the field, as Lola won the overall sales battle from March. Penske also had an advantage in more power from the team's British-sourced Ilmoor four-cam V8 engine. These engines bore the Chevrolet badge, powering the cars of both Sullivan and second-placed March driver Al Unser Jnr. A further variation could then be seen in the Judd V8-

powered Lola of third-placed Rahal, Michael Andretti running both March and Lola chassis as Cosworth's front-runner in sixth place. All three engines were produced within a few miles of the March and Lola factories, emphasizing the strength of the British motor racing industry.

Enter Porsche

A further assault on Indycar racing was also made by Porsche, which now had little new to win after several years' domination in sports car racing. Initially their own chassis proved uncompetitive, but after switching to March, Fabi managed to take 10th place in the championship. Penske had proved that with lap speeds now in excess of 220mph (354km/h) on the fastest speedways, specialized chassis development paid off in terms of race wins. So when leading sports car racer Al Holbert was killed in an air crash, Porsche hired former Penske chief Derrick Walker to run their operation — and he, in turn, signed an exclusive contract with March in 1989.

The deal worked well with Fabi moving up during the season to give the emergent Porsche team their first win on the tight Mid-Ohio circuit where the ability of the chassis to put down the engine's considerable torque really paid off. Mears had been tipped to take the championship in Penske's front-running car, but hard driving by Emerson Fittipaldi with similar equipment in the rival Patrick team's lead car helped relegate Mears to second slot. Highlight of the championship for Fittipaldi was victory in the Indy 500, making him only the second living driver, with Mario Andretti, to win both the world Formula 1 championship and Indianapolis.

But CART faced problems as it entered the Nineties. Only the front-running teams were attracting enough sponsorship for this very expensive highly-specialized racing and there were strong suggestions — as Penske's Marlboro-sponsored three-car team looked like dominating the series in a similar manner to McLaren in Formula 1 — that the two disciplines should merge. Logically the Indianapolis 500 should become the United States Grand Prix. Such a merger would give Indycar racing the international exposure it needed to boost sponsorship, while dramatically improving Formula 1's relative failure to make the impact it should.

Below: Brazilian Emerson Fittipaldi won the Indianapolis 500 Miles in 1989, reminding the world that he had lost none of the talent that took him to the top in GP racing in the early Seventies

Senior Formulae after F1

Typical coverage of motor sport in the mass media suggests that there is little single-seater motor-sporting life after Formula 1. Nothing could be further from the truth. Throughout each sporting season numerous drivers and teams compete with great skill and commitment in the two formulae which lie directly 'beneath' F1: F3000 and F3. These are the current stepping-stone formulae to a GP drive. Formerly there was F2 and before that there was Formula Junior in which the talented driver could prove his skills.

These are generally not the formulae for the enthusiast racing for fun and recreation; they are now professional categories in which the racing is fierce and success is at a premium. Success in these 'junior' formulae is the only route to the top of the sport.

Grand Prix graduate Stefano Modena leads the field at the start of the exciting 1987 Birmingham street race for F3000 cars

In the early days of motor sport, competition was available to any brave soul who had access to a set of wheels. With the very concept of the car still in its infancy, potential participants were thus few and far between.

Over the ensuing decades, as the car has become ever more prolific, the sport has developed a clearly-defined route of progression. In theory, it is this which the ambitious must follow if they hope to achieve the status of a Formula 1 Grand Prix driver.

Before the sport was forced into a sabbatical between 1939 and 1946, it was still possible for wealthy amateurs to purchase a car with which they could contest contemporary Grands Prix. The final few years of pre-war Grand Prix racing were utterly dominated by Germany.

The Italians, who thanks to the likes of Alfa Romeo and Fiat had enjoyed long spells of motor racing dominance prior to the arrival of the German sledgehammer, became distinctly unhappy. Indeed, in 1939 they decided to run all their races to a formula for cars with a maximum engine capacity of 1.5 litres (supercharged), thereby excluding the more muscular German machines. It may have seemed a good idea in theory, but in practice it didn't work. Mercedes-Benz secretly developed a 1.5-litre V8, and turned up to sweep the board with a 1–2 in the 1939 Tripoli Grand Prix!

This 1.5-litre supercharged category was known as the *Voiturette* (literally small or light car) formula, and it had become popular throughout Europe in the years leading up to World War 2. At that time, it served as a useful training ground for young drivers; in effect, a forerunner of what would later be known as Formula 2, and now goes under the misnomer of Formula 3000.

One man who benefited from his success in voiturette events was Britain's Dick Seaman, whose achievements with an ERA (1935) and a Delage (1936) led to the offer of a test drive from Mercedes-Benz. On the strength of that, he was integrated into the team in 1937, winning the 1938 German Grand Prix. Sadly, he lost his life in an accident at Spa during the following year's Belgian GP.

Post-war developments

Recovery from the war was gradual, for facilities such as Brooklands and Donington had been commandeered by the forces to assist the war effort. The first events of the new era relied on pre-war machinery, and required new circuits.

The post-war years saw a shortage of building materials, and petrol was rationed. The economically minded saw the sense of building tiny, 500cc motor-cycle-engined cars, primarily for sprinting and hill climbing. With the reintroduction of circuit racing, the 500s adapted to a new environment and became hugely popular, bringing such luminaries as Stirling Moss to the attention of the racing public, particularly so when the skeletal racers were introduced as a supporting feature at the British Grand Prix. Eventually, the category was christened Formula 3, and what we now recognize as the 'motor racing ladder' was taking shape.

Up until the late Seventies, it was still possible for private entrants to run in Formula 1. The regulations allowed manufacturers to supply more than one team, and enthusiastic amateurs often took advantage of that in order to try and qualify for their home Grand Prix. The changing face of the sport, largely a reflection of increased professionalism, has put such eccentric hobbies firmly to rest. Now, in order to qualify for the relevant racing licence, an aspiring Formula 1 driver has to prove himself in a succession of junior categories, a system which guarantees that only the cream of young drivers filter through to the top of their chosen profession. Being supremely rich *can* occasionally outweigh a driver's lack of results, but by and large the 26 men busying themselves on a Grand Prix grid on a Sunday afternoon are there on merit.

A start on the ladder

For many years, Formulae 3 and 2 were recognizably the final two rungs on the ladder, although in 1952 and 1953 the lack of Formula 1 cars meant that the World Championship was run to F2 regulations, and in the mid-Sixties F2 cars were occasionally included to make up the numbers in Grand Prix fields. However, a number of peripheral categories have come and gone, some of them pushing forward stars of the future, others flattering only to deceive.

Although Formula 3 survives as a proving ground, Formula 2 is now extinct, although its spirit and dimensions live on in Formula 3000. The licensing system allows Formula 3 champions to graduate directly into F1, but those who do are rare. Usually, Formula 3000 is the next port of call, and it is here that Formula 1 talent scouts generally find what they are looking for.

Below: A typical Voiturette race for 1.5-litre cars from the Thirties. In fact this is June 1937 in Florence with ERAs at the front, followed by Maseratis, one of which, driven by René Dreyfus, won the race

Left: *A full F3000 grid takes the start at Brands Hatch in a round of the 1988 Championship*

Formula 3000

Since its inception in 1985, Formula 3000 has proved to be the most keenly-contested international single-seater category in the world. In that respect, Formula 2's replacement has been a huge success. On the other hand, the European Championship has suffered from chronic lack of promotion, and the category's curious name means that it is difficult for the general public to assess its importance in the overall scheme of things.

With interest in F2 dwindling in the early Eighties, F3000 was created to rekindle some of the sparkle that used to be associated with its predecessor. Chassis dimensions would remain the same as those outlined in the F2 regulations, but the highly-tuned, four-cylinder F2 racing engines were replaced by normally-aspirated 3-litre units, with a maximum of 12 cylinders. In order to increase longevity and reduce running costs, an electronic rev limiter was developed to keep engine speeds down to 9000rpm. The system was tested in a converted Williams F1 chassis late in 1984, and positive feedback led to the formula's introduction for the 1985 season.

With turbochargers now a prerequisite for F1 teams, there was a ready supply of V8 engines in the form of the once ubiquitous Cosworth DFV. Interest in the new category was high, but despite one Italian motor sport magazine predicting as many as 94 entrants, the first race at Silverstone produced just 15 cars, barely any more than had graced Formula 2 in its final European season.

To add fuel to the doubters' arguments, the Ralt team — totally dominant in F2's dying days — romped to a conclusive 1–2 result, thanks to Mike Thackwell and John Nielsen. However, it was soon clear that Formula 3000 was extremely competitive. Even at Pau, where only 11 cars started and five finished, the meagre field kept the crowd mes-

merized for 90 minutes, Christian Danner's privately-entered BS Automotive March gradually wearing down the similar works car of Emanuele Pirro, the first of four victories that would eventually clinch the inaugural championship crown for the respected German driver.

Going into the final race at Donington, the entry had risen to 21, and the title was up for grabs. Thackwell, Pirro and Danner were all in contention, but when the first pair collided at the very first corner, all Danner had to do was to finish third. He avoided the soft option, and went on to win the race and with it the championship crown. It was enough to land him an F1 drive, albeit with the humble Osella team, but by the end of the following season he had found a more acceptable place with Arrows, and he left behind him a population explosion in F3000.

Gearing up to greater things

The Italian press tempered their predictions for the 1986 season, but they needn't have bothered. In the course of 11 races, no fewer than 71 drivers tried their hand at least once, and around 34 cars turned up for each event. With a maximum of 26 permitted to start (only 22 on the street circuit at Pau), each weekend produced a lengthy list of non-qualifiers. It was just like Formula 2 had been around 10 years earlier; better still, it was a formula in which the underdog could come up trumps. To this end, one further element was introduced at the start of the season: it was decided to make F3000 a control-tyre formula. Rubber companies were invited to submit a tender for the supply contract, and eventually Avon was chosen to produce identical tyres for everybody. At a stroke, this eliminated the need to produce expensive, soft-compound qualifying tyres. Avon's monopoly ensured future stability, which came as a relief after the fierce competition between Bridgestone and Avon in 1985.

Above: Johnny Herbert in his Reynard 88D. Herbert's success in F3000 was the key to his move into GP racing

Lola, March and Ralt all produced competitive chassis, and Cosworth V8s were still readily available. Honda introduced an engine exclusively for the works Ralt team, but the restrictive regulations meant that the Japanese newcomer conferred no discernible advantage, and indeed it won just one race.

The championship again went down to the final race, when Ivan Capelli secured enough points to fend off the challenge of fellow Italian Pier-Luigi Martini. Two wins and a succession of points finishes were enough to give Capelli the crown, and his success neatly summed up F3000's appeal. Capelli's Genoa March entry was run from the workshop of his close friend, the late Cesare Gariboldi, and the team scraped through the year with just a couple of mechanics and barely sufficient sponsorship to cover all the races. Indeed, had a Japanese backer not appeared towards the end of the season, he would never have been able to maintain his challenge to the end. It was a popular triumph, and Capelli followed Danner's trail by graduating to F1 with March, a project set up with the assistance of Gariboldi, who continued to keep a fatherly eye on his protégé until sadly losing his life in a road accident two years later. By then, Capelli had become an established member of the Grand Prix circus.

The 1986 season provided a solid base on which to build, and the top three chassis manufacturers again provided closely-matched products for 1987. The Honda engines were renamed Judds after John Judd, who prepared them for competition, and life continued as before, with victories shared between March, Ralt and Lola.

In a fair world, the title would have gone to the Ralt-Judd of Brazilian Roberto Moreno, who had turned his back on a profitable American racing programme to try and re-launch his career in Europe, after earlier attempts to push through to F1 had led him up a succession of blind alleys. The lure of

the dollar wasn't enough to dissuade Moreno from an F3000 programme, and but for a series of mechanical failures his gamble would have paid off handsomely. As it was, it earned him a couple of late-season F1 races with AGS, but the F3000 title was settled — again at the last race — in favour of another Italian, Stefano Modena, who did just enough to snuffle out the hopes of Spaniard Luis Sala. However, both they and Mauricio Gugelmin, third in the final standings, moved directly into Grand Prix racing on the back of their successes.

The unfortunate Moreno would have to wait another year. There were significant developments in Formula 3000 in both 1988 and 1989. Firstly, there was the arrival of Reynard as a manufacturer. The success of this new car, most notably in Moreno's hands, brought a flood of orders. Lola kept pace with developments, particularly in the latter part of the season, but March and Ralt both struggled. By the end of the year, Ralt was absorbed into March, but the latter was struggling for customers after its own disappointing showings. Moreno romped to the championship title and that, inevitably, brought him the regular F1 seat he had craved for so long. And he was by no means the only one; no fewer than nine drivers went directly into F1 and another three progressed at a later stage.

Technical progress

The next significant technical development was the introduction of the Honda-based Mugen engine, of which great things were expected, on account of its alleged superiority over the Cosworth at the bottom end of the rev range. It was priced accordingly, and made available in limited quantities. In its first year it won seven of 10 races, with Cosworth taking just two and Judd one. On the chassis front, Reynard and Lola had the measure of each other for the most part, although the former took six wins to the latter's three, and once-proud March — winner of the first three championship titles — could boast just one. In the middle of the year, March's Formula 3000 division had been absorbed into the Leyton House group, the sponsor whose first association had been with Capelli back in 1986.

Severely increasing costs brought a slight fall in the number of entrants in Formula 3000's fifth season, but the racing was as close as ever, and the championship was tied on points between Frenchmen Jean Alesi and Erik Comas, Alesi taking the title by dint of three wins to Comas' two. Alesi didn't even have to wait until the end of the year for a job in F1; he was gainfully employed by July, long before he'd clinched the championship title. Several of his rivals progressed with him.

With 450bhp on tap, and top speeds of around 180mph (290km/h), Formula 3000 cars are spectacular to watch (and faster than their Cosworth-powered F1 forebears, which ran similar engines without rev limiters several years previously), and the regulations are designed to eliminate any significant performance advantages. That puts the emphasis very much on the driver, which is just one of the reasons that those who succeed are so highly rated.

In 1986, the series' title was changed from FIA European Formula 3000 Championship to FIA Intercontinental F3000 Championship. At the end of 1985, an end-of-season, non-championship race took place in Curaçao, and this was enough to convince the authorities of hidden extra-European potential. There was talk of races in Canada, America and New Zealand, but none came to fruition. Eventually, the official schedule featured Curaçao and two races in Brazil, but insufficient finance on behalf of the intended promoters saw all three collapse, and the first 'Intercontinental' series took place in Britain, France, Italy, Belgium, Austria and Spain! For 1987, it was simply known as the FIA International Formula 3000 Championship, thus covering all eventualities.

Facing into the future

Talk persists that the FIA series will eventually break out of Europe, but for the moment the Japanese and British are the only people who get to see pukka F3000 cars regularly. Japan adopted the category in 1987, two years after Europe, although they do things slightly differently in the Far East. If a European driver pits to complain of a handling problem, he and his engineer will fine-tune the chassis in an effort to cure it. In Japan, they throw on a different tyre compound and send the car back out.

The leading tyre companies — Bridgestone, Yokohama and Dunlop — invest substantially in racing programmes, and the likes of Reynard, Lola and Leyton House apparently provide less significant components. The chassis have to be set up quite differently to their Avon crossply-shod European counter-

parts, to cater for the radial rubber used exclusively in Japan. On the engine front, Yamaha has produced a competitive V8 with which to tackle Mugen and Cosworth.

The races, usually around nine per season, attract enormous crowds, and while European Championship competitors often operate on a shoestring, the Japanese teams usually provide healthy salaries for seasoned professionals, a fact which hasn't been lost on a number of European drivers, many of whom are now based permanently out there. The national series is less likely to bring you to the attention of F1 teams, but you are unlikely to be left wanting.

Britain also has a national championship, instigated in 1989. Although this got off to a quiet start, with small fields, the quality of the racing was sufficient for FISA to grant a Formula 1 superlicence to the series winner, Gary Brabham.

Finally, America liked the idea of a powerful, competitive single-seater series to plug

Above: Similar power outputs for all the engines makes the racing in F3000 close and exciting. This is Marco Apicella in a Reynard

Left: The uninitiated might be hard pressed to tell the difference between F3000 cars and GP cars, especially where the sponsors are the same. This is Volker Weidler's Marlboro-liveried March 88B at Brands Hatch in 1988

the gap between Formula Super Vee and Indycars. Thus a batch of March chassis — based around the 1985 monocoque — was sent to the States, to be mated to a Buick V6 engine offering around 450bhp. The US version of F3000 was christened ARS — American Racing Series, and now acts as a curtain-raiser at important CART events. Since its first season in 1986, it has helped promote several drivers into CART, America's premier single-seater formula.

European Champions: 1985 — Christian Danner; **1986** — Ivan Capelli; **1987** — Stefano Modena; **1988** — Roberto Moreno; **1989** — Jean Alesi.

Japanese Champions: 1987 — Kazuyoshi Hoshino; **1988** — Aguri Suzuki; **1989** — Hitoshi Ogawa.

British Champion: 1989 — Gary Brabham.

ARS Champions: 1986 — Fabrizio Barbazza; **1987** — Didier Theys; **1988** — Dave Simpson; **1989** — Jon Beekhuis.

Formula 2

While Formula 3000 is most certainly a misnomer now, so — at one time — was Formula 2. In 1952/53, Formula 2 cars were adopted for the World Championship. It was decided that the existing F2 regulations, allowing for normally-aspirated, 2-litre engines or 500cc supercharged units, gave better scope for a more competitive and better-supported class than did contemporary F1.

Alberto Ascari overwhelmed the opposition in 1952, taking his Ferrari to victory in six of the eight events. Ferrari's only 'failure' was in the Indianapolis 500, which in those days counted for the World Championship, but whose different regulations made its presence in the series something of an anomaly.

Maserati put up stiffer opposition the following season, but even the legendary Fangio could muster only a solitary success, and Ascari stormed to the title once again.

Strong beginnings

Initially developed from the pre-war voiturette class, Formula 2 officially came into being in 1948, and peaked when it was adopted for the official World Championship in the early Fifties. While Italy stole most of the glory, thanks largely to Ascari, Ferrari and to a lesser extent Maserati, Britain was very much involved through the likes of Connaught, Alta, Cooper and HWM, while France pitched in with Gordini. The latter, incidentally, provided what was numerically the strongest challenge to Ferrari in 1952, although strength in depth was never going to be enough, despite the presence of the gritty Jean Behra.

When the new 2.5-litre F1 was introduced for 1954, Ferrari and Maserati went off to struggle against returnee Mercedes, and Formula 2 faded away for a couple of seasons.

It returned in 1957, this time as a 1.5-litre class, contested mainly by Lotus, Cooper, Ferrari and Porsche, but there was no officially recognized championship outside the UK. As Formula 1 switched to the same capacity in 1961, F2 was snuffed out yet again, before returning as a 1-litre, maximum four cylinders formula in 1964, the smaller engines ensuring that it remained in the shadow of Grand Prix racing, leastways in the eyes of the public. For the next three years, you would occasionally be hard pushed to spot the difference between respective entries for F1 and F2 races. While the latter was certainly bristling with aspiring youngsters, it also enjoyed the support of Grand Prix drivers in factory-entered cars (Brabham, Lotus, Matra and Cooper were regular entrants). Competitors were seldom dissuaded from participating on non-Grand Prix weekends, and indeed were often encouraged to do so.

Thus burgeoning talents such as Jochen Rindt or Jackie Stewart could measure themselves against contemporary F1 drivers. And not just any drivers either, for World Champions Jack Brabham, Graham Hill and Jim Clark were frequent F2 competitors. A modern parallel would be Ayrton Senna and Nigel Mansell taking part in an F3000 race on a free weekend. Contracts don't permit such frippery nowadays, of course, but the practice

carried on, albeit on a varying scale, into the Seventies. The high start money needed to ensure the continued participation of the Grand Prix stars eventually led to a limitation of the number of invitations issued, and for a few years the idea was dropped altogether. Now, it seems inconceivable that it should ever have been possible.

Into Europe

It wasn't until 1967 that F2 finally got the full recognition it deserved, when the FIA created the European Trophy. Everybody immediately labelled it 'European Championship', but the Trophy tag remained official terminology until 1971.

For the first season of authorized European competition, engines were enlarged to between 1301cc and 1600cc, up to six cylinders, and based around a recognized production block. To encourage youngsters, 'graded' drivers — ie established Grand Prix stars — were allowed to compete, although they weren't eligible for points.

It proved to be a tremendous success. The star names helped draw in the crowds, and the massed ranks of young aspirants keen to forge their reputation ensured quantity as well as quality. Belgian Jacky Ickx (Matra) was the pick of the non-graded drivers in 1967, thus becoming the inaugural European F2 champion. He would later score a record-breaking six wins in the Le Mans 24 Hours, although outright success in the World Championship narrowly eluded him. Ironi-

cally, no European F2 champion has *ever* gone on to win the World Championship.

Not that that should be taken as a criticism, for it wasn't as if Ickx was the first in a string of no-hopers. One year on, Jean-Pierre Beltoise, one of Ickx's principal opponents in 1967, leapt to the top of the tree, simultaneously retaining Matra's crown and defeating the likes of Henri Pescarolo and Derek Bell, who went on to record nine Le Mans wins between them. Beltoise would be a leading F1 racer for many seasons, although his only win came at Monaco, in 1972.

Matra clinched the hat trick in 1969, courtesy of Johnny Servoz–Gavin, but the Frenchman — whose previous, sporadic F1 appearances included a place on the front row at Monaco in 1968 — contested just two Grands Prix in 1970 before quitting the sport.

Matra pulled out on that winning note, leaving Swiss Gianclaudio 'Clay' Regazzoni to sweep up for Tecno. In third place, Emerson Fittipaldi gave a hint of the potential that would take him to two World Championships and — almost 20 years later — America's prestigious CART title.

Ronnie Peterson, widely acknowledged as one of the finest drivers never to win the sport's ultimate accolade, was the final champion of this era, new regulations being drafted for 1972, when the European F2 Championship was officially christened thus by the authorities.

During the glorious 1967–71 period, constructors inevitably came and went. One of

Before the advent of F3000, the premier formula after F1 was sensibly named F2. This is the field leaving the grid at Silverstone in 1981

Above: Renault were the dominant force in F2 in the mid-Seventies, running their effective V6-powered cars

Below: The Honda-powered Ralts were overpowering in 1983 and 1984. This is Mike Thackwell's 1984 Championship-winning example at Thruxton

the most significant developments was the arrival, in 1970, of March, soon to become the world's most prolific racing car constructor, and F2 champion in 1971 thanks to Peterson. Ferrari dabbled with the formula for a couple of years, as did BMW, but stalwart supporter Cooper, no longer a force in F1, faded away at the end of 1968.

The biggest change for 1972 was the adoption of 2-litre production-based engines, to a maximum of six cylinders, although these competitors were subjected to a greater weight penalty than their four-cylinder rivals.

The problem, though, was the shortage of suitable engines. Ford, whose FVA had been the thing to have during the latter days under the previous regulations, had homologated the 16-valve BDA for Group 1 saloon car racing in 1971, and this FVA-based four-cylinder was swiftly adapted for F2.

During the first season of the 2-litre formula, multiple motor-cycle-racing World Champion Mike Hailwood drove for former two-wheel rival John Surtees, and became the first British winner of the European F2 crown. It was to be Surtees' only major international success as a manufacturer, while Hailwood went on to become a more than competent F1 racer, although his career was terminated by an accident at the Nürburgring a couple of years later.

Ford had dominated on the engine front, but the return of BMW for 1973 heralded a new era. March drivers Jean-Pierre Jarier and Patrick Depailler used the German engine to good effect in the next two seasons, while Jacques Laffite kept the crown on French soil with his Martini-BMW in 1975.

In short, it was a time of total domination for French drivers, and rewriting the rules for 1976 did nothing to change that. It was decided to open the formula to any engine up to a maximum of six cylinders, thus removing the need for manufacturers to find a suitable production-based block. Renault launched a most effective V6, and swept to victory in 1976 and 1977 thanks to the efforts of Jean-Pierre Jabouille and René Arnoux, driving for Elf and Martini respectively. In 1975, the top five drivers in the final points table were French. For 1978, however, Renault pulled out, and the series returned to more cosmopolitan times.

The home straight

Two years of March-BMW success followed, for Bruno Giacomelli and Marc Surer, before the British broke the mould in 1980. The Toleman Group had sponsored Brian Henton in 1979, the Briton only losing the title to Surer after an appeal against disqualification from a race in Sicily failed. For 1980, Toleman commissioned Rory Byrne to design a chassis, Brian Hart to produce an engine, and Henton and Derek Warwick to drive. With support from BP, the all-British outfit stormed to a championship 1–2, Henton finally claiming the major honour that had eluded him for so long.

Late in the year, Honda — which had enjoyed much success with Brabham during the 1966 F2 season — returned on a small scale with the factory Ralt team. Geoff Lees and Nigel Mansell proved the effectiveness of the Japanese V6, and thus began the final stage in Formula 2's long and largely successful history.

Lees stayed with Ralt-Honda in 1981, and duly won the Championship. BMW responded briefly in 1982, when Corrado Fabi's March grabbed the spoils, but Honda had the last word.

By now, the spiralling costs of engine development were taking their toll. Even when Renault had steamrollered to victory in the mid-Seventies, Formula 2 fields were well oversubscribed. Now, fields were dwindling, and with Honda supplying only Ralt, who

completely dominated in 1983 and 1984, the death-knell was inevitable. Jonathan Palmer and Mike Thackwell won the final two European Championships, and meetings between interested parties led to the introduction of Formula 3000 for 1985, although Japan — which had held its own national F2 series for many years — kept the formula alive for a further two seasons.

At the time, F2's demise was inevitable, and the birth of Formula 3000 ensured that its best features would live on, under altogether more satisfactory regulations. The immediate success of F3000 proved the point.

But Formula 2 had done its bit. It produced a whole host of top-line F1 drivers, and World Champions who raced regularly in the formula before graduating to Grands Prix include Niki Lauda, Keke Rosberg and Jody Scheckter. Despite its excellent pedigree, it fizzled out through rising costs.

European Champions: 1967 — Jacky Ickx; **1968** — Jean-Pierre Beltoise; **1969** — Johnny Servoz-Gavin; **1970** — Clay Regazzoni; **1971** — Ronnie Peterson; **1972** — Mike Hailwood; **1973** — Jean-Pierre Jarier; **1974** — Patrick Depailler; **1975** — Jacques Laffite; **1976** — Jean-Pierre Jabouille; **1977** — René Arnoux; **1978** — Bruno Giacomelli; **1979** — Marc Surer; **1980** — Brian Henton; **1981** — Geoff Lees; **1982** — Corrado Fabi; **1983** — Jonathan Palmer; **1984** — Mike Thackwell.

British Champions: 1957 — Tony Marsh; **1958** — Jack Brabham; **1959** — Stirling Moss; **1960** — Jack Lewis; **1964** — Mike Spence; **1965** — Jim Clark; **1966** — Jack Brabham; **1967** — Alan Rees; **1972** — Niki Lauda.

Formula 3/ Formula Junior

Following World War 2, the immense popularity of 500cc racing led to its adoption by the sport's governing body, the FIA. They christened it Formula 3, which emphasized its role as a training ground for those who wished to move up eventually to Formulae 2 and 1.

That is a function it performs to this day. From the small, spindly, 440lb (200kg) racers that first highlighted Stirling Moss's ability, to the sophisticated, streamlined machines developed in wind-tunnels to keep pace with modern F3 trends, the formula has been through a variety of guises, each of which has thrown forward a succession of future Grand Prix winners.

Formula 3 has been part of the motor racing scene almost since its inception, being absent only for a couple of seasons at the start of the Sixties.

The 500cc formula enjoyed a marvellous

One step down the ladder from F2 was F3. Here, a healthy grid of 1970 1-litre cars starts a race at Snetterton

run, although its popularity in Britain wasn't echoed elsewhere in Europe. Towards the end of the Fifties, support was lapsing, and when Britain adopted Formula Junior in 1959, following Italy's lead, F3 took a back seat. It continued for a couple of years as a British club racing formula, but international attention focused firmly on Formula Junior.

When Formula 2 disappeared at the end of 1960, Formula Junior effectively assumed its mantle. Not only did the 1100cc racers provide an opportunity for the top up-and-coming drivers from all over Europe to come into contact, it brought smaller constructors into direct opposition for the first time. In the formula's Italian birthplace, Fiat engines were the obvious choice, although the FIA allowed in 1-litre engines to encourage variety, those using the larger engines suffering an 88lb (40kg) weight penalty.

Ironically for Italy, so accustomed to motor racing success, most of the glory during Formula Junior's brief life fell to Cooper and Lotus. As for drivers, the considerable talents of Jim Clark, Jo Siffert, John Surtees, Lorenzo Bandini, Ludovico Scarfiotti, Denny Hulme and the Rodriguez brothers, Pedro and Riccardo, all emerged as future F1 stars, Clark, Hulme and former 'biker Surtees going on to win the World Championship.

Formula Junior's elevation, in the wake of F2's temporary disappearance, made it more costly and thus less accessible. When Formula 2 was reintroduced for 1964, it was time for a rethink. At the end of the 1963 season, the FIA decided to reintroduce F3, and the Formula Junior name died, although it was revived by historic racing enthusiasts who dusted off some of the old cars for British club meetings in the late Seventies. It may only have been around for a few seasons, but Formula Junior pumped a glittering array of stars into Sixties motor sport.

1989 F3 runner-up Allan McNish leads Paul Warwick and Mika Salo in a typically hard-fought F3 race at Brands Hatch

One-litre, production-based engines to a maximum of four cylinders graced the reborn F3, and it was the start of another epic era. The engines were soon labelled 'one-litre screamers' on account of their free-revving nature, and races were characterized by frantic, slipstreaming battles all over Europe. Grand Prix support races were commonplace, and overall driving standards were high, although the close nature of competition inevitably led to fraught moments.

A certain Jackie Stewart reigned supreme during the first season of the revised formula, at the wheel of his BMC-engined Cooper. In the ensuing years, Emerson Fittipaldi, Ronnie Peterson, Tim Schenken, Tony Trimmer, Carlos Pace, Reine Wisell, François Cevert, Patrick Depailler, Jean-Pierre Jabouille, Henri Pescarolo and John Miles raced to the front of the slipstream, all of them going on to drive in F1, although not all of them ultimately realized the potential they had shown in their F3 days.

On the chassis front, there were significant contributions from Alpine, Brabham, Chevron, Cooper, Lola, Lotus, March, Martini and Tecno. It was a healthy, progressive environment, which was wound up at the end of the 1970 season, in favour of a production-based, 1.6-litre formula. The new engines were strangulated by an air inlet restrictor; after the exciting wail of the previous era, the new, muffled sound failed to provide aural stimulation, but the quality of the racing made amends, and reliability would be considerably improved. On the flip side, arguments over incorrectly-set restrictors led to several events being settled in the scrutineering bay, rather than on the race-track, and protests against fellow competitors became quite frequent.

Unhappiness over the formula's relative lack of pace led to the adoption of a slightly wider air inlet aperture in the middle of the 1971 season, but despite significant competitor support the rules were changed more radically after just three seasons.

During that time, Ensign and GRD joined the established band of constructors, both enjoying success, while Ford almost inevitably hogged the engine bays, their dominance only occasionally interrupted by Renault. And there was no stemming the tide of naturally-gifted participants; the formula attracted truly enormous support from drivers of all nations. Roger Williamson, Alan Jones, Jacques Laffite, Ian Taylor, Conny Andersson, Tony Brise, Brian Henton, Masami Kuwashima, Larry Perkins, Jochen Mass, Tom Pryce, Patrick Depailler . . . the list was long and impressive.

Changes and chances

For 1974, the FIA dictated a switch to 2-litre, production-based engines, and it almost brought the formula to its knees. Anyone attending an F3 championship race in 1973 would have seen an entry so large that it needed two heats to determine the finalists. When the new formula started at Oulton Park in March 1974, you could count the F3 cars on the fingers of one hand. The organizers chucked in a few makeweight Formula Ford cars, the quality of which was such that they hadn't qualified for their own feature race!

Things improved during the course of the year, and the introduction of a fully-fledged European Championship gave the formula extra credibility in 1975. Gradually the category regained its former strength and, having dropped it for a few years in favour of Formula Super Renault, France eventually readopted it. With strong national series in Britain, Germany, Italy, France and Scandinavia, the European series was deemed surplus to requirements in 1984, and was killed off. Meanwhile F3's international appeal was emphasized when the organizers of the Macau Grand Prix introduced it as the feature event in 1983, creating a prestigious showpiece in which Grand Prix drivers were happy to put their reputations on the line against the cream of the world's rising stars.

Such was the pace of chassis development, with the introduction of composite materials and extensive use of wind-tunnel testing, that year-old chassis were quickly rendered obsolete by their successors. To reflate the value of older cars, and to give drivers the opportunity of a gentle introduction to the category, Britain launched Formula 3 Class B in 1984. The growth in entries continued apace, and by the end of the Eighties it was often necessary to precede the main race with a qualifying event.

March, for so long the backbone of Formula 3, was gradually eased out by the arrival of Ron Tauranac's Ralt chassis. Tauranac's RT1 was an instant success, but its successor, the RT3, eventually achieved a virtual monopoly. In 1985, Reynard appeared and won its first race, and the Ralt domination was over, although the two companies continue to trade wins. In Europe, Martini and Dallara have proved as effective as their British counterparts. There were neat designs too from Chevron, Modus and Argo; 10 years after it first made an impact, the latter was planning a comeback for the Nineties.

For a long time, the Toyota Novamotor engine seemed impregnable, but VW and Alfa Romeo eventually assumed control, leaving Toyota to reply with a 16-valve unit. Other Japanese too got in on the act, with the Honda-based Mugen, and the wide choice of options, and associated development costs, have escalated costs enormously.

The formula's original purpose, however, has never changed. You need look no further than the subsequent successes of Nelson Piquet, Derek Warwick, Nigel Mansell, Stefan Johansson, Jonathan Palmer, Alain Prost, Riccardo Patrese, Ayrton Senna, Michele Alboreto and countless others for evidence of that . . .

Drivers who accede to F1 without any experience of F3 on the way are few and far between indeed.

British Champions: 1966 — Harry Stiller; **1967** — Harry Stiller; **1968** — Tim Schenken; **1969** — Emerson Fittipaldi; **1970** — Dave Walker; **1971** — Roger Williamson; **1972** — Roger Williamson, Rikki von Opel; **1973** — Tony Brise, Ian Taylor; **1974** — Brian Henton; **1975** — Gunnar Nilsson; **1976** — Rupert Keegan, Bruno Giacomelli; **1977** — Derek Daly, Stephen South; **1978** — Nelson Piquet, Derek Warwick; **1979** — Chico Serra; **1980** — Stefan Johansson; **1981** — Jonathan Palmer; **1982** — Tommy Byrne; **1983** — Ayrton Senna; **1984** — Johnny Dumfries; **1985** — Mauricio Gugelmin; **1986** — Andy Wallace; **1987** — Johnny Herbert; **1988** — J. J. Lehto; **1989** — David Brabham.

European Champions: 1975 — Larry Perkins; **1976** — Riccardo Patrese; **1977** — Piercarlo Ghinzani; **1978** — Jan Lammers; **1979** — Alain Prost; **1980** — Michele Alboreto; **1981** — Mauro Baldi; **1982** — Oscar Larrauri; **1983** — Pier-Luigi Martini; **1984** — Ivan Capelli.

French Champions: 1981 — Philippe Streiff; **1982** — Pierre Petit; **1983** — Michel Ferté; **1984** — Olivier Grouillard; **1985** — Pierre-Henri Raphanel; **1986** — Yannick Dalmas; **1987** — Jean Alesi; **1988** — Erik Comas; **1989** — Jean-Marc Gounon.

Italian Champions: 1976 — Riccardo Patrese; **1977** — Elio de Angelis; **1978** — Siegfried Stohr; **1979** — Piercarlo Ghinzani; **1980** — Guido Pardini; **1981** — Mauro Bianchi; **1982** — Enzo Coloni; **1983** — Ivan Capelli; **1984** — Alessandro Santin; **1985** — Franco Forini; **1986** — Nicola Larini; **1987** — Enrico Bertaggia; **1988** — Emanuele Naspetti; **1989** — Gianni Morbidelli.

German Champions: 1985 — Volker Weidler; **1986** — Kris Nissen; **1987** — Bernd Schneider; **1988** — Joachim Winkelhock; **1989** — Karl Wendlinger.

Formula 5000

Formula 5000 was spawned from America's Formula A in 1969. One year before, during its maiden season, Formula A had proved tremendously spectacular. John Webb, head of what was then known as Motor Circuit Developments, had always been an innovator, and he decided to import the 5-litre formula to Europe, albeit under a new name.

Chassis were powered by production-based V8s, which gave them a theoretical horsepower advantage over the F1 cars of the time, although F5000 cars were larger and heavier. Even so, they weren't far off F1 machines in terms of speed, and the category's arrival was eagerly awaited.

In order to ensure full grids, Formula 2 cars were permitted to compete during the first year, albeit in lightened form. McLaren, Surtees and Lola built new cars, although only the latter was in a position to supply customer chassis in any quantity.

After a shaky start, the formula gradually found its feet, and Peter Gethin clinched the title after he and Trevor Taylor tangled in the final race at Brands Hatch. Graded drivers were not permitted to take part, and with the attraction of several races in Europe, F5000 was viewed as a real alternative to Formula 2 for the coming men.

F5000 met F1 head to head in the Oulton Park Gold Cup, and the raucous newcomers were outpaced, although Andrea de Adamich took his Surtees to third place. But in 1973, Gethin scored a victory in the Brands Hatch Race of Champions, his Chevron passing Denny Hulme's ailing F1 McLaren to give F5000 its first and only success in a combined race of this type.

F1-style chassis and thumping great production-based V8 or V6 engines made F5000 cars an impressive sight and sound. This is the 1972 Surtees coping with the rain at Silverstone

Somehow, the category always promised to be better than it was, and although there were some very good seasons, notably in 1973 and 1974, it never really became the breeding ground it was intended to be. Although one or two exponents went on to F1 (Gethin won the 1971 Italian GP for BRM, but two years later he was back in F5000), the serious-minded racers were frequently outnumbered by enthusiastic amateurs. Alan Jones, World Champion in 1980, raced in the formula in 1975, the last season in which it ran to established Formula 5000 regulations.

The competitive nature of the 1974 season had promised much, and the following season several teams experimented with Cosworth's 3.4-litre V6, which made up for what it lacked in power against the V8s with its compact dimensions and lighter weight. It was hoped that this new option would encourage new faces to the class, but F5000 continued on its erratic way. A fair number of established drivers appeared during the course of the 1975 season, but seldom more than five or six of them ever ran together.

In the middle of the year, it was announced that *any* car of up to five litres would be eligible to compete in 1976, although the series ran for one more year as the ShellSport 5000 Championship. It quickly became more of a glorified club racing formula, and interest dwindled. In 1978, it was replaced by the British Formula 1 Championship, and surviving Formula 5000 cars were left to go and play in Formula Libre races at low-key club meetings. The British F1 series was scrapped after the 1980 season, being revived briefly and rather embarrassingly in 1982.

In the United States, Formula 5000 attracted support from a number of leading teams, and many of the country's top drivers took part on occasions. At the end of the 1976 season, however, CanAm was reinstated on the US racing calendar, and that meant scrapping F5000. In Australia, home of one or two promising F5000 designs, notably the McRae, it ran from 1970–1979, forming the basis of the once-prestigious Tasman Cup until 1975. From 1976, the Antipodeans admitted F1 cars, but with the Tasman Cup title having been dropped, this series soldiered painfully on with elderly F5000 chassis until somebody saw sense and knocked it on the head, promoting Formula Pacific to the role of senior national formula.

The formula certainly enjoyed bright moments on both sides of the Atlantic, although it never achieved the status that had been predicted so optimistically back in 1968. Only Lola stayed faithful to the end, although the early McLarens saw service for several seasons in the hands of privateers. Chevron produced stern competition in Britain, while Eagle produced an effective chassis in the USA. Ultimately, however, European crowds wanted to see Formula 1 cars, and no amount of hype could change their minds. Formula 5000 should

Right: Early days of Formula Ford 1600, still thriving and still the traditional first step for the aspiring professional driver

have been allowed to die with dignity in 1975, but the futile attempts to revive it didn't even allow that.

British Champions: 1969 — Peter Gethin; **1970** — Peter Gethin; **1971** — Frank Gardner; **1972** — Gijs van Lennep; **1973** — Teddy Pilette; **1974** — Bob Evans; **1975** — Teddy Pilette.

American Champions: 1968 — Lou Sell; **1969** — Tony Adamowicz; **1970** — John Cannon; **1971** — David Hobbs; **1972** — Graham McRae; **1973** — Jody Scheckter; **1974** — Brian Redman; **1975** — Brian Redman; **1976** — Brian Redman.

Tasman Champions: 1970 — Graeme Lawrence; **1971** — Graham McRae; **1972** — Graham McRae; **1973** — Graham McRae; **1974** — Peter Gethin; **1975** — Warwick Brown.

Formula Atlantic/ Formula Pacific

Following the introduction of America's Formula A to Europe, under the guise of Formula 5000, in 1969, Formula B followed suit in 1971. Under its new name of Formula Atlantic, it was designed to bridge the gap between F3 and F2.

It looked good in prospect, with F2-sized cars featuring 1.6-litre engines purporting to give out around 200bhp. The regulations for Britain were slightly different from those in America, in that the Ford BDA engine was made eligible. Reliability problems during the first season meant that the consistent Vern Schuppan won the title with his twin-

cam BRM-powered Palliser, and despite the performance differential between the pace-setters and an abundance of makeweights, the new category was adjudged a success. Indeed, by 1973 there were two national championships.

In some ways, Formula 3's struggle to get going under 2-litre regulations played into Formula Atlantic's lap, and in 1974 the latter received a massive boost with the announcement of support for one of the two national championships from John Player. In mid-season, the sponsor's F1 team Lotus had signed championship contender Jim Crawford as a test driver, and in the welter of publicity all looked rosy. It stayed that way for one more season, and then all of a sudden it was dropped in the UK, the promoters claiming that participants were demanding too much money. The cars raced in mainland Britain in 1976 under the Indylantic banner, but no number of promotional ideas could save it, and it sunk without trace. In Northern Ireland and Eire, the formula continued uninterrupted, remaining as the premier category until the early Eighties.

It also continued to be popular in America, where to this day there are a number of well-supported regional championships. In Australia and New Zealand, where it runs as Formula Pacific, it forms the basis of the major national single-seater championships. The Australian GP was held to Pacific regulations in the early Eighties.

With the plethora of formulae that already compete in Britain there is little chance of its reintroduction. It returned in 1979, but after a few poorly-supported seasons it was quickly dropped again. Its continued existence overseas keeps Ralt gainfully employed building chassis, but the British firm's monopoly has been broken by Reynard and Swift.

In the early days, March, Lola, Brabham, Modus and Chevron produced competitive cars, and the formula certainly turned out some decent drivers, notably Gilles Villeneuve, Tony Brise, Gunnar Nilsson and Alan Jones. In America, it continues to do so.

British Champions: 1971 — Vern Schuppan; **1972** — Bill Gubelmann; **1973** — John Nicholson, Colin Vandervell; **1974** — John Nicholson, Jim Crawford; **1975** — Tony Brise, Ted Wentz; **1979** — Ray Mallock; **1980** — David Leslie; **1981** — Ray Mallock.

Formula Super Vee

The success in Europe and the United States of the VW-powered Formula Vee led to the introduction in 1971 of an uprated version. While the British national series was always feebly supported, generous prize money from VW ensured huge interest elsewhere.

The originally specified, air-cooled Beetle engines gave way to the 1.6-litre, water-cooled motor derived from the VW Scirocco. In 1975, aerodynamic aids were allowed for the first time, and Super Vee's visual similarity to F3 was immediately apparent. Despite that, the European series enjoyed healthy support until the early Eighties, when VW's interest in the rosy F3 market led to its decline.

In America, the category has produced a number of future Indycar stars, and continues to attract support from drivers, although occasional attempts to introduce sweeping regulation changes have threatened its existence more than once.

One of the few drivers to progress to GP racing from F5000 was Peter Gethin, seen here relaxing in his Chevron before the 1973 Race of Champions

Beginners' Single-Seater Formulae

In the Twenties and Thirties it was enough that well-heeled young men could buy themselves cars and go motor racing. Come the late Forties this hit-and-miss approach to entry into an important and growing sport was no longer satisfactory. From this dissatisfaction sprang the idea for a 'cheap' starter form of single-seater racing to which the 'average' enthusiast could realistically aspire and in which he could learn his trade and then progress to greater things. The idea was proved viable with 500cc racing in 1947. This has a direct lineage with today's Formula Ford which for many years has been the entry-level formula for stars of tomorrow. Along the way many other starter formulae have sprung up; some have survived and others have blossomed and then died.

A huge grid of Formula Ford 1600 cars starts a race at the 1988 Formula Ford Festival, staged at Brands Hatch

Beginners' cars

When motor sport was gathering its thoughts after World War 2, the creation of the 500cc racing car class, later to become Formula 3, introduced a new concept. Here was a small, relatively affordable car in which new drivers could gain a feel for the sport. And if they were any good, they could progress to more powerful machines in greater safety, having acquired useful tactical awareness and knowledge of their own limitations in a slower, more forgiving environment.

The durability of the 500 class, which ran from 1947 to 1960, proved the value of the concept. But as racing benefited from quantum leaps in technology, the lessons learned in Formula 1 were quickly passed on down the line to lesser formulae. When F3 was phased out in favour of Formula Junior, the international status it was accorded quickly pushed costs beyond the means of many potential competitors. Formula Junior was renamed F3 once again in 1964, but this bore little relation to the 500 formula that had existed only five years previously.

In short, there wasn't much the single-seater rookie could do other than jump straight into the ultra-competitive world of Formula 3. As costs continued to spiral, the lack of a relatively cheap start-up formula was becoming increasingly obvious.

Formula Vee, the consequence of an experiment in the USA in the late Fifties, was just starting to find its feet, having been introduced as a class in its own right in 1965. Then, quite by chance, there arose an idea that would revolutionize single-seater motor racing. In July 1967, the first ever Formula Ford race took place at Brands Hatch. Over 20 years later, Formula Ford is established in virtually all motor-sporting countries.

Its introduction was something the sport sorely needed, and the concept has been copied with various degrees of success all over the world. Some categories, like Formula Renault, have flourished. Others have en-

joyed brief success, but for every category which has come and gone, there has inevitably been a new idea to take its place.

Formulae for success

The technological advances in Formula Ford during the Eighties inflated prices so much that it was felt necessary to introduce a new, lower-cost formula in the spirit of the original Formula Ford ethic. Formula First was to Formula Ford what the latter had been to F3 in the Sixties. Nowadays, there are if anything too many choices for intending racers, though there is a clear dividing line between those which are intended to be fun, and those which are designed to educate the Grand Prix stars of the future. Formula Vee has survived all this time, too, and remains an enormously popular club racing formula, although its days of producing a stream of future Grand Prix drivers appear to be over.

Increased involvement from manufacturers such as Renault and General Motors, and the seemingly endless support of Ford, means that young racers have seldom had it so good. Although the majority of promotional formulae are common to several countries, there are a few categories unique to their country of origin outside the UK. Italy, for instance, has Formula Alfa Boxer, similar to Formula Ford in spirit, albeit with slicks, wings and a common chassis.

The sport will always be relatively expensive, but now there is a realistic number of possibilities to suit a whole range of bank balances.

Below: Big crowds at Oulton Park in 1954 enjoy the excitement generated by the 500cc racers who supported the main race of the day

Left: *The start of the first ever Formula Ford race, held at Brands Hatch in 1967. The formula is still going strong more than two decades later*

Formula Ford

The birth of the most successful formula in the history of motor racing was a mixture of chance and opportunism. Motor Racing Stables, one of the country's leading racing schools in the Sixties, was finding it tough to run and maintain a fleet of Formula 3 cars. For one thing, maintenance costs were on the increase; for another, novice drivers tended to leave a fair bit of necessary maintenance in their wake, damaging engines with missed gears and occasionally reprofiling the bodywork against any ancillaries that might be lying around the circuit.

Eventually, at the suggestion of instructor John Tomlinson, MRS replaced one of its costly race engines with the unit from an Austin A35 van, found in a breaker's yard! To the pupils, a racing car was a racing car, no matter what nestled behind it. The next step was to ditch the second-hand slick tyres, when supplies from a racing team dried up. Tomlinson persuaded his colleagues to try a set of road-going radials, and the perfect school trainer was born, the progressive nature of the road tyres making the car much easier for novices to control.

After a severe winter ravaged MRS's Finmere base, the school moved to Brands Hatch, and acquired three Lotus F3 cars, which it modified to its new specification, albeit with 1.5-litre Cortina engines replacing the experimental item from the A35 van.

John Webb, Managing Director of the Kent track, thought what he saw at MRS looked like a good base for a cheap single-seater formula. After a meeting between Webb, MRS and Ford, Ford agreed with him, and the wheels were set in motion.

The first public race, at Brands Hatch on July 2, 1967, was won by Ray Allen, and the close competition behind him gave a small hint of the cut-and-thrust action that the new concept could provide. The price ceiling for the chassis was fixed at £1000, and a surge of prospective competitors loomed into view with an eye on the first national Formula Ford series, in 1968.

After the series of pilot races in 1967, it was decided to replace the Cortina GT powerplant with Ford's 1.6-litre pushrod Kent engine. Much of the formula's success can be attributed to its stability over the years. While chassis and suspension technology have advanced enormously, the same Kent engine continues to give sterling service, even though it hasn't been used in any of Ford's range for a number of years! Nowadays, it is produced purely for racing.

Another stabilizing influence has been the retention of the control-tyre regulation, which ensures that competitors receive identical equipment. The contract has changed hands over the years, and the latest Dunlops are actually a race rather than road compound, albeit fully treaded like the Firestone F100s on which the formula was launched. The lack of rivalry between rubber manufacturers also

Above: Modern Formula Ford cars in action at Brands Hatch. The current machine is a much more sophisticated device than its 1967 ancestor

helps to keep costs down. In America, however, Formula Ford cars compete on full racing slicks.

In terms of entries, the national championships peaked in the early Seventies, when it was not unusual to find around 100 drivers on the entry list. Three heats were frequently required to determine 30 or so finalists. The oil crisis knocked the stuffing out of most forms of racing for a while, but Formula Ford continued to attract an enormous number of participants. In the Eighties, the trend was to regionalize the formula. The national championships still flourish at two levels, following the introduction in 1976 of 'junior' championships for those new to the category. In addition, almost every circuit in Britain has its own championship, so that those with a limited budget can chase a meaningful reward without having to travel. And just to make sure that the Formula Ford chassis of yore aren't left to rot, there are numerous championships for which cars are eligible according to their age, so cars built before 1974 can still race compete against their contemporary rivals. Other series cater for cars built between 1974 and 1978, before 1985, and for those with straightforward wishbone suspension rather than the more sophisticated in-board arrangements developed during the early Eighties. If you have a Formula Ford car, there is a championship in which you can race it, no matter how old it is.

Britain is alone in having such a labyrinthine network of championships. In other countries, there tends to be just one national series to chase, although France — where the category has blossomed in the face of the equally prominent Formula Renault since its launch there in 1984 — runs a B class within its main framework, catering for drivers of cars that are over one year old.

Regulations have differed little over the years. Chassis must be of spaceframe construction, but different applications of this technique have led to stronger, faster cars. With the engine tuners, of whom there are many, similarly restricted in what they may and may not do, the racing is always heart-stoppingly close, and inexperience on the part of some drivers inevitably leads to a high number of incidents. Formula Ford has witnessed some truly horrifying accidents in its time, yet such is the strength of the cars nowadays that injuries are a happily rare consequence.

Constructors' challenge

The increasing complexity — relatively speaking — of Formula Ford cars has left the market to those who are able to keep abreast with technological progress. Lotus and Brabham supplied most of the cars in the early days, but other constructors quickly joined the fray. Agent, Russell-Alexis (later just Alexis), Delta, Dulon, Elden, Hawke, Image, Laser, Martlet, McGregor, Merlyn, Nomad, Quest, PRS, Palliser, Rondeau, Royale, Sark, Sparton, Titan and Zeus have all built cars at one time or another, though their products are nowadays seldom seen outside series for older cars.

The battle for supremacy between Hawke and Royale during the mid-Seventies furthered the formula's technical progress, but ultimately neither survived. The most successful manufacturer of all has been Van Diemen, launched by Ralph Firman in 1973 and still supplying countless championship-winning chassis every season. Van Diemen has always specialized in this end of the motor racing market, to the point where it has enjoyed long periods of monopoly. Reynard and Swift provide the main opposition, while there is still scope for the smaller manufacturer, as Cooper, Elden, Jamun, Mondiale or Ray will testify. Crosslé too has enjoyed success, particularly in its native Ireland.

Popular opinion has it that Britain is home of the most prestigious championships, which explains why young Brazilians like to move to the UK to further their careers. Yet Ayrton Senna, dominant in 1981, was the first Formula Ford champion to win a World Championship Grand Prix, when he paddled home at Estoril in 1985. All the same, the list of F1 drivers who started the learning process in Formula Ford is long and impressive. Emerson Fittipaldi was the first graduate to take the world title (in 1972 and 1974), and he has since been followed by Hunt, Scheckter and Senna.

Over 20 years after it was first introduced, the Formula Ford success story shows no sign of abating. The subsequent results of those who shine in major Formula Ford championships are testimony to the importance it places on driver ability. Quite simply, it requires a special talent to win in such competitive surroundings.

Formula Ford 2000

With Formula Ford entries running at an all-time high in 1974, Formula Ford 2000 was conceived to attract drivers who wanted to move up, but who either felt they weren't ready, or who didn't have the budget, for Formula 3.

Like its elder forebear, the accent was placed on developing close racing at reasonable cost, hence the retention of tubular, spaceframe chassis and a single tyre supplier. Unlike Formula Ford, the new formula featured slick racing tyres and wings, thus enabling drivers to learn more about the art of setting up a car to suit a particular circuit, a talent which they would need when progressing to F3 and beyond. Ford's 130bhp, 2-litre Pinto was chosen as a suitable engine, and tuners were allowed to introduce strictly-limited modifications.

A pilot race took place late in 1974 at Oulton Park, when the category ran as a separate class within an F3 race. The handful of cars generated considerable interest, and a national championship was implemented for 1975, Derek Lawrence becoming the first winner in his Crosslé.

Within a couple of years, Britain had two national series and there was also a European Championship. Although it didn't have quite the same level of support as its smaller-engined brother, the quality of the competition was enough to suggest that the latest Motor Circuit Developments brainwave had created a worthwhile new stepping-stone.

Donington Park initiated its own one-circuit series, and there were several regional competitions. The level of support continued unchanged for several years, but by the mid-Eighties the formula had fallen on harder times. Part of the blame could be put at the

door of Formula 3's Class B, introduced in 1984, which offered a higher profile at little extra cost, and which didn't put drivers under quite the same pressure as the main F3 class.

In order to boost its flagging fortunes, Formula Ford 2000 itself created a B class for older cars, and by the late Eighties this contained the bulk of the entry, as drivers who might previously have considered FF2000 either went straight into F3, the profile of which had been further enhanced by TV coverage, which made sponsorship easier to come by, or into better-promoted new categories such as Formula Vauxhall Lotus. The latter had replaced FF2000 in Europe, and had the added benefit of several races on Grand Prix support programmes.

Championships for older cars, ie those old enough not to be competitive in Class B of

Above: Formula Ford 2000 was created in 1974 as a 'big brother' to Formula Ford 1600. Bigger engines, wings and slick tyres are the main differences, as revealed in this 1977 shot at Mallory Park

Below: Formula Ford 2000 had begun to decline in popularity by the late Eighties, although there was still some good racing. These cars are about to start a race at Snetterton

Above: Formula Forward cars in action during the modestly-supported inaugural 1989 season

the national series, continued to provide amusement for a respectable number of club racers, but the days of FF2000 as a prominent European formula were over, although manufacturers still had a healthy market place in Canada and the United States.

Many established Formula Ford 1600 constructors have done well in the nominally senior Ford category, Van Diemen, Delta, Royale and Dulon amongst them. Adrian Reynard, European FF2000 champion in 1979, has enjoyed greatest success as a manufacturer, his company's supremacy challenged occasionally by Swift in the latter part of the Eighties. Perhaps the most charismatic success came in 1978, however, when Syd Fox won the Allied Polymer title at the wheel of a lightly-modified Palliser, which was entered for the whole season as The Old Nail.

A number of drivers have starred in FF2000 before going on to greater things higher up in the sport, David Leslie, Tommy Byrne, Ayrton Senna, Martin Brundle, Bertrand Gachot, Mark Blundell and J.J. Lehto to name but a few.

In 1984, John Webb announced his intention to extend the Formula Ford concept still further, when he unveiled Formula Turbo Ford. The theory was that this would offer a cheaper option than F3 to FF2000 graduates, while also providing turbo experience at a time when the normally-aspirated engine was dead in Grands Prix. Few people showed much interest, however, and despite an intensive development programme with a Reynard test hack, a Formula Ford 2000

chassis boosted by a Garrett turbocharger, the project was quietly shelved. Only a few seasons later, it seemed that there was a similar fate in store for FF2000, leastways in Europe.

Formula First/ Formula Forward

Although Formula Ford's popularity has never diminished, the high costs involved in running a full season of around 40 races, together with essential pre-race testing, caused its creators to wonder whether it wasn't time for a rethink. After all, it had started out as a low-cost formula with a chassis price ceiling of £1000, and things had escalated somewhat in the intervening 20 years.

And so, in 1986, Brands Hatch Leisure, essentially comprising the old Motor Circuit Developments management, announced Formula First, for which a complete car would be available, ready to race, for under £6000. Furthermore, there would be no costly inter-manufacturer rivalry, as Van Diemen was commissioned to design and produce a chassis for all competitors. It was, in effect, a one-make, single-seater formula. The one-make concept had been a roaring success in saloons for many years, so why not here?

Predictably, Ford supplied the engine, a 1.6-litre unit giving around 73bhp, and Dunlop supplied control tyres. The regulations were stabilized for a minimum of three years, so theoretically cars would hold their value well when sold on at the end of the season.

The rush of orders for the new, wedge-shaped cars justified BHL's optimism, although it did mean that there were several total novices taking part, and destructive tendencies during the first season, 1987, were alarmingly widespread. Races were frequently red-flagged because of accidents, and the formula's reputation took several serious knocks.

Fortunately, things calmed down in the following seasons, and entries settled at a healthy level, leading to the introduction of regional championships to support the main, national series.

BHL was sufficiently pleased with the way things turned out to evolve a higher-spec one-chassis formula, Van Diemen again being called upon to develop a challenger for Formula Forward, a step up from Formula First employing slicks and wings. The category first appeared in 1989, but despite an encouraging initial response from potential competitors, the actual turn-out was modest. During its darkest days, Formula Ford 2000 always attracted a quality entry for its traditional winter series at Brands Hatch, thanks in part to the lure of television coverage. When Formula Forward took FF2000's place in that part of the racing calendar, entries remained at a low level, although they picked up at the start of the following year.

Formula Vauxhall Lotus

Proof of what can be achieved if you have the assistance of a major manufacturer came with the emergence, in 1988, of Formula Vauxhall Lotus (known as Formula Opel Lotus in mainland Europe).

With Formula Ford 2000 having become relatively stale, the European Formula Drivers' Association was looking for a way to inject some sparkle into a pan-European series for drivers from all nations. Reynard agreed to design a chassis, Lotus agreed to act as a consultant and GM set up a production line to turn out racing versions of its potent, 150bhp, 16-valve 2-litre engine, first seen in the road-going Vauxhall Astra GTE. The result was a car capable of lapping circuits within a few seconds of F3 machines, and which was relatively forgiving to drive to boot.

The ambitious scheme included the establishment of national championships in Britain, Germany, Scandinavia and the Benelux countries, together with a Euroseries featuring several Grand Prix support races.

The appeal of racing before F1 team managers and crowds predictably brought a flood of entries, and scepticism about the likely success of the project was quickly quashed when more than 20 cars appeared for the first race.

Throughout the year, all GM Lotus races maintained a respectable entry level, and the presence of two-car teams from the major tobacco sponsors added extra credibility. Its usefulness was emphasized when, only 12 months after clinching the British Championship, 19 year-old Allan McNish was employed for testing work by the McLaren Grand Prix team.

The tobacco companies withdrew their sponsorship after just the one season, but the formula was well enough established by then to exist without them, and the opportunity to experience several Grand Prix circuits in the course of a season gave it a unique appeal which guaranteed its continued popularity.

Formula Renault

Ford's decision to launch Formula Ford into France in 1984 seemed incredibly brave, given that Formula Renault had been established for so many years in its homeland. Yet Formula Ford flourished without taking anything away from its French rival, which differed in its use of slicks, wings and the turbocharged Renault 18 engine.

If anything, the decision to introduce Formula Renault to the UK five years later seemed even more foolhardy. It coincided with a change in the regulations, replacing the trusty turbo engine with Renault's newer, normally aspirated 1.7-litre unit. But while the modification would make precious little difference in France, where there was an established market, it was difficult to see Renault finding a gap in Britain, where those fresh out of Formula First or Formula Ford

Below: Formula Vauxhall Lotus was introduced in 1988 and offered a lower-cost alternative to F3. The driver of this car is Justin Bell, son of Le Mans star Derek

Right: Formula Vee for Volkswagen-engined single-seaters was big business in some countries but remained a club formula in the UK

Below: Monoposto racing offers fast single-seater sport to club-level enthusiasts with various different car and engine combinations taking part

already had FF2000, Formula Forward and Formula Vauxhall Lotus to choose from if they were after a slicks-and-wings formula. But with all the main UK constructors announcing plans to enter the market, perhaps there was a point to it.

However, when only five cars contested the first British race, in May 1989, the cynics saw justification for their reasoning. Although the numbers never really picked up, the racing was generally good, the cars proved reliable, and by the end of the year over 50 deposits had gone down on cars for the 1990 season. Renault stepped in with generous support, and suddenly everybody wanted to know about it.

In France, the formula's usefulness was common knowledge. After all, Alain Prost and countless others had moved up the ladder on the back of what they had achieved in Formula Renault. Just because Renault hadn't marketed the product all over Europe, there was no reason to doubt its effectiveness.

France leads the world in its motor racing scholarship system. Each year, a handful of promising young drivers is picked by the country's numerous racing schools, and given fully-sponsored drives in one of the junior categories, usually Formula Renault, although some schemes now use Formula Ford. If the candidates prove successful, the benefactors will then assist them up into F3, and beyond into F3000 and Grands Prix when the time is right. Formula Renault has been an integral part of this process for many years, and can take due credit for the continued proliferation of French drivers in the sport's higher echelons.

Its introduction into Britain is the first part of a plan to broaden interest in Formula Renault throughout Europe.

Formula Vee

First conceived in the USA, Formula Vee has its roots back in the Fifties, when an Italian company produced a VW-engined single-seater at the initiation of a Florida-based VW dealer. America recognized the formula in 1963, and by 1965 it had races in its own right. It has since enjoyed huge popularity both there and in the Antipodes, while it has produced some notable champions in Europe. World Champions Niki Lauda and Keke Rosberg both served apprenticeships in the category.

Using mostly standard VW components, including the 1.3-litre Beetle engine, the spindly Formula Vee chassis produce lap times within a few seconds of those achieved by Formula Ford cars, and competitors will rub their hands with glee while they tell you about the comparatively fractional cost of a season in Vee.

Following its transatlantic crossing in 1967,

support from VW ensured the popularity of Formula Vee in several European countries. Such incentives were not available in Britain, where it has stubbornly remained a low-key club formula. Even so, 1971 champion Brian Henton would go on to race in Formula 1 with March, Tyrrell and Toleman, and 1975 title-holder Ian Flux has since forged a fine reputation as an all-rounder with excellent performances in a wide range of single-seaters, saloons and sports cars.

Part of Formula Vee's charm lies in its lack of development over the years, which has led to cars remaining competitive for years on end. In the 1986 British season, an Austro built in 1968 was still winning races!

Despite most F1 aspirants preferring the higher-profile pastures offered by such as Formula Ford, Formula Vee's simplicity and minimal running costs coupled with paddock camaraderie saw it gain in popularity during the Eighties, with full grids of cars the rule rather than the exception.

The 750 Motor Club took the formula under its wing in 1980, and in this happy environment it has flourished. Many manufacturers have constructed Vee chassis, most notably McNamara, Kaimann, Austro, Veemax and Scarab. The latter has been the most prolific in the UK in recent years, supplying cars either in kit form or ready built.

With spare parts easy to come by in most scrapyards, Formula Vee makes good sense for the amateur racer. Although there was a general lack of enthusiasm for the formula in the Seventies, it has since found a secure footing.

Other Formulae

No other country shares Britain's wide range of options for hobby racers. In addition to the classes already covered, the Monoposto Formula and Formula 4 offer sport at relatively low cost, and both categories encourage DIY.

Monoposto was conceived back in 1958, in an effort to develop cheap racing for the amateur. Thus home-built cars are strongly favoured, although mass-produced chassis are permitted so long as they are at least three years old. Competitors may run 1-, 1.6- or 2-litre engines in the faster of the two classes, each modified suitably to ensure parity with its alternatives. The second class (in which mass-produced chassis have to be at least five years old) allows mildly uprated Formula Ford 1600 engines, and the wide range of possibilities has made it a popular home for older F3 and FF2000 chassis, which can continue to give competitive service for years.

Formula 4, which began life as a motor-cycle-engined category, was fostered by the efficient 750 Motor Club in the early Seventies,

and now uses either a Ford 1.3-litre pushrod engine in restricted form, or a 1-litre Chrysler Imp motor in full race trim. In the interest of its amateur status, major commercial sponsorship is outlawed.

And if there is still nowhere to race your particular car, several clubs organize Formula Libre races, which permit absolutely anything to run, providing it is in raceworthy condition. Formula Libre actually enjoyed moments of considerable glory in the early Fifties, when the World Championship ran to F2 regulations and F1 cars had few other places to play. Nowadays, it is an increasingly rare feature of club meetings.

Finally, to prove that not all motor racing ideas are bound to succeed, no matter how bright they seem, there was Formula Talbot, launched in 1980. An interesting concept if ever there was one, Formula Talbot chassis were powered by a 1.6-litre Talbot Sunbeam engine, converted to run on methanol. It was a bold attempt to prove the sport's willingness to adapt in the wake of an international fuel shortage. There was also a major marketing coup when the Prime Minister's son Mark Thatcher signed up to take part.

The cars themselves were basically Formula Fords, with modified suspension to cope with the extra cornering forces generated by slick tyres. Although never well supported, there was some fabulous racing, notably during the final season in 1982. There were also less memorable moments, such as when three of the five starters spun off together at Oulton Park on the first lap. One restarted, and spectators had to endure 10 laps watching three cars spread equidistantly over 1.6 miles... Days like that were not a good advertisement.

Sparton, whose attractive FF1600 designs had never found great favour, became the dominant constructor, but despite the exciting racing customers were few and far between. It never came close to attracting the required support, and its demise came as no surprise to anyone.

Below: *Britain's top GP star, Nigel Mansell, seen here back in 1977 at Brands Hatch, began his career in the cut-and-thrust world of Formula Ford*

Sports Car Racing 1920–1990

It is a brave pundit who offers a definition of a 'sports car'. At one time all cars involved in competition could be considered 'sports', but soon there developed a separate branch of racing for purpose-built single-seat racers. Competition vehicles with two seats then came to be considered as 'sports cars'.

This remains true to this day. However, gone is the time when you could drive Le Mans-type sports cars on the road or go into a showroom and buy a similar car for road use. The modern sports racer is every bit as specialized and as finely engineered as its GP racing counterpart and the racing can be just as thrilling. Of course there is plenty of sports car racing below international level and contests between road-going sports cars, modified or otherwise, remains one of the healthiest areas of club competition in the UK and USA.

The most famous sports car race of them all is the Le Mans 24 Hours. This is the start of the 1989 event with the victorious Mercedes team leading off, ahead of the Jaguars

It has taken the best part of a century to work out exactly what is a sports car and what is not. During the early days of motoring, virtually any form of motorized transport could be called a sports car because you had to have a pretty sporting nature to be able to drive it. Progress was such, however, that by the turn of the century there were sub-divisions extending from commercial vehicles designed and built purely to carry loads that earned money to cars built purely for racing or record breaking. Weight is the implacable enemy of high performance, so this sort of machinery invariably had the minimum of equipment needed to convey a human being to whatever goal was in sight.

It was at this early point that confusion arose. The most obvious place to race cars was on the road, although there were some events on beaches and dirt tracks constructed specially for the British sport of horse trotting which had become such a craze in America and Australia. The main problem about the early roads was that they tended to be extraordinarily rough and the cars that had to traverse them were quite complicated to control, especially as bigger and bigger engines were mounted in ever more flimsy lightweight chassis with next to no bodywork.

As a result these fire-breathing monsters normally needed a crew of two, one with his hands and feet fully occupied operating the steering wheel, brakes and gears, and the other working such items as a plunger to work up fuel pressure and helping to change the frequently-punctured tyres. Most of the excitement came from driving the car, so that role was often the province of the owner. The second member of the crew then tended to specialize in mechanical care.

This all meant that the earliest racing cars had to be two-seaters. But very soon they became so specialized that they were of little use for anything other than racing. A typical example was the large Mercedes of 1904 which raced with a skimpy two-seater body, and then needed a team of workers to remove its bodywork and to replace it with a far more accommodating affair for touring. Such tasks were tiresome, so the wealthy people who could afford to race cars often kept them just for that purpose and bought another for general activities.

The Tourist Trophy

The publicity achieved by racing, or record breaking, could be quite crucial to sales, so manufacturers then began to enter their touring cars in competitions to prove they were better than rivals' products! These early events included what would become the world's longest-running motor race, the Tourist Trophy, first held by the British in 1905, the year before the French started

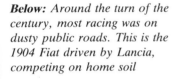

Below: Around the turn of the century, most racing was on dusty public roads. This is the 1904 Fiat driven by Lancia, competing on home soil

Grands Prix for purpose-built racing cars.

The first TT consisted of four long laps of an Isle of Man circuit totalling just over 200 miles (322km). It had to be held away from the mainland as road racing had been effectively written out of the English constitution. Part of the deal to promote this tourist attraction on the Isle of Man was that the competing cars would not be real racers.

The general rule then was that the biggest and most powerful engines used the most fuel, so the organizers put them at a disadvantage by framing their regulations around petrol consumption. They also stipulated that the cars would have to have some form of bodywork like real touring cars.

Entries were led by the Hon. Charles Rolls who distinguished himself by becoming the first retirement when his car stripped a gear soon after the start. Hinting darkly that somebody might have tampered with his mount, Rolls then protested that the winner, John Napier *on* — rather than *in* because, in those days, the occupants always rode on top of the car, like a horse — an Arrol-Johnston should be disqualified because a broken exhaust had not been repaired properly. Protests and rule bending have been part and parcel of motor sport ever since . . . and the Honourable Charles's Rolls-Royce went on to great commercial success after winning the next TT in 1906.

The commercial problem of being unable to unleash monstrous racing cars on the public roads worried British patriots like hotel builder Mr H. F. Locke King. As a keen driver, he felt strongly that the fledgling British motor industry should be able to test its products in the manner of the French who closed their long straight roads to hold Grands Prix. So he promptly resolved the matter by building a banked track on his estate at Brooklands, near Weybridge in Surrey. In next to no time at all, and by dint of the not inconsiderable expenditure of £150,000, Brooklands — the world's first track designed specifically for high-speed motoring — sprang into action in 1907. The TT was held only spasmodically for a while after that as firms like Rolls-Royce used long-distance reliability trials to promote the merits of their touring cars. One of the most significant of these events was the Austrian Alpine Trial, which had its roots in the German Herkomer Trophy events of similar concept to the TT.

Now that Alpine passes were being used for competition, racing cars became ever more impractical for road use and touring cars continued to be too heavy to be effective on the track. Quite soon, enthusiastic drivers began to realize what they were missing and what they wanted: a road machine that was a joy to drive, as nimble and fleet of foot as any sprinter, yet blessed with the unflagging stamina of a mechanical marathon runner. If this is the definition of a sports car then the Hispano Suiza Alfonso was the first real one. All sporting vehicles that had gone before were designed primarily for competition; it was merely a happy coincidence if they could be used for anything else. Quite naturally, the Alfonso was spawned from a racing car, the Hispano Suiza voiturette, which won the 1910 Coupe de l'Auto in France.

One of the early patrons of these cars from Barcelona was the teenage King Alfonso XIII of Spain. He could often be seen dashing around in helmet and goggles, a military aide by his side. The roads of the day, particularly in Spain, were appallingly rough and dusty, so his cars had to have their wheels covered to protect the occupants. There was also no telling what time they might complete a journey, so they needed lights as well. Already, the definitive sports car was taking shape: a machine with a performance as rewarding as that of a racing car, but with accommodation for at least two people, shrouded wheels and lights. For years, good King Alfonso was never without one or two examples of what was to become the Spanish national car, their first pure sports machine being named after him in 1912.

Hispano Suiza's Swiss designer, Mark Birkigt, was an uncommonly artistic engineer matched only by a French-domiciled Italian, Ettore Bugatti. Every part of a Hispano Suiza, even the pedals, displayed an exquisite feeling for form. It was also incredibly well balanced, the weight of the Alfonso being carried almost equally by each wheel. In stark contrast to the brute force and ugliness of the average racing car, its weight was modest because everything was designed with such elegance. The swan's neck spring hangers, for instance, looked delicate by the standards of the day, yet they were so well stressed they never showed signs of strain. Because the Alfonso weighed less than a ton, Birkigt was able to use a reinforced steel chassis which did not need to flex like those of its heavily-laden rivals. As a result the Alfonso could use softer springs, which gave it a ride more like that of a modern car and made it extraordinarily agile. Its engine was equally enjoyable to use because it had an uncommonly long stroke, giving it a great deal of pulling power. As if that was not enough, the gearbox was exceptionally sweet in operation. In those days before the invention of synchromesh, considerable skill was needed to change ratios without grinding the gears. As a manufacturer of magnificent guns, Hispano Suiza had the ability to machine cogs so precisely that they slid in and out of mesh in near silence.

Early evolution

The cars that raced at Brooklands were a complete contrast. Whereas many of the early ones had been powerful touring cars stripped of nearly all their coachwork, they were now beginning to acquire new bodies based on the streamlined fuselages of the aircraft which flew from the centre of the track. Riding mechanics were soon discarded

Above: A Vauxhall coping with the dust of the 1914 French GP. The road surface was better than in previous years but the surface was still not sealed

as unnecessary, partly because of their weight, partly because of their bulk, and partly as the cars were now never far from their base. By the time Hispano were producing their Alfonso, real racing cars were single-seaters.

They became even less like road cars in 1913 as Louis Coatalan started a trend by removing the 9-litre V12 engine from an aeroplane and inserting it in one of his Sunbeam chassis. From that point on, the general public began to have a harder time associating racing cars with anything which could be driven on the road.

The conflict of World War 1 so accelerated engine development that smaller and more efficient units became more than competitive because they were lighter. They also became attractive to racing car makers because they were cheaper and bore a closer resemblance to products which could be sold in quantity.

Le Mans and the Targa Florio

In addition, the success of 24-hour racing in America had not gone unnoticed. Soon after peace was declared in 1918, Parisian entrepreneur Eugene Mauve began to devise ways to make money out of the spectacle in France. His first *Bol d'Or* in 1922 was won by André Morel in a dainty 1100cc Amilcar. The organization was less impressive than the idea, which inspired the better-disciplined Automobile Club de l'Ouest to promote their own endurance race on roads around their base at Le Mans the following year. Like the TT, it was intended for touring cars, but was dominated from the start by the faster and more practical sports cars.

The roads were closed, as they were in Grands Prix, to get over the problems with crowd control that had bedevilled the early road races. These had survived — just — in modified form, typified by the Targa Florio organized by Sicilian tycoon Vincenzo Florio since 1906. The roads around this Mediterranean island were so rough and narrow that overtaking was frequently impractical, so the

cars started at one-minute intervals, the contest being resolved on elapsed time. On roads as tortuous as those in the Alps, outright racing cars were impractical, so entries were limited to what was termed standard cars. This meant that at least 10 identical examples had to have been manufactured. Weight-saving modifications, such as removing the wings, were allowed, but — in essence — this event would soon be dominated by sports cars. Initial entries for a race in such a remote spot were small, but the drivers found the course so challenging that they soon came back for more — encouraging thousands of Sicilians who soon decided that motor racing should become a national sport. Early races tended to be titanic battles between entrants from France — an acknowledged leader in motor sport at the time — and the fiercely-nationalistic Italians.

By 1919, however, the touring car concept had taken a back seat as leading manufacturers vied for the publicity that surrounded winning one of the toughest races imaginable. Front-runners included an Indianapolis Ballot, full-race Peugeots, Alfa Romeos, Italas, and a little-known Lancia driver, Enzo Ferrari, in his first motor race (hill-climb experience notwithstanding). The cars still had two seats because riding mechanics were an absolute necessity, but they were pure racing cars.

But when Mercedes returned to the motor racing fray in 1921 the Targa demonstrated once and for all that reliability and roadholding were more important on Sicilian roads than sheer power. With typical Teutonic thoroughness, the Germans had decided to

back every avenue of development. They entered two modern 1.5-litre supercharged sports cars, two modified 1914 Grand Prix cars, and two other big six-cylinder chargers. Backing came from another four-cylinder car driven by the Florentine Count Giulio Masetti, who had outrun Max Sailer's semi-works 7.2-litre six-cylinder Mercedes to win the previous year's race. The big Mercedes tore themselves and their tyres apart, leaving the wily Count to hound Jules Goux's French Ballot to near destruction on his way to a second victory.

With Italy's honour on the line, Alfa Romeo uprated their RL sports car to RLTF (for Targa Florio) specification for Ugo Sivocci to win the 1923 race, backed by the similar machines of Antonio Ascari, in second place, and Masetti, fourth, Ferdinando Minoia's big Steyr splitting the team as it took third position. By 1924, big cars were almost a thing of the past as only André Dubonnet's 8-litre Hispano Suiza could be considered a contender for overall victory. The Germans had learned their lesson well, however, concentrating on 2-litre super-charged cars, ranged against teams of Peugeots and Alfas, plus a lone Ballot. Masetti's Alfa led a drama-packed race until he was relegated to second place at the finish by Christian Werner's Mercedes, Dubonnet wrestling sixth place as the rugged course took its toll in shredded tyres, mechanical mayhem and the inevitable accidents.

Meanwhile the French found consolation as André Lagache and René Leonard won the first Le Mans 24-Hour race in their 3-litre Chenard & Walcker. A subtle change could be seen here in that, although the cars had to have at least two seats, only the driver was on board. At least two drivers were needed, however, because of the length of the event.

The spectacle of pit stops to change drivers and refuel was heightened when only three of the 33 starters failed to finish, partly because these production-based cars were more durable than the highly-tuned racers. But they had to be tough because the roads were still rough — although not as bad as those of the Targa Florio — and, even in 1923, the winning car covered 1372.9 miles (2209.4km) against the Targa's 268 (431km). The length of the French straights was also reflected in the winning average speed of 57.2mph (92.1 km/h), the Targa's countless corners taking their toll at 39.67mph (63.84km/h).

This undoubted test of endurance closer to main centres of car ownership than a remote island, where donkeys were the main form of transport, quickly captured the imagination of major manufacturers. The roads were also a lot easier on the machinery, so front-running cars soon became heavier and faster. The organizers tried to restore some balance in favour of smaller machinery by instituting an index of performance handicap award as early as 1926, but the lion's share of the glory still came from crossing the line first.

Enter the Bentley

The Isle of Man TT, meantime, had been extended to motor cycles, capturing the imagination of many, including a former rider, engineer Walter Owen Bentley. So when he began producing cars under his own name to replace the French DFPs he had been importing before World War 1, he was quick to gain publicity by entering a team in the 1922 TT — with a fourth car going to Indianapolis, probably as a result of American subsidies aimed at retaining an international flavour for the race. Such was the reliability of this near-standard 3-litre sports car that star driver W. D. Hawkes took 13th place!

The Bentleys followed up by taking the team prize in the TT with works test driver Frank Clement second place behind the vastly-experienced Frenchman, Jean Chassagne, in a Sunbeam. With the proprietor, W. O. Bentley, fourth and Hawkes fifth, the emergent team was filled with enthusiasm for events like this which could demonstrate the undoubted speed and durability of their very expensive sports cars. The publicity was of far more benefit than anything they might expect from shorter races at Brooklands, where an Edwardian system of handicapping was much in evidence.

The rather reactionary management at Brooklands had also banned the glamorous new idea of racing all night, so it was hardly surprising that the emergent Bentley team decided — at the insistence of motor trader Capt. John Duff — to go for glory at Le Mans. They had a lot to learn in the first year, especially about the way the road surface

Left: Italy's Targa Florio, pictured here in the Twenties, was first run in 1906 and took place on the mountain roads of Sicily

broke up as a result of being pounded non-stop for 24 hours. Repairs to the damage caused by flying stones cost a lot of time and they finished fourth.

But when Duff and Clement returned in 1924, their car was better prepared, with coconut matting and laths protecting the vulnerable petrol tank, stone guards for the lights and double fuel lines. There was nothing that could live with the Bentley, which ran like a train — which, in turn, was hardly surprising because 'W. O.' had learned his trade on locomotives. Niggling problems led to French Lorraine-Dietrichs winning the next two races at Le Mans, by then established as the most prestigious event in Europe. But four consecutive victories by Bentleys between 1927 and 1930 left ever bigger and more powerful cars, with capacities as high as 6.5 litres, dominating the decade so far as publicity was concerned.

With only the odd exception, such as Clement and convert Chassagne, the Bentley Boys, as they became known, were mostly very well-heeled amateurs. The most spectacular was financier and diamond millionaire Woolf Barnato, who scored a hat trick by winning the only three times he entered. And semi-professional Sammy Davis, a motoring journalist, partnered Harley Street consultant J. Dudley Benjafield to the other win, in 1927, nursing home the doctor's battered car after it collided with — and helped eliminate — its two team-mates at the notorious White House Corner. Performances like this by the heavyweight British Racing Green chargers raised patriotic feelings to a fever pitch and led disgruntled rivals like Ettore Bugatti, with what had become the French national racing car, to snipe that Mr Bentley made the fastest lorries around . . .

He had good reason to be annoyed. His beautiful little cars won the Targa Florio five times in succession during this period to nothing near like the acclaim. Part of the reason, however, was that the 2.3-litre straight-eight blown Bugattis were so ideally suited to this circuit that, at times, they made up half the field. But the cars they beat, works Alfa Romeos and the new Italian Maseratis, were formidable to say the least.

The birth of the Mille Miglia

Meanwhile, mainland Italians were smarting at the continuing success of the Targa Florio. This was despite the area around Brescia, where many great cars were built, having become the centre of Italian motor sport by the Twenties, hosting the country's first Grand Prix in 1921. Local blood was further curdled when that race was won by a Ballot, and a new track established at Monza, in the rival city of Milan, to help develop world-beating Italian competition cars. The citizens of Brescia were even more upset in 1923 when France took the new initiative at Le Mans. If Brescia was to regain its status, it would have to have an even greater race.

There was a lot of talk, but no effective action until four well-heeled patriots met in 1926. They were the aristocratic racing drivers Count Aymo Maggi and Count Franco Mazzotti, long-distance trial organizer Renzo Castegneto and journalist Giovanni Canestrini. They rejected a rally format like that of the Alpine as being too long and complicated, and open-wheel racing cars were barred because they were in decline. Sports cars were chosen to encourage the development of better production machines.

First thoughts about the route centred on Brescia to Rome because that was the capital of Italy. But Brescia wanted all the glory, so the route settled on Brescia–Rome–Brescia, in a figure of eight to take in all types of road. All that remained was to find a name. Mazzotti, who was putting up the money, asked: 'How long is the course?' 'Sixteen hundred kilometres,' said one of the others. 'That's a thousand miles,' said Mazzotti. 'We'll call it the Coppa della Mille Miglia.' 'Won't politicians be offended by us using Anglo-Saxon measurements?' asked another. 'Hardly,' replied Mazzotti. 'The Romans measured their distances in miles.' And the second great sports car race began.

All Brescia went wild as local OM cars finished first, second and third after 21 hours of flat-out racing on roads partially closed for the event. Next came two Lancia Lambdas, and Maggi and Bindo Maserati in a giant Isotta Fraschini. The leading Alfa Romeo

was driven by Brescian Arturo Mercanti under the assumed name of Isnoto because he was considered a traitor in his home city for helping to establish Monza. Motor-cycle ace Tazio Nuvolari achieved the 'impossible' by finishing 10th in a slow and unwieldy Bianchi. The winner, Minoja, was feted for bringing glory — and work — back to Brescia.

In 1928, foreign manufacturers, such as Lorraine-Dietrich, Chenard & Walcker, Bentley and Sunbeam, refused to enter the Mille Miglia, preferring the easier Le Mans race. But Bugatti, anxious to emphasize that his cars really were the best, sent supercharged straight-eights, along with Chrysler and La Salle from America. Nuvolari took an early lead for Bugatti, only to be overhauled by inspired Alfa Romeo test drivers, Giuseppe Campari and Giulio Ramponi, in Milan's 'secret weapon', a supercharged version of Vittorio Jano's new 1500cc sports car. Glory swung back to Milan.

By 1929, Campari and Ramponi were doing it again in a 1750cc blown Zagato-bodied Alfa Testa Fissa. But they were severely rattled by Baconin Borzacchini and Ernesto Maserati in a new straight-eight 1700cc supercharged Maserati which led at Rome before consuming its transmission. The TT was beginning to fall from international significance despite having moved to a demanding new course around Ards, south-east of Belfast. The fastest finishers invariably drove an Alfa Romeo, Bentley or Mercedes, but the winner was worked out on a handicap system favouring small British MGs, Rileys and Austins.

The Brooklands scene

Their development had been encouraged by the Junior Car Club's 200-mile (322km) races run at Brooklands since 1921 for equally-diminutive two-seater racing cars. But it was not until 1927 that the ambitious Essex Car Club, stimulated by Bentley Boys Benjafield and Davis, were able to stage a six-hour race at the track for production sports cars including larger and more glamorous examples. Although there was a strong element of horse-race-style handicapping in the regulations, Barnato managed to get away with donating a cup to the entrant whose car covered the greatest distance.

George Duller's Grand Prix-inspired Sunbeam ran away with the race which was adjudged to have been won the following year by Ramponi's Alfa Romeo, despite the larger Bentleys of Sir Henry Birkin, Bernard Rubin, Barnato and Clement finishing ahead of the Italian car. Falling attendances goaded the Brooklands club into providing more stimulating events in 1929 and resulted in the first Double Twelve — two 12-hour races run in daylight to TT rules on consecutive days. The endurance element was heightened by locking competing cars overnight in a 'parc fermé' so that they could not be repaired. Ramponi's Alfa won again on handicap after Davis put up an astonishing display of faster driving in a Bentley. The British factory team had consolation in the next year when Barnato and Clement's normally-aspirated Speed Six won convincingly as rival supercharged Bentleys, developed privately against the advice of W. O., failed.

The Mille Miglia's rules were changed the following year to give standard cars a chance against exotics from Alfa Romeo and the thinly-disguised Grand Prix Maserati. Bentley, by now beset by financial crisis, still refused to enter because the roads were too rough, but Mercedes sent a fabulous supercharged SSK for Rudi Caracciola and Werner. Intense rivalry in the Alfa team led to Nuvolari — who started 10 minutes behind Varzi — chasing his team-mate through perilous mountains at night with headlights switched off, to catch him by surprise and win at a 62mph (100km/h) average.

Into the Thirties

As Bentley's finances finally ran out they were taken over by Rolls-Royce, who felt threatened by the rival firm's new 8-litre touring cars. They refused to become involved in motor sport again as the might of German industry was geared up. Mercedes made enough exotic cars to enter even more fabulous SSKL super-light Mercedes for Caracciola, possibly the only driver in the same class as Nuvolari. Rival aero-engine makers Alfa responded with a power unit up to 2.3 litres for Nuvolari; Varzi switched to a fearsome 5-litre Bugatti.

The pace of development in such an emotive arena was not confined to mechanical matters. Carrozzeria Touring boss Felice Bianchi Anderloni invented a new system of super-

leggera bodywork for Alfa Romeo, to make their cars even lighter than those clothed by the dominant firm of Zagato. At the same time Itala produced a Type 61 for the novice Piero Taruffi. In the race, Varzi's engine blew up after only seven miles (11km). As Caracciola raced ahead, Nuvolari almost set his Alfa's tyres alight in pursuit. The battle raged, but Caracciola won, the near-demented Nuvolari bloodied by off-road excursions. An extra perspective to a race in which cars started at one-minute intervals was added by one of the new Maseratis, driven by Guerino Bertocchi. Unfettered by handicapping, it won the 1100cc class by 1 hour 40 minutes from Britain's Charlie Goodacre in an Austin Seven. Alfa Romeo took the closed car class with an ordinary saloon, but it was the exotic sports cars that captured everybody's imagination.

Grand Prix racing was dull by comparison and needed stimulus that was not forthcoming during the great depression that followed the Wall Street crash. Private owners often took the place of factory entrants at all levels and could race almost anything they liked providing they put on a spectacle for the promoters. Sports cars mixed with outright racers in many events, often running without their easily-detached wings and lights in Grands Prix as pure-bred racing cars sprouted such appendages in road races. As ever, regulations were open to 'interpretation'. When Bugattis began to be beaten with some regularity, the French turned their Grand Prix — the oldest in the world — into a sports car event so that their national car stood a chance of winning.

Valuable publicity could also be achieved

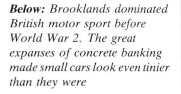

Below: Brooklands dominated British motor sport before World War 2. The great expanses of concrete banking made small cars look even tinier than they were

by the more direct association of marque names with production cars. The man behind the Blower Bentley project, Sir Henry Birkin, switched to Alfa Romeo to win the 1931 Le Mans race with Lord Howe. Then, in the following year, the Italian firm, who would go on to dominate a decade of sports car racing, developed the world's first grand touring car — a supercharged 1750 GTC *berlinetta* (small saloon) — for the closed car class in the Mille Miglia to back up the open cars. It took fourth place for Minoja behind open Alfas led by Borzacchini after Nuvolari crashed. The French were far from happy when Varzi's Bugatti blew up. And the Britons, Lord Clifford, in an MG, and the Hon. Brian Lewis, driving a Talbot, put up a noble display. By now, however, the Double Twelve had lost impetus without star attractions like the Bentleys, and the Earl of March won the last such race in an MG.

The Sicilians were not to be outdone by the mainland Italians, and enlisted the support of dictator Benito Mussolini to build a new loop road which helped form a more practical Piccolo Madonie circuit. Soon, however, the domination by Alfa Romeo — despite having to save money by handing over the works cars to Ferrari's private operation — discouraged other factory teams and the spectacle faded. The final four pre-war Targas were run round a city centre car park.

The Mille Miglia continued to provide most of the technical stimulation for sports car development, however, and Le Mans the lion's share of international publicity.

In 1933, as Scuderia Ferrari took over Alfa Romeo's hardware, the hot-blooded Nuvolari had to obey the autocratic Enzo Ferrari and win the Mille Miglia at a canter after the expiry of team-mate Borzacchini's car and the Mercedes of Manfred von Brauchitsch. English aristrocrat Lord Howe took over MG sponsorship for a team of supercharged Magnette K3s to be driven by himself, Birkin and Rubin, and land speed record ace George Eyston. Sports car racing had become so important in Europe that this British national team was received by the King of Italy and his new political boss Mussolini in an attempt to encourage an Anglo–Italian axis. Eyston replied by demolishing Bertocchi's Maserati opposition to win the 1100cc class with local ace Count Giovannino Lurani pointing the way from the passenger seat. MG won the team award and returned to Britain for another royal reception. Back in Italy, Fiat had invented the Balilla to win the 'utilitarian car' class and provide learner drives for the Villoresi brothers. It was the most significant Mille Miglia for years and Nuvolari's subsequent win at Le Mans seemed almost an afterthought.

The following year, the Mille Miglia became an elitist race, with the utility — or touring — cars occupied in a rival Tour of Italy. OM, Lancia and Mercedes — fully occupied with Grand Prix development — withdrew, but it mattered little to the spectators. A full-blooded battle raged between Varzi, signed by Ferrari to replace the rebellious Nuvolari, and 'The Flying Mantuan' as he was known, in a lone works car kindly supplied by Alfa Romeo. It was MG versus Maserati again in the small car class, and Balillas for learners.

Technical developments were more than significant. Pirelli produced the first wet-weather tyres for Varzi, leaving Nuvolari and the MGs handicapped in heavy rain by outdated Dunlop rubber. Nuvolari drove like a madman to overtake Varzi, before being beaten back into second with Monaco's Louis Chiron third, one hour behind, in a second Scuderia Ferrari car! Howe wrapped his MG round a pylon as Taruffi raced ahead in a Pirelli-shod Maserati for fifth place, Lurani's MG holding off Gilera's Fiat for second in class. Again, Le Mans seemed like an anti-climax although another Franco-Italian pairing, Phillipe Etancelin and Chinetti, won that race, too, for Alfa Romeo.

Changing times

The over-complicated Tour of Italy was abolished and production cars returned to Mille Miglia in 1935. Aerodynamic thinking was in evidence for the first time on a Balilla-based Fiat-Siata bodied by co-driver Nuccio Bertone. Alfa Romeo converted a P3 Grand Prix car into a very cramped two-seater for the only able driver who could squeeze in, the slimline Carlos Pintacuda. The equally tiny, and imperturbable, Marquis Della Stufa was stuffed in beside him. Peace broke out between Enzo Ferrari and Nuvolari, leaving

Below: The sport offered by events such as the TT, held on roads in Ireland and shown here in 1914, was impossible in mainland Britain as the roads couldn't be closed without parliamentary permission

Varzi to switch at the last moment to a ferocious new Grand Prix-based 3.7-litre supercharged Maserati. It blew up, leaving Pintacuda to win. Bertocchi's 1100cc Maserati outpaced fellow class winners, the Britons Clarke and Falkner, in a 1500cc Aston Martin for seventh place overall as the Villoresi brothers won the small car class. Britain made a comeback at Le Mans, however, as test pilot John Hindmarsh and Luis Fontes outlasted all the Alfa Romeos to win in their very Bentley-like Lagonda. It was ironic that Lagonda, just about to go into receivership, lacked the cash to advertise the success. But it brought them new finance and the ability to secure the services of W. O. Bentley, finally released from a contract enforced by Rolls-Royce!

Le Mans had to be called off the following year because of extensive industrial unrest and Italy was embroiled in the Abyssinian war — so there were few foreign entrants in the Mille Miglia. Alfa Romeo adapted 3-litre Grand Prix cars to run with new-fangled independent front suspension so the Marquis Antonio Brivio could hang on to win by 32 seconds from team-mates Nino Farina, Pintacuda and Biondetti. Bertocchi gained glory for Maserati, however, by taking fifth place with a proper 1500cc sports car.

Sports car racing returned to somewhere near normal in 1937 with the all-French team of Jean-Pierre Wimille and Robert Benoist winning at Le Mans in a controversial new streamlined Bugatti Type 57S. The French were ecstatic, as it was the first time in 10 years that an all-French team had won their own race. The British were happy, too: Aston Martin won the efficiency cup.

Peace in Africa meant foreigners returned to the Mille Miglia, notably driving French Delahayes and Talbots. But the air was thick with political intrigue. The Duce's son, Vittorio Mussolini, took the wheel of an aerodynamic Fiat and his father's personal car, a Touring-bodied Tipo B Alfa, was driven by Guidotti. His passenger, however, was the dictator's chauffer, Boratto, who was given the credit for fourth place. First- and second-placed Pintacuda and Farina escaped political wrath by explaining they had to do it to make sure that the third-placed Delahaye did not win. Industrialist Carlo Dusio won the small car class with a Topolino-Siata.

Pre-war developments

Technical innovation reached new heights in 1938 with Pinin Farina, Touring, Zagato, Ghia and Bertone vying to produce the lightest and most aerodynamic bodywork on Italian chassis, all of it much better-looking than that of the tank-like Le Mans Bugatti. The French Delahayes were just as ugly, but fast because they had Grand-Prix-based 4.5-litre V12 engines. Pintacuda and Farina were given well-tried Touring-bodied Alfa Romeos, Clemente Biondetti taking a more powerful machine powered by a prototype Grand Prix engine. Fiats, including examples driven by Taruffi, Mussolini's son Vittorio and grandson, Vito, faced small class opposition from advanced new Lancia Aprilias, including a lightweight version driven by Luigi Villoresi. Works BMW 328 rally cars were entered in the 2-litre sports class with Englishman Tony Fane as the leading driver.

Record speeds ensued as Biondetti kept the experimental Alfa together to win from Pintacuda and Dusio, Pierre Dreyfus bringing in a Delahaye fourth, and Fane winning his class and eighth overall place. Taruffi provided the star turn among the Fiats and 'Gigi' Villoresi's Lancia won its class.

It was the last Mille Miglia to be won by such an exotic car as an amateur-driven Aprilia crashed into crowds, killing 10 spectators and injuring 23. Until 1938, towns and cities en route had insisted on competing cars using narrow city-centre streets for the maximum spectacle and commercial profit. The outcry that followed forced a voluntary ban on superchargers, abandonment of the 1939 Mille Miglia and no more city-centre racing in Italy.

The spectators were better controlled at Le Mans where public roads were sealed off to form the track. In 1936, an accident that resulted in death and injury to spectators at Ards had led to the TT being transferred to a relatively tame circuit in Donington Park on the mainland. The handicap racing was still relatively tame, too, nothing near like as dramatic as a Grand Prix despite the admission of prototype — rather than just series production — cars from 1938 when the French had further reason to celebrate as Eugene Chaboud and Jean Tremoulet won Le Mans in a Delahaye.

The 24-hour race once more became the technological focus of sports car racing with what would be the temporary demise of the Mille Miglia. By now, Rolls-Royce and Lagonda were engaged in a propaganda war as W. O. Bentley produced an exciting new V12 road car. Against his better judgement, Bentley was persuaded to prepare works cars for Le Mans to be driven by Arthur Dobson-Charles Brackenbury, and the Lords Selsdon and Waleran, with the enthusiastic backing of surviving Bentley Boys. The opposition from Bugatti, Delahaye, Darracq and Delage was formidable but the relatively untried British cars ran superbly to take third and fourth places behind the winning Bugatti of Wimille and Pierre Veyron.

Italy adopted a policy of non-belligerence, allowing domestic motor racing to continue in 1940 as World War 2 brought it to a halt everywhere else in Europe. Adventurous enthusiasts like Lurani took advantage to reorganize the Mille Miglia on the more easily-policed 104-mile (167km) road circuit around Brescia. There was still a strong element of sportsmanship in the motoring world. Alfa Romeo remained as the favourites, however, despite the very high speeds

attained by the streamlined BMWs. Enzo Ferrari, having fallen out with Alfa Romeo, fielded his first cars, which were officially called Fiat 815s. But in the race itself, the BMWs outpaced the Alfas for Baron Huschke von Hanstein to win, team mates Brudes, Brien and Wencher dropping back among the Alfas so that Germany's Italian allies should not be humiliated!

Picking up the pieces

The publicity generated by the Le Mans 24-Hour race continued to dominate sports car racing after the war, although there would now be far more of it. Numerous nations — especially the United States, which would begin to import European sports cars in large numbers — would organize events along the lines of Grands Prix to eventually start a World Championship.

But once more it was the Mille Miglia that led the way in 1947 as a morale-booster for war-torn Italy. The course was lengthened to 1823 kilometres (1000 nautical miles) to take in as much of the country as possible. A huge entry was guaranteed as competitors were offered cut-price fuel and Pirelli tyres, normally on ration. Most of the cars were Fiats, or Fiat-based, including one driven by Maggi. Prototypes included fabulous Cistitalias built by Dusio, a new 125 from Ferrari, and an A6GCS Maserati for Gigi Villoresi. Nuvolari rose from his sickbed to lead the race in an open 1100cc Cisitalia before a downpour swamped his ignition and

Biondetti's 3-litre two-stage supercharged grand touring Alfa swept by to win. Second-placed Nuvolari returned, cursing and spitting blood, to his sickbed.

Pain-wracked and bereaved, the 55-year-old Nuvolari was courted by Alfa Romeo and Ferrari to drive again in 1948. Eventually he emerged from his confinement to take the wheel of an open Ferrari. The crowds went wild as Alberto Ascari took the lead for Maserati, only to be overtaken by Franco Cortese's Ferrari, then Consalvo Sanesi in an Alfa and Taruffi's Cisitalia. But the late-starting Nuvolari beat them all to Rome, losing a front wing in a crash en route and the bonnet in another. A third crash cracked his car's chassis, but failed to slow him. Enzo Ferrari placed a priest in the middle of the road to implore him to stop, but Nuvolari swerved past, speeding on in a disintegrating car. As the suspension collapsed in sight of the finish, he retired, howling in anguish, to his sickbed. Another great veteran, Biondetti, won for Ferrari; Fiat drivers included tractor mechanic Ferrucio Lamborghini who crashed into a restaurant and gave up racing on the spot. A British contingent was led by pre-war rally ace Donald Healey, ninth in his own car.

The passion that led Italians to go motor racing resulted in the Sicilians literally moving mountains so that the Targa Florio could continue around the original 600 miles (965km) of their battered coastline. Biondetti won again for Ferrari in 1948, his average

Above: The Chinetti/Selsdon Ferrari that won the first post-war running of Le Mans in 1949

Right: *The famous duel between the Jaguar of Hawthorn and the Mercedes of Fangio in the opening hours of the tragic 1955 Le Mans race, before the infamous crash that led to Mercedes' withdrawal*

of 55.1mph (88.6km/h) an improvement of 16mph (26km/h) on the previous round-the-island race in 1914.

Despite intense opposition from Alfa Romeo, he repeated the trick on the long circuit in 1949, having won the Mille Miglia for a third time following a battle royal with two other works Ferraris driven by Taruffi and Bonetto. By now the AC de l'Ouest was back in action at Le Mans, accepting prototypes of production sports cars on the grounds that hardly any new ones had been produced since the war. This line of thinking would be highly influential for the next four decades. As it was, France provided most of the heavy metal in the form of Delahayes, Talbots and Delages, but Chinetti, partnered by Lord Selsdon, won in a Ferrari.

Onward and upward

Entries reached a record 60 for Le Mans in 1950 with another record, 750 cars, taking part in the Mille Miglia. There were numerous crashes, and three drivers were killed, but the Italian transport ministry produced figures proving that more would have died on a day in which normal traffic ran! Wealthy Ferrari GT driver Giannino Marzotto won, clad in an immaculate pin-striped suit. Teammate Dorino Serafini, in an open Ferrari, finished second. Already the days of the traditional open sports car were dated, although it would be more than 30 years before they disappeared from front-line racing. Juan-Manuel Fangio demonstrated world-championship driving ability by taking third place in a perspiring Alfa Romeo touring car

with Britain's Leslie Johnson fifth in a Jaguar XK120 production car.

The romantic appeal of Le Mans had by now spread to the United States where sports car racing was being organized on a strictly amateur basis by the fledgling Sports Car Club of America. They would soon be running an international race for professional drivers and works teams, and the TT would return to Northern Ireland, where roads could be closed to make up the new Dundrod circuit near Belfast. Emergent hero Stirling Moss celebrated his 21st birthday a day in advance by winning both on scratch and handicap in a Jaguar XK120.

By 1951, sports car racing was hitting new heights with 26 Ferraris lined up against two works Alfa Romeos, three Jaguars, two Aston Martins, an Allard and a Frazer-Nash among the faster cars in the Mille Miglia. Works Stanguellini driver Sighinolfi, battling against numerous 1100cc OSCAs, built by the Maserati brothers, crashed near Ferrara, uprooting three kerbstones. But there was still room for the amateurs: Giannino Marzotto, in one of the leading Ferraris, retired with tyre trouble, rather than change the wheel himself. Fellow Ferrari driver Villoresi took the lead, only to leave the road at the same spot at Sighinolfi. But he was able to continue with just a jammed gearbox as there were now no kerbstones to impede progress. With such luck, he won the race from Giovanni Bracco's new Lancia Aurelia — a production GT car. Lancia sales soared after that, Enzo Ferrari preferring to concentrate on pure competition cars rather than get involved in larger-scale production. As

some measure of the progress made by road cars, Felice Bonetto could finish only sixth in a pre-war Alfa Grand Prix car.

Cortese won the Targa Florio, back on the shorter Madonie circuit, in a British Frazer Nash — equipped, like Bonetto's Alfa Romeo, with cycle-type wings and a narrow cigar-shaped body. It would be one of the last victories for this type of sports car. Future racers would have to have all-enveloping bodies in a bid to outlaw road-going Grand Prix cars like the Lago-Talbot.

Le Mans became especially significant as swift development work in Coventry led to Britons Peter Walker and Peter Whitehead winning in a special-bodied C-type competition version of the XK120 as Talbots and Ferraris fell by the wayside, a new Volkswagen-based German marque, Porsche, running home 20th with an 1100cc coupé.

In the United States, Sebring's first 12-hour sports car race, run on an airfield circuit and won by a Le Mans-style French Deutsch-Bonnet economy car, joined the Indianapolis 500 as North America's second international event. In Mexico a great open-road race, the Carrera Panamericana, was staged for virtually any type of car.

Most of the works teams had stayed in Europe, with Bracco — now in a prototype Ferrari 250GT and comforted by swigs from a Chianti bottle — driving like a demon through thick fog to hold off Karl Kling's Mercedes 300SL and veteran Luigi Fagioli, driving his last great race for Lancia. Fellow veterans Caracciola, in a Mercedes, and Brivio, running in a brand-new Ferrari 250GT, took fourth and ninth places. Lurani won his

class for Porsche with the Volkswagen gearbox jammed in third. Porsche went away, designed some new synchromesh, and would begin making millions from patents as others adopted their system.

The speed of the new Mille Miglia Mercedes led Jaguar to revise hastily the C-type bodywork with the result that overheating eliminated their Le Mans cars, leaving victory to Mercedes. They would not make that mistake again. Sebring leading light Briggs Cunningham drove 20 hours unaided in a car of his own creation as French veteran Levegh's Talbot expired while he was in the lead after 23 hours at the wheel.

Ferrari had a less successful year, Lancia sending a works team of Aurelia GTs — based on a design initiated by Jano — for Bonetto to win the Targa Florio from teammates Valenzano and Anselmi. But Ferrari managed a win in the Monaco Grand Prix — demoted to sports car status — after Moss's C-type Jaguar was disqualified, much to the crowd's disgust. Porsche were rapidly becoming more serious, with Walter Glockler debuting a new sports racing car, the Type 550 Spyder, at the Nürburgring. Guatemalen Jose Herrate demonstrated its durability by winning his class in the Carrera.

Mid-Fifties developments

Six million spectators were on hand to watch 481 starters, including the by now traditional 26 Ferraris, in the 1953 Mille Miglia, part of a new Manufacturers' Championship. Giannino Marzotto, still in collar and tie, won from Fangio in an Alfa Romeo Disco Volante and Bonetto's Lancia. Britain's Reg Parnell took fifth place for the rapidly-emerging Aston Martin team, using engines based on a W. O. Bentley design. Marzotto's race average at last topped that of Biondetti's supercharged Alfa Romeo in 1938.

As rivals concentrated on all-out speed, Jaguar looked to the brakes, ever more tortured now that all-enveloping bodywork shrouded them from a cooling air-stream. As the pundits predicted a Ferrari-Alfa duel for the lead at Le Mans, the British team adopted aircraft technology. Their new disc brakes were so superior that the C-types of Tony Rolt and Duncan Hamilton, Moss and Walker, easily outran Ascari and Villoresi in a howling 4.5-litre Mille Miglia Ferrari coupé. It had seemed like magic when Jaguar won at an average of 93mph (149km/h) in 1951. Now they had raised the speed to 105mph (169km/h) with little extra power and the same bodywork.

Jaguar lost the new World Championship by the narrowest of margins to Ferrari, who added the Spa 24 Hours and the Nürburgring 1000-Kilometre races to their Mille Miglia victory. Lancia also became a formidable challenger to Ferrari when Umberto Maglioli won the Targa Florio — and Jaguar suffered a similar fate when their team were defeated by Aston Martin in the TT. It was then left to

Above: Stirling Moss in the 300SL Mercedes on his way to a record-breaking win in the Targa Florio with Peter Collins

cars and the American Cunninghams played a waiting game. Moss was the British team's pacemaker, though he could not pass the Italian cars, which had a power advantage of more than 100bhp. Then clogged fuel filters and mechanical trouble eliminated Moss and team-mate Ken Wharton. But Rolt and Hamilton ploughed on relentlessly until there was only one Ferrari left, driven by the Argentinian Froilan Gonzales and Maurice Trintignant from France. The 'Pampus Bull' drove his machine like Ben Hur in a chariot race, but both man and machine were weakening. Gonzales had neither eaten nor slept for two days and the thundering V12 was down on compression. It took longer to restart after every pit stop and the Jaguar crept closer until it was delayed by an accident with a baulking backmarker. Still the relentless pursuit went on until Gonzales called on the last reserves of his enormous strength to win by little more than 1 minute.

Jaguar had revenge when Wharton and Whitehead won the Reims 12-hour race the following week, but had to be content with fifth place in the TT as special 2.4-litre engines intended to beat the handicapper failed to run well. Laureau and Armagnac were the official winners in a tiny French Panhard but, so far as the Italians were concerned, the Ferrari of Mike Hawthorn and Trintignant, first on the road, was the winner. They advertised the fact so extensively that the TT was turned into a normal scratch race the following year.

1955: tragedy and triumph

If the 1955 sports car racing season will always be remembered for the world's worst motor racing crash in which 82 people were killed at Le Mans, followed by further fatal crashes, it also deserves to be remembered as the year Moss, and other Britons, emerged as the greatest drivers. It became their most successful season, right from March, when Hawthorn shared victory with the American Phil Walters at Sebring in a Jaguar, to the Targa Florio in October when Moss and Peter Collins won in a Mercedes at a shattering 59.2mph (95.2km/h) average. This victory also brought Mercedes the World Championship — and of the five title races in which British drivers competed, they won them all.

Moss's greatest victory that year was in the Mille Miglia, partnered by Denis Jenkinson. Moss and Jenkinson wore out two Mercedes in reconnaissance of the route before winning at 98.5mph (158.5km/h) in their 300SLR from team-mate Fangio with Maglioli third in a Ferrari. At the same time, Cipolla averaged 49.6mph (79.8km/h) to win the bubble car class, 1.25mph (2.01km) faster than Minoja's 1927 race average. The once seemingly-invincible Ferraris were eclipsed, not only by Mercedes, but by Maserati, whose brilliant number one driver, Jean Behra, won several races, and by Jaguar at Le Mans.

Lancia to take the first three places in the 1934-mile (3112km) Carrera race from Tuxtla Gutierrez to Juarez.

Ferrari won the World Championship again in 1954, entering five of the six title races while Jaguar concentrated on building a stunning new D-type with aircraft-style bodywork designed specially for the ultra-high speeds of Le Mans. Lancia and Aston Martin provided the most consistent opposition around the world, although Moss and American Bill Lloyd caused a sensation by taking victory at Sebring in a tiny 1.5-litre OSCA from the Austin-Healey of Lance Macklin and George Huntoon when the other works cars suffered mechanical mayhem. The Mille Miglia was rerouted through Nuvolari's home town of Mantua, where he had died a lingering death through years of inhaling exhaust fumes. Entries included seven of the new Isetta bubble cars, lined up against works Ferraris, Maseratis, Lancias, Aston Martins, Austin-Healeys, Jaguars, Triumphs and Porsches.

Ascari won for Ferrari with team-mate Vittorio Marzotto second only nine seconds in front of third-placed Luigi Musso's Maserati. Another Ferrari was fourth, driven by four-times winner Biondetti in his last great race before he died the following year. Numerous serious accidents resulted in two deaths.

But the most dramatic race of the year, and perhaps of the decade, came at Le Mans despite the withdrawal of Mercedes — concentrating on Formula 1 development — and Lancia, whose new 3.8-litre cars were not ready. Taruffi had won the Targo Florio at record speed with a 3-litre car, but Lancia knew that it was not fast enough for the French circuit's long Mulsanne straight. As heavy summer storms swept the Sarthe, the race became a straight fight between Jaguar and Ferrari as Aston Martin lost all five of its

Yet another thrilling duel had developed between Hawthorn's D-type and Fangio's 300SLR until disaster struck when Levegh's Mercedes ran up the back of Macklin's Austin-Healey, and was launched into the crowd. Moss took over the leading Mercedes and Ivor Bueb jumped into the Jaguar, in place of a shocked Hawthorn, who had been involved in the incident leading up to the crash. Gradually their rivals, Maglioli, Castellotti and Trintignant in Ferraris, Tony Brooks and Roy Salvadori in Aston Martins, the Jaguars of Walters and Don Beauman, retired. Then Mercedes withdrew, leaving the Jaguar to win from Valzano's Maserati.

The tragedy had far-reaching effects. Many races were cancelled on safety ground, including two World Championship events, so the next round, the TT at Dundrod, assumed even greater importance. All the top sports cars were there, including one D-type for Hawthorn and Ulsterman Desmond Titterington. Disaster struck again — three drivers were killed in crashes. But the D-type led until the last lap, when its engine seized — leaving Moss and John Fitch to lead home two other Mercedes.

Small cars were banned from the Mille Miglia in 1956 in the continuing outcry which led to Mercedes quitting motor racing. But the remaining sports racing cars were so spectacular that five times as many races were organized for them as were for single-seaters. The expense of competing in so many far-flung events became too much for many manufacturers, however, and the World Championship developed into a half-hearted battle between Ferrari and Maserati, resolved in favour of Ferrari after Castellotti's Ferrari led home five others in the Mille Miglia when Moss crashed in his Maserati.

By now Jaguar had acquired a supporting team, the Ecurie Ecosse, running ex-works cars, which came more than good at Le Mans, providing the winner for Ninian Sanderson and Ron Flockhart. And small, nimble Porsches were starting to make their presence felt at the front of the field as Maglioli won the Targa Florio in a works RS. The car had made its debut in the Nürburgring 1000-kilometre race, to be nearly upstaged by another Porsche special. This was an old and battered Type 550 fitted with a large wing by its Swiss engineer-driver Michael May. The wing worked so well that his car went far faster than the works machines. Team manager von Hanstein promptly protested, and it was banned. Strangely, nobody followed up this line of development for more than a dozen years until wings suddenly appeared in all forms of racing ... Enzo Ferrari, for instance, was so reactionary — preferring to concentrate on ever more powerful engines — that his cars did not yet have disc brakes.

The end of the Mille Miglia

Ferrari won the World Championship again in 1957, but more on sheer power, durability and driver ability than anything else. Jaguar did not race officially, but Flockhart again swept to success (with Bueb) at Le Mans in a D-type, its advanced aerodynamics proving a great advantage on the Mulsanne straight. Its overall weight and relatively antique suspension made it less competitive on the tougher course, however, and it was significant that the good-handling Aston Martin DBR1 of Brooks and Noel Cunningham-Reid was able to beat the mighty Maserati and Ferrari

Below: Jaguar won Le Mans again in 1957 with a D-type driven by Flockhart and Bueb

around the tortuous Nürburgring. Entries in the Mille Miglia which followed were cut to 350 in an attempt to eliminate incompetent amateurs. White-haired Taruffi won at his 14th attempt for Ferrari, flagged in, as ever, by Castegneto. He kept a promise to his family and retired before learning that 10 spectators, the Marquis de Portago — a member of the Spanish royal family — and American Ed Nelson died when their Ferrari crashed as a tyre burst 25 miles (40km) from the finish. The storm of protest which followed ended the Mille Miglia. Diplomatically, the Targa Florio was run as a regularity trial that year.

In the aftermath of the Mille Miglia, a 3-litre limit was set on World Championship sports car racing in an attempt to slow the cars — which proved a great advantage to Aston Martin, which had been running cars of this capacity for six years. By then, Maserati had dire financial problems and it was left to Ferrari to provide the British team with strong opposition. Ferrari's new Testa Rossa won the first three events, the Anglo-British team of Collins and Phil Hill taking the Argentine 1000 Kilometres and Sebring, with Luigi Musso and Olivier Gendebien winning the Targa Florio. Moss's Aston Martin made the fastest lap before retiring in Sicily and then, capitalizing on its superior chassis, won the Nürburging 1000 Kilometres with Jack Brabham.

Ferrari won the Championship again, but the Nürburgring was just a taster for what was one of the greatest years in British motor racing history when Cooper won both the Formula 1 and 2 World Championships and Aston Martin took the sports car title — and Le Mans.

But it did not start that way, two Ferraris leading in five Porsches at Sebring when the lone Aston Martin expired. Porsche's championship hopes brightened when they filled the first four places in the Targa Florio before Moss and Jack Fairman dominated the Nürburgring 1000 Kilometres race with the only works DBR1. But Aston Martin had

three cars on hand for Le Mans where Salvadori and Texan Carroll Shelby ran to a strict schedule to lead in second-placed teammates Trintignant and Frere. The strategy worked perfectly as all the faster Ferraris expired — along with Moss's pace-setting DBR1 — and, to Porsche's anguish, none of their six cars finished. Ferrari still led the Championship, with only three points separating them from Aston Martin and Porsche. The last round, the TT at Goodwood, developed into a mighty battle between Moss's DBR1, Jo Bonnier's Porsche and a Ferrari shared by Phil Hill and Brooks. Despite a fire in the pits, the Aston won, with the Porsche and Ferrari only two seconds apart.

Interest flags

By 1960, however, interest was evaporating in the World Sports Car Championship as so few marques were competing in this very expensive series. The general feeling was that if a manufacturer was going to spend this much, he might as well go for Grand Prix racing because competitive sports racing cars were becoming far removed from road-going products. Only the publicity generated by Le Mans remained as a star-studded attraction, although the Italians still took the Targa Florio seriously. Maserati's new 'birdcage' Tipo 61, a weird-looking machine featuring an ultra-light chassis made from a network of spidery tubing, emerged as the fastest car, although the Ferrari Testa Rossa and smaller Porsche RS60 — handicapped by engine size from gaining outright victory of really fast circuits — were more durable.

A broken fuel line eliminated the Maserati of Nino Vaccarella while leading the Targa, the Porsche of Herrmann and Bonnier then

Below: Stirling Moss in the Aston Martin DBR1 at Goodwood on his way to the victory in the 1959 TT that clinched the World Sports Car Championship for Aston Martin

More significant for sports car racing than the CSI's moves, however, was a decision by Ford to change an image of utter dependability gained by producing stodgy cars. They decided to aim for a more youthful market by going for a high-performance image. Such campaigns have to be world-wide, so they started looking at world championships rather than just American domestic racing.

The great revival

This decision coincided with a great revival in sports car racing as the low contemporary engine capacity in Formula 1, and lack of a Formula 2, made single-seaters far from spectacular. For those teams who wanted to graduate from Formula Junior and could not afford the immense costs of Formula 1, and those who were uncertain of the junior formula's future, sports cars were attractive.

This all meant that Ferrari, Porsche and Abarth faced more opposition: clandestine General Motors backing saw Chaparral prototypes at Sebring, and Chevrolet Corvette String Rays in the GT category, with Ford supporting teams of AC Cobras. Grand Prix front runners Lotus and Cooper produced ultra-lightweight sports racers, along with newcomer Brabham, as an exciting new Lola-Ford made its debut at Silverstone. Jaguar produced lightweight versions of its E-type production car to give some opposition to Aston Martins and Ferraris while Rover produced a gas-turbine car for Le Mans as a result of experiments which had been going on since the end of World War 2.

Meanwhile Shelby had begun a new trend in professional sports car racing in the United States by inserting the Cobra's Ford V8 in a lightweight Cooper chassis. Such was the power-to-weight ratio of such cars that John Surtees' prototype Ferrari 250P could finish only fourth in the relatively short-distance Californian Riverside Grand Prix.

But at the end of the day, it was Ferrari which had won again at Le Mans (and the Targa). Ford tried to buy Ferrari as a quick way of changing its image, but — having been rebuffed — ploughed money into the Shelby's Cobras and the Lola GT, Colin Chapman of Lotus proving almost as much of a problem to handle as Enzo Ferrari.

Cobras won the opening race at Sebring in 1964, but after that Ferrari's better-handling Testa Rossa-engined 250GTO carried on winning GT races as it had done the previous year. Porsche's 904GTS became unassailable in the 2-litre class, winning the Targa Florio in the process while the Alfa Romeo GTZ vanquished Lotus's Elan in the 1600cc category. Prototype racing was another Ferrari demonstration, the 275P and 330P scoring numerous successes, including 1–2–3 victory at Le Mans, a Cobra slotting in fourth before two of the inevitable 250GTOs. Brabham's BT8 became the most successful sports racer, dominating the 2-litre class while, in America, big V8s appeared in all sorts of European

Left: Drivers Dan Gurney, seated on roof, and A. J. Foyt, waving on Gurney's left, celebrate their 1967 Le Mans win in the Ford GT40

outlasting all the Ferraris to win. The Birdcage of Moss and American Dan Gurney disappeared into the distance, leaving the rest of the field far behind, in the Nürburgring 1000 Kilometres. Bonnier and Gendebien were second in a Porsche, however, giving the Germans enough points — with a Sebring win for Herrmann and Gendebien — to show their sports cars were the best in the world. This was despite six Ferraris filling the first seven places at Le Mans, Gendebien and Frere winning, with the Aston Martin DBR1 of Salvadori and Jim Clark third.

The CSI then decided to reorganize the 1962 World Championship for grand touring cars only in the hope of attracting more manufacturers, leaving Le Mans as the principal outlet for sports racing cars. But Ferrari still had by far and away the fastest cars and few other manufacturers were interested. So prototypes were admitted as well, and Ferrari — which was producing front-engined sports racers, mid-engined prototypes, and very rapid GT cars — again scooped the Championship, winning Sebring from Porsche, who then took the Targa Florio. Somehow the American drivers Lucky Casner and Masten Gregory kept a Birdcage in one piece long enough to win a snow-hit 1000 Kilometres at the Nürburgring before Ferrari Testa Rossas took the first two places at Le Mans from one of their 250GTs. This gave them a long enough lead in the Championship to give the TT — for GT cars only — a miss with the works car and leave victory to Moss in a private Ferrari. Porsches won the medium class in GT racing with Fiat-Abarths mopping up the smaller championship, the same three marques going on to dominate their classes in 1963.

chassis. The home-brewed Chaparral was the most successful, however, although a new marque was emerging in McLaren-Oldsmobile — the result of another Anti-podean Cooper driver, Bruce McLaren, deciding to follow Jack Brabham's line by going it alone. The new Lola-inspired Ford GT gave nothing but trouble, despite leading early laps at Le Mans, matched only by Chapman's underdeveloped Lotus 30.

Ford made a massive effort to thrash Ferrari with sports prototypes the following year, but failed miserably through inexperience in Europe. Ferrari's strength lay in the fact that they had raced everywhere before, and so had their drivers, many competing regularly in Grands Prix. The only satisfaction that came Ford's way with the GT40 — apart from a home win in the Daytona 12-Hour — was the World GT Championship for a British-run team of AC Cobras — a hollow victory because they faced little or no opposition. Ferrari's successes at Monza, Spa, Le Mans, Reims, Austria, at the Nürburgring, in the Targa Florio and South Africa, were shared by four-cam P2 proto-types or the 250LM — a mid-engined version of the 250GTO that, like the GT40, could not find enough well-heeled customers to make it worth building 100 to qualify it as a GT car.

Although there was no official world championship for sports cars, this form of racing had never been stronger. McLaren-Elva, Chaparral and Lola all scored numer-ous wins with their lightweight mid-engined machinery which could easily outrun heavier Fords and Ferraris. They suffered a lot of trouble with their production-based Chevrolet or Ford V8 engines, however, pure racing engines like the Coventry-Climax used in Denny Hulme's TT-winning Brabham BT8 and the Porsche that powered George Follmer's US Road Racing championship-winning Lotus 23 proving far more reliable.

Ford topples Ferrari

Towards the end of the year, new regula-tions were framed in an attempt to bring the specifications of European and American sports racing cars closer together so that there could be a real world championship. But the racing would become so fast and furious in 1966 — with the biggest sports cars sprouting wings — that the gap became even wider. Cars for the Canadian–American (CanAm) championship on airfield circuits became open single-seaters with full-width bodies covering the massive fuel tanks needed to supply ever-larger V8 engines. The machinery used in European races, on the other hand, developed along more tradi-tional lines. More coupés were in evidence, however, because their aerodynamic super-iority on long straights outweighed the better visibility of an open car which could also prove very wearing for the drivers as speeds grew ever higher in long-distance races.

F1 driver John Surtees, in a Lola-Chevrolet, emerged the winner of the CanAm series, scooping $70,000 in prize money — more than he would have got for winning every Grand Prix that year. These cars became the lifeblood of big-time American racing, F1 racers being regarded as mere novelties that

Below: Ford's attack on Le Mans didn't come good until 1966 when their GT40s at last had the speed and reliability to win. In fact they filled the first three places

raced once a year at Watkins Glen. The only single-seaters that Americans really understood were the Indianapolis-style track cars. These big sports cars — built to the international Group 7 rules — struggled in Europe, however, where there were so many categories and classes. Formula 1 took most of the money here, leaving Group 7 to vie with Formula 2 for what was left.

The result was that hardly any Group 7 racers appeared outside North America, although Britain started an industry exporting more than £500,000-worth of Lolas and McLarens, only Chaparral offering any opposition. Imagine the surprise, however, when one of these Texan racers, driven by Bonnier and Phil Hill, won the Nürburgring 1000 Kilometres at its first attempt after Surtees' Ferrari P3 retired!

But it was Le Mans that provided most of the drama in Europe as Ford opted for reliability with a slow-revving 7-litre engine for its fleet of modified GT40s ranged against the more sophisticated 4-litre four-cam P3 prototypes. This clash of the titans ended in a 1–2–3 victory for Ford — breaking Ferrari's six-year domination — after most of the Italian cars suffered from transmission trouble. Ferrari, pouring time and money into Formula 1 development, was becoming overstretched. The point was emphasized by the way Porsche took the next four places with their 2-litre Carrera 6 cars, leaving Ferrari's only finisher, a 275GTB, struggling in eighth.

Ford, running 7-litre GT40s in Group 6 against Ferrari's 250LM, was able to add that title to its prototype championship, although

Porsche became unofficial world champions by scoring more points in the smaller-capacity Group 4 than Ford and Ferrari put together. Persistent performances by Porsche's 911S also took the Group 3 GT title from Ferrari 275GTB and Ford Shelby Mustang opposition.

Ford had kept its new J-car on the sidelines in 1966, but one of the American firm's Le Mans drivers, Bruce McLaren, used its technology to good effect to produce a new M6A version of his CanAm car to dominate the Group 7 series in 1967 as power outputs soared and tyres became ever wider. Overall champion Hulme and McLaren were able to scoop huge amounts of prize money simply because their cars had far more downforce in slow corners than the rival Lolas and Chaparrals. As the Chevrolet and Ford V8 engines became ever larger, even Ferrari's new lightweight P4 was left behind.

1968: Ford stays ahead

The P4s could not keep up the following year at Le Mans either as Ford hung on to win again with a revised version of the heavy 7-litre. The Ferraris were second and third, however, and took the Manufacturers' Championship — which had been reconstituted along conventional lines — by a narrow margin from Porsche. A full season in Europe by Chaparral added a new dimension to the series. They had a power superiority but suffered from being unable to produce a gearbox that could cope with all the torque produced by a CanAm-style 7-litre Chevrolet V8. Porsche's cars, varying between 2 litres and 2.2, proved far more reliable than Alfa Romeo's new 2-litre Tipo 33, a fact that the Italian firm found hard to bear as the Germans carried on winning the Targa Florio, and took the first four places at the Nürburgring. Lola suffered from using an underdeveloped Aston Martin V8 but an interesting car emerged in the Ford Mirage — a lightweight version of the GT40, developed in Britain.

This would prove a highly significant car when the CSI decided to outlaw the outrageously fast 7-litre cars from the World Sports Car Championship in 1968 on safety grounds. They decreed that the series could be contested only by 3-litre cars with a minimum weight of 650kg (1433lb), or 5-litre 800kg (1764lb) cars of which at least 50 had been built. This figure was soon reduced to 25 so that at least some 5-litre cars would appear, but it was not envisaged that they would present much of a problem to the prototypes as the power output of their Grand Prix-style engines would be more adequate for their reduced weight.

Nobody thought that any manufacturer had the resources to develop and build 25 identical 5-litre racing cars for Group 4 — normally the province of production cars — quickly enough to make them competitive. But Porsche, with one eye on the lucrative CanAm series, saw it as a chance to steal a

Above: A great sight from the 1970 sports car racing season as Porsche 917s and Ferrari 512s fight it out at Monza

march on their rivals. The initial stage of the plan would be to build a 3-litre engine — in essence an eight-cylinder version of their existing six-cylinder 2.2-litre — and then expand it to a 12-cylinder 5-litre and 16-cylinder of 6 litres or more for CanAm! The 3-litre ran into all sorts of problems in 1968 but the plan still went ahead, notably because Ferrari was thinking along similar lines.

Ferrari actually made it to the last CanAm race of the season with a 6.3-litre V12-powered P5, but it was eliminated in a first-corner crash that left Hulme champion again, McLaren's 7-litre Chevrolet outpowering Lola's Le Mans-style 7-litre Ford engine — on the limit of its development. The Italian firm was far too occupied with the threat of the Cosworth DFV in Formula 1 to compete in the World Sports Car Championship, however, and it was left to Porsche to take on the continuing might of Ford, using the light-weight 5-litre Mirage. Matra, Alfa Romeo, Alpine and Ford also built prototypes, but they needed development, along with very thirsty Howmet turbine cars. This meant that the private British-run JW Automotive team was able to retain the championship for Ford with their well-tried GT40-based machine. Lola provided some opposition with their 5-litre T70, but it was half-hearted. The Championship race was a close-run thing, however, as they scored only 51 points from 10 events against the 67.5 of Porsche, who lost out because only five scores counted.

Porsche domination

Porsche started the first part of the 1969 season with 3-litre Type 908 cars — winning the Targa as usual — before the exciting new 4.5-litre 917 could be made ready for Le Mans. Engine development — and building so many cars — had taken so much time that this 525bhp coupé had to use basically the same chassis as that of the 350bhp 908, so it was hardly surprising that handling problems developed. It took brave men like Rolf Stommelen, Kurt Ahrens, Vic Elford and Richard Attwood to fight for the lead at 230mph (370km/h). In the end their clutches failed, and a 908 driven by Herrmann and Gerard Larrouse battled on to lose out on first place to the JW Mirage of Ickx and Jackie Oliver by only 200 yards!

Apart from Daytona, won by a Lola-Chevrolet, and Sebring, taken by a Mirage, Porsche won every round of the World Championship, the 917 finally coming good for Jo Siffert and Ahrens to win the final round in Austria. Ferrari — beset by labour and financial problems — managed only a second place at Sebring in their new 3-litre 312P prototype with Matra's 650 prototype managing a couple of fourth places.

McLaren, running exotic 7-litre Chevrolet engines that were no longer production based, were even more dominant in CanAm racing, winning every round with constructor Bruce McLaren winning the title. Towards the end Ford were running at the same pace, however, Mario Andretti using a new 8.1-litre engine in a McLaren chassis when Ford-constructed cars and their new 3-litre prototype proved uncompetitive. Ferrari were up to 6.9 litres with their 612P towards the end, but it was really only being run as a development car for their planned new 5-litre Group 4 machine. Siffert's open 917PA was not far off the pace, though, and he was looking forward to a capacity increase.

But it did not materialize in 1970 because Porsche were too busy with other developments, including turning the 917 into a guaranteed endurance race winner. In pursuit of this ideal, they hired John Wyer's JW outfit to run a team of 917s in company with a works Porsche Salzburg equipe. It was Wyer's brilliant development chief, John Horsman, who solved the 917's aerodynamic problems by cutting off its long tail and building up what was left into a wedge shape. Although this reduced the maximum speed, it gave so much more downforce that the car was easier to drive and lapped faster. Lightened and more nimble 908s were retained for tricky courses like those of the Targa Florio and Nürburgring 1000 Kilometres.

The result was that Porsche won nine out of 10 Championship rounds with Ferrari — which had expected to be competitive with its Group 4 512S — winning only one race, at Sebring, by a fluke. They preferred to concentrate development on the 312P as the CSI had decided to abolish the 5-litre Group 4 and get rid of the big cars in 1972.

A new championship was launched at the same time for the smaller 2-litre cars — as a parallel to the contemporary Formula 2 — which had begun filling the vacuum left by Porsche. Abarth were early leaders until the British constructors got in on the act, Redman clinching the Championship for Chevron with a new open B16.

In the meantime, Hulme had a harder time winning the CanAm Championship again for McLaren because General Motors made 8.1-litre alloy-blocked V8s generally available — with the result that a far wider variety of constructors used them. Ferrari toyed only fitfully with the Championship, but new cars emerged, notably, from BRM, March, Shadow and Autocoast. Chaparral, which had been struggling with advanced technology which did not work, suddenly came good with a revolutionary 'fan' car in which a fan literally sucked the car down onto the track to give it greater grip. This car took a number of pole positions in practice, but suffered mechanical failures in races in which Oliver's titanium Autocoast became the closest challenger to the works McLarens of Hulme and Peter Gethin.

Again with CanAm in mind, Porsche continued to develop the 917 for the Gulf-sponsored JW team and Martini, who were financing the Salzburg effort. The engine was uprated to a full 5 litres, Porsche again winning the World Championship although Ickx's Ferrari 312P — in reality the contemporary Grand Prix car with all-enveloping bodywork — took pole position at Brands Hatch with Stommelen's 3-litre Alfa second. Ickx was eliminated by an accident and Alfa won their first World Championship race for 20 years. Local hero Vaccarella also took the Targa for Alfa Romeo, to the Sicilians' delight, but Porsche won everywhere else.

Down among the highly competitive 2-litre cars, Lola turned the tables on Chevron with their Ford-powered T212, Fiat-Abarth trailing in third place, and Austrian Helmut Marko clinching the Drivers' Championship.

The Seventies: change and decay

As Wyer started to build his own Mirage cars for the 3-litre championship in 1972, Roger Penske replaced his lightweight Ferrari 512Ms with a new open 917-10 turbocharged Porsche producing 850bhp in 4.5-litre form. Normally–aspirated 917s went up to 5.4 litres and 660bhp to counter the 730bhp which had been extracted for McLaren. The British team, along with Shadow — the former Autocoast operation — frantically turbocharged their Chevrolet engines, but could not afford the very high development costs, and became also-rans to Mark Donohue's Porsche. Many of the former CanAm cars were then transferred to a similar series in Europe, called Interserie, which promptly suffered from the same problem as CanAm, Leo Kinnunen winning the first title in 1972 with a Porsche 917-10. Porsche decided to concentrate on developing their 911 GT cars rather than to continue pouring money into farcical championships — especially as Ferrari and Matra were spending a fortune on the new 3-litre formula.

As a last fling, they stepped up the turbocharged car's capacity to 5.4 litres for CanAm in 1973 to produce more than 1000bhp in a lengthened 917-30 which won six races in succession in 1973 leading to the withdrawal of McLaren, Lola, March and BRM. This led to the SCCA body governing CanAm racing to introduce a new fuel consumption formula as the easiest way to limit power outputs without forcing competitors to change equipment. Porsche, committed to developing turbo-chargers for their road cars, then withdrew from CanAm. Ironically, the world's first energy crisis followed soon after the SCCA's decision, making it look highly prophetic. But it was a disaster as UOP-Shadow were the only team able to find the money to compete seriously and the series — which had been attracting record crowds the year before — was cancelled after only five rounds.

Meanwhile Ferrari were taking advantage of huge amounts of new-found Fiat finance to turn their 312Ps into endurance race winners. They easily took the World Championship in 1972, winning all 10 races that they contested — including the Targa Florio, to more Sicilian joy. The exception was Le Mans, where Matra, having withdrawn from Formula 1, spent the equivalent of an entire season's budget in testing and development to produce the first winner for France since 1950. Ferrari's reason for non-starting at Le Mans was that their Grand Prix-based engines could not be expected to last 24 hours . . . and Matra did not compete in any other races because Ferrari were so dominant in these 1000-kilometre (621.4 mile) 'sprint' events.

Above: The Targa Florio survived until 1973 when at last the authorities decided that it was too dangerous. This is the Porsche of Rodriguez heading for second spot in the 1970 race

Only Alfa Romeo looked like giving Ferrari worthwhile opposition and they ran into all sorts of trouble although they eventually took second place overall. Gulf Mirage and Lola cars powered by Cosworth Grand Prix-style engines suffered from a lack of development, leaving only Reinhold Joest's coupé version of the ex-works Porsche 908/3 — ballasted up to the new 650kg (1433lb) minimum weight — anywhere near the Ferraris, most frequently winning in the hands of Ickx and Andretti.

More Fiat finance — although on a far smaller scale than enjoyed by Ferrari — helped ensure that Abarth won the 2-litre championship from Lola and Chevron opposition using Ford or BMW power units.

Hard times ahead

The 1973 season was hard fought as both Ferrari and Matra contested most races. The World Championship developed into a duel between Ferrari's 312P and Matra's V12 as Gulf Mirage won one event, at Spa, and Alfa Romeo's new flat-12 failed. Porsche's Carrera RSR — a GT car running as a prototype with 917 tyres and brakes — and Chevrons fitted with Ford or BMW 2-litre engines got very close to winning on a number of occasions as the sports racers failed to last the distance. It was the staying-power of the RSRs that finally landed the Targa Florio for them after the faster Ferraris and Alfa Romeos

eliminated themselves. But it was the beginning of the end of an era for sports car racing. The CSI decided that the narrow Sicilian roads were unsuitable for modern sports cars and turned the event into a rally the next year, the only event of comparable age, the TT, having long been confined to touring cars.

By the end of 1973, Matra — who won again at Le Mans — emerged winners from a war of attrition leading Ferrari to abandon sports car racing and concentrate on Formula 1. Soon the rot set in, leaving only Le Mans to maintain a high level of interest in sports racing cars. The world's first energy crisis, which hit car sales very hard, did not help.

Matra, however, had enough money from Chrysler-Simca to carry on for another season and won everything in sight for Larrousse and Henri Pescarolo, Beltoise and Jean-Pierre Jarier. The only serious opposition in sports racing cars came from Gulf, placed second in the World Championship, and Alfa Romeo, which had the power but little else that was effective, plus makeweights in the form of French Ligier chassis running with Citroën-Maserati production engines. The financial problems that followed the energy crisis practically killed the 2-litre championship as Chevron's B26 proved by far the fastest car, often dicing with the 3-litre prototypes, and leaving Renault's Alpine, the odd Lola and March, far behind. Porsche, meantime, transferred their turbocharging development to the 911RSR, running two Turbo Carrera cars at a 2.1-litre capacity which qualified them as the equivalent of 3-litre prototypes in the World Championship. Van Lennep and Herbert Muller took them to several high placings — including second to Pescarolo and Larrousse at Le Mans — and third in the Championship.

By the turn of the year, it looked as though long-distance sports car racing might go the way of the CanAm series as the FIA delayed the introduction of new regulations for a year. They had good reason: the new turbocharged Porsches looked as though they would be so far ahead of other teams that potential rivals were scared off.

Times were hard, however, and initially only Alpine-Renault, which had converted their 2-litre car into a 3-litre prototype by turbocharging it, and Ligier, which had inserted a Cosworth DFV in their JS2 chassis, showed any real interest in a further year of the existing series. But Germany was still prosperous and privateer Willi Kauhsen found enough money to lure back Alfa Romeo, Georg Loos beefed up Gulf, and a mysterious Dr Dannesberger resurrected a couple of Porsche 908/3s with Turbo Carrera power, with Joest following a similar path. Then, after a slow start, Alfa won seven out of eight races to take the World Championship, the most successful drivers being Arturo Merzario and Jacques Laffitte. Porsche took second place by dint of their wide variety of runners, far more entertaining racing being provided by the numerous RSRs in the GT categories. Gulf raced only spasmodically, preferring to concentrate on Le Mans which became a non-championship race run to fuel consumption rules. These eliminated most of the 3-litre cars and the Gulf GR7s ran with detuned DFVs and super-slippery bodies. Gearbox problems almost robbed Ickx and Derek Bell of victory, but they held out from Ligier for the one win that mattered most of all to them. Alpine-Renault, meantime, treated the season as a learning exercise ... with grids made up in general by Chevron, March, Lola, Toj-BMW, and Abarth 2-litres now that they had no championship of their own.

Reaching the end of an era

By 1976, the FIA could not hold out any longer waiting for other manufacturers to match Porsche — and BMW, which had been catching up with turbocharging technology. So, in a vain attempt to revitalize the World Championship, the FIA introduced their new regulations, splitting the Championship into individual titles for Group 4 GT cars, silhouette versions in Group 5 (so called because they had to keep a near-standard appearance) and prototypes (which could use any two-seater bodywork) in Group 6. Porsche's armoury was impressive: a 934 — based on their new turbocharged road car — in Group 4, a 935 — a highly-modified version of the 934, developed from the Turbo Carrera — in Group 5, and a new prototype 936 for Group 6. This had been produced as a frantic last-minute effort when it looked as though the FIA might amalgamate Groups 5 and 6 because there were so few potential entries. Had this happened, Porsche's work would have been wasted as the production-based 2.8-litre 935 was outrun by lighter prototypes. The 936 that resulted had 917 transmission and brakes, a small-capacity 935 engine, and chassis based on both the 908 and 917. Joest helped make up the numbers by fitting his timeless 908/3 with a lot of 917 and Turbo Carrera hardware.

The opposition was still meagre in numbers, but enough to stop the FIA amalgamating Groups 5 and 6: BMW had 700bhp turbocharged 3.5-litre versions of their saloon-based CSL coupé in Group 5 with further 2-litre modified saloon back-up, and Renault had an ambitious new Alpine in Group 6. Apart from the prototypes, it all began to look very much like the American GT racing being run by the International Motor Sports Association (IMSA), a professional organization which had broken away from the CanAm organizers, the SCCA, when they wanted to remain amateur in concept. Meanwhile, the SCCA had revived CanAm for a while, but now confined to converted single-seaters rather than sports cars.

Despite strong opposition from BMW, and very little from the unreliable Alpine as Renault was just starting to learn about

turbocharging technology, the Porsches mopped up the GT titles. The AC de l'Ouest showed that long-distance sports car racing still had a future, however, by abandoning their fuel consumption regulations and allowing a mixture of Groups 4, 5 and 6, and anything else that looked viable, including American racing saloons, plus a new GTP (for Grand Touring Prototype) category which would prove significant. A Porsche 936, driven by Ickx and van Lennep, still won, but it was far more dramatic.

Renault had high hopes of winning Le Mans in 1977 as Porsche concentrated on developing the 935 with a twin-turbo system to reduce throttle lag, leaving Alfa Romeo to win everything in Group 6 — well, almost. As BMW made only a token appearance in Group 5 while they were developing their new mid-engined M1 in conjunction with the Italian Lamborghini sports car manufacturer, Porsche had found little opposition, and time to dust off the 936 for Le Mans. Once more, it outlasted all the opposition for Ickx to win, with Hurley Haywood and Jurgen Barth, much to Renault's chagrin.

Works Porsches contested only two events in the 1978 World Championship, but they still won it. Private teams of 3.2-litre 935s run by Loos and the Kremer brothers shared seven victories with uprated 935s as the factory produced an incredible 935-78 featuring

Above: In the Seventies Porsche developed a range of winning racers related to the road-going 911. The 935, seen here at Silverstone in 1979, was the ultimate expression of the theme

a long 936-style nose and tail, and nicknamed Moby Dick after the legendary white whale. Its 3.2-litre engine was no less exotic, using water-cooled cylinder heads to supplement its normal air-cooling, and produce as much as 750bhp. This car won at Silverstone in a dress rehearsal for Le Mans, where three 936s were also entered. But Renault found form to outlast the lot, although Didier Pironi and Jean-Pierre Jaussaud's fastest time along the Mulsanne straight was only 228mph (367 km/h) — far less than the 240mph (386km/h) achieved by 917s and the 243mph (391km/h) to come from Moby Dick-styled cars.

By then Renault reckoned they had learned enough about turbocharging to go Grand Prix racing, leaving private Porsches to make up most of the endurance racing fields, Fiat entering only intermittently with works Lancia Beta Monte Carlos. The BMW M1 was mostly occupied with a new Pro-Car series aimed, forlornly, at getting F1 drivers interested in sports cars. The Porsche factory still ran 936s at Le Mans, but these prototypes ran into trouble, leaving a private 935 — featuring ground-effects bodywork developed by the Kremers — to win.

The AC de l'Ouest, had shown they could still run an attractive race, so Le Mans was taken back into the Championship, which was now thrown open to prototypes of any engine capacity in an attempt to bolster grids. Le Mans kept its own rules, however, once again reflecting fuel economy in a bid to level out competitors' speeds! Local constructor Jean Rondeau took the 24-Hour race to the eternal joy of the organizers.

Such was the lack of factory involvement in the World Championship that the British driver, Alain de Cadenet, was able to win two rounds with a 3-litre special loosely based around a Lola. Lancia won the Championship, however, through running their turbocharged Beta Monte Carlo coupés in the 2-litre class. Porsche were much more occupied with Indianapolis development and running small Carrera GTs at Le Mans. The most popular front runners continued to be private 935s of varying specification, although Joest carried on racing his 908 with 936 bodywork, and German dentist Sigi Brun became a front runner with the 1970 Targa-winning 908/3 resurrected from Porsche's museum!

When the Indycar hierarchy changed their rules to outlaw Porsche's new engine even before it could be entered, the German firm quit in disgust and installed it in modified form, with 917-30 transmission, in a 936 for Ickx and Bell to beat the Rondeau at Le Mans in 1981. The Kremer brothers continued to develop the 935 into a K4 form for the German domestic Group 5 championship with even more downforce. They then took a close look at the Le Mans regulations, borrowed an old European-specification 917 from a British enthusiast, copied it and produced an even more formidable front runner than Brun's 10-year-old car.

FISA worked hard on new rules to revitalize the World Sports Car Championship, but failed to reach agreement with the ever more powerful IMSA, which was running a successful GT championship. This was dominated by the 935s, which bore a far closer resemblance to the touring cars that featured in IMSA's other championships than to prototype sports cars. As a result, the IMSA series attracted a lot of American interest, and FISA tried to capitalize on this by including touring car races in the World Endurance Drivers' Championship. This was duly won by Californian Bob Garretson in a 935 K3.

On the upturn

Meanwhile the World Sports Car Championship entered its last season on a tragic note as Muller, driving Brun's 908, died in a crash at the Nürburgring that left Lancia with an unassailable lead. High hopes for the future emerged in the last race at Brands Hatch, however, with Ford's new C100 prototype for what would be next year's Group C powered by a long-stroke 3.9-litre DFL version of the Cosworth DFV Grand Prix engine. It did not finish the race, won by Guy Edwards and Emilio de Villota in a Lola T600 Group 6 prototype, and struggled to beat the Pescarolo and Bob Wollek in the 'old' 917 during qualifying, but it demonstrated a vigorous new interest in sports car racing.

Essentially the new regulations were based around the Le Mans GTP class for two-seater

Right: North America developed its own form of 'big banger' sports car racing with the CanAm series, epitomized by this 1968 McLaren at Riverside

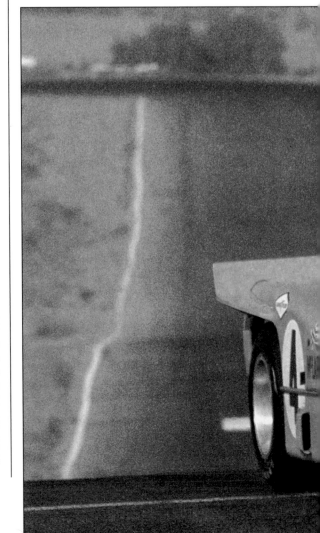

racing cars using an engine from a manufacturer which already had products in series for mass-production cars. The theory was that it would attract major manufacturers rather than small specialists who had rarely been able to command much media attention: Ford versus BMW, for instance, would make far more attractive headlines than URD versus Rondeau . . .

This category did not become popular, however, until IMSA adopted it, giving potential entrants more than one race (Le Mans) in which to compete. The GTP class allowed the organizers to adapt the rules which would make cars other than 935s competitive. These moves were reasonably successful, so FISA combined them with fuel consumption regulations intended to appeal to environmentalists. Meanwhile, the SCCA, in an attempt to revitalize their ailing single-seater CanAm series, offered to admit the new Group C cars, while IMSA refused because it would render their existing GTP cars uncompetitive!

Group C was intended to be the pinnacle of new categories for cars with which the general public could identify, single-seaters — especially F1 cars — having become too far removed from anything that a normal person could dream of driving: Group N for *Normale* would be for mass-production cars in substantially standard trim, Group A for the same cars, mildly modified for competition, Group B for logical developments of these cars, and Group C for cars using engines made by manufacturers who built enough cars to qualify them for the basic categories. A junior, Group C2, category emerged in 1983 for lighter sports cars using less fuel, Group 5 and 6 cars being allowed to compete to make up fields and provide extra points for the Drivers' Championship.

There were teething problems with the regulations, but the first year proved successful. This was despite Porsche using a stunning new 956 to win the World Championship for a ninth time and Le Mans for a seventh as Lancia went against the spirit of the contest by running *new* cars built to the old Group 6 regulations in an attempt to scoop publicity by finishing first on the road and winning the Drivers' title. The drama of who won what went on to the last lap of the last race at Brands Hatch — and beyond — as the two major manufacturers argued over details in the regulations. But the spectacle was great as not only Porsche and Lancia fielded cars, but Ford, Aston Martin-Nimrod, Joest-Porsche, WM-Peugeot, Sauber, Lola and Rondeau scored points and Ickx took his first individual world title.

Early Eighties confusion

IMSA reinforced its hold on American endurance racing by going it alone with its own GTP formula — and a GTX category loosely based on the old Group 5 — which meant they could not stage world championship

events. While the cream at the top of IMSA's traditionally large fields was sometimes thin, there were always enough cars to race. By the end of the season, Porsche had agreed to lend technical support to teams wanting to use their engines in GTP chassis, which proved highly attractive to the drivers of the heavy and dated 935s. The 22-year-old John Paul Junior became the youngest champion, driving both a Chevrolet-powered Lola T600 GTP car and a lightweight 935 special. As other competitors used a variety of cars ranging from Marches and a Rondeau to BMW M1s, Jaguar financed the development of an XJR-5 GTP car. Despite being overweight and behind schedule, this V12-powered machine made a promising debut at Elkhart Lake by taking third place for Bob Tullius and Bill Adam.

The dispute with IMSA continued to disfigure the World Championship in 1983 but, while the GTP category continued to be well supported, it was in the FIA arena that the real technological advancement was made. Porsche won virtually everying, including Le Mans, in the main Group C category, but now there was immense variety, with 28 constructors using 19 different engines. Main points scorers in Group C1 were Porsche, of course — with Ickx winning the Drivers' title again — Lancia (who won the only race in which the works Porsches did not compete), Aston Martin-Nimrod, Nissan-March, BMW-Sauber, Toyota-Dome and BMW-URD, the Group C2 cup going to the Italian Giannini-Alba team from Mazda, Mazda-Harrier and Toyota-March.

Although IMSA continued to follow its own path, there were strong signs that the two sides would soon get together. The Camel GT championships developed into a battle between March 83G cars with either Chevrolet or Porsche power, the odd Lola, and three Jaguar XJR-5 cars. Eventually Holbert ran out the winner, switching between March-Chevrolet, March-Porsche and a 935 to beat the tenacious Tullius in a Jaguar.

1984: Porsche domination continues

Repeated rule changes to accommodate the IMSA cars led to a lot of confusion in the 1984 World Championship, although it was again won by Porsche, Lancia's cars remaining fast, but fragile. The Porsche factory, which was investing a lot of time and money into research with Bosch into electronic engine management systems for improved fuel economy, left virtually all chassis development to privateers. The most notable of these were Joest and the British GTI team, which even constructed a lighter and more rigid honeycomb chassis. Despite Porsche's continuing domination, however, and another win for Giannini-Alba in Group C2, there were still 19 chassis powered by 10 different engines. But it was left to Stefan Bellof to win the World Drivers' Championship from team-mates Jochen Mass, Ickx and Bell,

although Joest's drivers, Klaus Ludwig and Pescarolo, took Le Mans.

The Jaguar GTP cars, despite being a little underpowered and overweight for Group C, actually managed to lead Le Mans at one point, only to fail through tyre and transmission problems. Meanwhile Porsche had to accept that IMSA would not budge from marginally different footwell regulations to those in Europe and began building 962 versions of the 956 for the US market. They performed just as well, so gradually the younger 962 took over in Europe too. The admission of the latest Porsche into IMSA racing did not result in a walkover, however, because rules covering weight and so on could still be adjusted. This resulted in a three-way battle between March chassis powered by Chevrolet V8s, the 962 and Jaguar's XJR-5, resolved in favour of Randy Lanier's March.

Porsche's continuing World Championship domination in 1985 masked the real facts. The Championship became one for teams, as opposed to makes, because so few makers stood a chance of winning it. The Rothmans-backed works team started the season off at the pace set by the Lancias and private 962s run by Joest, Kremer, Walter Brun and RLR/Canon (formerly GTI). Even when they fought back into contention, they faced strong challenges and ultimately had to rely on their highly-disciplined race organization to win what would be very closely-fought races, with the Drivers' Championship being shared by Bell and Hans Stuck.

Lancia, who won only at Spa, were afflicted largely by mechanical problems while the Jaguar operation, by now moved to Britain with a new XJR-6 chassis, became ever more challenging with a second place in the last race at Shah Alam in Malaya. Meanwhile the British Canon-backed 956GTI emerged as the fastest private Porsche although Joest's faithful 956B won again at Le Mans for Ludwig, Paolo Barilla and John Winter. Nissan's March C1 car had the consolation of winning at Mount Fuji when the European teams refused to race on a flooded track. They had only European wet-weather tyres against specialized Japanese rubber, developed in their domestic Group C series, which was frequently run in appalling weather. Mass also won the final year of the German endurance racing championship which would now become a series of sprint races to reduce costs.

There were also C2 teams and drivers' championships where the stranglehold by Giannini (now renamed Carma) was broken for Spice Engineering's DFL-powered car to win for constructor Gordon Spice and Ray Bellm to win from the reconstituted Ecurie Ecosse, running its own chassis.

Widening the field

Porsche, having been almost wiped out for the first time since 1971 in the previous year's IMSA championships, struck back with a

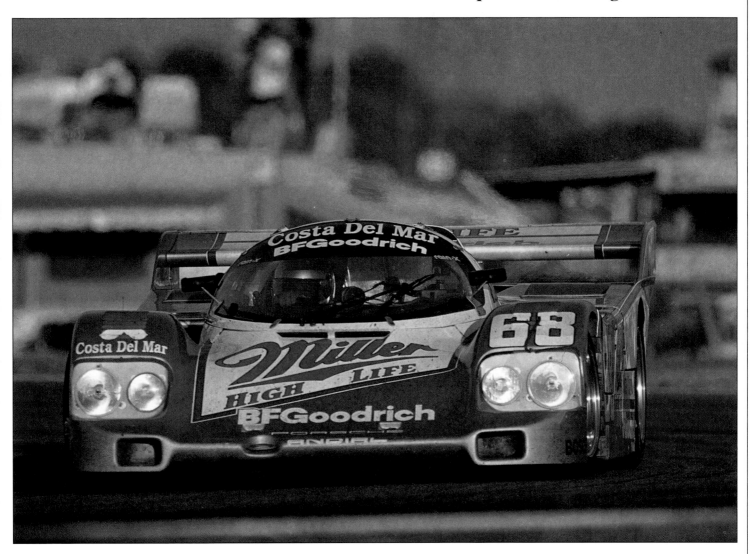

vengeance in 1985. Holbert, the company's North America motor sport boss, won a record-breaking nine races in a 962, mostly partnered by Bell, with other Porsches winning seven out of the remaining eight races. No team was worse hit than the Jaguar XJR-5s led by Tullius, still handicapped by transmission problems. A new Camel Lights class — along similar lines to C2 — became a benefit for the Mazda-powered Argo cars led by Jim Downing.

Until 1985, the GT40 which won Le Mans on two consecutive years — 1968–9 — could be called the most famous individual car in world endurance racing. Then its feat was equalled by the Joest 956B, which went on to top the GT40's record by remaining the best car on the tracks for much of 1986! It was even set to score a hat trick at Le Mans, vying for the lead with the works 962C, before the engine expired late in the race. But it finished the rest of the season, having scored 44 top-three finishes from 55 races.

It was Bell, in the winning Rothmans Porsche, who took the C1 World Drivers' title again — but the teams prize fell to Brun's private Porsches while the C2 crown was taken by the Ecurie Ecosse, now with a power unit from Austin-Rover's normally-aspirated Group B Metro 6R4 rally car,

although driver and constructor Ray Mallock was beaten into third place for the individual title by Spice and Bellm. The spirit of innovation was never greater than in C2, with no less than 27 different chassis-engine combinations appearing.

The newcomers were becoming more of a threat in C1, too, as old-stagers Lancia quit while taking pole positions in order to concentrate on world championship rallying. But Jaguar, who became Porsche's most serious rival, were plagued by mechanical mishaps, winning only on their home track, Silverstone.

To intense surprise, the small Swiss team Sauber then won at the rain-soaked Nürburgring with a Mercedes stock-block engine as the leading Jaguar retired and most of the Porsches crashed or were withdrawn. Porsche, meantime, concentrated on developing their own Group B project, the 959 rally car, as a mixture of 962s and 956s took the first seven places in the Japanese series from Toyota's Dome project, and all except Jaguar's third place in the German championship's top ten.

IMSA racing, meantime, was booming as never before with Porsche still winning but Chevrolet, Ford, BMW and Jaguar taking events while Nissan and Buick were close.

Above: An IMSA-racing version of the Porsche 962 which carried on the dominance of the 956 in sports car racing on both sides of the Atlantic

Holbert took the GT championship again with Chip Robinson's Jaguar getting among the Porsches in fifth place. Downing's second Camel Lights championship in the rotary Argo was achieved on a shoestring against the Pontiac-backed Spice project.

1987: breaking the records

Now that more manufacturers were involved with European racing, more stability of regulations could be expected ... and the Silk Cut Jaguar team broke all world championship sports car records in 1987. Their XJR-8s won eight of the 10 for the British manufacturer to take the main title for the first time with four of its five drivers topping their points table. The feat was made even more remarkable in that they were still using a normally-aspirated engine in the same V12 configuration as those in their road cars. There was only one snag: Porsche broke another record. They won at Le Mans for the 11th time, although their cars saw little development as the factory concentrated on the CART Indycar programme.

Bell won at Le Mans for a fifth time, but had to cede the Drivers' title to Raul Boesel. Sauber could offer to compete in only five races, but the speed of their Mercedes-powered cars was enough to take pole position at Spa. Frustration was felt by the Championship organizers, however, that Japanese manufacturers like Toyota and Nissan refused to enter the entire series, preferring to concentrate on local races and Le Mans. Group C2, however, continued to grow in stature although it was now dominated by Spice rather than Ecosse, back with DFL power, although Will Hoy was usually the fastest driver in Martin Schanche's Argo.

In the Camel GT series, Robinson drove a Holbert Porsche to win a season-long battle with Price Cobb's Dyson Racing 962. But the Bayside team with two Porsches driven by the all-star line-up of Mass, Rahal and Ludwig won the highest total of four events despite Brun's European team looking dangerous.

As Porsche privateers fell back, Jaguar managed to snatch a season of glory with their XJR-9 before Mercedes backed Sauber to the hilt, finally taking over the team to haul in the Britons fast. Jaguar took the teams title they had chased so hard by finishing second to a Sauber-Mercedes at Spa before Martin Brundle wrested the C1 Drivers' Championship from the leader, Jean-Louis Schlesser of Sauber, by winning at Fuji. But after the bonus of winning at Daytona, the real achievement was recapturing the glory of the Fifties by winning at Le Mans with Dutchman Jan Lammers and British drivers Johnnie Dumfries and Andy Wallace. The fact that their task was made easier by Sauber's withdrawal because of tyre problems mattered little: the victory was achieved as the result of a race-long duel with the Porsche 962C of Bell, Stuck and Ludwig,

who were among the first to congratulate Jaguar team-manager Tom Walkinshaw. But after that Mercedes' twin-turbo engine began to reel in Jaguar's 7-litre V12, taking 120 points in the second half of the season to the 80 of Jaguar and winning the final race at Melbourne. Almost as a sideline, Spice and Bellm stayed on top of Group C2, finishing as high as fifth overall in Melbourne.

The other great battle — Porsche versus Jaguar — billed for the Camel GT series never came off, as Nissan found form and won nine of their 14 races, giving Geoff Brabham a 46-point advantage over John Nielsen's Jaguar. It was especially surprising because the Jaguars had started by trouncing the Porsches at Daytona and Nissan's first win came only in the fourth round. It was not without significance that the 3-litre turbocharged V6 Japanese engine in an Electramotive-developed Lola chassis was running at 750bhp against the 600-odd of Porsche and Jaguar, which had been restricted to 6 litres by IMSA rules. In Camel Lights, Tom Hessert's Tiga powered by either a Chevrolet V8 or Buick V6 finally dethroned Downing's second-placed Argo-Mazda against Spice-Pontiac and Alba-Ferrari opposition.

Heading for the Nineties

FISA then decided to revamp the world sports car series by turning it into a similar

televised package to Formula 1. This involved making races shorter and using similar 3.5-litre engines to those in Grand Prix cars. It was not possible to persuade manufacturers to change engines overnight, so those regulations were slated for 1991. In the meantime, the races — with the exception of Le Mans — were reduced from six hours to around two and a half hours. Heavy fines were also instituted if teams failed to run in sufficient events. The idea behind this move, to draw in the Japanese, proved effective with far more varied grids at all events. It also became essential to have at least one race on the American continent if the sports car package was to be promoted as a world championship. But there was no persuading IMSA to adopt the same regulations, so Mexico was persuaded to run the last round of the Championship in 1989, which turned out to be a great success.

Spice took advantage of the entire 1989 season to run with 3.5-litre Cosworth racing engines in their chassis, before Jaguar — whose production-based 7-litre V12 was near the end of its development — moved on to first, the 3-litre inspired by the Metro 6R4 power unit, and ultimately, 3.5-litre turbocharged racing engines. Toyota and Nissan followed similar lines, but Mercedes stuck to their by now well-tried 5-litre stock-block turbos. This enabled them to win virtually everything, including Le Mans, as Jaguar gradually became faster and faster despite development problems during the races. The shorter events also became more closely contested, as Toyota and Nissan started to show promise, and private Porsche teams like Joest continued to run Mercedes close.

FISA were happy, however, as Mercedes won the teams title only towards the end of the series and the battle for the Drivers' Championship went to the final round in Mexico before Jean-Louis Schlesser won from team-mate Mauro Baldi. Part of the FISA package was that Group C2 would be eliminated to make the racing easier to follow for a mass audience, resulting in Chamberlain team Spice drivers Fermin Velez and Nick Adams becoming the last champions in this category.

Brabham carried on winning IMSA races throughout 1989 to take the Camel GT title for Nissan as Jaguar became ever more threatening, Price Cobb eventually winning the last round at Tampa after an accident eliminated Jan Lammers, the British team's front runner on both sides of the Atlantic. Spice also became dominant in Camel Lights through Buick-powered Scott Schubot and Linda Ludemann, leaving sports car fans throughout the world with the prospect of traditional racing on one continent and a new form spreading from the others.

Left: *Jaguar found success again at Le Mans in 1988. Here the winning Lammers/ Dumfries/Wallace XJR9 leads home the other team cars of Daly/Cogan/Perkins and Sullivan/Jones/Cobb*

Saloon Car Racing

Saloon or 'touring' car racing, as it is sometimes known, is a vital branch of motor sport, offering road car manufacturers an obvious way of demonstrating the superiority of their products over those of competitors.

In the pre-war period the dividing line between sports cars and touring cars was fuzzy, to say the least, and it wasn't until 1949 that the difference was sufficiently distinct for a major race to be staged in the UK especially for modern-style saloon cars.

This race led to a whole new avenue of motor sport which operates at an international level. Beneath the top league of international Group A saloon car racing is a huge volume of national and club competition offering perhaps the most accessible form of motor sport to the would-be competitor.

Ford Sierra Cosworths head the field at the start of a Brands Hatch round of the 1989 British Touring Car Championship

At Silverstone's International Trophy meeting of 1949, an experimental one-hour race was held for production cars. The entry was dominated by some of the popular sports cars of the period, such as Jaguar XKs, but a number of hardy souls turned out in saloon cars. The Rileys and Jowett Javelins entertained the crowd and performed respectably, even though the event regulations oddly insisted that they had to compete with the offside window down and the rear windscreen removed!

The race proved popular, and was repeated one year later with an increased saloon contingent. By 1952, interest was such that Silverstone hosted separate races for production sports cars and production touring cars. Stirling Moss won the latter in his lightly-modified Jaguar Mk VII, and saloon car racing — in the form in which it would become recognized internationally — was born. Subsequently, it has expanded into a colourful variety of classes, popular the world over.

No matter how much one appreciates the art of the Grand Prix driver, or how much one is impressed by the staggering grip and colossal average lap speeds of Formula 1 chassis, saloon car racing — or touring car racing as the official jargon has it in the case of most major national championships — enjoys a huge following.

Its popularity is easy to understand: for one thing, racegoers can relate far more easily to the familiar shapes they might see in their supermarket car park, no matter how different they may be under the skin. A Grand Prix single-seater looks like nothing else on the planet. The fact that modern-day touring cars will touch in excess of 170mph (274km/h) given a long enough section of straight track, tends to create quite an impression, particularly when the exterior looks precious little different from a road-going Ford Sierra.

Something for everyone

Saloon car racing exists in a variety of forms at all levels of motor sport. Humblest of all are Britain's road-going saloon championships, designed for cars which must be licensed for everyday use, taxed, and in possession of an MOT. In some series, it is compulsory to drive your car to and from the meeting in which you are competing, always providing that it is still in one piece at the end of the day. At the other end of the scale, America's NASCAR (the formative years of which took place before the last war, thus giving it the slight edge on developments elsewhere in the world) has provided some of the closest, most exciting racing to be found anywhere. On banked oval circuits, the NASCAR machines are capable of lapping at an *average* speed in excess of 200mph (322km/h); in a race the pace eases a fraction, but with cars slipstreaming each other in groups of anything up to 20 vehicles, you would hardly expect anything else. Even so, they lap, inches apart, at 180mph (290km/h) plus during races which vary from 200–500 miles (322–805km) in length. And they do it for the best part of 30 weekends every season . . .

In between such extremes, there is a wide diversity of saloon categories. Most countries run their premier national series to slightly different rules, more often than not based rather loosely around guidelines laid down

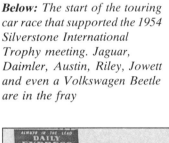

Below: *The start of the touring car race that supported the 1954 Silverstone International Trophy meeting. Jaguar, Daimler, Austin, Riley, Jowett and even a Volkswagen Beetle are in the fray*

by the FIA, the sport's governing body. Since the latter killed off the popular World Touring Car Championship (after just one season!) and followed up by abandoning the European Touring Car Championship, the need to retain a common formula diminished somewhat, for competitors no longer had the option of combining their major national championship with a programme abroad. While the multitude of permutations covering lower-key categories are fine for club racers, the lack of a championship for a clearly-defined, world-wide touring car formula does the sport no favours. When Australia, after years of running a set of rules unknown outside the Antipodes, switched to the internationally familiar Group A, interest in the annual 1000-kilometre (621-mile) classic at Bathurst reached epidemic proportions. Suddenly, the highlight of the Australian racing calendar achieved celebrity the world over, and became an integrated part of the short-lived World Touring Car Championship. Happily for the Australians, Bathurst didn't need the WTCC as much as the WTCC needed it, and so it continues to bring in teams and drivers from all corners of the globe.

The regulations governing major international events have varied considerably since the idea of racing 'tin tops' was first mooted. The vagaries of the rulebook have permitted such as the Porsche 911, Mazda RX-7 and Jaguar XJ-S to compete at the forefront of international touring car (as opposed to *grand* touring, ie GT) events over the years, all taking honours at the expense of vehicles which most spectators would identify to be a more typical saloon. In the 1968 British Saloon Car Championship, run to what were then known as Group 5 regulations, Vic Elford's 911 met Lotus Cortinas and twin-cam Escorts in the same class! Nonetheless, the ability to interpret regulations shrewdly has always been a useful talent, and has served a number of manufacturers and entrants well.

Sometimes, different interpretations of the same rule are so varied that protests and counter-protests leave race results in doubt for several months. In the most celebrated instance, the 1983 British Touring Car Championship scaled such acrimonious heights that the outcome wasn't known until the end of a lengthy case in the law courts! Similarly, the technical commission of the same series was unable to give a verdict on who had won the main class in the 1989 Championship, which finished in October, until January 1990. And this controversy dated back to the previous June . . .

A run for your money

It isn't always like that, of course. For all the grey areas which torment scrutineers, there are countless more bright ideas. Generally, events the world over are divided into classes. Thus, although a Ford Sierra Cosworth will quite clearly see off a Honda Civic, the Civic will be racing against similarly-powered cars within the same race. In effect, it is a race within a race, and although the crowd will identify most readily with the outright victor, the effort which goes into winning one of the smaller classes demands just as much commitment from participants. It also means that drivers can enter prestigious national championships at lower cost and, having forged their reputation in a

Below: Modern saloon car racing in the United States means NASCAR stockers, seen here on the Charlotte raceway

Above: In the mid-Sixties the only cars that could offer real opposition to the Lotus Cortinas were the big American Galaxies, in one of which Jack Sears is seen here leading at Goodwood

smaller car, they then have something concrete with which to woo potential sponsors before they move up a division.

It is significant that racing drivers' schools, which for many years used only single-seaters, have recently introduced saloon courses. As an increasing number of European drivers now earn a living in touring cars and sports cars (their American counterparts have enjoyed such a privilege for years), perhaps that is no surprise. With Grand Prix racing having closed its doors to all but an elite few, many talented drivers have to look to other forms of the sport to earn a living. Outside Formula 1, only a handful of aspiring single-seater racers will draw a living wage from sponsorship deals. Yet most national touring car championships are contested by a number of salaried professionals, particularly in Germany, where intensive competition between manufacturers has attracted a cornucopia of established stars . . . and wages to match. And over in the United States, investment in NASCAR is such that drivers who have never won a single race can become dollar millionaires simply through being consistent.

So, in addition to being a crowd puller, saloon car racing can be big business. At the other end of the scale, however, which is just as good a piece of news for the sport in general, is its relative accessibility. Although the budget required to run an international touring car team might look longer than your telephone number, there are several easier places to start.

Britain

Late in 1982, a keen amateur racer named Tim Dodwell had a bright idea. He had his fun by driving an elderly Mini to circuits, racing it against cars which were often prepared to a far higher degree of sophistication, and then driving it home again. What a cheap form of motor sport it would be, he thought, if there were a category for cars which *had* to be driven to and from the track, and thus had to be road legal, just like his faithful Mini.

His scheme was publicized in *Motoring News*, a British motor-sporting weekly newspaper, and he was inundated with enquiries. He named his idea Road Saloons, formed a register of potential competitors, and within a year — after a successful series of pilot races — a national championship was announced. The variety in the entry lists was astonishing: highly-tuned Capris, elderly Hillman Hunters which met a tool kit for the first time when they were fitted with a roll cage, hordes of Minis in various states of modification. . . In short, it was a huge success. Anybody who had a roadworthy car could now go and take part in a motor race, if the mood took them. Inevitably, the competitive nature of motor racing led to the creation of some quite extraordinary road-legal cars, and after a couple of years even this simple formula had to sub-divide into two categories to weed out the sledgehammers.

Even so, it provided saloon car competition on the cheap; furthermore, it introduced a great many people to the pleasures of competition, many of whose 'racing' cars had previously graced the spectator car parks at race circuits up and down the country.

Britain is lucky in that it has a plethora of saloon classes, most of which are well supported, although fashions come and go. After the exploratory races of the early Fifties, it didn't take long for British club racing to adopt saloons as a regular feature, events being divided into four classes: up to 1200cc, 1200–1600cc, 1600–2700cc and over 2700cc, for instance. By 1958, there was a British Saloon Car Championship, run to international regulations, while club racers relied on their own ingenuity to gain extra performance. This became the basis for the Special Saloon class, which was enormously popular in the Sixties, when all manner of odd hybrids competed head-to-head.

By the Seventies, the arrival of light-weight bodywork based around spaceframe shells added a new dimension, and it soon became essential to base your Special Saloon around a second-hand Formula 1 or 2 chassis. Thus you had something which *looked* vaguely like a Skoda, yet which could turn in lap times only a couple of seconds shy of those of top-class Formula 3 cars.

Costs soared, impecunious amateurs ran away to race something else, and by the late Eighties the category — which boasted several healthy national championships a couple of decades previously — was reduced to a trickle of support. By then, the dedicated saloon enthusiast was positively swamped with alternative options.

In 1981, the original Special Saloon concept was revived by the introduction of Modified Saloons, which insisted on retention of original steel bodyshells, production block engines and other penny-saving restrictions. Although it has never brought support back to the level Special Saloons once enjoyed, it has none the less been well supported at a time when sizeable investment from manufacturers has made one-make saloon series ever more appealing to competitors.

One-make racing in ascendance

As its name suggests, one-make racing caters for one particular type of car. In 1966, the Mini Seven Racing Club teamed up with the 750 Motor Club to develop a relatively cheap saloon formula. Mini Seven racing, for 850cc Minis with limited modifications, was born, and thrives to this day. The concept expanded with the introduction in 1970 of a 1-litre Mini formula, Mini Miglia, which also continues to attract huge support, despite the Mini's age. Any fears that the lack of visible variety on the grid would detract from the spectacle were quickly quashed by the intensity and excitement of the competition, not to mention the camaraderie and value for money.

So successful were these original, humble one-make series that similar concepts followed, albeit for cars closer to their standard production cousins than the Minis could claim to be. In 1971, Ford launched the Escort Mexico challenge, which lasted for 10 seasons through two different Escort evolutions, eventually being replaced by a similar challenge for the Ford Fiesta. The latter is still going strong.

The Renault 5 Challenge started in 1974, and eventually switched from the rather tardy 1-litre TL model to the nippier 1.3TS. Even though the Mk1 Renault 5 has long since been superseded on the production line, the old 5TS series continues, and incredibly attracts more support by the year, even if suitable vehicles for race preparation are harder to come by. Renault naturally withdrew support when the model became obsolete, and in its place substituted a national championship for the newer 5GT Turbo. Predictably, this too is an enormous success. When a manufacturer such as Renault creates a range of bonus schemes to benefit all competitors, not just winners, taking part becomes a matter of common sense.

The Mini empire spread its wings with the launch of the 1275GT Challenge in 1976, and this has developed over the years into the Metro Challenge and, finally, Metro Turbo Challenge. Honda promotes a healthy series for its astonishingly rapid CRX coupé, but just occasionally there are lame ducks. The BMW M3 appeared an obvious, albeit expensive, choice for a one-make challenge, but after a handful of races the lack of entries told its own tale, and the idea was scrapped.

In addition to the plethora of championships dedicated to a specific model, there are

Below: Minis have been raced since they were introduced in 1959. This is a Mini Seven battle at Brands Hatch in 1990

also series for particular marques, such as those for BMWs, Fords, Jaguars and — in Ireland — Fiats. Each is split into classes, according to the engine capacity and potential performance of competing cars.

In addition to providing an inordinate amount of fun-per-pound for the clubman (although the close racing inevitably leads to bills for fresh body panels), the one-make series are excellent training for those who want to go on to a career in saloon car racing. The regulations are designed to produce close racing, and the emphasis is very much on the driver. (Theoretically, nobody should have any significant performance advantage, and those whose results suggest otherwise frequently have their car checked over by the eligibility scrutineers.)

Steve Soper, who first made his name by winning in Minis and Fiestas, went on to become a leading light in the British, European and World Touring Car Championships. When the two international series were axed, he was snapped up as one of the top performers in the high-profile German national series.

Above and beyond the mass of classes which serve both the ambitious and the amateurs, there is a logical path of progression up to the British Touring Car Championship, the pinnacle of tin top racing in the UK.

Production Saloon Cars first appeared in the early Seventies, and swiftly became a popular feature of meetings. Crowds were well used to the varied fields of Special Saloons, and it was initially feared that the slower newcomers would not provide the same spectacle. However, the specified road tyres gave them a lot less grip than that enjoyed by the slick-shod saloon classes, and the lurid cornering antics of early Capris, Chevrolet Camaros and — in the smallest class — two-wheeling Moskvitches proved an instant hit.

The face of Production Saloons has changed in the intervening period, if only because the list of eligible cars changes from year to year. In order to be eligible, at least 5000 units must have been produced within a consecutive 12-month period, and a car must have been on sale at some time during the three years prior to the start of a particular season.

The class system changes, too, to suit changing trends amongst manufacturers. At one point in the Seventies, a maximum capacity ceiling was introduced to outlaw the muscular Camaros, and encourage greater competition between more readily-available Capris, BMWs and Opel Commodores.

For 1990, Britain retained its traditional Production Saloon formula, but also adopted Group N regulations, which had seen active service in several mainland European countries for a number of seasons. Although similar to Production Saloon specification, Group N cars differ in the use of proper racing tyres, which thus make them a little

Right: Daytona Speedway is the home of NASCAR racing in the United States. The cars pass the huge main grandstand at around 200mph (322km/h)

closer to the Group A machines which contest the British Touring Car Championship.

The BTCC has always followed the international saloon regulations, laid down by the sport's governing body, and over the years that has led to a number of significant rule changes. Classifications such as Group 1, Group 2, Group 5 and Group A make little sense unless you have a copy of the FIA's annual yearbook to hand. Even then, you may need an interpreter to explain what may and may not be done in order to prepare a car for competition.

The ins and outs of classification

Essentially, it has always been a requirement that cars should have been built in reasonable quantities, thus preventing manufacturers from producing limited editions with the intention of dominating touring car racing. In general production terms 5000 units may be small beer in the overall scheme of things, but if a manufacturer is prepared to go that far, the chances are that the car will be eligible for homologation. In recent years, the Ford Sierra Cosworth and BMW M3 are two examples of road-going cars presented to the public in limited numbers, in order that the manufacturer might reap some benefit on the racetrack.

Although the days of Groups 2 and 5 produced some stirring contests, initially between Ford Falcons, Lotus Cortinas and Mini Coopers (the latter would frequently embarrass more powerful opposition at tight,

classes, which over the years had produced many outright champions (points for a class win had parity with those for an outright success), were axed.

Here to stay

Despite all the chopping and changing that has shaped its sometimes chequered history, saloon car racing still appeals to the masses. To the casual spectator, what goes on under the bonnet is incidental. It's what the cars look like, and the closeness of competition, which counts.

Most famous of all British Touring Car Champions is undoubtedly Jim Clark, who took the title in 1964 in a factory Lotus Cortina. The easygoing nature of Grand Prix racing at that time allowed him to dovetail saloon and single-seater commitments in a way that would be unthinkable nowadays. Many well-known figures in British racing have possessed the trophy: Roy Pierpoint, John Fitzpatrick, Sir John Whitmore, Andy Rouse, Bernard Unett, Richard Longman and Chris Hodgetts have all earned the respect of the industry for their efforts in saloons.

The successful attempts by the Classic Saloon Car Club to revive the spirit of the early days have demonstrated the popularity of the concept. Nowadays there are championships for cars of all ages, so the Austin A35s, Ford Anglias and Lotus Cortinas that produced so many thrills all those years ago have another chance to entertain.

As is the case with single-seaters in Britain, if you have a racing saloon of almost any type, there will be a category in which you can race it.

twisty circuits), and ultimately between Chevrolet Camaros, BMW 3.0 CSLs, Ford Escorts, Capris and Hillman Imps, the relatively high cost of preparation forced a rethink in the early Seventies. Britain subsequently adopted Group 1, for less overtly modified cars.

However, liberalization of the regulations in the interests of extra speed and spectacle (the class was soon dubbed Group 1½ by cynics) meant that it wasn't long before costs escalated there too. At least the involvement of several manufacturers and top-notch drivers lent the BTCC a quality image, even if bickering off the track led to a number of unseemly protests and occasionally ruined the aura of professionalism.

After 10 seasons, during which time the FIA had once again redefined international touring car regulations, Britain opted to fall in line and took to the theoretically less radical Group A. Although the initial response from manufacturers was minimal, with only Rover taking a serious interest, the advent of regular television coverage brought back hitherto undreamed-of levels of support, and the Championship flourished once more. But after two sometimes oversubscribed seasons, the spectre of the rule-book rose again. For 1990, the BTCC consisted of just two classes, the first retaining the structure of the existing Group A Class A (for cars with an engine capacity exceeding 3 litres, or 1.7 litres for turbocharged engines), the second for 2-litre production-based engines. The smaller

Europe

At the end of the 1988 season, the axe fell on the European Touring Car Championship. The FIA hoped it would strengthen individual national championships; for drivers, it was the end of a fascinating international championship to which they could aspire.

There were moments in the history of the ETCC when you wondered why the FIA bothered to keep it going, but at the time of its execution it was in a reasonably healthy state thanks to fierce competition between BMW and Ford, who had done much to enliven the series over the years.

The ETCC provided leading saloon car drivers with a rare chance to race against their foreign counterparts. Although the single-seater ladder gives young drivers the chance to test themselves against crack continental opposition at a relatively early stage (for instance in the Formula Ford Festival, an end-of-season confrontation for FF1600 champions, or in the European Formula Vauxhall Lotus series), saloon racers got precious little chance outside the ETCC.

In 1987, the ETCC took second place to

the new World Touring Car Championship. Within two years both were gone, and with their disappearance such famous old races as the Spa 24 Hours, the equivalent of Le Mans for the saloon fraternity, and the Silverstone Tourist Trophy, the world's oldest motor race, instigated in 1907, lost much of their appeal. Spa survived the loss by holding a non-championship race for a mixture of sports and saloon cars; Silverstone, despite attempts to keep the TT going, had to admit defeat, at least for 1989.

Among the notables who took outright or class wins in the ETCC's early history were Sir John Whitmore, Jacky Ickx, Andrea de Adamich, John Handley, John Rhodes, Toine Hezemans and Jochen Mass. After some glorious battles between BMW's 3-litre CSL and Ford's Capri RS in the early Seventies, when Group 2 regulations were in force, the series took a serious dip in fortunes in the middle of the decade, leaving privateer BMW drivers to mop up in what had become little more than a club championship, albeit one held on a European stage.

The eventual switch to Group A regulations signalled a return to happier days, with Jaguar arriving on the scene to give BMW a run for its money. The epic battles between the XJ-S and the 635CSi rejuvenated the ETCC, and following Jaguar's withdrawal at the end of 1984, when Tom Walkinshaw lifted the drivers' crown (although class-winning consistency gave Alfa Romeo a third consecutive manufacturers' award), Rover stepped in to take on the Germans.

After two more seasons, Rover dropped out to be replaced by the returning might of

Ford, and the BMW 635 was overtaken by the M3. The arrival of the World Touring Car Championship made the 1987 ETCC a very low-key affair, but the demise of the former restored some of the ETCC's popularity and prestige. And then it got the chop.

Roberto Ravagalia, WTCC champion in 1987, collected the ETCC crown one year later, and may well be the last man to wear it.

United States

Although the USA boasts a variety of saloon car classes, and shares some common ground with Britain (Showroom Stock is similar to the UK's Production Saloon class, for instance), the States possesses one jewel which is unlikely to be approached by any other form of 'saloon' car racing anywhere in the world — NASCAR.

The National Association for Stock Car Auto Racing was founded in 1947 by Bill France, an active stock car race promoter before World War 2. Brought up on a diet of dirt and sand tracks, France envisaged developing a well-financed form of entertainment. Before France took the reins, drivers occasionally used to find that race organizers didn't hang around to pay the promised prize money. As a competitor himself, France saw to it that that all changed. The first NASCAR-sanctioned race took place at Daytona Beach (actually on the beach!) in 1948, while the first official Grand National event, forebear of the modern 200mph (322km/h) slip-streaming battles that typify today's main NASCAR features, was at Charlotte in 1949, Jim Roper taking his Lincoln to victory.

The first of the big, banked, paved superspeedways which form the backbone of modern NASCAR competition opened in 1950 at Darlington, South Carolina. Twenty years later, Buddy Baker set the first lap in excess of 200mph (322km/h), in Alabama, and the NASCAR Grand National aces raced on dirt for the very last time, in Raleigh. Quite simply, NASCAR has become bigger and better by the year.

Since becoming a part of mainstream American motor sport, NASCAR's Grand National Championship has developed into the richest and most spectacular class of racing in a nation which isn't noted for penny-pinching when it comes to dishing out prize money.

The accent has always been on entertainment, so if any manufacturer has ever been seen to gain an advantage, NASCAR introduces a rule to restore equilibrium. There have been some celebrated instances of attempted cheating. One driver built a seven-eighths replica of his race car in a bid to find an aerodynamic advantage, and it was only when somebody parked a standard, road-going version of the same model alongside that anybody spotted the difference. Or

Below: The BMW CSLs were the leading cars of the early to mid-Seventies, racing against Ford Capris, Alfa Romeos and Chevrolet Camaros. This example is seen during the 1974 Spa 24 Hours

there was the driver who, having had his fuel tank removed for inspection by the eligibility scrutineers, allegedly drove off ... He had a supplementary reservoir inside his roll cage.

Generally, the series is well policed, and the racing is as close as any in the world. With 30 races a year, support from major manufacturers and million-dollar sponsorship, it is a healthy, vibrant environment.

Cars are strengthened considerably, and with average qualifying speeds of well over 200mph (322km/h) around some banked ovals, that's no bad thing. With cars racing at such high speeds, usually just fractions of an inch apart, accidents are common, but the solidity of the machinery is such that injuries are few and far between.

In addition to outright speed, tactical awareness is also a prerequisite. In the course of a 500-mile (805km) race, several pit stops will be required, and making them at the most opportune moment is imperative. If there is an obstruction on the circuit, such as a damaged car, racing proceeds under yellow flags, at which times all competitors must follow a pace car, and overtaking is prohibited. At such times it is beneficial to make a pit stop, in the interest of losing as little time as possible. Speed is essential, and NASCAR pit crews are renowned for their efficiency and resourcefulness. Mid-race engine changes, for which the record is 11 minutes, have now been outlawed!

The appeal of NASCAR isn't limited to the excitement it brings to the crowds. Drivers tend to stay around for a number of years: Richard Petty débuted in 1958, took his 200th win in 1984, and was still turning up to race five years later, at the age of 52 ... And he's by no means the oldest man to have competed regularly in top NASCAR competition, despite the length of the events, the hectic annual schedule and the frenetic pattern of the races (it is not uncommon to see over 20 lead changes per contest!).

NASCAR also covers a variety of junior categories, in which those aspiring to this specialized discipline may learn the ropes.

Australia

In 1984, something significant happened in Australian motor sport. The Bathurst 1000km, the nation's top racing event, incorporated a class for Group A cars. Previously, Australia's own hugely popular touring car series ran to what the locals called Group C regulations. To Europeans, Group C meant Le Mans-style sports cars; as far as the Aussies were concerned, it was all about highly-modified saloon cars, outwardly similar to something you might buy yourself, but somewhat different beneath the shell.

The sound and speed of the Australian musclecars was best emphasized at the undulating 3.9-mile (6.3km) Bathurst circuit, which created national heroes every year. When the Group A cars came in 1984, as a preview of what to expect in 1985 when Australia adopted international Group A regulations full-time, the locals were ready to witness the sterilization of a national institution.

To their mild surprise, the namby-pamby Eurospec cars didn't disgrace themselves, the fastest — the Rover Vitesse of Jeff Allam and Armin Hahne — being less than 10 seconds slower than the fastest Holden Commodore, shared by Bathurst legend Peter Brock and Larry Perkins.

Far from bringing about the death-knell for Australian touring car racing, the arrival of Group A gave it a world-wide appeal, one which strengthened the determination of European teams to conquer Bathurst, this particularly Australian tradition.

The introduction of the World Touring Car Championship in 1987 saw Bathurst's status elevated when it was included on the schedule, although a protest against the fuel used in the winning Ford Sierra Cosworth ultimately saw the outcome of the WTCC decided by a court. Ford eventually lost.

Although Bathurst is the jewel in Australia's crown, a healthy national championship takes place at less celebrated circuits such as Sandown, Symmons Plain, Wanneroo, Surfers Paradise and Oran Park.

But it is at Bathurst that reputations are forged. In Australia, racers like Brock, Dick Johnson, Allan Grice, George Fury and Allan Moffat are household names, their popularity enhanced by their willingness to speak, live, to TV viewers from inside the cockpit whilst in the middle of a race.

Below: *The Jaguar XJ-S was the dominant car of the mid-Eighties in Group A, its weight more than compensated by the ample power of the V12 engine*

Historic Cars in Competition

There was a time when most old cars used to be scrapped as a matter of course because few people wanted them, except for some British enthusiasts. This was even true of competition cars. Far from being regarded as being of particular merit and value, ex-works race or rally cars were widely viewed as particularly undesirable as they were probably worn out! Nowadays the Classic car movement is in full swing and even the mundane cars of a couple of decades ago are prized by some. Few vehicles are now cherished more than historic competition cars and there has been an explosion in the amount of motor sport available to them.

From humble Austin Seven Specials up to Maserati 250Fs or Jaguar D-types, there is sport aplenty.

A typical scene from an Eighties VSCC race meeting at Oulton Park with a Ferrari Dino and a Lotus 16 leading the pack. The great values placed on these cars today does not prevent their owners from driving them with verve

Historic motor sport is almost as old as motor sport itself. Its origins can be traced to the opening of the Brooklands motor track in 1907 when many of the competitors drove old touring cars stripped of their original heavy bodywork. Ever since then the British have been nostalgic about old cars, even though they were soon outpaced. By the Thirties, mass-production methods pioneered by manufacturers like Ford had wrought such changes in the motor car that many enthusiasts were fearful that they would soon lose sight of thoroughbreds made by traditional means. Cars that only a few years before carried the most magnificent coachwork, or provided outstanding performance, were either being scrapped, or thrashed to death by impecunious owners. In the United States, young people went to extreme lengths modifying outdated machinery to make Hot Rods — frequently based on old chassis, propelled by far more powerful engines from modern wrecks. Old cars in their original form were disappearing fast . . .

The British, long imbued in the antique trade, were horrified by such trends. Their Veteran Car Club had been organizing Emancipation Day runs from London to Brighton for real antiques since 1904 when drivers had been liberated of the necessity of having a man carrying a red flag walk in front of them to warn the local populace of the approach of their infernal machinery. Thus, cars made before Emancipation Day which qualified for this run became known as veterans. One of the first speed events in which they could compete was, not surprisingly, held at Brighton. Ever anxious to improve out-of-season trade, local dignitary Sir Harry Preston persuaded the town council to close the seaside resort's tarmac promenade for standing-start speed trials over a timed kilometre. Natural grandstands for what would become the world's first drag race were supplied by double-tiered walkways above the promenade. This event for 200-odd competitors has been going on ever since, with only the odd break for war, and frequently featuring nostalgically outdated machinery.

The Vintage Sports-Car Club

But the first real effort to provide a club and serious competitions specifically for historic cars followed a letter by two cousins to *The Light Car* magazine in 1934 suggesting meetings with fellow enthusiasts 'of the right type of car.' The flavour of their letter was

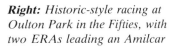

Right: Historic-style racing at Oulton Park in the Fifties, with two ERAs leading an Amilcar

distinctly Brooklands, long proclaimed to be the Mecca of 'the right crowd and no crowding.' These rather self-righteous people wanted, quite simply, to meet like-minded individuals wanting to preserve cars they considered to be classics: those of impeccable breeding made before the advent of mass-production. Quite arbitrarily, they selected the end of 1930 as their cut-off date. Initially, the club that resulted took the name Veteran Sports-Car Club, although this was soon changed to Vintage Sports-Car Club to avoid confusion with the Veteran Car Club.

Their first speed event — a time trial — was held up the gravel drive of the Howard Park Hotel at Aston Clinton in Buckinghamshire, with the first race meeting to be organized, in conjunction with the Bugatti Owners' Club, at Donington Park in 1937. Already one-make clubs like the BOC were running hill climbs and sprints, and were keen to join in racing where enough money could be raised to hire a venue. These marque clubs were typified by the MG Car Club, formed in 1930, whose events soon gained a strongly historic flavour because the vehicles for which they catered tended to be so nostalgic. In the same way, the Midland Automobile Club, which had run hill climbs

at Shelsley Walsh since before World War 2, catered well for historic cars because they did not have to compete directly with more modern machinery as would have been the case on a racing circuit.

In the same way, some regular events began to adopt a distinctly historic nature. The best example is the Six-Hour Relay race which has become the classic of British club racing. It has its roots in a unique series of races started in 1931 by members of The Light Car Club — for owners of machines of no more than 1500c — few of whom could afford to compete in such glamorous long-distance races as the Double Twelve at Brooklands. They did not even stand much chance of finishing, such was the punishing nature of the circuit and, quite frequently, the age of their cars. So the club devised an event for teams of three cars (of no more than 1500cc capacity), each of which was scheduled to complete 30 laps, or 90 miles (145km). Should any one car fail to finish its quota, the next in line could take over the sash which had to be carried to the end. And to give everybody a decent chance, the final result was run in typical Brooklands style, to a handicap. Early enthusiasm was immense, the teams of Austin Sevens battling with Morgans and the like. As the VSCC continued to organize meetings at Donington, the LCC carried on at Brooklands until war intervened.

The post-war scene

One of the main problems before the war had been finding anywhere to race because

Above: *Brooklands pioneered the club-style meeting that allowed owners to exercise their own cars in competiton on the track*

Top: The 750 Motor Club's Six-Hour Relay race is one of the major club events of the British season. This is the start of the 1957 race with an impressive mixed grid at Silverstone

Above: Since its inception, the Vintage Sports-Car Club has organized events for old cars. Here a typical mixed field awaits the start of a ten-lapper at Silverstone in 1963

1940 and 1960. Within these classes, racing cars are defined as those built for racing or speed events, or sports cars running stripped; sports cars must be road-equipped with at least two seats; touring cars are open ones accepted by the club committee as being such; light cars are standard small vintage cars of modest performance; and saloon cars are saloon cars. They are not allowed to race, but they can take part in trials and rallies. There are further divisions for standard cars, ones with minor modifications, period-modified specials and hybrids.

In the meantime, the Six-hour Relay race had been taken over by the 750 Motor Club — a low-cost racing organization that initially catered for the owners of specials based on Austin Seven parts — to be run, mostly from the new Silverstone airfield track, from 1951. Crowds were up to Grand Prix standards by the mid-Fifties, with contemporary front-line sports racing cars such as Lister-Bristols fighting it out with Austin-Healey 100Ss, although there were still pre-war Invictas.

Into the Sixties

The VSCC continued to control historic motor sport into the Sixties in a reasonably informal and steadfastly amateur manner that reflected their true origins. Other, individual, events tended to be run by national motoring organizations as sideshows for major events like Grands Prix. The trouble was that motor sport was evolving so fast that cars were rapidly becoming obsolete. Some of them were such works of art that it seemed a crime not to preserve them — and then museums started to run out of space as well! The VSCC could not cope with any more cars and refused to budge from its established rules.

So a nucleus of enthusiasts, led by photographer Guy Griffiths and former racing driver Betty Haig, found support from the Frazer Nash Car Club, whose members owned highly competitive, yet obsolete, machinery, to promote races for sports cars built between 1940 and 1955. These were run under rules called the Griffiths Formula to include such classics as the Jaguar C-type and D-type, Aston Martin DB3S, and Frazer Nash Le Mans Replica, the first, promoted by the Porsche Club GB and the Frazer Nash CC, being held on another former airfield, Castle Combe, in 1966.

At that point, the appearance of sports racing cars was changing rapidly as they started to run on slick tyres, with all sorts of aerodynamic devices, notably wings. This meant that the Griffiths Formula cars looked very nostalgic although some were only 10 years old. The fact that they were now obsolete so far as any other form of racing was concerned meant that they were relatively cheap, D-type Jaguars which now fetch more than £1 million changing hands for around £2,000. Grids were large then for

roads could not be closed for such events on the mainland and events for more modern cars took precedence at Brooklands, Donington and the newly-opened Crystal Palace Park track. But the opposite situation applied after the war: many newly-built airfields became redundant with no war to fight and it was soon discovered that their perimeter tracks could be adapted for racing. The only problem, apart from petrol rationing, was a scarcity of modern cars, let alone racing ones. This enabled the VSCC, along with old-established clubs like the Bentley Drivers' Club and MG Car Club, to play a vital part in organizing the first post-war races to be held in Britain because their members had plenty of competitive cars.

Gradually the VSCC worked out categories for its members' cars that have developed into today's classes for Edwardians, made before 1919, Vintage, made before 1931, Post-Vintage, of the same character but made between 1931 and 1941, and, more recently, Historic Racing Cars made between what amounted to a cheap, and highly enjoyable, form of motor sport.

These cars then became known as Classics to distinguish them from Vintage sports cars. As these races became ever more popular in the late Sixties, a new club — the Historic Sports Car Club — was formed in 1969 to cater for their racing activities, along similar lines to the VSCC. The 10-year cut-off date for Classic sports cars now meant that cars built before 1960 could compete, with further races for the road-going historic sports cars that most members used as everyday cars, Post-Historic Classic Sports Cars built between 1960 and 1964 and later Historic Special GT cars built before 1968.

Soon after, races were organized for Thoroughbred cars of the type that raced in the popular *Autosport* championship in the late Fifties. In this series, only certain models were allowed to compete as a way of keeping grids big and racing close; such events were now re-created for cars like Aston Martins, Austin-Healeys, Jaguar XK120s and MGs and would eventually be run by the old-established Aston Martin Owners' Club. At the same time the AMOC, Bentley Drivers' Club, Jaguar Drivers' Club and MG Car Club continued to hire race tracks to promote meetings for their members, often including rounds of the HSCC and Thoroughbred championships to add variety.

Single-seaters made before 1960 still found a home with the VSCC, with the Monoposto Racing Club — a low-cost 1958 development along 750 Motor Club lines — promoting events for racing cars that were either home-built or more than five years old if professionally made. The Formula Junior cars made before 1965 were given their own series

under the wing of the Monoposto Club when they became too old to be competitive with more modern machinery. Age limits tended to remain static in other formulae, however, because there were plenty of cars.

The spread to Europe

By 1973, the rapidly-expanding classic car field had its own magazine, *Classic Cars*, with additional competititon categories being promoted by the Classic Saloon Car Club, founded in 1975. Initial cut-off dates were pre-1957, later expanded to pre-1965 and pre-1974. Soon after the HSCC would be catering not only for sports cars, but single-seaters that could not be fitted into other schedules. By the end of the decade the club had attracted major sponsorship, in the form of Lloyds & Scottish Finance, for its most prestigious Historic Racing Car series embracing front-engined single-seaters made between 1931–53, front-engined 1954–60 single-seaters, 1950–54 sports racing cars, 1955–57 sports racing cars and 1958–60 sports racing cars. Since then the seeds of this championship have expanded to become the FIA European Championship for Historic Cars with a separate FISA Cup for GT Cars, all with a 1965 cut-off date but many having undergone the most extensive restorations to make them more competitive. The spirit of the original series still survives, however, in the British national *Classic Cars* series in which originality is the keynote.

The movement had spread to Europe partly through one-off races for cars which had competed at Le Mans in 1973 to celebrate the 24-Hour race's 50th anniversary, feature races supporting the Monaco Grand Prix, and partly because the Lloyds & Scottish

Below: The MG Car Club organizes various forms of racing including a series for T-type MGs in road-going and modified forms, seen here at Donington Park

series demonstrated the viability of running a championship for such cars.

Interest in historic cars in the United States, however, had been largely confined to museums or *concours d'elegance* competitions where there was no danger of precious machinery being damaged. Repairs to cars, many of which were originally built in Europe, tend to be far more expensive in the United States, without the specialist racing car industry which thrives in Britain to make spare parts. It was only when race meetings were organized in the mid-Seventies to coincide with California's Laguna Seca concours on Labor Day that the historic racing movement really got under way in the United States. But there were strict rules governing driving which could put machinery at risk so events tended to be far less competitive. The long distances between locations in America have also governed the development of historic car racing in that it is organized on a regional basis. This has meant that events tend to be shaped so that almost any historic car can compete because there may not be sufficient of any one type in an area to make up a European-style race.

Soaring values, escalated by the provision of series in which historic cars can compete, led to many redundant racers returning to Britain from the United States. The HSCC then started catering for such cars with full grids for CanAm, Special GT and sports racers built between 1966 and 1971, the 2-litre sports racers built before 1975, and pre-1971 single-seaters. Enthusiastic owners such as former endurance racer David Piper then began to organize one-off 'Supersports' races to support major events — such as a Grand Prix — where sufficient sponsorship could be raised to import an entire field. This operation was then transformed into the Steigenberger Supersports Championship, run mainly in Germany — where the Steigenberger Hotel chain is based — with one round in Britain where many of the cars normally race.

Mainland European racing has developed into one-off international historic meetings at major circuits such as the Nürburgring, Zolder, Zandvoort, Monza and Montlhery with only the FIA, FISA Cup and Steigenberger series able to offer championships outside Britain for similar reasons to those that govern American events. But such is the thirst for competition that Americans and Australians are now transporting cars to Europe to take in a short series of events on consecutive weekends, typically in August.

Retrospectives take off

Britain also inadvertently started a historic rally car movement by running a retrospective event to mark the 50th anniversary of

Below: An evocative scene from the Mille Miglia Retrospective held each year over the classic thousand-mile route in Italy. This is the Alfa Romeo Disco Volante driven in 1987 by former World Champion Phil Hill and British journalist Mike McCarthy

their only world championship event, the RAC Rally, in 1982. This was then commemorated by a single-day Coronation Rally annually until leading organizer Phil Young launched the Classic Marathon for pre-1968 rally cars in 1988 on a 2000-mile (3218km) course through Europe to celebrate the 20th anniversary of the London-to-Sydney marathon. In turn, these events have generated a European championship for pre-1965 cars.

In the meantime, the success of the historic RAC Rally led enthusiastic Italians to re-run the Mille Miglia in 1983 as a regular event for cars of a type which competed in the great road race that ended in 1957. The big difference here, of course, was that the cars could not race on open roads, although considerable enjoyment resulted from just driving them in such circumstances.

Again the competitive instinct was strong, leading to the organization of the Coppa d'Italia in 1984, a series of races and hill climbs with linking road sections for pre-1965 cars, along the lines of the Giro d'Italia for modern machinery.

Within five years, further retrospectives like the Targa Florio were being run with most European countries staging historic versions of their traditional rallies and Mexico, where road restrictions are less severe than in the US, returning to the fore by re-running the fabled Carrera Panamericana.

Above: *Still fast after all these years, a Maserati 250F prepares to leave the line at Silverstone*

Left: *Racing for sports cars of the Sixties and early Seventies is very popular as typified by this impressive grid of Porsches, McLarens, Chevrons and Lolas contesting a round of the Steigenberger Hotels Super Sports Historic Championship at Brands Hatch*

Mobil Mobil Mobil
MULA I
ORLD
NSHIP
Shell
BOSS
HONDA
NACIONAL
HEIM
Mobil

The Personalities

With thousands of drivers having competed in tens of thousands of races in a century of motor sport, selecting just a few of them to comprise a chapter in a book is a thankless task. By far the majority of the drivers featured in the following section are winners of World Championship Grands Prix through to 1989. A handful of well-known non-driving personalities has been included too, plus the best known of the pre-war Grand Prix drivers and some post-war names who have achieved notable international success in sports cars.

The popular image of the latter-day star driver is often one of glamour and wealth. While this is part of life for some drivers, the reality is that becoming (and remaining) a top driver is hard work. For every hour spent in a race there are long days spent testing. The modern driver needs to be fully fit and intensely competitive to succeed. To win he needs to be in the right car at the right time and to drive it in a fashion that means it reaches the end of the race in one piece.

Choosing the right team for next season is as much a part of being a top driver as being able to post fastest lap, although of course it helps to be able to do that too!

Some of the drivers in the following chapter are indisputably 'great'; others perhaps are less so. The one thing they all have in common is that they were (or are) winners.

Three of the leading personalities of the Eighties and Nineties on the podium of the 1989 German GP. Left to right, Alain Prost, Ayrton Senna and Nigel Mansell

Right: *One of the most successful drivers ever in the history of motor racing, Mario Andretti*

Michele
ALBORETO
b.1956

A level-headed and thoughtful Italian driver from Milan, Michele Alboreto served his time in Italian national formulae, shining in Formula Fiat Abarth and Formula Italia before moving on to F3 in 1979. He became European F3 Champion in 1980 and his success in this sphere singled him out for a GP drive. His first taste of the Big Time came with Tyrrell in 1981 starting with the San Marino GP in May 1981, at Imola. His season progressed steadily although 10 starts resulted in no championship points at all. However, early in 1982 Alboreto finished fourth in the Brazilian GP and went on to score his first GP win at Las Vegas, later in the year, having figured already in the results in France and Italy.

He went on to win again for Tyrrell, once more in the USA, but this time in Detroit, demonstrating his liking for tight street circuits. In 1984 he achieved the ambition of many Italian drivers and moved to drive for Ferrari in the turbocharged 1.5-litre cars. He won the 1984 Belgian GP and, in 1985, won the Canadian and German GPs, but thereafter championship points were scarce. Despite some good showings, the Ferraris were off the pace in 1988 and the lack of form did not reflect well on Alboreto. He left Ferrari at the end of that disappointing season to drive for Tyrrell again in 1989. He managed six races and put up a couple of top six places but left after the Canadian GP, reappearing in Germany for the Larrousse team. Things became worse as the season wore on, culminating in a string of failures to qualify on three successive occasions, which is surely no direct reflection on Alboreto's innate talent.

Below: *Michele Alboreto, on left, chats with Alain Prost before the start of the 1987 Detroit GP*

Mario
ANDRETTI
b.1940

Winning the 1978 World Championship in a Lotus was but part of the incredible career of this total racing driver. He was born in Italy but moved to America in his teens, starting to drive race cars in the late Fifties, turning to single-seaters in the early Sixties. Although successful in domestic formulae, he was attracted to 'European' racing and was offered an F1 drive by Lotus in 1968 in the US GP at Watkins Glen. He led that race briefly but retired. He drove again for Lotus in 1969 and then battled with an STP March in 1970. Meanwhile he had improved on his 1965 second place at Indianapolis with a win in this premier event in 1969. Andretti's first GP win came in a Ferrari in South Africa in 1971 in one of 10 drives he had for the Scuderia.

Despite this success in F1, Andretti opted to concentrate on US racing during 1973 and 1974 with just the occasional foray into F1. This developed into a disappointing full season with the US-based Parnelli team in 1975. However, success was not too far away as Colin Chapman offered Andretti a Lotus ride in mid-1976. This was the beginning of a golden era for Andretti and Team Lotus, not least the result of a great relationship between Chapman and his new number one driver. Andretti was the right man in the right car at the right time. Starting with the 1976 Japanese GP, Andretti went on to win a further 10 times for Lotus, taking the Championship in 1978.

The Lotus was quickly eclipsed after 1978 and 1979 saw little success; likewise a year with Alfa Romeo in 1981. Thereafter Andretti returned to Indycar racing at home in the United States, with consistent success that continues today.

Elio de ANGELIS
b.1958 d.1986

A fatal testing accident at Paul Ricard in 1986 ended the career of a popular and pleasant Italian driver who had confounded his critics by proving he was no mere rich playboy by winning two GPs: the Austrian in 1982 and the San Marino in 1985.

Coming from a well-heeled background, motor racing was not his only interest, but his commitment was sufficient to see him move from kart racing to F3 and victory in the influential Monaco F3 race in 1978. He progressed to the Shadow team in 1979 and drove the uncompetitive car faster than many observers expected. He went to Lotus in 1980 alongside Nigel Mansell, winning an exciting Austrian GP by a small margin from Keke Rosberg. He stayed with Lotus until the end of the 1985 season, scoring one more win for the team in the turbocharged Renault-engined car. He moved to Brabham for 1986 but the team was struggling for form. His contribution was brief as he died just a few months into the season.

René ARNOUX
b.1948

Frenchman René Arnoux gave all the indications of having a long and glorious career in front of him. It has certainly been long and there have been moments of glory but several less than impressive seasons at the end of the Eighties have tarnished his reputation.

He entered F1 in 1978, coming from F2 as European Champion. He started with the Martini team, progressing to Surtees at the end of the year. Then came the offer from Renault of the second seat in their new-generation team of turbocharged cars. As the cars came good, so did Arnoux's performances and he scored wins in Brazil and South Africa during 1980. He scored two more wins for the team before moving to Ferrari in 1983 where he enjoyed his best season. Three victories and several placings left him just a short way behind eventual champion Nelson Piquet when the final scores were added up.

Arnoux's relationship with Ferrari soured and they parted in 1985. Arnoux then moved to Ligier where the cars, like his form, have not impressed beyond a few placings in 1986. Despite Arnoux's years in the sport and his great experience, 1989 yielded up only two Championship points and added six DNQs to his long and, at some points, impressive record.

Alberto ASCARI
b.1918 d.1955

Alberto Ascari was among the greatest drivers of the immediate post-war era. His father was a well-known racer but was killed in an Alfa Romeo when his son was just seven. However, this did not prevent his talented son from deciding to follow in his footsteps. Before he was 20, Alberto had started racing motor cycles and made his move onto four wheels in 1940 with the first model of Ferrari, the Type 815, entered in the Mille Miglia.

The war then intervened and it was not until 1947 that Ascari was able to get back on the track. His talent was obvious to observers and he was soon driving works Maseratis with measurable success. He remained with Maserati until early 1949 whereupon he embarked upon five glorious years driving Ferraris. A huge tally of wins in the Ferrari 500 resulted in the World Championship in 1952 and 1953, years when GPs were run to F2 regulations. For 1954 Ascari moved to Lancia to drive the D50 but the cars were not ready until 1955. His patience was duly rewarded with two wins early in the season but he crashed during the Monaco GP and ended up in the harbour. He was not badly injured but just four days later he crashed fatally while testing a sports Ferrari at Monza.

Giancarlo BAGHETTI
b.1934

Twenty-seven-year-old Baghetti caused a sensation in 1961 when he won the first three GP races in which he took part. Sadly this meteoric success was not sustained and the Italian quickly faded from the motor racing scene thereafter.

He started racing in 1956 and progressed through success in Formula Junior to a seat in an F1 Ferrari for 1961 in a team run by a consortium of Italian car clubs. In the non-championship races at Syracuse and Naples he won fair and square and for his first fully-fledged championship race, the French GP at Reims, he fought with Gurney's works Porsche, winning by a fraction of a second. Such form did not continue into 1962 and he left Ferrari for 1963, moving to the ill-starred ATS team and thence to the equally unsuccessful Centro-Sud team in 1964, driving a BRM.

Baghetti drove just occasionally thereafter and his final event before retirement was at the London-Sydney Marathon in 1968. He is now a professional photographer.

Italian driver Giancarlo Baghetti enjoyed a meteoric start to his career but thereafter enjoyed little success and faded from the scene

career fully got started with a seat in the F2 Gordini of 1951. He quickly achieved success, remaining with the team until 1954, before signing to drive for Maserati in single-seater and sports cars. He won two non-championship races in a 250F but had a better season the following year when, as number two to Stirling Moss, he was second once and third no fewer than four times in Championship rounds.

Maserati withdrew from racing in 1958 and Behra moved to BRM with little joy, although he was still successful in sports car racing with a Porsche RSK. His year for Ferrari in 1959 started well with victory in the non-championship Aintree 200 but degenerated thereafter. He left in July after a final argument with team manager Dragoni. Just two weeks later, France's most successful driver of the Fifties was killed racing his Porsche Special at Avus, in Berlin.

Top: British Le Mans star and former Ferrari works driver Derek Bell, with his son Justin, now also involved in the sport

Above: *Hero of Italy Lorenzo Bandini who remained in Surtees' shadow for much of his career at Ferrari but enjoyed significant successes before his death at Monaco in 1967*

Lorenzo BANDINI
b.1935 d.1967

Lorenzo Bandini, once an impoverished youngster who dreamed of driving a Ferrari, worked his way up from being a garage mechanic to making his mark in Formula Junior. He came close to securing the F1 Ferrari drive that instead went to his contemporary, Giancarlo Baghetti. However, he was chosen for a seat in the Centro-Sud team for 1961, driving a Cooper Maserati. He enjoyed several good placings and became a reserve Ferrari driver in 1962. His first championship points came with an impressive third place for Ferrari at Monaco. Bandini became number two Ferrari driver to John Surtees in 1963, scoring some good places in GPs, although not actually winning. He did win Le Mans for Ferrari in 1963 in a car shared with Ludovico Scarfiotti. His first GP win came at Zeltweg in Austria in 1964 but he remained as number two to John Surtees into 1965 and 1966. He scored points but further GP victories eluded him. Bandini's talent in sports cars was marked by 1967 wins in the Daytona 24 Hours and the Monza 1000kms. His front row grid position at Monaco in May 1967 boded well for Ferrari's season but Bandini crashed on lap 82 while in second place and sadly died from terrible injuries.

Jean BEHRA
b.1921 d.1959

Jean Behra's 10-year career saw him achieve great heights of popularity in France, his home country. Having driven an elderly Maserati and various touring cars, his racing

Derek BELL
b.1941

Britain's most successful sports car driver, Derek Bell, began his career in 1964 in a shared Lotus Seven. He graduated to F3 in 1966 and enjoyed a most successful season in 1967, leading to the offer of a seat in the Ferrari F2 team. Bell also drove for Ferrari in F1 but this was a bad time for the Scuderia and he returned home for 1969, running a Brabham in F2. Bell's best year of single-seater racing was 1970 when he was runner-up in the European Championship to Clay Reggazoni. He continued to drive occasionally in F1, competing in nine races in all up to 1974, his only point coming from a sixth place in the 1970 US GP, driving a Surtees.

It was to be in sports cars that Bell would find real fame, winning 21 events to date. Sharing a Porsche 917 with Jo Siffert, he won the opening round of the 1971 Championship and was placed at Sebring and Brands Hatch. He won again at Spa in 1973 driving a Mirage, repeating the trick the following year in an Alfa Romeo. In 1975, driving a Gulf Cosworth, he scored the first of five wins in the Le Mans 24 Hours, winning for Porsche in 1981–2 and 1986–7. He was World Sports Car Champion of 1985 and 1986.

Jean-Pierre BELTOISE
b.1937

Serious injuries while racing a René Bonnet sports car in 1964 did not prevent Jean-Pierre Beltoise from continuing a promising career that soon led him to F3 single-seaters with the newly-formed French Matra team. As Matra's number one driver, he took the team into F2 and ultimately into F1. On the way this hard-driving enthusiast won many races, taking the 1968 F2 Championship. Beltoise drove the new Matra V12 F1 car in 1968 but moved in 1969 as number two to Jackie Stewart in the Tyrrell Matra-Ford team while still driving the Matra V12 sports cars. In 1970 Beltoise returned to the Matra F1 effort and led the 1970 French GP until the engine expired.

After 1971 Beltoise moved to BRM and, driving for the British team, managed his only GP win, at Monaco in the rain in 1972. He stayed with BRM until his F1 career came to a close in 1974, after which point he restricted himself to racing saloon cars, an activity that he thoroughly enjoys.

Gerhard
BERGER
b.1959

Gerhard Berger's natural talent was sufficiently apparent right from the start of his racing career for him to make a quick progression through saloons and F3 straight into F1. His break came with ATS in 1984. Via the Arrows team in 1985 he moved to Benetton for 1986 and drove the Benetton-BMW to victory in the season's penultimate race, in Mexico.

Berger's move to Ferrari for 1987 as nominal number two to Alboreto culminated in two wins at the end of the year, in Japan and Australia, bringing to a close a long period without success for the top Italian team. His sole win in 1988 was in front of the Italian home crowd at Monza and, with a total of 41 points, Berger finished the season in third place in the championship. He remained with Ferrari for 1989, alongside Nigel Mansell. The season was marked by a long list of frustrating retirements; no fewer than 10 in succession. The high point of the season was a long-overdue win in Portugal and second place in Italy and Spain. For the first season of the Nineties, Gerhard Berger drives for McLaren.

Joakim
BONNIER
b.1930 d.1972

Having started his competition career as early as 1948, it was a cruel blow that the life of this wealthy, good-living and safety-conscious Swede should end with a crash in a Lola at Le Mans as late as 1972. In all Jo Bonnier competed in 104 GPs and hundreds of other races besides. Yet he scored only one GP win: the 1959 Dutch, driving a BRM.

Bonnier's first GP drives came with Maserati in 1958, having established a fine record in touring cars in 1955/6. For 1959 he moved to BRM and during the next 13 years he drove many different cars, including Cooper, Brabham, Porsche and McLaren.

Bonnier had a successful sports car career in parallel with his GP racing, winning the Targa Florio twice, in 1960 and 1963, both times in a Porsche. He was second at Le Mans in 1964 and won the Nürburgring 1000kms in 1965, among other sports car highlights, including a successful period running his own McLaren and Lola in 1968 and 1969.

Sir Jack
BRABHAM
b.1926

Jack Brabham built his first race car himself and used it to dominate Australian Midget car speedway racing between 1948 and 1951. He turned from the ovals to road racing in Australia and New Zealand and this inexorably led to a trip to Britain in 1955, launching this hard-driving and introverted racer on a glittering international career. Brabham's first GP win came for Cooper in 1959, at Monaco, and he won the British GP at Aintree too. Further points scored in Holland, France, Italy and Sebring were sufficient to secure his first World Championship. He won five straight races the following year to hold on to the crown.

In 1962 Brabham scored the first Championship points by a driver in a car of his own manufacture. He raced Brabhams from then

Sir Jack Brabham was a front runner throughout the Sixties, winning three World Championship titles. His sons David, Geoff and Gary continue the family racing tradition

on, making full use of the reliable Repco engine in 1966 to win the World Championship for a third time with four victories to his name. Brabham continued to be a front runner right up to his last season, in 1970. His 14th and final win came in the first race of the year in South Africa and he should have won both the Monaco and British GPs but for inexplicably crashing in the former and running out of fuel on the last lap in the latter.

Manfred von BRAUCHITSCH
b.1905

Manfred von Brauchitsch is best remembered as a member of the all-conquering Mercedes-Benz works team from 1934 to 1939. In many ways he was the unluckiest member of that select group of racers and he should have won more races than he did.

A record of his victory against powerful opposition in the 1932 Avus GP at an average speed of more than 120mph (193km/h) in a privately-entered, streamlined Mercedes survives on film. It was this drive that led to his place in the newly-formed works team. His start with the team could not have been better as he won his first race but thereafter he suffered cruel luck, including a near-fatal accident at the Nürburgring. He led the German GP the following year but lost the lead to Nuvolari on the last lap. 1936 was another bad year as the Mercedes team had been eclipsed by the Auto-Unions and von

Right: Vittorio Brambilla whose enthusiastic driving made him popular with the crowds. His only GP victory came in 1975

Below: Tony Brooks, centre, photographed during an Aston Martin reunion with fellow Aston team drivers Caroll Shelby, left, and Jack Fairman

Brauchitsch fnished in the top six not once.

His win in the 1937 Monaco GP stemmed the run of bad luck and in 1938 he added the French GP to his tally, although yet again he lost the German GP when his car caught fire during a pit stop when in the lead. Hermann Lang proved to be easily the fastest Mercedes driver in 1939 and von Brauchitsch never really shone again, his career effectively over with the coming of war, despite a half-hearted attempt at some immediate post-war races.

Vittorio BRAMBILLA
b.1937

That Vittorio Brambilla did not kill himself racing was perhaps the biggest surprise of his six-year career spanning 74 GPs. A rugged, hard driver of the old Italian school, he was fast but crashed frequently. An entertaining driver, Brambilla had a tendency to go faster than was safe and he had little mechanical sympathy for his car's gearbox or engine. He graduated via several seasons of F2 to the premier formula with March in 1974 and

remained with them until 1976. His single GP win and a few other places came during the 1975 season when he won the foreshortened Austrian GP from James Hunt's Hesketh. This victory is recalled by many, not simply because it was a surprise win but because the victor crashed after crossing the finish line, such was his delight at seeing the chequered flag.

A single point in the 1976 season marked his last year with March before a move to Surtees. His fourth place in the Belgian GP was the high point of his two-year stay until 1978. He failed to make any mark in the uncompetitive Alfa Romeo team for which he drove four GPs in 1979/80, before retiring from the sport.

Tony
BROOKS
b.1932

This quiet, thoughtful and highly-talented racer began competing with a Healey Silverstone in 1952 and had his first single-seater experience in 1955. Later that year he became famous overnight after his first F1 race by driving his works Connaught to victory over the works Maseratis in a straight fight for the non-championship Syracuse GP, held in Sicily.

He moved to BRM for 1956 but enjoyed little success although he concurrently continued to prove his mettle in sports cars and F2. Leaving BRM to join Vanwall was the turning-point for Brooks and he finished second in Monaco and shared the winning car in the British GP at Aintree with Stirling Moss. The following year saw Brooks win three further GPs and then he was offered a seat at Ferrari for 1959. He had another good season driving for the Italian team and won in Germany and France, missing out by four points on the World Championship.

Apart from his GP successes, Brooks enjoyed fruitful years with the Aston Martin sports car team, winning the Nürburgring 1000kms in 1957 and the Goodwood TT in 1958. Brooks returned from Italy in 1960 to drive the Yeoman Credit Coopers but the cars were not the best and he achieved little. The story was the same with BRM in 1961. He rounded off a poor season with third place in the United States GP and then retired.

Martin
BRUNDLE
b.1959

Eight F3 victories in 1982/83 set Martin Brundle on course for a GP drive with Tyrrell in 1984. He was showing well in the British Saloon Car Championship when just 17, in 1977. Ken Tyrrell recognized his talent and professionalism and Brundle repaid the team owner's faith by finishing fifth in his first F1 race, in Brazil, and second in the Detroit GP later in the year. However, an alleged infringement of the fuel regulations led to the removal of these points.

1986 saw Brundle remain with Tyrrell but it was a poor season. Things improved somewhat in 1987 and several placings resulted in eight points for the year's efforts, top place being fourth in Australia. Brundle then moved to the small German Zakspeed team for whom he scored their first points, at San Marino. He had the opportunity to stay with the team for 1988 but decided that he could do more for his reputation by switching to a top-line sports car drive.

His success in sports cars began in 1987 with a win for Jaguar at Spa. He continued this relationship for 1988, notching up five more wins for the team to gain him the World Sports Car Drivers' Championship. He kept his GP hand in with a one-off drive for Williams in the Belgian GP where he finished ninth. Brundle returned to full-time GP racing in 1989 with Brabham. His best result of the year was fifth place in Japan. For 1990 he elected to return to sports car racing.

Rudolf
CARACCIOLA
b.1901 d.1959

Apart from a brief interlude driving for Alfa Romeo in 1932, Rudolf Caracciola, a German, despite his Italian-sounding name, enjoyed all his successes driving various Mercedes-Benz sports and GP cars. He was universally admired for his outstanding ability and judgement at the wheel; his nickname was *Regenmeister* (rainmaster), such was his skill in the wet.

He joined the Mercedes team in 1924 and in 1926 won the German GP at Avus, the first of five victories in his home GP. He won many hill climbs and other races, including the Mille Miglia of 1931, driving a mighty Mercedes-Benz SSKL. Mercedes-Benz withdrew from racing in 1931 and Caracciola took up the opportunity of moving to Alfa Romeo for whom he drove a P3. He continued to be successful but injured himself badly in practice for the 1934 Monaco GP.

Below: Martin Brundle deserved to drive better cars in F1 but the chances never came. His main successes were found in Group C sports cars

Above: Colin Chapman kneels beside Graham Hill's Lotus to discuss the car's handling. Under Chapman's guidance Lotus conquered most avenues of front-line motor sport

Caracciola was out of the sport for a year but by the time he had fully recovered Mercedes-Benz had formed a new team and they had a place for him. He scored no fewer than seven GP wins in 1935, two in 1936 and, with the introduction of the legendary W125 model for 1937, won five more. The 1938 and 1939 seasons were not quite as successful but he still won the Swiss and German GPs and broke several speed records.

The war effectively brought an end to Caracciola's glittering career. He did race again, including a fourth place in the 1952 Mille Miglia, but several weeks later he crashed in Switzerland and did not ever compete again.

François CEVERT
b.1944 d.1973

François Cevert achieved a considerable amount in his five-year GP career, but most observers thought he was on the verge of much more when he crashed fatally during practice for the 1973 US GP at Watkins Glen. He was popular and gregarious and his loss was felt by many, not least his team-mate Jackie Stewart who did not race at Watkins Glen that day or ever again.

Cevert started racing motor cycles but moved to four wheels in 1966. He was French F3 champion in 1968 and moved up to F2 in 1969, finishing third in the Championship behind winner Johnny Servoz-Gavin who was signed to drive for Tyrrell in 1970.

Ironically it was 28-year-old Servoz-Gavin's retirement from racing that led to Ken Tyrrell's call to Cevert, offering him a seat in his March alongside Jackie Stewart. His first point came with sixth place in the Italian GP and that was that for the season. Things started to improve with the French GP the following year when Cevert finished a strong second to Stewart, repeating the trick at the Nürburgring a month later. Placings in the Italian and Canadian GPs paved the way to a clear win in the final race of the year — the US GP at Watkins Glen. He finished up third overall in the World Championship.

Through 1972 and up until that fateful day in October 1973 Cevert had a remarkable run of eight second places, plus a third. Posthumously he finished fourth in the Championship.

Colin CHAPMAN
b.1928 d.1982

Anthony Colin Bruce Chapman was one of those multi-talented men who achieved so much as to make some ordinary mortals feel terribly insecure. Apart from founding Lotus Engineering and designing and building a succession of world-beating road cars such as the Elite, the Elan and the Europa, he designed dozens of successful sports and single-seater racing cars. He introduced monocoque race car construction techniques and pioneered numerous other innovations, such as ground effects, to a racing world whose regulations he always followed to the absolute limit and, sometimes, beyond.

Apart from being a brilliant designer and far-sighted race team owner and manager, Chapman was himself a successful driver and raced his own cars at Le Mans in 1955 and again in 1956, also practising a Vanwall for the 1956 French GP but failing to start the race due to a crash in practice.

Chapman-designed cars had been dominant in most branches of racing since the mid-Fifties but it was not until 1963 that a Lotus won the World Championship with Jim Clark sweeping all before him, as he did again in 1965. More Championships would follow with Graham Hill in 1968, Jochen Rindt in 1970, Emerson Fittipaldi in 1972 and Mario Andretti in 1978.

Team Lotus and Lotus Cars were large organizations by the late Sixties and Colin Chapman had around him many talented engineers and designers who were able to develop and contribute to his ideas. Chapman persisted in his innovative approach to racing but Team Lotus suffered a lean few years and not until 1982 did a Lotus win a GP again. Lotus would win again in the mid-Eighties but Colin Chapman himself would not live to see it as he suffered an unexpected and fatal heart attack in 1982.

Jim
CLARK
b.1936 d.1968

Jim Clark was regarded as The Best, not just by the public who saw him race but by many of his fellow professionals at that time and since.

He started his racing aged 19 in 1955, but had his first busy season in 1958 with a D-type Jaguar in which he won many events. Then he drove a Lister Jaguar to great effect, continuing the run of success in a Lotus Elite. He moved to single-seaters in 1959 with a run in a Formula Junior Gemini. Thereafter Clark would spend the rest of his career in various Lotus cars after Colin Chapman signed him to drive for Team Lotus in 1960.

He started in Formula Junior and F2, winning nine races in his first year. He graduated to F1 midway through 1960 and scored his first points at that year's Belgian GP. Results were encouraging during 1961 and, elevated to the number one position in Team Lotus, victories followed in Belgium, Britain and the United States in 1962 driving the new monocoque Lotus 25. He won the Championship in 1963, winning seven out of the 10 races and finishing second and third respectively in two of the three other rounds.

John Surtees won the 1964 Championship but Clark was back in control for 1965, the same year in which he won the Indianapolis 500, at his third attempt. His victory in the 1966 US GP was a triumph of man over machine as he was the only driver ever to persuade the BRM H16 engine to last the distance. The arrival of the Cosworth V8-powered Lotus 49 in 1967 was the start of a new era in GP racing, and Clark went on to win four GPs that year. He tackled a successful 1967/68 Tasman series and started the 1968 World Championship season on a high note, winning the opening South African round, taking his tally of wins to a record 25. Then, on April 7, he was killed in an inexplicable crash in a Lotus during a minor F2 race at Hockenheim.

Peter
COLLINS
b.1931 d.1958

Peter Collins' path into motor sport was eased by his family background in the motor trade. He was a versatile and tremendously enthusiastic driver, just as at home in a rally car or a sports car as in a top-line GP machine.

His racing began in 1949, aged just 17, in the highly-competitive world of 500cc Formula 3. His success in this sphere took him on to F2 with HWM, coupled with sports car racing for Aston Martin, for whom he won the Goodwood Nine Hours in 1952.

His move to big single-seaters came in 1953 when he took Tony Vandervell's Thinwall Special Ferrari to several wins. He also drove the Thinwall's successor, the Vanwall, and appeared in a Maserati 250F. His performances were sufficiently noteworthy for Ferrari to offer him a place in 1956 driving a Lancia Ferrari. That year he finished third in the Championship, winning the Belgian and French GPs. Collins was joined at Ferrari by his great friend Mike Hawthorn for the 1957 season, but frustratingly the cars were not on the pace. They were better in 1958 and Collins won the British GP at Silverstone, where he had also won the International trophy earlier in the year.

Just two weeks after the triumph at Silverstone, Collins was killed when he lost control of his Ferrari during the German GP at the Nürburgring.

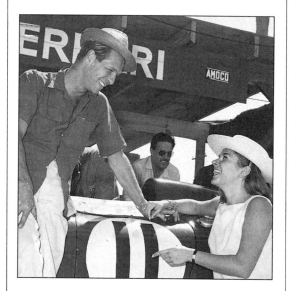

John
COOPER
b.1923

John Cooper, with his father, Charles, is credited with one of the major developments of post-war motor sport — the change from front- to rear-engined designs. They pioneered what amounted to mass-production of racing cars, building possibly 1500 examples through to 1969. John Cooper raced his own cars until 1952, thereafter concentrating on the roles of engineer and team manager.

Charles Cooper had been involved with Brooklands racing since the Twenties but it was not until after the war that the Coopers founded the Cooper Car Co., building diminutive rear-engined machines for the new 500cc Formula 3.

The enterprise quickly expanded and by 1952 the firm's front-engined cars were running in international events. Overcoming

Above: *Jim Clark at the wheel of one of the 1964 Lotus Indianapolis cars. He would win the great American race the following year at his third attempt*

Left: *Smiling Peter Collins with his wife, alongside the Ferrari that he would drive in the 1957 Sebring 12 Hours race. He died in a Ferrari GP car just over a year later*

Right: Frenchman Patrick Depailler was a hardworking driver who enjoyed success over several seasons before an untimely death in a testing accident in 1980

resistance from his more conservative father, John Cooper took the company towards building a proper GP-type car and, reverting to the familiar F3 layout, the first car running in 1955 was rear engined. For the F2 formula of 1957 and 1958, the rear-engined Coopers were winners and the cars could easily be uprated for use in GPs. If they were not sophisticated or light, they were strong, efficient and reliable. The culmination of this move to F1 and the start of some hugely successful seasons was Stirling Moss's victory in the 1958 Argentine GP; the first championship win for a car of this configuration.

John Cooper ran a fully-fledged, tightly-financed GP team in 1959 and 1960, with Jack Brabham winning the Championship both years. Cooper GP cars would win other GPs right up until 1967 but the growing sophistication of the sport had started to overtake the small and enthusiastic company. John Cooper sold his interests in the team soon after the death of his father in 1964, although he continued to act as technical director. John Cooper was also instrumental in the conception and development of the Mini Cooper in the early Sixties and was paid a royalty by BMC for each example sold.

Patrick
DEPAILLER
b.1944 d.1980

Patrick Depailler was something of a journeyman who worked hard but maybe lacked sparkle. However, he did graduate to F1 in 1973 and was active for eight seasons, winning two races and finishing second no fewer than 10 times.

Depailler was French F3 Champion in 1971. He moved up to F2 for 1972 and continued in that formula in 1973 and 1974, although in 1973 he had made his F1 debut for Tyrrell, in the French GP, completing a full season for them in 1974 alongside Jody Scheckter. He continued with Tyrrell for another four seasons, picking up several good placings. In 1977 he finished above his team leader, Ronnie Peterson, in the Championship. 1978 was even better with his first win coming at Monaco, taking him to the top of the Championship points table. The season ended with Depailler fifth in the Championship and he decided to move to the French Ligier team for 1979. He won the Spanish GP for the team in April but then broke his contract and several bones hanggliding, laying himself up for the rest of the year.

He moved to Alfa Romeo in 1980 but died from injuries received during a testing accident at Hockenheim in the summer.

Juan-Manuel
FANGIO
b.1911

Juan-Manuel Fangio's supernatural talent took him from obscurity in a small town in Argentina to become five-times World Champion and win a higher percentage of GPs contested than any other driver. In his nine seasons driving World Championship GPs he contested 51 races, finishing in the top six in 41 of them and winning 24 outright. Of course he won countless other non-championship races too. It is worth noting that Fangio did not have his first works drive until the age of 38. He was, and still is, a man

Below: Giuseppe Farina enjoying the acclaim for winning the 1950 British GP at Silverstone

of great charisma and charm, who is universally admired for his talent and achievements.

He learned his craft driving in pre-war South American road races. He came to Europe in 1949 and his early results were sufficient for Alfa Romeo to offer him a works drive for 1950. He won three races that year and three the next, plus the World Championship. Alfa withdrew from racing at the end of the year and Fangio had a poor 1952 which ended with a crash at Monza that put him out for the remainder of the season.

However he was back in 1953 with his skills undiminished. Driving a Maserati he won the Italian GP and was second in the French, German and British GPs and the Mille Miglia. His 1954 season started with two GP wins in a Maserati but then he moved to the new Mercedes-Benz team, for whom he won four of the six remaining GPs, winning his second World Championship. Four wins in 1955 were sufficient to retain the crown. Mercedes withdrew in 1956 and Fangio switched to drive the Lancia-Ferraris. Yet again he was Champion.

Fangio's skill at the wheel was matched by his skill at choosing the best team to drive for. His judgement was proved correct yet again in 1957 when four GP wins for Maserati in the old 250F were enough to bring him a record fifth world title.

Fangio, now 47, raced again in 1958 but then gracefully retired, returning to his native Argentina. He still appears at occasional race meetings, often donning his helmet to demonstrate one of his cars. His stylish, fast performances on these occasions show that this great man has lost little of his natural flair.

Above: Fangio, on left, assists in the presentation of an award to his former team-mate Stirling Moss, centre, assisted by fellow ex-World Champion Denny Hulme

Giuseppe FARINA
b.1906 d.1966

Dr Giuseppe Farina was one of the few drivers whose careers spanned the war. He used his experience to good effect, becoming the first winner of the newly-constituted post-war World Championship in 1950. A member of the Farina (later Pininfarina) coachbuilding firm, he was a Doctor of Political Science and a man of considerable culture and means. His confidence in his own abilities sometimes spilled into over-confidence and he crashed or broke cars more times than might be expected of a champion. His driving style was distinctive — fast but smooth and with a splendidly relaxed, straight-arm stance at the wheel.

Farina ran private Maseratis and Alfas from 1934 but joined the re-formed Alfa works team for 1938 at a time when Mercedes were the dominant force. However, he was Italian Champion for 1938 and 1939.

After the war Farina resumed his works Alfa drive but successfully drove Maseratis and Ferraris in 1948 and 1949. Back with Alfa Romeo for 1950 he won three rounds of the new World Championship, in Britain, Italy and Switzerland, placing him top of the points table ahead of team-mate Fangio.

Farina won four major races in 1951 but at 45 was being eclipsed by other and younger drivers. However, he proved himself to be still in contention in 1951 with wins at Monza and Naples driving a Ferrari 500. He drove for Ferrari again in 1952, winning the German GP plus several non-championship races. He was prominent in sports cars too, winning the Nürburgring 1000kms and the Spa 24 Hours in Ferrari 375MMs.

By 1954 it was widely recognized that Farina was overreaching his skill and trying too hard to prove himself. He crashed several times, burning himself badly in a particularly unpleasant accident while leading the 1954 Mille Miglia. He made a partial recovery and returned to racing in 1955, but his injuries had left him damaged and he reluctantly withdrew after the Belgian GP in June.

Two attempts to qualify for the Indianapolis 500 in 1956 and 1957 were unsuccessful and thereafter Farina officially retired. Ironically, having survived many accidents on the track, he was killed in a road accident in 1966 when his Lotus Cortina crashed.

Enzo FERRARI
b.1898 d.1988

Enzo Ferrari's incredible life spanned the whole of modern motor racing. Regarded as the patriarch of motor racing, he ruled his empire with a firm hand but was a great friend to those he liked and the drivers he respected. Ferrari ran his team autocratically but seldom went to races. His cars were rarely at the forefront of technical development, apart from their engines, and the team had more than its fair share of off seasons. However, the overall result has been one of unequalled success.

Ferrari had already driven competitively when, in 1920, he joined Alfa Romeo as an engineer and test driver, racing too whenever he could. He had talent at the wheel but his health was not up to rough Twenties-style racing and he began instead to concentrate on running Alfa Romeo's racing team.

When Alfa Romeo officially withdrew from racing, Ferrari left to run the Alfa team under his own Scuderia Ferrari banner, based in Modena and using his chosen Prancing Horse shield as the company emblem. This arrangement persisted until 1938, by which time Alfa had taken their racing effort back in-house and Ferrari concentrated on building cars of his own.

The first of these, for legal reasons not actually called Ferraris, appeared in 1940 but it was not until 1947 that the first Ferrari proper was unveiled. Enzo Ferrari had by then moved his company from Modena to nearby Maranello where it remains to this day. From that time, Ferrari cars have been constantly at the forefront of the sport. Enzo Ferrari's racing cars have won innumerable Constructors' Championships and many World Championships, and his cars and drivers have won all the great races, sometimes time after time.

Although Ferrari latterly sold interest in his company to Fiat, he was still very much in control of the racing team and remained hugely influential in motor sport right up to his death.

Below: The legendary Enzo Ferrari whose career straddled decades of motor sport and whose cars have won so many races and titles

Emerson FITTIPALDI
b.1946

Emerson Fittipaldi took the now well-trodden path from Brazil to Britain in 1969, having established himself as a promising talent racing at home. Despite his experience, upon arriving in Britain he visited a racing school to settle himself into the British way of racing and he launched into a meteoric career in Formula Ford and F3.

As early as 1970 he had his Formula 2 chance with Lotus and part-way through the season was in a Lotus GP car, albeit an old one, for the British GP. He scored points next time out and rounded off that extraordinary season by winning the penultimate championship round, the US GP at Watkins Glen. 1971 was a bad year as Lotus were off the pace but things were far better in 1972 with the arrival of the great Lotus 72. Five wins were enough to secure the Championship crown for the Brazilian who by now was enjoying the fruits of a great working relationship with Colin Chapman.

Fittipaldi was second in the 1973 Championship, despite winning three rounds, and then in 1974 he moved from Lotus to McLaren. The new M23 model was the car of the moment and Fittipaldi drove it convincingly to three wins and sufficient points-scoring positions to take the Championship for the second time. Lauda's Ferrari had the beating of the McLaren in 1975 but Fittipaldi won the British and Brazilian GPs. Then in 1976 he surprised the GP world by announcing his departure to join his brother's Copersucar team. He left the McLaren seat to James Hunt, who went on to win the 1976 Championship with it.

The five seasons spent in the Copersucar (later 'Fittipaldi') team proved a sad wind-down for a brilliant GP career. Apart from a sparkling second place in his 1978 home GP, Fittipaldi had little to show for so many years of effort in an uncompetitive team. He left GP racing, almost unnoticed, in 1978.

However, in the mid-Eighties he became something of a born-again driver in the United States, driving Indycars. He confounded all his critics by winning the biggest US race of them all, the 1989 Indianapolis 500, at near record speed, averaging 167mph (269km/h).

Richie GINTHER
b.1930 d.1989

Richie Ginther experienced his early racing teamed up with fellow American Phil Hill, and he went on to enjoy racing various sports cars on the West Coast of America. His first

European race was Le Mans in 1957 which he failed to finish. He had made a sufficient name for himself as a fast and thoughtful driver to be invited to Ferrari for the 1960 season as team member and test driver, in which capacity he had proved himself to be particularly accomplished. His GP career started well with a sixth place in the Monaco GP in the first rear-engined GP Ferrari. He drove just three GPs in 1960 but tackled a full season in 1961, finishing a close second at Monaco and third in Belgium and Britain.

Ginther moved to BRM in 1962 and stayed there for three seasons, enjoying successful years in 1963 and 1964, being placed on 14 occasions but not actually winning a race. Jackie Stewart replaced Ginther at BRM for 1965 and the American moved to the recently-formed Honda team for whom he scored a maiden GP win in the last GP of 1965, in Mexico. Ginther persisted with the problematical and heavy Honda through 1966, with a mere five points to show for his efforts. He retired at the end of the year and, although he retained an interest in the sport, largely disappeared from the scene.

He returned to Britain in 1989 for the filming of a documentary about BRM. He looked frail and ill and died just days after driving a racing car for the last time.

José Froilan
GONZALES
b.1922

This colourful, larger-than-life character came from Argentina in 1950, having earned his spurs racing back home. Gonzales replaced Fangio in the Scuderia Argentina Maserati after Fangio had moved to the works Alfa team. He quickly made his mark with a dramatic, wild and exciting driving style. He had a busy year in 1951, standing in for Taruffi in the works Ferrari team and taking his car up to second in the French GP. He drove for Ferrari again and took the 4.5-litre unsupercharged car to the flag in the British GP at Silverstone in convincing fashion, beating the works Alfas.

In 1952 he drove a variety of cars including the V16 BRM, Thinwall Special and F2 cars for Ferrari and Maserati. He stayed mainly with Maserati in 1953 with several good placings resulting. 1954 was to be his best year overall when he rejoined Ferrari. He was placed in all but two of the year's races, winning the British GP for the second time, plus the non-Championship International Trophy. In sports cars, the high point of the year was a win at Le Mans in the Ferrari 375, shared with Trintignant.

His exciting career was speeded to its close by a bad crash in practice for the Dundrod TT. Gonzales drove in Argentina occasionally in 1955, managing a hard-fought second

place in his home GP. He raced again once or twice in Europe in 1956 but thereafter did not appear in a race car outside his native country.

Dan
GURNEY
b.1931

Like Phil Hill and Richie Ginther, hard-driving American Dan Gurney's roots were in USA West Coast sports car racing. He was never World Champion but he was certainly world class and scored points in 34 of his 84 GP appearances. He was amusing, charming and popular with his fellow professionals.

Gurney came to drive at Le Mans in 1958 but didn't finish. He was recruited to the Ferrari works sports car team for 1959 but was soon driving the F1 cars as well. Success came with second place in the German GP in August and he was placed third and fourth respectively in the Portuguese and Italian GPs. His win, with Stirling Moss, in a Maserati in the 1960 Nürburgring 1000kms demonstrated his versatile talent.

Gurney's 1960 season with BRM coincided with one of the team's low points. However, he joined the Porsche F1 effort for 1961 and took three second places, scoring the team's first and only F1 win a year later, in France. In 1962 he tried his hand at Indy racing and successfully drove stock cars too.

Gurney's years with Brabham in 1963/4/5 were his most consistently successful and he won at Rouen and Mexico City. Concurrently he pursued an active programme of racing back home in the USA.

Above: Emerson Fittipaldi was a double World Champion whose career looked to be over but he now enjoys great success racing in the USA

Below: Richie Ginther, a tough and talented American driver who was a front-runner for Ferrari but won just one GP, in a Honda, in 1965

Above: Graham Hill, who enjoyed one of the longest and most successful careers in motor sport only to retire and die in an air crash

By 1966, Gurney's own car, the Gurney Eagle, was in full swing. He scored only twice that year in it, but things came good in 1967 and he took the attractive Weslake-powered machine to victory in the Race of Champions at Brands Hatch and memorably in the Belgian GP at Spa. Gurney also gave Ford their second win at Le Mans, teamed up with A. J. Foyt. That year he also won in stock cars and Indy cars in the States.

Gurney drove several times for McLaren in 1968 but opted out of F1 in 1969 to concentrate on Indy racing at home. He went back to McLaren to drive sports and GP cars in 1970, but the return was short-lived and Gurney returned to the States to concentrate on running his Indycar team.

Mike
HAWTHORN
b.1929 d.1959

Blond, bow-tied, jovial Mike Hawthorn is remembered in the same breath as his great friend Peter Collins. Whereas Collins died racing, Hawthorn retired from the sport but was then killed in a freak road accident.

Hawthorn started racing Rileys in 1950 but it was his driving of an F2 Cooper Bristol that shot the 23-year-old to fame in 1952 with several non-championship wins and points in three GPs. He created such an impression that Ferrari offered him a drive in 1953 and in July he won the French GP in exciting style from Fangio's Maserati. In sports cars he won at Spa in the 24 Hours. In 1954 he was second three times for Ferrari and won the Spanish GP. His wish to stay in England for 1955 to run the family garage business led him to forsake Ferrari for Vanwall. This resulted in a barren year as far as GPs were

Right: Mike Hawthorn aged 25, photographed after his strong second-placed finish in the 1953 Monza GP, five years before his Championship-winning season

concerned but he won the tragic 1955 Le Mans race for Jaguar, plus the Sebring 12 Hours.

Hawthorn spent 1956 with BRM suffering absolute frustration at the car's unreliability and lack of performance. To stem the tide of misfortune he rejoined Ferrari for 1957. Refreshed, he re-established himself as a front runner. His win in the 1958 French GP and his placings in all the other races except Portugal and Monaco were enough to win him the Championship, even though his nearest rival, Stirling Moss, had won four races that year. But it was also a year of tragedy: Hawthorn's friend and team-mate Peter Collins was killed in the German GP. At the end of the season in October, Hawthorn announced his retirement. He was killed driving his road-going Jaguar in January 1959.

Graham
HILL
b.1925 d.1975

Graham Hill didn't pass his driving test until he was 24. Mike Hawthorn had won his first GP by that age but this slow start didn't prevent Graham Hill carving himself a hugely successful career in the driving seat. He was a charismatic man, an engaging and amusing speaker whose popularity extended far beyond the world of motor racing.

As a trained engineer, his first brush with racing came in 1954 and the enthusiasm thus ignited led to his becoming a mechanic for Team Lotus and generally starting to offer his services around in exchange for one-off drives in races. He enjoyed a challenge, was a hard worker and his efforts reaped rewards. He soon built up a useful reputation that ultimately led to GP outings with Team Lotus driving the Lotus 16 in 1958 and 1959 but with little to show for it apart from experience.

Hill moved to BRM in 1960 and his luck began to improve. But it was not until 1962 that things truly came right when he won the first of the five Monaco GPs that would be his. He also won in Germany, Italy and South Africa, beating Jim Clark to the Championship. Jim Clark was Champion in 1963 but Hill was second with two wins. He was runner-up again for BRM in 1964 after winning at Monaco and in the US GP. Yet again Hill was second in 1965 with two wins; Monaco, as usual, and the US GP for the third year running. No GP wins came Hill's way in 1966 but he was still there in the reckoning. His move back to Lotus as team-mate to Jim Clark for 1967 came as a surprise for some.

Apart from GPs, Graham Hill won the TT in 1963 and 1964. He won the 1966 Indianapolis 500 in a Lola and would go on to win the Le Mans 24 Hours in 1972 for Matra.

Lotus was the class of the field in 1967 but it was Clark who took four wins, leaving Hill to suffer dispiriting retirements apart from a couple of second places. When Jim Clark was killed early the following season, it was Hill who took up the challenge, kept the team together, won three races and scooped his second Championship at age 39. Graham Hill's last GP victory came at Monaco in 1969. The season did not continue well, ending prematurely with a bad crash at Watkins Glen which had him in hospital for weeks.

However, Hill did not announce his expected retirement, competing with decreasing degrees of success right through to the 1975 Monaco GP, in a Lola-based car run by Hill's own team. Hill then faced the inevitable and retired to become team manager. Sadly, he and five members of that team, including his promising driver Tony Brise, died in an air crash later in the year.

Phil
HILL
b.1927

American Phil Hill worked his way up through more ordinary sports cars to race Ferraris. He came to Europe to drive for the works Ferrari sports car team in 1956 and progressed in the elite company to win Le Mans, with Gendebien, in 1958, also winning at Sebring with Peter Collins. He went on to win at Sebring again in 1959 and would win Le Mans two more times, in 1961 and 1962.

Hill's first GP drive came with Maserati in 1958 but later that year he graduated to the Ferrari GP squad alongside Mike Hawthorn after the deaths of Musso and Collins had depleted the team. His debut at Monza was impressive as he led the race and finished third. Four good seasons with Ferrari followed with Hill's first win coming in the 1960 Italian GP. This was a memorable occasion as he was the first American to win a GP since

1921. Sadly, Phil Hill's 1961 World Championship win came about directly as the result of the death of his team-mate Wolfgang von Trips. Trips crashed fatally during the last race of the year, leaving the title with his fellow Ferrari driver.

The new World Champion stayed with Ferrari for 1962, but it was not a particularly successful year and Hill left to join the new but ill-starred ATS team for 1963. His switch to Cooper for what would be his last full season in 1964 produced barely more success, although right through to his retirement in 1967 he continued to prove his prowess in sports cars, including the remarkable Chaparrals. He retired to his native California where he now runs a successful Classic car restoration company among other interests.

Denny
HULME
b.1936

Denny Hulme proved that you don't need a daredevil approach to motor racing to make it to the top. By his standards you don't even need to work terribly hard. He was safety conscious and laid-back in his approach to his sport but the record shows that in 1967 he was World Champion, having won two of the most demanding races of the year, Monaco and Germany.

This agreeable Kiwi came to European racing after several busy seasons at home as the New Zealand 'Driver to Europe' for 1959. This was not a key to the top but a handy start and he ran in Formula Junior through to 1964, having a marvellous year in 1963. By 1964 he was having occasional F1 drives but drove mainly in F2. Only in 1966 did Jack Brabham offer him a full works seat in GPs and a place with the works F2 effort.

Left: *New Zealander Denny Hulme had a relaxed approach to the sport but this did not prevent him from becoming World Champion in 1967*

Above: Driver turned commentator James Hunt, who combined hard work with good fortune to win the 1976 Championship in a McLaren

Hulme's first year of GP resulted in fourth place in the Championship while his mentor and team leader Jack Brabham took the top spot. However, Hulme was at the top of the pile the following year. He won twice as against Jim Clark's four wins, but Hulme's other points brought him out on top. In his second season he had won the Championship!

Despite his success with Brabham, Hulme elected to join the new team created by his countryman Bruce McLaren, doing much to keep that team going after the death of its founder. Hulme would remain with McLaren for the remainder of his career up to 1974. In various GP McLarens he was a consistent points scorer and won a further five GPs, including the Argentine race in his final year. Apart from success in GPs, he enjoyed extensive success in CanAm racing, an avenue of sports car competition that he pursued right up to his retirement.

Right: Although Jackie Ickx retired from F1 at the end of 1979, he successfully combined careers in both GP and sports car racing for many years

James HUNT
b. 1947

James Hunt still has his critics who dislike his independent attitude or his opinions, or detract from his driving skills. But the record tells the real story. True, Lauda crashed in 1976 and relieved Hunt of much pressure in the fight for the Championship crown. But it was Hunt who blew the others off in impressive style in six of 1976's GPs, taking the crown for himself by the narrowest of margins.

He enjoyed his early years in the sport, finding the high-speed lifestyle to his high-living and fun-loving taste. Few drivers would have survived the accident-ridden traumas of his early competition years but he had the character to keep going, and to secure the backing from Lord Hesketh to provide the cars for him to keep going in!

His achievements in Formula Ford and F3 were modest, although he proved himself a fast, if sometimes rash, driver. But as the stakes increased, so his driving matured. Hunt's first taste of F1 came in 1973 with Lord Hesketh's March in the Race of Champions where he finished third. Entries in GPs followed and by the end of the year Hunt had become a force to be reckoned with, finishing a strong second in the last race of the year.

The first of the Hesketh GP cars appeared for 1974 and by the middle of the year it had started to show promise. Hunt scored points in the Swedish, Austrian, Canadian and US GPs. 1975 was better still, the high point being a straight win in the Dutch GP over Lauda's Ferrari. Two more second places, a fourth and a fifth rounded off a great year.

But greater things were in store. 1974 World Champion Emerson Fittipaldi had vacated his seat at McLaren, and Hunt stepped in. He won in Spain, France, Germany, Holland, Canada and the US, snatching the Championship from Lauda by one point.

In 1977 Hunt added three more victories to his tally, but the McLaren was being gradually overtaken by other manufacturers and the Championship went back to Lauda. The downhill slide was not arrested in 1978 and a disillusioned Hunt joined the Wolf team for 1979. He lasted for just seven unsuccessful races with the team, and retired in his seventh season.

Jacky ICKX
b. 1945

Belgian Jackie Ickx is usually thought of as a great sports car driver but he was also an accomplished and successful Grand Prix driver whose talent in single-seaters deserves not to be forgotten. He was a craftsman at the wheel, handling any car smoothly and stylishly.

Ickx was given his break by Ken Tyrrell, driving for him in both F3 and F2, making European F2 Champion in 1967. He drove for Cooper in F1 later that year and was taken up by Ferrari for 1968. He won that year's French GP and was placed in five other races, reflecting the 23-year-old's prodigious talent. He left Ferrari to join Brabham for 1969 and finished the year second to Jackie Stewart's Matra with two GPs under his belt. Ferrari called him back for 1970 and he won in Austria, Canada and Mexico, missing the Championship by just five points. He would win again for Ferrari and be a consistent points scorer right through to the end of his stay there. In 1974 he moved to Team Lotus for two seasons. Although still under 30, Ickx gave the impression of having mellowed and his driving was less impressive, with just the occasional glimpse of greatness. He continued in F1 with Williams, Ensign and Ligier until the end of 1979 before announcing his retirement. He seemed to have done so much but was still only 34.

In parallel with his F1 programme Ickx had developed into an accomplished sports car driver, winning 34 Championship races from 1967 onwards, more than any other driver, including six famous victories at Le Mans.

Innes
IRELAND
b.1930

Innes Ireland won only one GP but enjoyed other successes and lived life to the full, and beyond, during his 14 years in the sport. He was fast but seemed to have a lot of accidents. He triumphed in 1960 and 1961 but thereafter suffered from lack of a top-line car.

He began racing a Riley and a Bentley but had his first real successes with his home-assembled Lotus 11 in 1957. More sports car racing and more victories followed in 1958 and for 1959 he joined Team Lotus, making fourth in his first GP, in Holland. He took the Lotus 18 to two non-Championship GP wins early in 1961 and also secured the first GP win for Team Lotus, at Watkins Glen.

Colin Chapman's apparent reward to Ireland for this result was to drop him for 1962 in favour of Jim Clark. Ireland moved on to drive the UDT Laystall Lotus for 1962, with little luck, although he did win the TT that year in a Ferrari GTO among other sports car successes. He stayed with the team for 1963, driving a Lotus 24, but only two fourth places resulted from GPs. A BRM replaced the Lotus for 1964 with slightly improved results but the works teams ruled the day. After persisting in uncompetitive machinery until the end of 1966, Ireland decided that there was no longer a place for him in the sport. It had changed from the easygoing jovial group of friends that it had been and he left to become a journalist and develop his business interests. His talent with the pen is considerable and he continues to write regularly for *Road and Track* in the USA and *Classic Cars* in the UK, among other journals.

Jean-Pierre
JABOUILLE
b.1942

Jean-Pierre Jabouille was a highly competent and modest French driver whose driving skills were a significant factor in the ultimate success of the turbocharged Renault GP cars. His career began in 1966 in saloon cars and he became a prominent F2 driver in the mid-Seventies. His first taste of F1 came with Tyrrell in 1975, but he truly found his niche as part of the Renault F1 effort in 1977. He drove the team's sole entry in the British GP that year and retired having qualified near the back of the grid. Four more appearances that season also ended with mechanical failure.

However, Renault were quickly pushing back the frontiers of turbocharger technology with their innovative car and with continued development of the engine, Jabouille appeared in the points for the first time in the US GP towards the end of 1978.

For 1979 the big result came in Jabouille's home GP in July. From pole position, he won a superb race from Villeneuve's Ferrari. Jabouille did not finish in the points again that year, nor for the first half of 1980, until he came through to win the Austrian GP. In September Jabouille injured his legs in a crash in Canada and, although he raced again for Ligier in 1981, he decided to retire after the Argentine GP early in the year.

Below: Innes Ireland won the US GP for Team Lotus in 1961 and was prominent in the sport for several seasons before turning to journalism

Alan JONES
b.1946

Son of a well-known Australian racer of the Fifties, Alan Jones was never short of confidence and bravery. He also had a gritty determination that served him well, netting him a dozen GP victories and a World Championship crown.

Jones began racing in his late teens in the Sixties and then, taking the usual path for ambitious Antipodean drivers, he came to Europe and F3 racing. He managed three seasons in that formula before moving on to bigger single-seaters with two now-defunct formulae, Formula Atlantic and Formula 5000. Jones was quick in both types of car and the graduation to F1 was inevitable. His first taste of Cosworth-DFV power came in 1975 and his first points in a Hill GH1 in the German GP that year, although frankly he didn't look very impressive at times.

Jones drove for Surtees in 1976 without much success but moved to Shadow in 1977, replacing Tom Pryce who had been killed in a tragic accident at Kyalami. Grasping the opportunity, Jones started to improve in leaps and bounds. His first GP win came in Austria in August 1977. James Hunt looked like winning in the rain but his engine expired and it was left to Jones, who had worked himself up to second place with brave overtaking manoeuvres from a mid-grid position, to take the chequered flag.

This result, plus his obvious pace for the rest of 1977, was sufficient to earn him a place in the Williams team for 1978. He didn't win that year but made the most of having the best car in the new FW07 to take four clear wins in 1979, three of which came in a row.

Despite having won more races than anyone else in 1979, Jones was not Champion. For that crown he had to wait until 1980 when five more wins took him to the top of the table. For all his success in the new-generation ground-effect cars, Jones didn't enjoy driving them very much and after two further wins for Williams in 1981 he announced his retirement from the sport.

However, he did reappear in sports cars and money appeared to lure him back for occasional one-off F1 appearances, culminating in a full season with Beatrice-Lola in 1986. Little resulted from this return and Jones finally left the F1 stage.

Jacques LAFFITE
b.1943

In 1986 Jacques Laffite came within one race of being the most experienced GP driver ever up to that time. But a quirk of fate saw his Ligier involved in an accident not of his making. His hapless car pitched into the Brands Hatch barriers and the injuries to his legs ended the long career of this popular and accomplished driver whose love of life and sense of humour made him one of the most popular figures in the GP world.

Laffite was a product of the system of the early Seventies that aimed to produce a French World Champion. He moved through Formula Renault to F3 and then F2, combining this latter racing with some GP drives for Frank Williams' team. In the 1975 German GP he scored the team's best result to date with a sound second place behind Carlos Reutemann's Brabham.

After this initiation with Williams, Laffite began the first of seven seasons with the French Ligier team. A third, two fourths and a second were his rewards and he kept plugging away in the V12 Matra-powered cars until 1977 for a win. This came in an otherwise fruitless season when luck was on Laffite's side and he was there to capitalize on leader Andretti's Lotus running out of fuel. For 1979, Laffite drove the new Ford-engined Ligier JS11 and initially looked like running away with the Championship. He won both the opening South American rounds in fine style. But, apart from a few other placings, that was that for the year and he wound up fourth in the Championship.

Laffite enjoyed some good finishes in 1980 with a win at Hockenheim in the German GP as best result. With Ligier switching back to Matra power for 1981 Laffite continued in his customary manner, picking up placing and scoring two good wins in Austria and Canada, finishing third in the Championship, just six points behind the winner, Nelson Piquet. Compared with 1981, 1982 was a dismal year

Below: Alan Jones was the son of a well-known Australian racer. He worked hard to get to the top and was Champion for Williams in 1980

with just five points to show for 16 races. Switching back to the Williams team for two years improved things marginally, and Laffite returned to the revamped Ligier team in 1985. Driving a French car again, and now in his forties, Laffite showed that he was still quick on his day but he did not win again up to his accident-enforced retirement in July 1986.

Hermann
LANG
b.1909

Hermann Lang was the only one of the elite pre-war Mercedes team to make a successful post-war racing comeback. Having raced motor cycles and sidecars, he joined Mercedes in 1934 as a mechanic but applied himself so completely that he soon earned a drive. That was in 1935 and he immediately proved team manager Neubauer's judgement of him to be correct by finishing strongly in his first race.

Two years later he was given his first full season of racing, winning the Tripoli GP from Rosemeyer's Auto-Union. Lang went on to make this event something of a speciality, winning again in 1938 and 1939.

1939 was Lang's best year, scoring seven outright wins in circuit races and major hill climbs. With the coming of war, Lang would not race again until 1946. Clearly he was older and some of the fire had gone but he was still a great driver. Despite the lack of a top German GP team he tackled a variety of racing, including a 1951 Argentine outing in one of his pre-war GP cars when he finished second to a car 12 years younger.

Lang drove GPs twice for Maserati in 1953 and tackled his last race, the German GP, in one of the new works W196s for the re-formed Mercedes GP team in 1954, making second place behind Fangio before retiring. His best post-war result, also for Mercedes, was victory in the Le Mans 24 Hours in 1952 in a car shared with Fritz Riess.

Niki
LAUDA
b.1949

Before his courageous return to racing after a terrible crash in his Ferrari at the Nürburgring, Niki Lauda was respected by most followers of the sport; but his austere approach and clinical driving allowed other drivers to become more popular.

Lauda's entry to GP racing exemplifies the point. He had raced in junior formulae and sports cars in 1969 and 1970 but rightly saw that the quickest way to progress was to get an F1 drive. The simplest way to do that was to buy it. He hired a March for races in 1971 and 1972 and then he was on his way with BRM. Not that the way was easy in his first year with a team, as the P160E BRM was a dismal car and Lauda scored just one point. However, a Ferrari contract was waiting at the end of the year and Lauda was properly on his way to the top.

He was second first time out in the new Ferrari 312B and in April he won his first GP, in Spain. Success came again in Holland. In 1975 Lauda was clearly the best driver in the best car and he won five times, taking his first Championship in convincing style. The script for 1976 seemed to be the same, with two wins to open the season's account and three more by the time the British GP came around in mid-July. However, James Hunt's McLaren at times had the beating of Lauda's Ferrari and the result was not a foregone conclusion.

The fact that Lauda survived a massive fiery crash during the German GP at the Nürburgring is perhaps only slightly less remarkable than his return to the cockpit just two months later. Still in pain and badly

Left: Hermann Lang was one of the elite band of GP winners for Mercedes in the 1930s. He resumed a successful career after the war

Below: A dedicated and analytical driver, Niki Lauda reached the top and retired but staged a totally successful comeback before retiring again in 1985

Above: Bruce McLaren won his first GP aged just 22 in 1959. He was successful in sports cars and single-seaters right through to his tragic death, testing, in 1970

scarred, he finished fourth in the Italian GP and was third in the USA a month later. The final result of the Championship came down to the last race in Japan. Part-way through the race Lauda decided that the conditions were too dangerous to continue and retired his car, leaving the glory to James Hunt.

However, the challenge was resumed in 1977 and Lauda took the Championship back from Hunt with three wins and six second places to his credit. Moving to Brabham in 1978, he won in Sweden and Italy before enduring his worst season in 1979 with only four points scored. Disillusioned with racing and increasingly preoccupied with his airline business, he decided that the time had come to hang up his helmet.

The helmet would remain hung up for just two years. A new challenge and a big new contract saw Lauda at the wheel of a McLaren for 1982. The new-generation cars were difficult to master but Lauda was up to the job. He won twice in 1982 and used the new Tag-Porsche McLarens to clinch his third Championship in 1984, winning five GPs. The Dutch GP in 1985 took his tally of wins to 25, where it will remain following his final retirement in November that year.

Bruce McLAREN
b.1937 d.1970

New Zealander Bruce McLaren was widely respected as one of the safest drivers around as well as being one of the best and most intuitive test drivers. So it was doubly ironic that his 20-year career should end with an unexplained fatal crash during a CanAm car test session at Goodwood. He was a popular, calm driver, said by some to lack the killer instinct needed for prolonged success.

With his victory in the 1959 US GP at Sebring, 22-year-old McLaren became the youngest-ever winner of a GP. He'd been involved with the sport since his mid teens and had come to Europe as the first beneficiary of the New Zealand 'Driver to Europe' scheme in 1958. He immediately drove in F2 for Cooper, with whom he progressed to F1 alongside Jack Brabham. The US GP victory came with the last race of 1959 and McLaren won the 1960 season-opener in Argentina as well, again in a 2.5-litre Cooper. The latter result, plus some good places, left him runner-up to Jack Brabham in the Championship.

McLaren stayed with the Cooper team until the end of 1965, replacing Brabham who left to form his own team. McLaren's results in this period were consistent, rather than spectacular. He always seemed to be in there somewhere, finishing third or fourth, but no longer in real contention for a win.

In 1966 McLaren left Cooper to drive for his own team, a project he had been developing for several years. It was a fraught year as far as GPs were concerned and the sole bright spot was a sixth place in the Serenissima-powered McLaren M2B in the British GP. However, McLaren's interests went beyond GP racing and he drove a works GT40, shared with Chris Amon, to win the 1966 Le Mans 24 Hours. He won too in CanAm racing in the USA, driving sports racing versions of his own cars, winning the 1967 CanAm Series, a feat he repeated in 1969.

It was McLaren himself who would take first blood in the GP car bearing his own name with a win in Belgium in 1968. His team-mate and compatriot Denny Hulme would score two more wins for the team that year and Bruce McLaren seemed quite content to be regarded as number two driver.

The 1969 season produced a string of top-six placings in GPs to supplement half a dozen CanAm wins. 1970 was going well too with a second-place result in Spain. Then on June 2 came that tragic accident at Goodwood, cheating McLaren of the many years he would doubtless have spent directing his own team to further successes.

Nigel MANSELL
b.1954

Nigel Mansell's no-nonsense approach to racing and his determination to overcome have brought him success against the odds. A successful kart racer in the late Sixties, he fought his way through injury that beset his highly successful years in Formula Ford. He then endured a largely depressing time in F3 but seized the chance of a Lotus F1 testing contract offered after a test session at the end of 1979. He made his GP debut in Austria in 1980 where he made an instant impression.

Nigel Mansell stayed with Lotus for 1981 but this was a fraught season with the banning of the new Lotus 88 twin-chassis car. However, Mansell made it to the winners' podium for the first time, in Belgium, with a good third place, two positions up on his team leader, Elio de Angelis. 1982 was another mediocre year for Mansell with just seven points to show for a busy time. Colin Chapman died late in 1982 and Team Lotus suffered a great blow, although for the latter part of 1983 they at least had the turbo-charged Renault engine to use. This put Lotus back in the hunt and Mansell secured some top-six finishes to boost his flagging morale.

But success was shy in 1985 and Mansell's tally during his final season with Lotus was just 13 points. He moved to the Honda-powered Williams team in 1985 and his personal breakthrough came with his superb victory in the European GP at Brands Hatch. He won again in South Africa two weeks later.

Having proved that he was a winner, Mansell used the FW11 Williams in 1986 to win more GPs than anyone else that year, but lost the Championship to Alain Prost by two points. In 1987 Mansell won six GPs, better even than the five of 1985, but still he didn't win the title which went to team-mate Piquet who won only three races but finished more consistently in the points.

The Williams team lost the use of the Honda engine for 1988 and reverted to normally-aspirated Judd power, and Mansell had only his superb second place in the wet British GP to show for the year before taking the decision to move to Ferrari for 1989. The year started well with a win in Brazil. There followed a spate of retirements before a brilliant summer with two thirds, two seconds and another win, superbly taken, in Hungary. Retirements and a disqualification for reversing in the pit lane during the Portuguese GP were a disappointing end to an encouraging season.

Jochen MASS
b.1946

Jochen Mass was a good, solid, likeable German driver who enjoyed some sound seasons as number two with McLaren, culminating in a single GP win, Spain in 1975. While his GP career may not have placed him among the greats, his sports car career was certainly exceptional with more than 20 outright victories in Championship races.

Mass began his sport with domestic German formulae before racing internationally in F3 and then F2, in which latter category he was runner-up in the 1972 Championship for Team Surtees. Surtees gave him his first taste of F1 in July 1973, bringing him in full-time for 1974. Not a single point resulted, however, and it took a move to McLaren for 1975 for this to change with third place in the Brazilian GP. Mass qualified 11th for the Spanish GP in April but was the lucky one who capitalized on the trail of misfortune and disaster that befell most of the field. In a race shortened after an accident involving spectators, Mass was leading as the flag fell.

Mass continued with McLaren for two further seasons, notching up a string of finishes in the points, the best being a second place in the 1977 Swedish GP. After leaving McLaren, Mass persisted until 1982, driving for ATS and RAM with little success. He retired to concentrate on driving sports cars, latterly for the Mercedes team.

Stirling MOSS
b.1929

It now seems unimportant that Stirling Moss didn't ever win the World Championship because today he is far more famous than most drivers who *have* done so. In each of his active GP years he was either second or third in the title race by a few points. As a driver he was the ultimate all-round professional and succeeded in everything he tackled. He could make indifferent cars look good and good cars look unbelievable.

He shot to fame in the early F3 years of 1948 and 1949 but won his first major race in 1950 — the Tourist Trophy in a Jaguar XK 120. From then on he never looked back and drove a bewildering variety of cars in an incredible number of events. His GP debut came in an F2 HWM in 1951 when he survived the horribly wet conditions to finish a good eighth ahead of some very powerful competition. Other GP drives came his way but successes came instead in single-seater races at home, in sports cars and as part of the Rootes works rally team.

Above: *Germany's Jochen Mass made a solid number two driver at McLaren, winning a GP for the team in 1975 and being placed on many occasions*

Left: *Britain's top driver of recent years has been Isle of Man-domiciled Nigel Mansell who has won for Williams and Ferrari although the Championship has so far eluded him*

Above: Never World Champion but better known to the public than most who were, Stirling Moss enjoyed an incredibly successful career that encompassed many types of motor sport

A desire to drive a British car in the senior formula delayed Moss's rise to real stardom, but eventually he relented and appeared in a Maserati 250F in 1954, scoring notable successes on British circuits and putting up several fine efforts in GPs, latterly as part of the works effort.

The showings in the Maserati led to the number two seat at Mercedes alongside Fangio and a crushing year for the team in the Championship. Moss won his first GP, the British, and was second to Fangio in two others. 1956 was indeed a great year as Moss also won the Targa Florio, Mille Miglia and TT, all in Mercedes 300SLRs.

Mercedes pulled out of racing again in 1955 and Moss returned to Maserati as team leader for 1956, a year of two Championship GPs and many other non-championship wins for the Italian team.

Having won the Daily Express Trophy race at Silverstone for the British Vanwall team in late 1956, Moss moved to them in 1957. It was a good decision and he proceeded to win the British and Italian GPs. He stayed with Vanwall in 1958 and the success continued, interwoven with dozens of other races in Aston Martins, Listers, Ferraris, Maseratis and Coopers. The Cooper connection was developed for 1959 and the string of successes continued with the Nürburgring 1000kms and TT in Aston Martins thrown in, among others, for good measure.

There was no let-up in the frantic pace for 1960 and 1961, in which years Moss's major victories came in Lotus 18s, including Monaco (twice), the US GP and the German GP among the plethora of wins. His final year in competition started in characteristic fashion with three wins in New Zealand but then at Easter 1962 came the serious crash at Goodwood. He survived, but the edge had gone and he decided to retire while still at the top.

Alfred NEUBAUER
b.1890 d.1980

Alfred Neubauer's role was a key one in the success of Mercedes in GP and sports car racing in the pre- and post-war periods. His mastery of team personnel and team tactics was the cornerstone of many great victories.

This physically huge German with a personality to match started his competition career in the cockpit with but modest success before undertaking to manage the Mercedes-Benz racing team in 1926. He masterminded the emergence of the company as a dominant force in the sport in the Thirties, during which time 34 wins were notched up. He was responsible for driver selection and development and while carefully bringing out the best in some characters, could crush the egos of others, when he judged it necessary.

After the war it was not until 1952 that Neubauer was able to exercise his management skills again. Victories at Le Mans in 1952 and in other classic sports car races were under his aegis but his hatted figure is best remembered in the pit lane during the incredible years of 1954/55, when the W196 GP cars ruled the roost until their withdrawal at the end of their second season. 1955 in particular was a year of great success, but also great tragedy with the Le Mans disaster in which a team car had been involved.

Gunnar NILSSON
b.1948 d.1978

This gregarious and friendly Swedish driver managed just two F1 seasons before dying of cancer, aged just 30. He is remembered fondly by those who knew him and there is a single GP win on his racing record to hint at what he might have achieved had he lived longer.

Nilsson didn't race until he was 25, but achieved the British F3 Championship in 1976 and a Lotus contract for 1976 as number two to Mario Andretti. The team was just pulling through a bad patch. Nilsson's third place in the 1976 Spanish GP was, however, ahead of the real recovery which began at the end of the year when the Lotus 77 began to come good. The 78 was even better and Andretti won twice with it before Nilsson's day came at Zolder when he overtook Lauda's Ferrari to lead the final 20 laps.

Nilsson took third in the British GP in July, but thereafter his season tailed off as he suffered more and more from the disease which would kill him. He ran well in Japan in October, reaching second place at one point, but on lap 64 he retired with gear selector failure from what was his last race.

Tazio
NUVOLARI
b.1892 d.1953

An Italian driver still revered as one of the greatest ever, Tazio Nuvolari, 'The Flying Mantuan', showed his brilliance in a remarkable career that lasted for 27 years, even though he didn't tackle his first motor race until the age of 31. Small and thin, he seemed dwarfed by some of the cars he drove. He danced at the wheel, executing huge four-wheel drifts and shirking the use of brakes yet somehow keeping the car on the road.

Nuvolari began racing motor cycles in 1921 and cars a year later. The two sports would run together until he gave up motor-cycle racing in 1930. His first four-wheeled successes were in domestic Italian events driving a Bugatti T35, but it was when he switched to Alfa Romeos run by the Scuderia Ferrari that bigger wins started to come his way. The Mille Miglia and the TT were among the tally from 1930 and in 1931 he won the Italian GP and the Targa Florio. He would win both the Targa and Mille Miglia again in 1932 and 1933 respectively. His win in the other great sports car race, Le Mans, came in 1933, in an Alfa Romeo 8C 2300.

A switch to the Maserati stable for the latter part of 1933 and the 1934 season produced more successes but it was a switch back to Alfa Romeo in 1935–1937 that yielded a string of wins including his most famous victory. This came at the Nürburgring in his outmoded P3 when he beat the might of the German teams in their home GP.

Nuvolari then showed that he was one of few drivers capable of mastering the fearsome rear-engined Auto-Unions. His wins for the team included the Italian and Donington GPs in 1938. His final season with Auto-Union was 1939 before the war. He drove again post-war with one or two good results, including a win in the 1946 Albi GP and second in the 1947 Mille Miglia. But he was ill and frail and could not re-create his pre-war sparkle. Aged 58 and very sick, he won his class in his last race in 1951. He died in Mantua in mid-1953. A statue and piazza plus a dedicated museum in his home town commemorate the career of this great driver.

Carlo
PACE
b.1944 d.1977

This talented, elegant Brazilian driver died in a light aircraft accident six years into an F1 career that seemed to be on the verge of something special. As it was he managed just one GP win in his fourth season but at least it was in front of his home crowd, at Interlagos.

Pace was one of many drivers given a break by Frank Williams who had watched him in F3 and F2 and been impressed. He managed a couple of placings in that first season driving Williams' March before moving to Surtees to drive a TS14 and notching up a few more points in what was a fairly dismal year. Things improved in 1974 when before the British GP the Brabham team called upon Pace to replace the rich but moderately-talented Rikki von Opel, who had failed to qualify the BT44 for the French GP a fortnight before. Pace qualified easily and finished ninth while the best result of the season was second in the US GP in October.

Pace was brilliant in the second race of the 1975 season in Brazil. He beat the challenge of fellow countryman and reigning World Champion Emerson Fittipaldi's McLaren to take his Brabham across the line first. Several more good results followed in what was his best season. Things were difficult in 1976 when Brabham turned to the new V12 Alfa Romeo engine and just seven points came Pace's way. 1977 was just as frustrating and sadly Pace would not live to see the benefit of the endless development hours that he and the team had put into making the Brabham-Alfa work properly.

Ricardo
PATRESE
b.1954

With 14 years' F1 experience and around 200 GPs under his belt, Ricardo Patrese is the most experienced F1 driver in the sport. After initially looking to have all the ingredients that make a great driver he never seemed to deliver the goods. Certainly he

Above: *Nuvolari, the Flying Mantuan, was a legend in Italy whose driving style delighted the crowds and made him a national hero. His career spanned thirty years*

Left: *Carlos Pace was a talented driver whose death in an air crash came before he had fully realized his talents at the wheel*

Above: Didier Pironi celebrates his win in the 1982 Dutch GP. Ironically, after retiring from racing he lost his life in a power-boating accident

Right: Ronnie Peterson was the fastest man in GP racing for several seasons and would have made a worthy World Champion

won two GPs for Brabham, but thereafter he became at best a midfield runner for four seasons and was largely disregarded as a serious contender. However, in 1989 his drives for Williams were mature and impressive and he came home six times in the top three, finishing third in the Championship.

Patrese honed his car control skills in karts and dominated Italian and European F3 in 1976, tackling F2 the following year. He joined the Shadow GP team for the Monaco GP in 1977 as they were recovering from the tragedy of Tom Pryce's death. Patrese drove again as F2 commitments allowed. His first point came in the last GP of the year, in Japan.

Moving to the newly-formed Arrows team in 1978 saw a second place in the Swedish GP but little else by way of success before two lacklustre seasons of the odd point here and there. Patrese's headstrong driving gained him some criticism from fellow drivers and he was actually banned, perhaps unfairly, from the 1978 US GP.

Patrese's two years with Brabham in 1982/83 saw him win the Monaco GP in his first season and the final race of 1983, in South Africa. He then moved to Alfa Romeo where a miserable eight points in 1984 looked almost healthy compared with a complete duck in 1985. He went back to Brabham for two more desultory seasons and then went to Williams in 1988, partnering Nigel Mansell in the Judd-powered cars. Points were few and far between for Williams that year as they struggled against turbocharged cars. However, things were on a more equal footing in 1989 with the enforcement of normally-aspirated engines. Boutsen may have won two races for Williams but Patrese was consistently in the points and finished above his team-mate in the Championship.

Ronnie PETERSON
b.1944 d.1978

Ronnie Peterson, known as 'Super Swede', was a driver with star quality. The crowds liked him for his extrovert style while his fellow drivers admired him for his car control and general demeanor. He would have made a good World Champion and looked set to be one but he never quite pulled it off. Nevertheless, the record books show an impressive string of victories in a variety of cars.

Peterson followed the time-honoured route through karting and junior formulae to F1 in 1971, driving a private March but with no success. He moved to the works March team for 1971 and a string of second places took him to second slot in the Championship, albeit a long way behind the winner, Jackie Stewart.

Peterson remained with the March team, alongside Niki Lauda, for 1972, but the 721

series cars were poor, as were the results, and it took a move to Lotus before Peterson hit a winning streak. He was already widely regarded as the fastest driver in F1 but it wasn't until the 1973 French GP that he took the elusive chequered flag. He won again in Austria, Italy and the USA but was only fourth in the Championship.

Team Lotus stayed with the ageing 72D model for 1974 but this didn't prevent Peterson taking three more wins. Lotus attempted to find a fifth season in the 72D, and even Peterson could do nothing with it that year. He could do little with the new 77 and left the team in early 1976 to drive for March once again. He pulled something of an ace out of the hat by winning the Italian GP in fine style from Reggazoni's Ferrari.

The March had little more to offer for 1977 so Peterson tried his hand with the Tyrrell six-wheeler which looked a good bet. But the expected domination of 1977 did not happen as these unique cars were beset by problems and had lost their advantage. So it was back to Lotus in 1978 as number two to Mario Andretti, where Peterson at last got his hands on a competitive car again with the Lotus 78. He won in South Africa and again in Austria.

Then came that disastrous day in Monza when a first-lap shunt left Peterson with multiple injuries and blood clots that would take his life. He posthumously finished second in the Championship, having notched up 10 wins in an entertaining career.

Nelson
PIQUET
b.1952

An enthusiastic, natural driver, Nelson Piquet has suffered a diminished reputation in recent seasons as the results have failed to keep coming.

He came from Brazil to embark upon a very successful programme of F3 in Europe and, as seemed to happen to most talented Brazilians, he was quickly on the road to F1 stardom. His first GP experience came with Mo Nunn's small Ensign Team in July 1978 when he managed 32 laps of the German GP. Piquet then drove the BS Fabrications McLaren M23 in Holland and Italy, recording his first finish in the latter event, in ninth place. His third car of the year was a Brabham Alfa in Canada in the last race of the year.

This led to a full-time seat with Brabham for 1979 but the BT48 was unsuccessful and the BT49 needed development so real success had to wait until 1980. Three wins in the now very quick Cosworth-powered Brabham BT49, starting with victory in the US West GP from pole position, left Piquet runner-up in the Championship. He was immediately on the pace in the 1981 season and notched up three more wins, beating Reutemann to the Championship by one point.

The 1982 season brought only one win as Brabham made the change to turbocharged engines. These were fully on song for 1983 and Piquet topped the tables for his second Championship. He remained with Brabham until the end of 1985, winning three more races before switching to Williams to drive with Nigel Mansell. Piquet won four races that year and three the next, just pipping his team-mate for the 1987 Championship, despite scoring fewer wins. Mansell winning so many races and on occasions beating him fair and square was probably one of Piquet's reasons behind his decision to decamp to Lotus for 1988, besides which Williams were losing their Honda engines.

Sadly Team Lotus was not in good shape for 1988, nor indeed the following year, and Piquet gradually lost form, along with the cars, and slowly slipped from the leader board. The final ignominy was the failure of the three-times Champion to qualify for the 1989 Belgian GP.

Didier
PIRONI
b.1952 d.1987

Another product of the French GP-driver 'production line', Didier Pironi brought considerable flair to his sport, but underlying it was confidence verging on the arrogant.

So many French drivers have been brought on by Ken Tyrrell and Pironi was among them, joining the Surrey-based team in 1978. He qualified last for his first race but improved as he came to grips with the 008 model. However, that first season tailed off in mechanical failures. 1979 was a little better but Pironi moved to the French Ligier team for 1980. The move worked and he won the Belgian GP in May, driving with superb style and confidence and leading from start to finish. A second, three thirds and a fourth left him with a useful end-of-season score and fifth place in the Championship.

With Jody Scheckter retiring in 1980, Ferrari called upon Pironi to partner Villeneuve at Maranello for 1981. Moving to the Italian team was a brave move as the results from 1980 had been poor. However, the cars proved themselves capable of winning, but it was Villeneuve who was getting the results. In the fourth round of the 1982 Championship the friendly relationship that had existed between Villeneuve and Pironi evaporated when Pironi ignored team orders and took the lead and victory from his team-mate on the last lap. The rivalry thus inflamed would cost Villeneuve his life, trying too hard to out-qualify Pironi during practice for the Belgian GP just two weeks later.

Below: Nelson Piquet upheld the tradition of Brazilian driving talent by winning three World Championship titles

Above: *Alain Prost, on right, captured on film during a rare moment of harmony with one-time McLaren team-mate Ayrton Senna*

Pironi was second in Monaco, third in Detroit and then came his second win for Ferrari after a fine drive at Zandvoort. The accumulation of points continued with second in the British GP and third in the French. Pironi was looking good for the Championship with four rounds to go. Then, in practice for the German GP at Hockenheim, his Ferrari drove into the back of Prost's slowing Renault and launched itself into the air. In the resulting accident Pironi's legs were broken so badly that he never raced again.

Cheated of his speed thrills in cars, Pironi moved to powerboats and sadly he was killed in an accident in 1987 when his craft flipped during a race.

Alain
PROST
b.1955

With more GP victories to his name than any other driver, and three World Championships to boot, Alain Prost must rightly be regarded as being among the greatest of all F1 drivers. His delightfully simple, single-minded approach to winning and the apparently trouble-free manner in which he achieves it may not make him the crowd's favourite but everyone must admire his professionalism and craftsmanship.

Prost dominated Formula Renault and F3 in his formative years and, having won the Euro F3 title, went straight into F1 with McLaren for 1980. McLaren was not the dominant team at that period so Prost worked hard for a few points that first year, driving the last of the old-style chassis. He moved to the French Renault team for the 1981 season to see if he had more luck there.

The season started poorly until the arrival of the new RE30 models. Then the results started to come, beginning with Prost's victory in the all-important French GP. This was the start of three good seasons with Renault during which Prost would win nine GPs altogether. Not even four wins in 1983 were enough to win him the Championship, though. Nor were a remarkable seven wins once Prost was back racing for McLaren in 1984. By now the McLaren team was on the upswing and their professionalism exactly dovetailed with Prost's approach to the sport. The combination was formidable.

Prost had to wait until 1985 for the Championship to be his. He held on to it in 1986, narrowly keeping it from Nigel Mansell. By Prost's standards 1987 was an average year with 'just' three wins and fourth place in the Championship. But in 1988 he equalled his record with another seven wins, topped only by team-mate Ayrton Senna who notched up just one more and took the Championship.

Many observers felt that Prost's business-like, unruffled manner might suffer as a result of this rivalry with Senna, yet ultimately it was Prost who won the 1989 showdown. He took four wins, in America, Britain, Italy and France, and added sufficient other points to beat even the six GP wins posted by Senna. Prost became Champion for the third time. His seven years with McLaren had brought an incredible 30 GP wins, taking his total to the end of the 1989 season to 39 Championship GP victories. He took the start number 1 to Ferrari for 1990.

Clay
REGGAZONI
b.1940

This characterful Swiss driver notched up five wins in a variable career. He was fast yet unpredictable, but he was also a winner on his day.

His F1 career lasted exactly 10 years and started in 1970 with Ferrari for whom he had driven F2 in 1969. He joined the F1 effort part-way through the season at a time when the flat-12 312B was still being sorted out. Teamed with Jackie Ickx, Reggazoni was soon putting in good performances and these culminated in his win at Monza in September. He made other good results, including three second places, and ended up third in the Championship in his first year. His only 1971 win was in the non-championship Race of Champions in Britain; otherwise it was a disappointing year. In 1972 the Ferraris were off the pace apart from a few good showings and ultimately the team would withdraw to regroup in 1973.

Regazzoni meanwhile left to join BRM for 1973 but suffered a miserable time. He was therefore happy to be back on the strength at Maranello in 1974. He embarked upon his best season and, although he only won one GP, in Germany, he was placed in 10 others and missed the Championship by a mere three points. He was in there pitching again in 1975 with a second win in the Italian GP top of his results. One GP per year seemed to be the Reggazoni norm and in 1976 it duly came at Long Beach, USA. However, his 31 Championship points weren't enough to keep his seat at Ferrari and he departed for Ensign in 1977.

Five points for his new team in 1977 reflected more on the car than on Reggazoni but he was similarly out of luck with the Shadow team in 1978. Some onlookers might have suggested that retirement was on the cards for the 38-year-old but nothing was further from his mind; or from Frank Williams' mind for that matter.

Duly settled in to the number two Williams FW07, Reggazoni embarked upon his final good season. He was a fine second at Monaco and then came his customary single GP win, at Silverstone, the first for the Williams team. For 1980, Reutemann replaced Reggazoni at Williams, as indeed he had done at Ferrari. Reggazoni went back to Ensign for his 11th season of F1. Just four races into the year it all ended sadly with a crash at Long Beach when the brake pedal failed and the car hit the barriers at speed, damaging Reggazoni's legs and leaving him wheelchair bound.

Carlos REUTEMANN
b.1940

This complicated, serious-minded Argentine driver with a real dedication to racing seemed to lack the final grain of determination it needs to succeed. He was nearly World Champion several times and should have pulled it off in 1981; but he failed to score in the last two races and lost by one point. When he felt like it he was brilliant; at other times he was feeble. His heart for racing disappeared completely in 1982 and he retired early in a season when he was still quite capable of winning races.

Reutemann moved to Europe in 1970 to drive F2 in a Brabham and it was with this team that he moved to F1 in 1972. In his third season with them he won the South African GP and more than a year later won again at the Nürburgring. 1975 was a good year and Reutemann was third in the Championship.

During his fifth season with Brabham, Reutemann became disillusioned with the team's new Alfa Romeo engine and bought himself out of his contract to stand in for the injured Lauda in the Ferrari team for the Italian GP. Lauda was back in time to race and the Scuderia ran three cars for that event only, with Reutemann finishing ninth.

He joined Ferrari full-time in 1977, putting on a sound showing but being overshadowed by team-mate Lauda who took the World Championship. When Lauda left in 1978, Reutemann took over as number one, winning four GPs. Sadly for him, Andretti won six and with them the title.

Reutemann made a bad move in 1979. His transfer to Lotus was initially promising but as the season wore on, so the cars moved backwards down the grid. Reutemann's final team in F1 was Williams who always provided him with a competitive car. He won at Monaco in 1980 and then started an amazing run of 15 points finishes that lasted until the middle of the 1981 season. These results included two 1981 wins, at Rio and Zolder, and it was that 1981 tally that so nearly won him the Championship. He retired after the Brazilian GP in March 1982.

Peter REVSON
b.1939 d.1974

Peter Revson was heir to a fortune and raced for fun in the early Sixties in America, but the fun developed into a serious career. His first stab at GP racing in a non-works Lotus BRM came in 1963 but he failed to qualify at Monaco. He tried again in Belgium, qualified midfield but retired. The story was similar in the other four GPs he attempted in 1964 so Revson stepped back to F2 and F3 to gain more experience.

By 1965 he moved back to the States and drove sports cars, stock cars and Indy single-

Above: *Clay Reggazoni who enjoyed 11 seasons in the premier formula before a crash at Long Beach ended his colourful career*

Left: *American Peter Revson worked hard to shed the 'playboy driver' image and proved that he was a significant talent at the wheel of a GP car*

Right: Mexican Pedro Rodriguez during his 1968 season with BRM for whom he secured a great win at Spa, two years later

seaters for the rest of the decade, establishing himself as a very useful driver and scoring some notable successes.

Revson's performances in McLarens during 1970 gained him a place in the McLaren Team for CanAm and USAC racing for 1971 and this became a contract for the F1 season in 1972, alongside Denny Hulme in the M19s. Revson showed well from the off and scored his first points in South Africa with third spot. He placed in a further five rounds and was fifth in the Championship even though he had missed two rounds due to Indianapolis commitments.

In 1973, the misfortune of another McLaren team member assisted Revson in gaining his first win. Jody Scheckter spun across the front of the field at Silverstone, causing a multiple pile-up that necessitated a re-start. Revson seized his opportunity and drove his new M23 skilfully through a rain shower to win his first GP, leading home Peterson and Hulme. He won again at Mosport and for the second time was fifth in the Championship.

However, all was not well in the McLaren team and Revson departed for Shadow in 1974. His obvious potential would never be fully realized as he was killed in a testing accident after suspension failure before the South African GP in March.

Jochen
RINDT
b.1942 d.1970

In someone less talented and exciting to watch in a racing car, the arrogance displayed occasionally by Jochen Rindt would have been unforgivable. As it was, the entertainment value of this Austrian once seated in a car was sufficient to outweigh his manner out

Right: Jochen Rindt in pensive mood before the start of the 1968 German GP. He was posthumous World Champion in 1970

of it. He is remembered for several brilliant GP victories and the sad record of being racing's only posthumous World Champion.

Rindt was in F2 by 1964 where he started to be impressive. A full year in F1 for Cooper followed, but the Cooper-Climaxes were off the pace and Rindt did well to finish fourth in the German GP. Meanwhile he had co-driven the Le Mans-winning Ferrari and put on more good showings in F2. Cooper switched to Maserati engines in 1966 but they were unreliable and heavy and made the T81 difficult to drive. Nevertheless, Rindt put in some fine drives, coming second at Spa in June.

Rindt, however, was not a gentle driver and it was his team-mate John Surtees who scored the first win for the Cooper Maserati. Pedro Rodriguez did it it again with the first race of 1967, South Africa. Annoyed and frustrated, Rindt's GP performances tailed off. Nevertheless he continued to dominate F2 through 1967 and into 1968, scoring a record number of wins. A move to Brabham for F1 in 1968 proved to be a bad decision as their Repco engines were terribly unreliable.

A move to Lotus in 1969 reversed the trend. The Lotus 49s were potentially fast, but fragile, and it wasn't until the end of the year that Rindt won at Watkins Glen in a race marred by a bad accident involving team-mate Graham Hill. Rindt took over as number one at Team Lotus for 1970. Initially the results were still elusive, the new 72 model needing more work. Saddled with an aged 49 for the Monaco GP in May, Rindt produced his best-ever drive and won brilliantly. The 72 came good from the Dutch GP and Rindt won four times on the trot. He went to the Italian GP in September with a huge lead in the Championship. In the second practice session his car veered into the Armco barrier and Rindt was killed, just three races before his expected retirement, as World Champion.

Pedro
RODRIGUEZ
b.1940 d.1971

Pedro Rodriguez was the more successful and longer-lived of two Mexican racing brothers. He was a passionate, fearless racer whose car control was legendary. He was killed aged only 31 but he had packed in more than 12 years of competitive driving.

Both Rodriguez brothers drove various cars in Mexican events before racing sports cars in North America. Brother Ricardo initially made the best progress and drove GPs for Ferrari in 1961 and 1962. However, he lost his life in a practice accident in 1962 and Pedro was left to carry on alone.

Driving Ferraris for the North American Racing Team, Rodriguez established himself as a top-flight sports car driver, interlacing this racing with the odd GP outing. After a poor 1966 season, his big break came in 1967 with a one-off drive for Cooper in the South African GP. He showed he was not just fearless but also considerate about cars and he brought the Cooper Maserati home first, earning himself a contract for the rest of the year. He didn't win again but was the most successful Cooper driver that season.

Rodriguez moved to BRM in 1968 and ran consistently. His Le Mans victory in a GT40 was the high point of the season. 1969 was a bad season in a non-works BRM but, returning to the works team to drive the P153 V12 cars in 1970, he won his greatest victory in a wet and treacherous Belgian GP at Spa.

On that day Rodriguez was uncatchable, as he was often through 1970 and 1971 in the Porsche 917 sports cars. He won four Championship rounds in each season but the latter one was cut short by his fatal crash in a minor German event in July.

Keke
ROSBERG
b.1948

Finn Keke Rosberg proved that becoming World Champion wasn't necessarily all about winning races. He won just one GP in his Championship year but finished high up in enough other races to take the title. In later seasons he won a handful more GPs but he is remembered best for his exuberant driving style and his hard-working yet unconventional approach to being a racing driver.

He reached F1 via junior formulae which culminated in Formula Atlantic and F2 where his driving was always exciting and the car was permanently on the limit of adhesion. He rose to F1 in 1978 with ATS and Wolf and his struggles with unsuccessful cars didn't get any easier when he moved to the Fittipaldi team

for 1980 and 1981. He had one good finish in 1980 but it was a desperate couple of years.

The turning-point came when Alan Jones left the Williams team at the end of 1981 and Rosberg was drafted in as replacement for 1982, driving as number two to Carlos Reutemann. Handed a good car, Rosberg immediately moved from the back to the front of the grid. He was fifth in the opening South African race and second in Brazil and America although the Brazilian result was scratched after the FW07 Williams was found to be underweight. Then Reutemann abruptly retired and Rosberg found himself as number one in a top team. He grasped the opportunity to score a string of seconds and thirds. He finally won a race, the Swiss GP held at Dijon. Come September he was World Champion, having scored not one point the previous season.

Rosberg enjoyed three more good seasons with Williams, winning at Monaco, Dallas, Detroit and Australia before moving to McLaren for 1986. Whereas the Williams had suited Rosberg's wayward driving style, the McLaren did not. While his team-mate Alain Prost won four races and the Championship, it was a very disappointing year for the Finn who didn't win a race and retired at the end of the season.

Bernd
ROSEMEYER
b.1909 d.1938

Bernd Rosemeyer was another of those great pre-war drivers who became a German national hero in the Thirties. His career was short and brilliant and he never raced anything but an Auto-Union. It was certainly one of the most difficult cars to drive, its rear

Left: Heavy-smoking Finn Keke Rosberg, whose energetic driving style took him to the World Championship

Above: One of the biggest stars of the pre-war Auto-Union team was Bernd Rosemeyer, pictured here at the start of his second race, at Montlhery, in 1935

victories. 1937 was an even greater year as he won the Eifelrennen again and the Vanderbilt Cup in the USA, and thrilled the British crowds with a breathtaking win in the Donington GP. Sadly he died in a record attempt on a new German autobahn the following January.

Ludovico SCARFIOTTI
b.1933 d.1968

Ludovico Scarfiotti was an urbane Italian from a wealthy background. He matured into a top-rank sports car driver and drove well in 10 F1 races, winning a single GP, his home event at Monza.

After eight years racing small sports cars and Formula Junior single-seaters, Scarfiotti found his way into the works Ferrari team at Le Mans in 1962. He remained with the team to drive in hill climbs, winning the European Mountain Championship that year. In circuit racing he enjoyed a good 1963 season co-driving the winning cars at Sebring and Le Mans, and coming second in the Targa Florio. His pace in sports cars earned him his first F1 drive at the Dutch GP in June where he managed sixth place before crashing a week later at Reims and missing the rest of the year.

His success in sports cars continued through 1964 and 1965 and brought him back into the Ferrari F1 team in 1966, first in the German GP and then with the third team car entered in the Italian GP. The cars for Monza featured the new, powerful V12 and Scarfiotti used it well to win from Mike Parkes' similar car. Being an Italian, winning in a Ferrari in Italy made him a hero. But Scarfiotti was not given a permanent place in the F1 team and it wasn't until the death of Bandini in 1967 that Scarfiotti found himself back in the team. However it was a poor year in the premier formula although Scarfiotti still returned some good results in sports cars.

He parted with Ferrari at the end of 1967 and signed to drive for Cooper in GPs and for Porsche in sports cars. Two fourth places were the early-season rewards in F1 before Scarfiotti fatally crashed his Porsche in a hill climb at Rossfeld in Germany.

engine and tricky handling making it a knife-edge job keeping the immensely powerful machine on the track. It is said that his lack of experience in cars helped him drive the Auto-Unions; simply he didn't know any better and just got on with the job of going as fast as possible.

Rosemeyer drove motor cycles for the DKW division of Auto-Union and from there made his way to the four-wheeled racing team. Despite his lack of car racing experience he was tenacious and his first drive came in 1935. From this race he retired but in his second event at the Nürburgring he led, being passed by Carraciola within sight of the finish. His talent in the Auto-Union was undeniable and he embarked upon three glorious seasons with the team.

He won his first GP at the end of 1935 and the following season added the German, Swiss and Italian GPs to his growing list of

Jody SCHECKTER
b.1950

Jody Scheckter survived several seasons of living life on the edge to mature from an impulsive, reckless driver into an aggressive but successful one.

His route to F1 was brief and direct.

Right: 1979 World Champion, South African Jody Scheckter, during his Tyrrell years

Saloon racing in his home country of South Africa brought him to England for part of a Formula Ford season in 1970, then F3 in 1971 and onwards into F1 with McLaren who took him on board for the US GP in October. He drove for them again in 1973, leading the French GP for a time in July and crashing spectacularly at Silverstone later that month.

Ken Tyrrell thought that something could be made out of this raw talent and signed up the young South African for 1974. His first finish in the points came in Spain; just five weeks later he was first in Sweden. He won again in the British GP at Brands Hatch and came third in the Championship in his first proper year of GPs. Tyrrell stayed with the 007 model for 1975 and the results started to slip slightly, although Scheckter did win his home GP, at Kyalami.

Tyrrell then startled the Grand Prix world with the remarkable six-wheeler P34 in 1976. It turned out to be more successful than most observers expected. It was soon working effectively and Scheckter went on to win the Swedish GP and was second on four occasions.

In the light of the Tyrrell's potential, Scheckter's move to the new Wolf team for 1977 seemed strange. But he had chosen well and won the first race of the season at Buenos Aires. This was no fluke as he won again at Monaco and in Canada. Lauda was Champion but Scheckter was next up. The Wolf was no longer a front runner in 1978 and, with the lack of results, it surprised many that Scheckter received the call from Maranello for 1979, to drive the 312T4.

Scheckter found himself back in a very competitive car — so competitive, in fact, that he won three GPs and beat his team-mate Gilles Villeneuve to the Championship by four points. In contrast to 1979, 1980 was a dire year for Ferrari. Having scored just two points all season, Scheckter retired after the US GP in October, aged just 30.

Richard
SEAMAN
b.1913 d.1939

Richard Seaman was a well-educated and attractive driver who became the sole Briton to find a place in the great German GP racing teams of the Thirties.

Seaman's first successes came racing an MG Magnette internationally in 1934. This led to the acquisition of an ERA single-seater which he ran for two seasons with success, including several wins. He then made a famous decision to abandon the ERA and run instead a modified version of a 1927 GP Delage, despite its considerable age. The gamble paid off and Seaman notched up notable successes in major races in Britain and Europe running in the 1.5-litre class and under Formula Libre.

His interests had by now expanded to take in other cars, including the Alfa Romeo which he co-drove to victory in the 1936 Donington GP. Seaman's successes, particularly in the Delage, brought him to the attention of Mercedes-Benz team manager Alfred Neubauer. This resulted in Seaman joining their mighty Mercedes team for 1937, revamped after a poor 1936 season.

The Mercedes-Benz GP cars were larger and more powerful than anything Seaman had driven but after a spate of crashes he mastered the driving technique. He was top Mercedes driver in the 1937 Vanderbilt Cup in the USA, reputed to be the world's richest race. In 1938 Seaman had his greatest moment when he won the German GP, beating Lang and Caracciola to the flag. He also led the Swiss GP in great style before ceding to Caracciola and finishing second.

With war on the horizon, Seaman remained in Germany for the start of the 1939 season. It was to be his last. While leading the wet Belgian GP at Spa he crashed with 13 laps to go and died from terrible injuries.

Ayrton
SENNA
b.1960

Admired by some for his consummate skill and detested by others for his ruthless, totally confident driving style and offhand manner, Brazilian Ayrton Senna has proved himself to be one of the greatest talents ever in F1. He shattered Jim Clark's record of 33 pole positions in 1989 and in 1988 set the record for the most GP wins in a season, eight.

He began karting and came to Britain in

Above: Richard Seaman was the most successful British driver of the Thirties, graduating to the world-beating Mercedes GP team

Above: Record-breaking Brazilian star Ayrton Senna in thoughtful mood before embarking upon another winning drive

Below: Swiss driver Jo Siffert whose best win was the British GP in 1968 in a Lotus, although he also built up an impressive tally of successes in sports cars

1981 to shine in Formula Ford. This led to a dominant year in F3 with a record number of wins. A single season with Toleman in 1984 allowed his talent to shine occasionally in a difficult car. He almost won in Monaco and finished third in the last race of the year before moving to Lotus under a flurry of legal action alleging breach of contract. Teamed with de Angelis, Senna enjoyed the best Team Lotus season for several years. He won convincingly in the wet in Portugal and was first again in Belgium. He started seven of the 16 races from pole position.

Two more GP wins came in 1986 before Lotus switched to Honda power for 1987. The car was not as consistent as the Williams opposition: Senna won three races and was third in the Championship.

Senna's move to McLaren in 1988 saw him find his real niche and thus began a shatteringly dominant period for one make of car. Given the right equipment and a brilliant team back-up, Senna won a straight eight GPs and the World Championship along with them. He would have won more races but for occasional recklessness and errors of judgement. 1989 saw more races in the same brilliant fashion and Senna notched up a further six wins. Yet Alain Prost was equal to the challenge and had fortune on his side. With the greatest reluctance, Senna had to relinquish his Championship to his team-mate, until the next time.

Jo
SIFFERT
b.1936 d.1971

Mild-mannered and diminutive Swiss-born Jo Siffert was a tiger at the wheel of a racing car. He was exciting to watch but not as precise as a consistent winner needs to be. Nevertheless, he won races and was a favourite with the crowds who saw him in F1 and sports cars.

Like so many successful drivers before him, his taste for speed was first sated on motor cycles before switching to four wheels. From 1960 to 1962 he was prominent in Formula Junior before flirting with F1 in 1963. He ran his own Brabham-BRM in 1964, managing a good fourth in the German GP in August and a fine third at Watkins Glen at the end of the year, his efforts by then under the managership of Rob Walker.

With the coming of the 3-litre F1 formula for 1966, Siffert switched to a Cooper Maserati but had a poor time, scoring just a handful of placings through to the end of 1967. 1968 brought Siffert's F1 breakthrough in the Rob Walker Lotus 49. He convincingly won the British GP after the retirement of the works Lotus entries and set the fastest lap for good measure. 1969 was not so good but Siffert was still in there driving hard and produced one or two finishes in the points.

Supplementing his success in GP racing, Siffert had a good season driving works Porsches, winning four rounds of the series. Six major wins in sports cars followed in 1969 and three the next year. His last win came at the start of 1971, although he was subsequently second at Spa and Watkins Glen.

For the 1970 GP season, Siffert broke with Rob Walker to drive for the new March team. It was a miserable year and he didn't appear in the results again until turning to BRM in 1971. His season built up as the P160 improved and culminated in a win at record speed in the Austrian GP. The season ended on a high note with a second place in the US GP in October just three weeks before Siffert crashed in a non-championship race at Brands Hatch and died from his injuries.

Jackie
STEWART
b.1939

Jackie Stewart's professional and sensible approach to his race driving was a key element in the move of GP racing forward into the new era. This jovial and sometimes truculent Scotsman didn't believe that motor racing owed him a living; he knew that he had to earn it from his team, his sponsors and the crowd. Earn it he did during a great career.

His ability was evident from early competitive outings in a variety of road cars and it took him to tremendous F3 success with Ken Tyrrell in 1964, finding time to tackle some F2 races as well, rounding off the year with a good showing in a non-championship F1 race in South Africa.

He accepted BRM's offer of a full season in GP racing for 1965 with Graham Hill and was in the points first time out as indeed he was in the next five races that season. In Italy, fate smiled on Stewart; Clark's Lotus stopped with fuel pump trouble while leading, leaving the two BRMs of Hill and Stewart in control. With one lap to go Hill made a slight mistake and Stewart was able to go past to win his first GP. The second win came at the start of the 1966 season in Monaco following victory in the Tasman series earlier in the year. The 1966 season was marred by an accident in Belgium, costing Stewart a lay-off and missing two races. However, he was back in July to wrestle with the unsuccessful 16-cylinder BRMs for the remainder of that season and the next, with little to show for it, despite taking over as number one with the departure of Graham Hill to Lotus.

While struggling with a poor car in F1, Stewart was winning regularly for his old team manager Ken Tyrrell, now in F2. It was this renewed association that would lead the Tyrrell team into F1, with the specially-conceived Elf-sponsored Matra-Fords. The new car was a delight and Stewart won in Holland, Germany and the USA, finishing Championship runner-up to Graham Hill.

1969 was even better and a crushing six GP wins saw Stewart wrest the Championship by a huge margin. Matra wanted Tyrrell to use the Matra V12 for 1970 but Ken Tyrrell had other plans and opted to run a March until the first of his own Tyrrell chassis was ready. Stewart found the car a handful but defended his title manfully, notching up a win in Spain and a couple of seconds elsewhere. But it was a poor year by his standards, even after the new Tyrrell appeared in the autumn.

For 1971, the new Tyrrell had been sorted and Stewart set out to get his Championship back. He was successful and won six times. Four wins in 1972 were not sufficient to hold the title in a season where Stewart suffered stress-induced health problems. He pulled through and won his third title in 1973, taking his tally of GP wins to 27. He announced his retirement at the end of the year to concentrate full-time on his varied business interests that take him constantly round the world and keep him in the public eye.

John
SURTEES
b.1934

Straight-talking John Surtees was already famous before he ever drove a racing car in anger. His seven World Motor Cycle Championships for MV had seen to that. The transition to cars was made without catching breath and through Formula Junior he shot to F1 prominence with a startling second place in a works Lotus in the 1960 British GP.

More F1 drives followed in 1961 in the Yeoman Credit Cooper team with just four points from eight races. His 1963 season with his own Lola improved mid-season with good second places in Britain and Germany, but then the results tailed off.

When Enzo Ferrari renewed an offer to drive for the Scuderia in 1963, Surtees accepted. The first year in Italian colours produced one win and some placings; but in 1964 Surtees won the German and Italian races and added enough points to take the Championship. He thus became the first man to be two- and four-wheeled World Champion. He was also the hero of Italy, not least for winning the Italian GP in a Ferrari!

There were no GP wins for Surtees in 1965 and the good start to his 1966 season with the new V12 312 model was wiped out when his already fragile relationship with the team manager exploded and Surtees walked out. Nevertheless, he finished the season on a high note by winning the Mexican GP in the bulky Cooper Maserati. He turned to the Honda team in 1967, devoting himself to what was a rather half-hearted factory project. With Surtees' input, a Lola-inspired revised chassis was developed for the second part of the season. Surtees used it well, winning the Italian GP in September. He had one more season with Honda before the project folded rather messily at the end of 1968.

While the F1 scene may not have held many pleasures for Surtees in 1965–67, he fared well in sports cars, particularly driving his Lola T70 in the United States; in all he recorded seven major wins in this model.

Surtees suffered a miserable F1 season with BRM in 1969 and this led him to decide to build and drive his own F1 car. This was a logical extension of the existing Team Surtees F5000 and Lola racing project. The F1 TS/

Below: Jackie Stewart brought a new brand of professionalism to motor sport. He directed his considerable talent to maximum effect and remains a popular figure much in the public eye

made its debut in July at the British GP in 1972. The car showed promise, but in two seasons racing it the results sheets revealed very little. Surtees retired from driving after two races in 1972, concentrating full-time on running the Team Surtees through to its demise in 1978.

Patrick
TAMBAY
b.1949

This debonair and sensitive Frenchman had a changeable career that saw him with some great opportunities but some bad breaks. He won only two GPs but they were good ones to win, and he is remembered with affection in the sport that he left at the end of 1988.

Tambay made the most of the excellent opportunities and schemes to encourage French talent in the early Seventies. Via Formula Renault he was in F2 in 1974 and stayed there for three seasons. His move to CanAm racing Stateside and the 1977 Championship enhanced his good reputation and made him ripe for an F1 drive. It came with Ensign in 1977 and things seemed to be looking up with a move to the top-line McLaren team for 1978. But McLaren fortunes were on the wane and two seasons produced just a few points.

Deciding that this was doing him no good at all, Tambay elected to return to CanAm racing for 1980 and won the Championship for the second time. Second time around in F1 he tackled six races for Theodore in 1981, but the cars simply weren't on the pace and he moved to Ligier for the last eight races of the year. This gamble failed miserably

Below: Patrick Tambay who had a changeable career with the high points coming during his seasons with Ferrari

and Tambay didn't finish again that year.

When his friend Gilles Villeneuve was killed practising for the Belgian GP, Tambay was called upon to fill the vacant seat at Ferrari and drive the competitive 126C2. He rose to the challenge and was soon finishing in the points, beginning with a third at Brands Hatch. His first win came in Germany in August and he was second in the Italian GP later in the year. René Arnoux joined Tambay at Ferrari in 1983 and would ultimately win three races for the team that year. Tambay would win just one. But it was an important one to him for it came in Italy, at San Marino, where Villeneuve's win had been 'stolen' by Pironi the year before. Tambay featured in the results many more times in 1983 before moving to Renault.

Renault had passed their best by 1984 and two seasons of hard work were not particularly productive. For his final season Tambay joined the Lola F1 effort, but it was a year of struggle with a troublesome car and he retired at the season's end.

Piero
TARUFFI
b.1906 d.1988

Piero Taruffi was a multi-talented driver/engineer of the old school who led an incredibly varied life of which motor sport was but a part. Yet it was a significant part and was enjoyed on both two and four wheels.

He started competing aged just 17 and, assisted by his father, embarked upon a career that would last for more than 30 years. He drove Bugattis, Alfas, Italas and Maseratis from 1930, all the time maintaining a busy and successful schedule of motor-cycle racing. His results in cars were consistently good rather than spectacular and his best results would come after the war.

Driving a little Cisitalia, Taruffi enjoyed excellent seasons in 1947 and 1948 and by 1951 he was at last in the works Ferrari team. That year he won the gruelling Carrera Panamericana and scored points in Championship GPs for Ferrari. His first GP win was in the 1952 Swiss GP (held to F2 regulations) and he was consistently quick through the year, finishing third in the Championship.

Driving Lancias in 1953 brought little joy, but a win in the 1954 Targa Florio was an overdue reward. He drove once in a GP for Ferrari that year and again in 1955 before joining Mercedes-Benz for the final events of the year. He was fourth in the team's 1-2-3-4 at Aintree and second to team-leader Fangio in Italy. Nearing his fifties, Taruffi appeared in two 1957 GPs, in a Maserati in France and in a Vanwall in Italy, retiring both times.

Taruffi's remarkable racing career ended in splendid fashion in 1957 with a fine win for Ferrari in the last ever Mille Miglia.

Maurice
TRINTIGNANT
b.1917

A patriotic French driver of considerable talent, Maurice Trintignant gained his first motor racing experience before the war but enjoyed a long career after it ended. He raced his own Bugatti initially and then joined the Gordini team to drive for France in single-seater events and in sports cars.

Outings in a private Ferrari in 1952 led to a works contract in 1954 and victories in several non-championship races. In May 1955 he was the surprise winner of an exciting Monaco GP but then he failed to score again for the rest of the season.

Vanwall made use of Trintignant's services through 1956 with an agreed break for him to drive the GP Bugatti in July for the French GP. He managed 18 laps in the race but retired the car from its only appearance. Interestingly enough, it was his temporary departure to Bugatti that gave Colin Chapman the chance to drive the Vanwall, although he was a non-starter after a practice accident. Trintignant was back in the Vanwall for the British GP but his list of retirements lengthened. Indeed, he would not score a single point that year. A few points came Trintignant's way in 1957 when he drove one of the Lancia Ferraris in the first five races of the year.

Driving for Rob Walker's private Cooper team in 1958, Trintignant won his second Monaco GP after a fine, consistent drive. He had only one more result that year. He appeared in Walker's dark-blue Coopers again in 1959, enjoying five finishes in the points to add to his successes in F2 and his second place at Le Mans for Aston Martin.

From 1960, Trintignant raced numerous different cars with little success. IIis final race was in an ex-works BRM in 1964 which retired on lap 22 of the Italian GP. He had taken this same car to fifth place in the German GP a month previously to score the last points of his long and varied career.

Wolfgang von
TRIPS
b.1928 d.1961

A German aristocrat, Count von Trips simply loved to drive and started racing sports cars. His fearless style marked him out as a potential winner but it would take several years of sports cars racing before he would graduate to GP racing.

He started racing a private Porsche which led to outings in works examples, centred around Le Mans. He also drove sports cars for Mercedes in 1955 and for Ferrari in 1956.

Left: Maurice Trintignant was a successful GP driver but won in sports cars too and is seen here in his 1954 Le Mans-winning Ferrari after the big race

This led to a place on the grid for the 1957 Monaco GP in a works Ferrari. The race ended 15 laps from the finish and that taste of F1 had to last until the Italian GP later in the year. This race went much better and Trips finished third; first Ferrari home. Trips' best sports car result of the year was second in the Mille Miglia.

There followed three more difficult but occasionally encouraging seasons with Ferrari in GP racing coupled with some good results in sports cars both for Ferrari and Porsche.

Trips was still in the works Ferrari team for the 1961 season and from the start it seemed that at last it was really coming good for him. His bravery saw him win the Dutch GP from Phil Hill and again beat his team-mate to the flag for the British GP. Suddenly Trips was favourite for the Championship. Second place

Below: German count Wolfgang von Trips, happy after winning the Syracuse GP. In 1961 he looked set to be World Champion but was killed at Monza

Above: Achille Varzi with typical staring expression sits at the wheel of an Auto-Union

Right: Canadian Gilles Villeneuve was popular with the crowds and had a massive talent but he lost his life in a tragic accident in Belgium

in the German GP in August helped his cause and he sat on pole for the Italian GP at Monza a month later. Two laps into a tightly-contested race Trips' Ferrari touched Clark's Lotus under braking for the Parabolica. The Ferrari flew off the track and Trips was thrown out of the cockpit, causing fatal injuries. The errant car landed among spectators and 14 of them died. It was a tragic end to the gentlemanly career of a fine German driver.

Achille
VARZI
b.1904 d.1948

Italian Achille Varzi's racing record places him among the truly great drivers of the Thirties. His career paralleled that of his greatest rival, Nuvolari, but Varzi's unsmiling face and staring eyes contrasted with Nuvolari's chirpy demeanor. Varzi was a technician at the wheel and looked unspectacular although he was exceptionally fast.

Varzi's wealthy background helped him make his name on motor cycles and quickly switch to cars, driving first a Bugatti T35 and then, in 1929, an Alfa P2 with which he won many Italian races. He alternated between Alfa Romeo and Maserati in 1930, winning the Targa Florio for Alfa and the Spanish GP for Maserati. Between 1931 and 1933, Varzi was with the Bugatti team to drive the T51 and later the T54, winning races with both, including a record-breaking Avusrennen in 1933 at the wheel of the 4.9-litre T54.

In 1934 Varzi moved to Scuderia Ferrari,

driving a P3 to many wins including the Targa Florio and the Mille Miglia. This successful season made him very marketable and it was Auto-Union who signed him on. His superb reactions enabled Varzi to get to grips with the difficult and powerful Auto-Union very quickly. In his first season he won at Tunis and Pescara, was second at Tripoli and third at Avus. In 1936 he was first at Tripoli, second at Milan, Monaco and Berne and third at Pescara and Budapest.

His latter performances for Auto-Union seemed to tail off, due to his ill health. He drove infrequently in 1937 and 1938 before fading from the scene until 1946. Then he reappeared in the Alfa team, driving one of the dominant Type 158s. He proved he was still a force to be reckoned with by an early win in Milan. He raced on until in 1948 he lost control of his car in practice on the fast Berne circuit. The car overturned and Varzi lost his life, aged 44.

Gilles
VILLENEUVE
b.1952 d.1982

Gilles Villeneuve's unpretentious manner and dislike of fuss gave little indication of the quality of his driving. His style was dramatic and attractive; he was supremely fast and sometimes reckless but he was a winner.

He burst into GP racing from several seasons racing at home in Canada. McLaren gave him his chance in the British GP where he immediately showed his class. The one-off McLaren experience led to a brace of races for Ferrari in Canada and Japan before becoming a full-time member of the Italian

team for 1978 as number two to Reutemann. He worked hard and showed his talent in a difficult car. The pay-off came at his home GP in Canada when he took the lead and clinched his first GP victory.

Equipped with the 312T4 for 1979 and now partnering Jody Scheckter, the results improved further still. Three wins came Villeneuve's way that season: South Africa, US West, and the second US round of the year. But perhaps Villeneuve's second place in the French GP will be the best remembered result of the year. The crowds at Dijon watched in disbelief as his Ferrari and Arnoux's Renault fought out the final lap with wheels interlocked; Villeneuve emerged the winner of this particular struggle.

Scheckter won the 1979 Championship but Villeneuve was a close second. 1980 was a lean year for Ferrari drivers and further success would have to wait until the arrival of the turbocharged cars in 1981. At Monaco, Villeneuve chased and passed Alan Jones' Williams with just four laps to go to take a great victory. Three weeks later he won again in Spain. The season was disappointing from then on despite Villeneuve's continuing displays of superb car control and great bravery. He drove at the limit all the time and seemed to get away with it.

He continued to get away with it until his ambition got the better of him in Belgium. He was flying in practice and took one chance too many. He clipped a slower car and his Ferrari was launched into the air, the resultant accident killing the 30-year-old star.

John **WATSON**

b.1946

Pleasant-mannered, softly-spoken Ulsterman John Watson seemed to be one of the unluckiest men in racing until well into his long F1 career. But he overcame the stigma to become a worthy winner of races and came within an ace of the World Championship.

Watson drove sports cars in his native Ireland before jumping straight to F2 in 1969. His first F1 experience came with a March in 1972 and, by way of one or two other non-championship outings, he made his GP debut in the 1973 British GP. His first full season was for Brabham in 1974. He was a consistent midfield qualifier and picked up points from Monaco onwards.

A move to Surtees in 1975 did not enhance Watson's career very much, apart from a second place in the Race of Champions. Surtees pulled out for the latter half of 1976 and when Ickx was 'rested' by Lotus, Watson filled in for the German GP only, but retired. Then for the last race of the year he moved to the Penske team to replace Mark Donohue, killed in Austria.

Above: John Watson who enjoyed a long career in GP racing and scored some notable successes before turning to sports car racing

That one-off drive turned into a full season for 1976 and with it Watson's performances perked up. In mid-season he was third twice running and then scored a well-judged win in the closely-fought Austrian GP, having started from the front row, gained the lead, lost it, fought back and stayed at the front to the finish. That win cost Watson his beard, as a result of a bet with Roger Penske!

With Penske pulling out at the end of 1976, Watson returned to Brabham who were running the V12 Alfa-powered cars. Time after time he suffered mechanical failures. He led at Dijon and Silverstone but his luck deserted him with the races almost in the bag. The cars were better in 1978 and Watson found himself in the points on seven occasions, team-mate Lauda winning two races.

Disheartened after two years of being robbed of success, Watson moved to McLaren. The team ran the M28/29/30 for 1979 and 1980 and Watson achieved little to speak of. With the first of the MP4 series cars the pinnacle of the 1981 season was Watson's British GP victory, and he added further 1982 wins at Zolder and in Detroit. Unfortunately the early-season form of 1982 deserted Watson until the final two races when he added to his points with a fourth and a second, just insufficient to keep the Championship from Keke Rosberg's Williams. Remaining with McLaren for 1983, Watson won at Long Beach in March after an exceptional drive, but further major success eluded him that season and he was out of the team for 1984, replaced by Alain Prost.

Rather than race on with a second-string team, he elected to retire from F1 and concentrate on endurance racing which he has done with some success.

The Circuits

More than 60 circuits are included in this survey of the world's best-known tracks. Most of those included are circuits of international status but a handful of others is mentioned because they have historic significance. Not all the circuits mentioned survive; many rose to fame and vanished after staging just one or two major events. Others, like Silverstone and Monza, have been in use for years, albeit in gradually changing form as the demands of the sport alter.

Circuits vary in nature from the simplicity of Indianapolis to the extreme length and complication of the old Nürburgring, the latter now replaced by a modern, far less interesting facility. Some tracks were tedious, others interesting and challenging, not to say dangerous, for drivers and spectators alike. Today most of the 'dangerous' circuits have been dropped from the Championship calendar or made much safer by slowing down the cars and providing run-off areas.

As circuits are improved and developed, so corners change and lap distances alter. This should be considered when comparing lap times from different years. For example, Alain Prost's fastest lap at Monza in 1989 was some 5mph (8km/h) slower than Jackie Stewart's best lap exactly 20 years previously!

The unmistakable sweeps and curves of Monaco, home of maybe the most famous of all the GPs

Argentina

Argentina was the first of the South American countries to stage a Grand Prix, back in 1953. There were another 16 Championship rounds held in the country through to 1981. The development of Argentina's post-war interest in motor sport was encouraged by President Peron, who was anxious to promote his country's international image. All Argentine GPs since that first one in 1953 have taken place at the **BUENOS AIRES AUTODROME**, which had been opened one year previously.

The site chosen for the construction of the new circuit was on empty land which was then on the outskirts of the city. It has since been surrounded by modern development and has a skyline of skyscrapers. Buenos Aires was designed as a versatile circuit capable of being used in many alternative permutations to suit the type of racing taking place but using the same pit and grandstand facilities.

GPs took place at Buenos Aires from 1953 through to 1960 with the only gap in 1959, in which year the Championship opened in Monaco instead of its traditional curtain-raising venue. The GP circus returned to a much-improved Buenos Aires circuit in 1972 and, missing only once, in 1976, ran through to the last GP in 1981. Sadly, the circuit was the scene of many bad racing accidents stretching right back to 1953 when 15 spectators were killed.

The version of the circuit used most recently for GPs is slower than the original open design with very high-speed corners. Its 3.7-mile (5.9km) lap comprises a short straight and a long straight linked by a fast, sweeping right-hand bend with a tight, twisting complex with two hairpins leading round to the pit straight.

Australia

The Australian GP was first staged in 1928 at Philip Island and in its early years was largely a domestic affair. In 1937 the event started to move among various other circuits, many now defunct. European opposition began to be attracted to this event, particularly in the early Sixties when the Australian GP formed an important part of the Tasman Series which was contested by many top European teams and drivers.

However, it was not until 1985 that the Australian GP became a round of the World Championship with the christening of a modern street circuit in **ADELAIDE**. Adelaide's 2.35 miles (3.78km) are a lot more interesting and better conceived than some of the other new-generation street circuits. Actually it is more of a parkland circuit than a street circuit in the American sense and rests in pleasant tree-filled surroundings that give it a permanent feel. The 0.6-mile (1km) straight allows cars to reach high speeds and the corners before the straight on the west side are fast. The pits are located after the slowest corner on the circuit and the pit straight leads to a chicane and a sequence of bends.

The Adelaide track and the revamped Australian GP came about more as the result

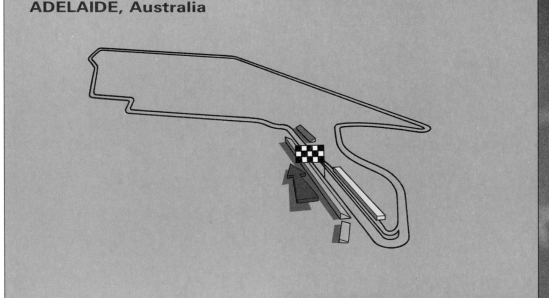

ADELAIDE, Australia

Right: The attractive circuit created in the streets of Adelaide, Australia
Far right: The Williams of Riccardo Patrese at Adelaide in 1989, sister car to that of winner Thierry Boutsen

of a desire of Adelaide city to promote its image than from a sudden growth of Australian interest in motor racing. Australian government support was enlisted by Adelaide in the negotiations with FOCA before the race became a reality. The result of all these efforts has been a superbly organized and very successful season-end event that is popular with the crowds and the teams alike and which has produced some good, exciting racing.

Another well-known Australian circuit is **BATHURST**, inland from Sydney, scene of the legendary James Hardie 1000 touring car race, formerly the Armstrong 500. This is easily Australia's best-known event after the Championship GP and is seen on television world-wide. In an earlier incarnation the Australian GP was staged at Bathurst three times.

This famous circuit dates back to the mid-Thirties, when it started life as a tourist drive through the picturesque Blue Mountains of New South Wales. The ups and downs of the hilly north-west end of the circuit give rise to spectacular racing, and sometimes some equally spectacular crashes. The famous con-rod straight, ending at Murray's corner, is nowadays broken with a chicane but the Bathurst circuit still retains much of its original exciting nature.

Austria

The first circuit of any note in Austria was at **ZELTWEG**, in the mountains near Graz in the east of the country. Created in 1958, it was a simple, uninspired airfield track with a poor quality, bumpy surface that became worse as the years passed. Several international meetings were staged leading up to a Championship GP in 1964.

The interlude in the Austrian GP up to 1970 was occupied with the construction of a new circuit near the original Zeltweg site. Known as the **OSTERREICHRING**, this 3.69-mile (5.94km) circuit is very fast and challenging and is one of the more popular venues among GP drivers. It is also one of the most picturesque of GP circuits, nestling in hilly pine-filled countryside.

Opened as Austria's premier circuit in 1969, Osterreichring is a combination of fast bends rather than fast straights although the one-time fastest of these bends, the legendary Hella Licht, immediately after the pit straight is now interrupted by a chicane. Niki Lauda considered this corner to be the most difficult and frightening of all, and this was his home circuit! Photographs of the Osterreichring give little indication of the steepness of some of the climbs and the abruptness of some of

the descents. Such variety of altitude make the Osterreichring an excellent spectator circuit with large sections of the track visible at any one time.

Parts of the Osterreichring were constructed to prevailing race standards of the late Sixties and the narrowness of the pit lane, for example, often caused problems, notably a start-line multiple accident during the 1987 GP. FOCA insisted that certain modifications be made to the circuit and the delay in completing these led to the Austrian GP being dropped from the calendar in 1988. However, it was back for 1989 and should remain a regular fixture.

The other circuit of note in Austria is the **SALZBURGRING** in the west of the country. A fast and fairly simple track, it hosts the occasional major single-seater race and was visited by international touring car events.

Belgium

Easily the best-known Belgian circuit is **SPA-FRANCORCHAMPS**, in the eastern part of Belgium, just before the German border. Spa can trace an almost uninterrupted history of top-flight racing right back to its founding in 1924. The first Belgian GP was held there in 1925 and the last one using the circuit in its

original form came in 1970. A revamped Spa won back the GP from Zolder in 1983 and it became a permanent fixture there from 1985.

The original circuit was conceived by Jules de Thier who laid out a route of just under 9 miles (14.5km) using existing roads in the hills adjacent to the picturesque town. The roads were improved over the years but essentially remained similar until the Eighties.

Spa was an exciting circuit and was very fast, calling for enormous skill and bravery from the drivers. Many were killed there, Dick Seaman and Archie Scott-Brown to name but two. Even Stirling Moss and Jackie Stewart had bad accidents.

The original course had its famous corners at La Source, Malmedy and Stavelot with the infamous Masta Kink in between them. The roadway rose and fell between the trees and had difficult cambers and a changing surface. Rain and mist was always a hazard at Spa and sudden cloudbursts could wreak havoc on a race.

By 1969 there were calls for improvements at Spa. Even the bravest drivers recognized that it could be a very dangerous circuit. Unable to react quickly to these calls and embroiled in a motor-sporting political dispute within Belgium, Spa lost the GP for 1969.

Almost 14 years later a remodelled and revitalized Spa would appear. Naturally

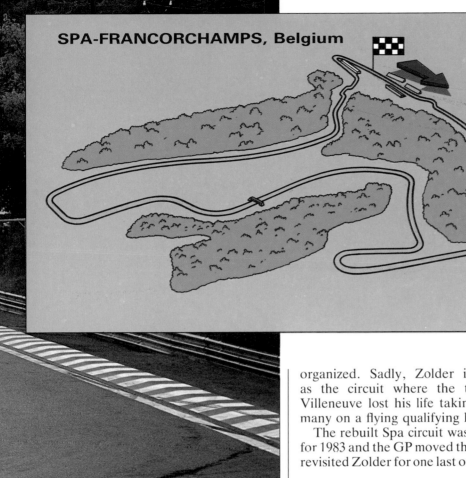

SPA-FRANCORCHAMPS, Belgium

Left: The McLarens of Ayrton Senna and Alain Prost emerge first from the ball of spray thrown up at the start of the wet 1989 Belgian GP at Spa

organized. Sadly, Zolder is remembered as the circuit where the talented Gilles Villeneuve lost his life taking one risk too many on a flying qualifying lap in 1982.

The rebuilt Spa circuit was back in action for 1983 and the GP moved there, although it revisited Zolder for one last occasion in 1984.

Brazil

This South American nation which has produced so many great drivers has two main circuits, both of which have hosted the Brazilian GP.

INTERLAGOS, near Sao Paulo, is the older of the two with a history that goes back to 1940. The circuit staged several important non-championship races before the Championship came to Brazil in 1973. It was a great day for Brazilian racing as Emerson Fittipaldi won, as indeed he would the following year too. The circuit is a masterpiece of packaging as it squeezes 4.94 miles (7.96km) into an extraordinarily compact space. It does this by doubling back on itself several times. In the centre of the circuit there is a point where five stretches of track almost run parallel to each other although they are actually at different levels.

For all its twists and turns, the corners at Interlagos were fast and the drivers seemed to like its challenging nature. However, in 1978 the GP circus was lured away to the more pleasant environment of Rio to race at a newly-constructed circuit called **JACAREPAGUA**, built on reclaimed marshes to the south-west of the city. The GP went back to Interlagos twice more, in 1979 and 1980, before moving permanently to the new well-equipped circuit. Jacarepagua was officially renamed Autodromo Nelson Piquet in 1987 but is still known by its original name.

some of the raw appeal of old Spa was lost, but the new circuit was characterful and still exciting. The old downhill pit straight and Eau Rouge corners were retained but thereafter the circuit made a new way through the hills and trees, reducing the lap distance to 4.35 miles (6.94km). The hairpin at La Source before the pit straight also remains although the lead in to it is now slowed by a strange double chicane just before a new alternative start line.

Spa is home to the premier saloon car race of the year, the Spa 24 Hours, and also a round of the World Sports Car Championship, the Spa 1000kms.

When the GP decamped from Spa it went to **NIVELLES**, a rather tedious airfield circuit directly south of Brussels. Two seasons were enough before **ZOLDER**, midway between Brussels and Antwerp, took over the running of Belgium's top race. Zolder staged its first meeting in 1965 and gradually built itself up to a standard suitable for GP racing. It is a relatively simple circuit of 2.64 miles (4.26km), roughly rectangular in shape with a loop off to the west at the top end. It was made a little more complicated by the addition of chicanes before GP racing went there, and these have since multiplied.

The GP teams did not rate Zolder among their favourite venues but the events staged were popular with the crowds and were well

MONTREAL, Canada

The circuit is flat, with predictable corners, and is dominated by a long back straight running parallel to the pit straight. There are twelve corners in its 3.126 miles (5.03km) but the heat and humidity make the Brazilian GP a hard event for drivers of modern cars which are thrown about by the circuit's surface bumps.

Canada

A country of massive land area and a thinly-spread population, Canada came to international racing quite late with the opening of **MOSPORT PARK**, near Toronto, in 1961.

With the exception of one tight pair of bends at the north end, Mosport was laid out as a fast, open track, offering a real high-speed challenge to drivers, particularly as it rained there frequently. The Canadian GP was added to the Championship in 1967 and the inaugural event was at Mosport, although it would alternate between there and the **ST JOVITE** circuit, also known as Mont-Tremblant.

St Jovite was opened in 1964 but increased in length to 2.65 miles (4.26km) in 1966, at which length it remained for all its years as a GP circuit. It was a narrow, tree-lined track that wound through the hills giving steep drops, dramatic climbs and tight corners. A bumpy surface complicated the job of keeping a car on the track and there were some serious accidents that eventually led to its abandonment for GP racing in 1970.

Mosport then kept the GP for its next six visits to Canada until that venue was also judged as too dangerous for the modern breed of GP car. The solution was to build a new circuit. This was duly done in record time. The site chosen was on an artificial island in the St Lawrence river at MONTREAL. The spur to the completion of the circuit was the rise to fame of Canada's only really successful GP driver, Gilles Villeneuve.

Villeneuve duly drove his Ferrari to a tremendous victory in front of a jubilant home crowd in 1978. The circuit used that year was subsequently modified and has now become the permanent home of the Canadian GP.

The circuit basically follows the half-moon-shaped outline of Ile de Notre Dame with a hairpin at the north end and a faster tight turn at the south. There are several small turns along the circuit's two legs that allow overtaking opportunities and can help to produce exciting racing.

France

France has more international-standard circuits than any other country except the USA; hardly surprising in the nation where the sport started and where today its governing body still resides. Motor sport in France dates right back to 1894 and there were vast circuits mapped out on public roads for races before the turn of the century.

The first, more modestly-sized circuit, was at **LE MANS** and was used for a French 'Grand Prix' in 1906. That circuit had little to do with the present track of that name but its presence established that town in motor racing legend. The circuit was subsequently modified and shortened to the first incarnation of its present form in 1919 and the GP was held there again in 1921 and 1929.

However, Le Mans would not become famous for GP racing but for being the site of the world's most famous endurance race, the Le Mans 24 Hours. That famous event has been run on a variety of permutations of the

Far left: Thierry Boutsen leads Ayrton Senna during the 1989 Canadian GP held at Montreal

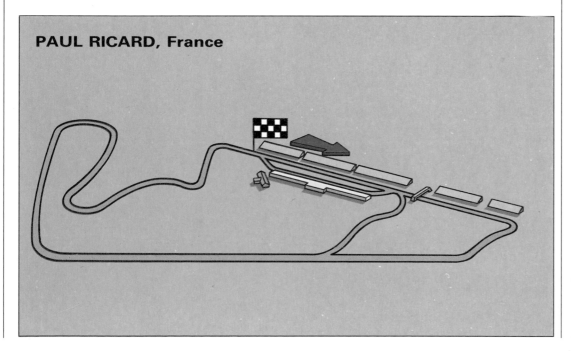

PAUL RICARD, France

Left: The circuit at Paul Ricard is favoured for testing by many GP teams as it is a challenging venue and enjoys a reliable climate

circuit known as the 'Sarthe', the more dangerous sections being gradually eliminated over the years.

The current circuit, as used once each year for the 24 Hours, is dominated by the famous Mulsanne Straight, comprising a stretch of Route Nationale with only a slight kink four-fifths of the way down to spoil its arrow-straight line. The corners at Le Mans are among the most famous in the sport: Tertre Rouge, Arnage and Dunlop. Each evokes memories of great moments and exciting duels in this most challenging of events. Controversy over the 1990 event hinged around the FIA's insistence that chicanes be added to the Mulsanne Straight where the modern breed of sports car can easily exceed 250mph (402km/h).

While Le Mans was among the circuits to stage pre-war versions of the French GP, **REIMS** was the site of the first race to be part of the new post-war World Championship. This circuit in northern France dates back to 1925 and the pre-war GP racers visited there in 1932. Reims was made up of closed public road and was designed to be very fast indeed, comprising a slightly deformed triangle with a total of six corners, only two of them tight, within the 5.18 miles (8.34km).

Even in pre-war events the average speeds at Reims exceeded 100mph (161km/h) and in the GPs of the late Fifties it was easily over 120mph (193km/h). The last French GP to be held at Reims was in 1966 and the circuit was used occasionally thereafter through to 1970 when the difficulties of closing public roads, plus financial problems of the organizing club, became insurmountable. The pit garages and billboards still survive by the roadside today as ghostly reminders of a glorious racing past.

Although Reims was the first French circuit to stage a post-war Championship race, another circuit sprang to prominence at this time and was the scene of the French GP five times through to 1968. This was **ROUEN** in Normandy. The circuit was cut out through the trees in the hillside on the west of the city of Rouen and it was an exciting place to drive a powerful car. It was modified and extended in time for the 1957 GP to become faster. The pit straight led downhill through fast bends to a difficult hairpin and the track then twisted back uphill through the trees along the two remaining sides of its basic triangle which measured just over four miles (6.4km) in its final form. Rouen first staged the GP in 1952 and was last used in 1968.

By 1965 yet another circuit had been found for the French GP, and a particularly challenging one it was too. **CLERMONT-FERRAND**, also known as 'Charade', nestled in the hills of the Auvergne in southern central France. It was a narrow and twisting circuit of more than 50 turns without a straight to speak of. Trees overhung the circuit, there were rock faces and drops behind barriers all within in its tortuous 5 miles (8km) which some drivers

loved and others hated. It seems remarkable that the GP went there at all. Yet it did, and went back again in 1969, 1970 and 1972. The circuit finally closed to racing in 1988.

While the GP racers were frightening themselves at Clermont-Ferrand, another purpose-built circuit was being completed right down in the south of France, at Le Castellet. Named **PAUL RICARD** after the popular French drink, the new 2.36-mile (3.81km) track was ready just at the right time to take over from the traditional venues for the GP in 1971.

The circuit was a sensible design with run-off areas in the modern style. It is good for spectators in terms of facilities and viewing and for the racers offers an ideal mix of corners to link one long back straight, plus the pit straight. Paul Ricard would ultimately assume dominance among French circuits, but not before a period of alternating as GP venue with **DIJON-PRENOIS**.

Dijon's simple and fairly short circuit in the middle of the Burgundy wine region first hosted the GP in 1974 and five more times thereafter, but had to give way to the faster and better-equipped Paul Ricard after 1984. The lap length was a little over two miles (3.22km) for the first GP but a northern loop added for the 1977 race helped spread the cars out a little more. Interestingly, both

Right: Thierry Boutsen's 1987 Benetton sweeps past the Hockenheim grandstand

HOCKENHEIM, Germany

Paul Ricard and Dijon hosted a Championship round in 1982, although the latter race was known as the Swiss GP, racing having been banned in that country since 1955.

Germany

Most famous and oldest of the circuits that still exist is the legendary **NÜRBURGRING**, built in the misty Eifel mountains in the Twenties. This extraordinary circuit in all its 14-mile (22.5km) and 184-corner glory was the scene of some of the greatest motor races of the Thirties. It lived on as a GP circuit in only slightly changed form to the Seventies.

The main circuit, known as the 'Nordschleife', originally had a southern extension but that has now gone; likewise, the main northern extension. The Nordschleife has been changed here and there, most notably in 1970, and it now has Armco barriers instead of hedges. However, a lap of the Nürburgring is something that most drivers never forget. Grand Prix cars did not visit the old circuit after Lauda's nasty accident of 1976 but it is still in use for German national races and the incredible International 24 Hours for touring cars each June. This is the largest motor race in the world with up to 180 starters flagged off in grids of 60 to drive on through the night and into the next day.

While the Nordschleife is nowadays deemed unsuitable for GP cars the adjacent new Nürburgring was built with them in mind. The new 2.8-mile (4.51km) circuit ate up a little of the old 'Ring and led to the demolition of some of the historic buildings left from the Thirties. The new circuit was greeted with dismay when opened in 1984 as it retains none of the character of the old circuit. Yet it is a fast, safe circuit and hosted the German GP in 1985.

Regardless of the run-off areas and splendid facilities at the new Nürburgring, the German GP has been held at **HOCKENHEIM** since 1985. Hockenheim is almost as old as the Nürburgring with a history stretching back to 1929. The circuit rests in woodland near Heidelberg and was little known outside Germany until the Sixties. Then it hit the headlines when Jim Clark was killed there in an F2 race. Others have died since and the safety measures have been progressively stepped up.

When the Nürburgring was being updated in 1970 the German GP came to Hockenheim for one year. It came back again in 1977 and has stayed there since, apart from in 1985. Hockenheim is an interesting design as it features a large grandstand loop aimed at giving the seated onlookers a good view of the cars as they turn in past the stadium, round the 180-degree Sachskurve and then back again to rejoin the main run of the track and turn through 90 degrees onto the start-line straight. Behind the stadium the large

back section of the track runs through the trees with the long straights and fast corners now slowed by the addition of three chicanes.

The only other German circuit to have staged a post-war GP is **AVUS** in Berlin which straddles the Berlin Wall. The GP cars visited this extraordinary circuit in 1959 and never went back again. Avus is Germany's oldest circuit, built in fits and starts between 1913 and 1921. It comprised two long straights alongside each other with banked curves of different radii at each. It was certainly no driver's circuit but with such small emphasis on handling or roadholding offered the opportunity for very high speeds to be achieved. Even in the Thirties cars were averaging 120mph (193km/h) plus.

Racing did not return to Avus until 1954 on a shortened circuit with an unbanked south loop to allow for the fact that the original banking was now in East Germany. The only German GP to take place there was in 1959 and it was won by Tony Brooks' Ferrari at an average of 143mph (230km/h).

Great Britain

Britain has almost 20 circuits in regular or part-time use and many others have come and gone in this most fertile of environments for motor sport. The development of so many circuits is partly due to the historic impossibility of closing public roads for racing as some European countries do.

BROOKLANDS at Weybridge in Surrey was the world's first purpose-built motor racing circuit dating back to 1906 with racing commencing in 1907. The vast open bankings and simple shape made Brooklands very fast and the overall concept of the track, with its excellent spectator arrangements and varied racing, allowed many thousands of people to watch and enjoy motor sport and many hundreds to compete in it. However, by the Thirties Brooklands was unsuitable for the modern style of GP road racing and, for all its merits, the peculiarities of its style of competition, frequently with handicapping employed, had taken Britain away from the mainstream of international GP competition.

Consequently, when international GP racing came to Britain it was **DONINGTON PARK** that would host what would become a display of German domination, in the Donington GP. Donington, near Derby, was opened in 1933 and in revised form is still very much in action today, making it the oldest working British circuit.

The track was built in the grounds of Donington Hall and swept through rolling, attractive parkland. In anticipation of the arrival of the German teams for the 1937 GP, the circuit was lenthened to 3.12 miles (5.03km) by the inclusion of a new loop which was approached over a brow that would have the great Mercedes and

Auto-Union cars leaping from the tarmac.

Like Brooklands, Donington Park was taken over for military use during the war years. But whereas Brooklands would never be used again for racing, Donington, having languished for more than 30 years, was rebuilt in the Seventies under the ownership of Tom Wheatcroft. The revitalized circuit, reopened in 1977, retained much of the appeal of the old and followed sections of its route closely, but it was a thoroughly modern track with ever-improving facilities. The original Melbourne loop survives but is detached from the main body of the circuit by a car park. A newly-added loop behind the paddock adds to the circuit length sufficiently for the circuit to be a contender for the staging of the British GP, although that has not yet happened.

Donington has not yet hosted the British GP because **SILVERSTONE** holds on to it these days with such tenacity. Silverstone was hardly an inspiring setting for a circuit, let alone the staging of the first post-war British GP in 1948. Like several other circuits that sprang up in the immediate post-war years, Silverstone was converted from an austere and bleak wartime airfield using the perimeter roads and runways, with some corners marked using oil drums and hay bales.

The fast, open corners of Silverstone reached a version of their current form in 1950 with a lap length of just under three miles (4.8km). The very first round of the newly-constituted World Championship was staged at Silverstone that year and, apart from years when the GP has been held at Aintree or alternated with Brands Hatch, it has been at Silverstone ever since.

SILVERSTONE, Great Britain

Left: Silverstone has seen the addition of a chicane at Woodcote corner since Peter Revson in a McLaren, below, won the 1973 event. The circuit is currently being further improved and modified

Silverstone has always offered the spectacle of very high-speed racing and Woodcote corner which led onto the pit straight was among the most dramatic at any circuit. Following a massive accident in 1973, the Woodcote chicane was introduced to slow the field down and other modifications have since been carried out to restrict speeds, although Silverstone remains one of the fastest circuits in the world. Various shorter permutations of the full GP are used for the numerous club race meetings that take place throughout the season.

The first circuit to wrest the British GP from Silverstone was **AINTREE**, opened in 1954 and running outside the famous Grand National horse racing course in Liverpool. At exactly three miles (4.8km) Aintree was a long circuit by British standards, but it was not a particularly fast one, with tight corners and just two significant straights in all its length.

The British GP visited Aintree five times between 1955 and 1962 and thereafter the circuit declined, being used for club meetings in much-shortened form through until the early Eighties.

The circuit that supplanted Aintree as the alternative GP venue to Silverstone was **BRANDS HATCH**. Located some 20 miles south of London, in Kent, Brands Hatch's natural amphitheatre started as a venue for pedal cyclists, then motor cyclists and then, in 1950, cars. By that time the circuit had been developed into a simple kidney-shaped

format, following the natural contours of the land.

In the mid-Fifties the Druids hairpin section was added and permanent spectator facilities started to appear in an attempt to make the venue more attractive to crowds. The process of improvement was continuous, with the most significant step coming in 1962 when the track length was more than doubled to 2.65 miles (4.24km) with the construction of an extensive back section through adjacent woodlands. Link roads meant that the circuit could be used in its original short form for club meetings.

By 1964 Brands Hatch was big enough and sufficiently well equipped for the GP to be staged there for the first time. It was to visit there a further 14 times, alternating with Silverstone, except in 1983 and 1985 when both circuits were given GPs.

Brands Hatch has seen some fantastic races but also some bad accidents. It was worries over safety that led the GP to Silverstone each year after 1985. Nevertheless, Brands Hatch management have been unstinting in their efforts to win back the GP and the track has been modified in several necessary ways. There is now more run-off at the first corner, the legendary Paddock Bend, while in the back section there are chicanes to slow cars through the quaintly-named Dingle Dell corner. Brands Hatch is liked by many drivers and is popular with spectators because not only are the facilities good, and getting better, but the viewing is much better than at flat, featureless Silverstone.

No other British circuit has staged the British GP but there are many other well-known tracks that have been the scene of excellent international and national racing. **GOODWOOD**, near Chichester, was another post-war airfield circuit and it enjoyed more than a decade of prominence from 1948. In many ways Goodwood was a better airfield circuit than Silverstone. Although narrow, it was more varied and had interesting corners in its 2.4 miles (3.86km). Goodwood was the scene of many prominent single-seater and sports car races but, by the early Sixties, its earth banks and ditches were outdated and major investment was needed in its fabric. In some ways it is good that such investment was not forthcoming since the track remains intact today as a pre-Armco atmospheric period piece, still used extensively for testing and club driving days.

OULTON PARK in Cheshire is best known for the Gold Cup meeting but it has been a consistently popular national venue since its opening in 1953. It is a tremendously picturesque and challenging circuit in the grounds of the disappeared Oulton Hall, although the lodge gates still remain at one of the corners.

SNETTERTON in Norfolk pre-dates Oulton Park by a couple of seasons and, like that circuit, is an important national venue. Its main claim to fame is the staging of

Below: *A grid of 500cc cars, including Stirling Moss in number 37, makes the start at Goodwood*

Britain's only 24-hour motor race each June — the Willhire 24 Hours for saloon cars.

THRUXTON also dates from the early Fifties but suffered such a shaky start that it closed in the mid-Sixties and reopened in 1968. Yet another airfield circuit, Thruxton's fast, gently curving 2.35 miles (3.76km) hosted an annual international F2 meeting through to the mid-Eighties.

Other famous names from Great Britain's tally of circuits include the now-defunct **CRYSTAL PALACE**, in South London. In fact this circuit is the third oldest in the country, dating back to 1937 and finally succumbing to problems over noise in the early Seventies. A compact track at 1.39 miles (2.16km), it was nevertheless a popular venue for major national F1 and F2 meetings throughout the Fifties.

More circuit names from the past and the present with which to conjure include Mallory Park, Castle Combe, Cadwell Park, Pembrey, Lydden Hill, Rufforth, Full Sutton, Croft and Boreham; Llandow in Wales, plus Ingliston, Knockhill and Charterhall in Scotland.

Racing on public roads had never been a feature of the British scene until the passing of a Birmingham Road Race Bill through Parliament in 1985. This historic measure allowed the staging of the first **BIRMINGHAM** street race. This televised spectacle which has proved popular with the crowds centres on an F3000 race round an interesting, fast course through the town centre of Birmingham. It is doubtful whether F1 cars will ever grace these street but the action is good and the circuit well conceived with good straights which allow high speeds to be built up and sensible corners that provide opportunities for exciting overtaking manoeuvres.

Hungary

Hungarian motor racing can be traced back to the Thirties when races were staged in a park in the centre of Budapest. The country's first purpose-built circuit, the **HUNGARORING**, was constructed as recently as 1985 and has been the scene of the Hungarian GP each year since.

The designers were able to make use of a natural bowl in open country east of Budapest to create a 2.49-mile (4.01km) circuit that is good for viewing. However, while it is true that it is the corners that make motor racing exciting, there are exciting corners and there are boring corners. Sadly most of those in Hungary fall into the latter category, or at least come at points in the circuit that make them thus. Consequently the Hungaroring is quite a slow circuit with few natural overtaking points. Nevertheless the basic concept is sound and will doubtless be improved in future years now that this race is a permanent fixture on the calendar.

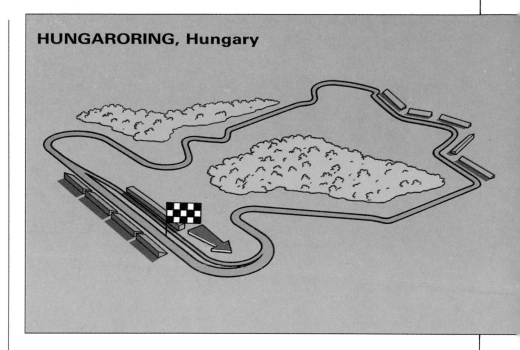

HUNGARORING, Hungary

Italy

While road racing in most countries died out many decades ago, it persisted in Italy right through to 1973 when the last **TARGA FLORIO** was run. The Mille Miglia had last taken place in 1957 when spectators plus a competing Ferrari's crew died in a terrible accident. Of course the roads were theoretically closed when the racing was on but the circuits were so huge that just about anything could happen and quite often did, ranging from meeting a hay wagon coming the other way to competitors being held up by Sicilian bandits.

The Targa Florio was first run in 1906 and by the time of its last running many different sections of the breathtaking mountain roads of northern Sicily had been used. Between 1951 and 1973 the event comprised varying numbers of laps of the Piccolo Madonie circuit which passed through the towns of Collesano, Caltavuturo, Cerda and Campofelice. Each lap was a little over 44 miles (70.8km) and for the last five years the winning average speed for the Targa was over 70mph (112.7km/h).

The Targa is now run in heavily-diluted form as an historic race-cum-rally, no longer racing through towns and villages with unprotected onlookers just feet away from the cars.

The spirit of the **MILLE MIGLIA** is also evoked by an annual historic regularity run around Italy but it would be impossible to recall exactly the sheer excitement and danger of the years 1927 to 1957 when the great race took place 24 times.

As the name implies, the route was of 1000 miles (1609km). It started in Brescia and headed south-east down the coast to Rimini then on to Pescara and Rome before turning back north through Siena, Florence, Bologna,

Above: The Hungaroring was created especially for the GP but might have benefited from the inclusion of some more challenging corners

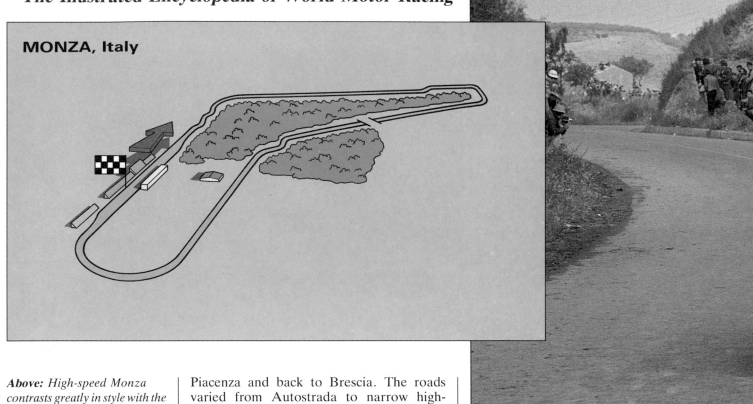

MONZA, Italy

Above: High-speed Monza contrasts greatly in style with the Sicilian road circuit once used for the Targa Florio, far right. Jo Siffert's 1970 race-winning Porsche braves the roadside spectators

Piacenza and back to Brescia. The roads varied from Autostrada to narrow high-mountain passes and were an amazing challenge to driver and machine.

Away from the public roads the first major permanent circuit to be built in Italy was in the grounds of the Royal Palace at **MONZA**, a little way from Milan. The original circuit with great banked corners at each side was demolished before the war and the first version of the post-war GP circuit was built in 1948; seven years later a new circuit with banking was added to the park, the two together producing a 6.21-mile (10km) lap. The average speed of every post-war Championship GP at Monza has been over 100mph (161km/h).

As the banking became bumpier so the risks of high speeds became greater and Monza has claimed more than its fair share of

lives. The full circuit was last used in 1961 and changes have been made regularly ever since in an effort to make it safer for the competitors.

The latest circuit of 3.6 miles (5.8km) is still fast but chicanes prevent the Curva Granda and the Vallone from being as blindingly fast as they were in the days of the Seventies when drivers averaged more than 150mph (241km/h) for a lap. Monza is a tremendously atmospheric place, even though

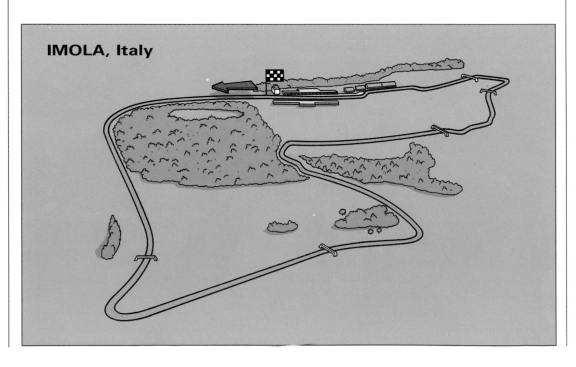

IMOLA, Italy

Right: Imola stages Italy's second Championship round, known as the San Marino GP

been taking place there since the Twenties. The race took place over more than 15 miles (24km) of closed roads along the coast and in the hills behind the seaside town of Pescara on Italy's east coast. Stirling Moss won this amazing event in his Vanwall and the GP drivers never went back again.

Japan

Japan's rise as a power in motor sport is quite a recent phenomenon. The Japanese GP was instigated as a round of the Championship only as recently as 1976 and after its second running in 1977 there was a 10-year gap until the Championship returned to become a regular annual event.

MOUNT FUJI was the scene of that first Championship Japanese GP in 1976. It was a memorable race as it was the one that clinched the World title for James Hunt as well as marking the re-emergence of Lotus as a winning team. The circuit is situated near the city of Yokohama, which is not far south of Tokyo on the eastern side of the country.

Mount Fuji was built in 1965 in the middle of a picturesque holiday region renowned for its changeable, misty and damp weather in the autumn. The circuit is but a part of the original concept which was hampered by financial problems. As used in 1976, the track is 2.7 miles (4.35km) of tricky tarmac. It does not look overly complicated as it is basically an oval with one side pushed in several times. However, the apexes are difficult and there are awkward changes in gradient which can catch the unwary.

Mount Fuji was not really suitable for the demands of a modern GP and Japan was without a Championship round until 1987. By that time an existing facility at **SUZUKA**, near Nagoya, 150 miles (241km) west of Tokyo, had been uprated to provide one of the best-served and most challenging circuits in the world today.

The circuit is owned by Honda and was designed by Dutchman John Hugenholz after a personal commission from Mr Honda himself in 1961. The track was intended mainly for vehicle testing and motor-cycle racing as part of an ambitious recreation park but was ideal for four-wheeled racing too. A programme of development was needed to gain a GP licence for 1987, notably the addition of a chicane before the pit straight. However, the circuit remains fairly true to its original design. It is very sinuous and crams 3.67 miles (5.91km) into a fairly compact area. The key to its compactness lies in the Scalextric-like figure-of-eight crossover in the middle but the corners are tight and all different while the straights are short. It is a challenging circuit, punishing on both cars and drivers, but it is generally liked by the teams who compete there.

the old pits have been partly demolished and the circuit now has all the trappings necessary for staging a modern race.

Italy's second circuit is at **IMOLA**. This picturesque venue manages to stage a GP through the dodge of calling the event the 'San Marino' GP, even though the principality of San Marino is some way away! The circuit was opened in 1950 but remained fairly low-profile until substantial upgrading and improvement led to it winning the Italian GP from Monza while a question mark hung over that circuit's safety record. Monza got the Italian GP back in 1981 but by that time the San Marino factor had come into the equation and both sides were happy, as were the Italian fans.

Imola is the nearest circuit to Ferrari's home at Maranello and in honour of Enzo Ferrari's son, who died in 1956, the circuit is also known as the Autodromo Dino Ferrari. There is also a Villeneuve corner, in memory of the most popular Ferrari driver of recent years.

Imola's varied and picturesque 3.13 miles (5.04km) are liked by the drivers as they give an interesting and challenging lap with a good mixture of corners and faster open sections. There is scope for talent to show through even though there are the inevitable chicanes to slow cars down before sections considered dangerous.

The only other circuit in Italy to have held a Championship GP post war was **PESCARA**, which hosted a GP in 1957 although racing had

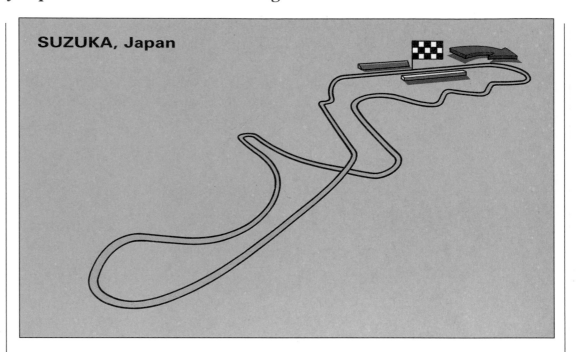

SUZUKA, Japan

Mexico

Mexico first staged an F1 GP in 1962 and the race was won by a Lotus shared by Trevor Taylor and Jim Clark. In 1963 the event was added to the Championship calendar and Clark again was first man home. The race was staged through to 1970 and then lapsed before returning to the calendar again in 1986. In its first years the Mexican fixture was traditionally the last race of the season; now it is among the first.

All Mexican GPs have been staged at **MEXICO CITY**. The circuit is in a city park and in its earliest form stretched for 3.1 miles (4.96km). Its design was roughly triangular with the longest leg of the triangle containing the bends. The circuit was built with little thought for safety and a feature of the race was always the frightening proximity of the crowds to the track. Often they used to spill onto the track and people had been known to run in front of cars. Added to this the track was very bumpy — altogether a recipe for dangerous racing. Perhaps it's surprising that more people weren't killed.

Mexico City circuit in its early form finally staged the GP in 1970 and it wasn't until major improvements had been made to the track and the spectator protection facilities that the F1 circus was enticed back in 1986. Run-off areas had been added, the sequence of corners changed and at last the spectators were protected by ample barriers and restrained by large fences.

A feature of Mexico City is its altitude which, at 7500ft (2286m) above sea level, robs normally-aspirated engines of large amounts of horsepower. In the years of mixed racing between turbocharged and atmospheric engines this always gave a great advantage to the drivers of cars with forced induction.

Monaco

This tiny Principality of **MONACO**, nestling on the coast in the South of France, has but one circuit, a temporary affair twisting its way between the houses and through the narrow streets of Monte Carlo.

The Monaco circuit was invented by one Antony Noghes of the Automobile Club de Monaco in 1928 and the first GP was staged in 1929. The first Championship GP was held in 1950, then there was a break until 1955

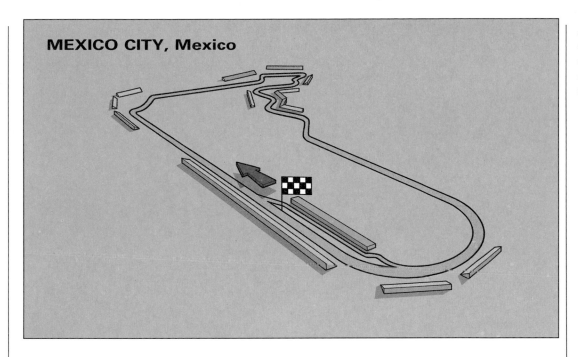

MEXICO CITY, Mexico

after which the GP has run there every year.

That the race has survived through to the Nineties is an amazing testimony to the glamour of Monaco and the pulling power of the event. Modern cars are much too fast and wide for the tight corners and cramped pits. Crashes are frequent at Monaco and the results are usually determined by grid position, as overtaking is so difficult.

The circuit has been changed over the years as parts of the waterfront have been redeveloped but there has been relatively little scope to do anything fundamental. A lap is now 2.06 miles (3.328km) and highest average speeds are around the 85mph (137km/h) mark.

A chicane at St Devote now slows the cars immediately after the start line and this has been the scene of many early-race incidents as the pack attempts to funnel through in single file. Casino Square, Mirabeau and Loews Hairpin are familiar corners to all who have seen this most televisable race on the small screen. Despite rebuilding, the famous tunnel still remains, longer than hitherto, taking the cars onto the harbourfront. The chicane before Tabac corner is now supplemented by a deviation after it to skirt a new swimming pool behind the paddock area.

There have been moves to stop the race but still it continues, such is the weight of tradition and influence.

Netherlands

Compared with the neighbouring countries of Belgium, France and Germany, it seems remarkable that Holland has just one circuit, **ZANDVOORT**. The track was built in 1948 using as its starting point a sequence of wartime access roads through the large sand dunes of this seaside resort. The first international event was the Zandvoort GP, run to Formula Libre and held in 1948. This ran again in 1949 and then the non-championship Dutch GP replaced it until the race was adopted as part of the Championship in 1952.

Zandvoort's 2.64 miles (4.25km) were designed to be fast and challenging to the drivers. It was arranged in a basic square with one corner distended to form a loop with a sequence of bends. Within the loop are the pits and paddock area. The hairpin bend which leads out into another fast section allows spectators to come exceptionally close

to the action. The back section of the circuit is now broken by a chicane but the final sequence of fast bends and the sweeping downhill right-hander onto the pit straight are exceptionally challenging sections.

Driving at Zandvoort is complicated by sea breezes and sand drifting onto the track. However, the main problem faced by the circuit has been one of noise, as it is very close to the resort town. It was this problem, among others, that meant that the 30th Championship Dutch GP, held in 1985, will be the last until a revised GP facility nearby is completed in the early Nineties.

Portugal

Although the town of Villa Real had staged annual pre-war races since the early Thirties, international motor racing in Portugal was largely a post-war phenomenon using fairly dangerous circuits laid out in city streets. The city of **OPORTO** was the first to stage a major post-war international race, for sports cars, in 1950. That race became known as the Portuguese GP in 1951, again a sports car event. **LISBON** was the next city to stage a major race, coming up with the Lisbon GP in 1953, held on a circuit in the streets at Monsanto.

When the Portuguese GP became an F1 event in 1958 it was held first at Oporto, with Stirling Moss the winner in a Vanwall. Next it moved to Monsanto in 1959 and finally was held again at Oporto before the event disappeared from the calendar as concern about safety of spectators and drivers overcame the excitement of racing around the city streets.

Not until the start of the Seventies was a purpose-built Portuguese circuit mooted. It was operational by 1972 at **ESTORIL**, a coastal town a short distance west of Lisbon. The track of 2.7 miles (4.35km) offered variations on a rough rectangle with a long main straight, fast corners and a twisting infield section. Estoril staged F2 races and national events through to 1984 when, after major redevelopment and improvement, the circuit was deemed suitable to host the first Portuguese GP of the new era. Alain Prost was the winner of the inaugural event, repeating the success in 1987 and 1988.

Estoril is favoured for winter testing by many GP teams as the circuit offers a variety of corners and a good straight as well as enjoying a pleasant climate that allows test sessions uninterrupted by the vagaries of the weather.

South Africa

Racing has taken place in South Africa since the Twenties but a modern-style purpose-built circuit was not constructed until 1959 to replace the original road circuits.

EAST LONDON on South Africa's east coast was a 2.43-mile (3.91km) track which staged non-championship South African GPs until this fixture became the last date on the 1962 Championship calendar. East London ran GPs again in 1963 and 1965, by which time its limited facilities were proving inadequate for the needs of front-line racing.

After missing a year, however, the Championship returned to the country in 1967 to make use of the improved facilities at **KYALAMI** near Johannesburg. This circuit had been built in 1961 and had staged the non-Championship Rand GP several times. It had been improved sufficiently by the mid-Sixties to be suitable for GP racing. The lap distance was 2.54 miles (4.08km) and the circuit was fast with a long start-line straight and very quick corners on the back section.

Kyalami witnessed some great races and was popular with the drivers despite the restrictions placed on engine power by the high altitude. Turbocharged cars dominated at Kyalami for several seasons. Missing only 1981, the South African GP remained in the Championship calendar until 1985. By that time the political pressures were becoming greater and some teams were opting not to race in South Africa. Additionally, the facilities at Kyalami were not being upgraded sufficiently quickly to keep pace with the needs of modern GP racing.

Although the South African GP was last run in 1985, the circuit was completely redeveloped in 1987. It is now an excellent modern facility used for domestic racing and testing by some GP teams. However, the

MONACO

likelihood of GP racing returning to that troubled country is remote in the present political climate.

Spain

The Spanish tradition of motor sport is among the oldest in the world with the Spanish GP, at first an event for touring cars, run as early as 1913. Many circuits were used for international races after that date, including the impressive banked circuit at Sitges Terramar. The designers calculated the angle of the bankings wrongly and it was all too easy for cars to fly over the top to disaster. Just one GP was staged there, in 1923.

Thereafter, pre-war GPs were run at **PEDRALBES**, to the west of Barcelona. With the interruption of both the Spanish Civil War and World War 2, there was a long gap in Spanish racing until 1950. The first Championship GP was held at Pedralbes in 1951, where it took place again in 1954 before GP racing departed from Spain until 1967. Pedralbes was an interesting mixture of park road and suburban streets, stretching for 2.77 miles (4.43km).

Grand Prix racing would not return to Spain until the completion of a new circuit at **JARAMA**, near Madrid. The circuit was first used for international racing in 1967 and the GP went there in 1968. For a circuit designed from scratch, Jarama was not a great success. It fitted a little over two miles (3.2km) of

track into a very compact area, the track being quite narrow and twisting and turning back on itself with just one straight. The Spanish GP visited Jarama nine times until the circuit's size and condition at last became inadequate for the GP circus.

While Jarama was being built in the mid-Sixties, another circuit in Barcelona was undergoing a revival after a long layoff. **MONTJUICH PARK** had been used in the Thirties and the park's roadways were re-worked to give an exciting circuit of 2.35 miles (3.76km): so exciting, in fact, that safety considerations saw the Spanish GP staged there just four times, alternating with Jarama, the last event being in 1975 when a dispute between the teams and the circuit organizers plus a fatal accident involving spectators were the last straw.

When Jarama lost its GP status, there was no alternative venue in Spain for a GP until the construction of a brand-new circuit at **JEREZ**, way down in the wilds of barren southern Spain. Jerez is an uninspired diet of medium-speed corners and just one straight. It doesn't make for exciting racing and, although its facilities are ample and modern, it is not popular with specators or drivers who find its 2.62 miles (4.28km) fairly tedious, praising only its suitability for out-of-season testing in pleasant winter sunshine.

Sweden

Scandinavia has more of a tradition of rally driving than racing although there was inter-national competition in the Fifties for sports cars and single-seaters at Kristianstad and Karlskoga. However, not until the Seventies was there a Championship GP in Sweden. It enjoyed a brief fling in the Seventies before ending not long after the lives of Sweden's

GP stars, Ronnie Peterson and Gunnar Nilsson. The only circuit used by the Swedish GP in its six-year life was **ANDERSTORP** in the middle of the country. The circuit was built in 1973 in anticipation of great things from a new generation of Swedish F1 aspirants. In the event, a Swede would never win the Swedish GP although Peterson came close in 1973. An airfield contributed part of its runway as the main straight of this very flat circuit, which comprised a loop within a loop as part of a twisting 'home' section leading on to the straight.

It was not a particularly interesting or challenging circuit despite the curves of its 2.5 miles (4.03km). What was perhaps more interesting was the surprising GP winners it threw up, including Jody Scheckter in the six-wheel Tyrrell in 1976 and Niki Lauda in the subsequently-banned Brabham 'fan car' in the last running of the event in 1978.

Anderstorp survives in a frayed state as a venue for national meetings and the occasional international touring car event.

Other Swedish circuits include **MANTORP PARK**, about 250 miles (402km) south-west of Stockholm. Part of this circuit is public road. It was sufficiently successful to attract rounds of the F2 Championship in the early Eighties but this was a brief spell of internationalism as national interest in motor sport declined.

United States

Motor racing in the United States is a much more complicated business than it is in Europe. The sport is divided in different ways and the types of circuit often vary with the nature of the racing. There are literally dozens and dozens of circuits of all shapes and sizes dotted throughout this vast country.

Oldest of all the race tracks is **INDIANAPOLIS**. The Indianapolis Motor Speedway, home of the famous '500', was built in 1908 and the first 500 took place in 1911, running right through to the present day with a break during both World Wars.

The circuit is simple in the extreme with just four banked corners and two straights in its 2.5 miles (4.03km). However, the corners are all different and, at the remarkably high average speeds attained by Indy cars (over 200mph/320km/h average), they all have a correct line and must be driven with precision.

At first Indianapolis was surfaced with tar-covered gravel but that was replaced by a brick finish in 1910; hence the nickname

ESTORIL, Portugal

Right: Estoril was opened in the early Seventies but didn't host a GP until 1984

JEREZ, Spain

Left: The short straights and many corners of Jerez and, above, the sweeping track in the parched hills during the 1989 GP

'Brickyard'. Gradually the surface changed totally to smooth tarmac but the layout remains the same today as it was originally.

Contrasting with the oval racing taking place at Indianapolis, more European-style road racing had to wait until 1956 for the construction of a specially-designed track at **WATKINS GLEN**. This was a logical development of various public road circuits that had been used for races in this area of New York State in the Forties and early Fifties.

In its early form, Watkins Glen was a fairly simple affair, measuring 2.3 miles (3.68km) and winding through a hilly wooded area. The circuit had been in use for five years before it attracted the US Grand Prix in 1961, an event it would retain for many years. The circuit was widened, lengthened and considerably redeveloped in 1971 to give a 3.37-mile (5.43km) lap. However, the facilities were still relatively poor and by the

late Seventies the track needed further substantial investment to keep it up to GP standards. Eventually the need for money and the problems of overstretched facilities caused the GP to go elsewhere in 1980.

Perhaps best known among the other road-racing circuits of the USA is **SEBRING** in Florida. This was the scene of the first US Championship GP in 1959, although idiosyncratically Indianapolis was a round of the Championship until 1960. Sebring was a long course, created from an airfield, and for much of its life offered a 5.2-mile (8.3km) lap in a simple format which harked back to the simplicity of the original runways. However, in 1987 Sebring was redeveloped and shortened with sections of modern tarmac replacing some of the original concrete runways.

Sebring's racing days started in 1950 and ever since the circuit has maintained a tradition of top-flight sports car racing. The GP visited just once before decamping to

Right: The midfield runners thread their way through the concrete walls of the Phoenix circuit used for the 1989 US GP

RIVERSIDE for another one-off event. This Californian circuit just east of Los Angeles was a versatile design with a long straight and a twisting uphill back section. This circuit staged many different forms of racing apart from the one Championship GP in its third year of operation. Best known for sports car and NASCAR meetings, Riverside succumbed to the pressure of urban expansion in 1988, leaving a smaller circuit of local interest only.

While Indianapolis is rightly famous throughout the world, another oval at **DAYTONA** also takes its share of the limelight. In fact Daytona, which measures 2.5 miles (4.03km), is not a simple oval as the pit straight is distended to give added interest. Also, there is a simple road circuit variation off the oval which takes cars from the banking into the infield and round two hairpins before rejoining the main track. This permutation gives an extra 1.31 miles (2.10km) of lap length.

Daytona has been an active venue since 1959. Outside the United States the 24 Hours sports car race is probably the circuit's best-known event. However, it is for NASCAR racing that the circuit is renowned within the USA. The annual Daytona 500 attracts a massive crowd during the week-long festival each February where average speeds are consistently above the 150mph (241km/h) mark.

With the inauguration of the United States West GP in 1976, another circuit came to the fore in Los Angeles. **LONG BEACH**, within sight of Hotel Queen Mary, was a well-crafted and challenging circuit of just over two miles (3.2km). It called for great concentration as the barriers and walls were close to the track and run-off areas were tight.

After a shaky start, Long Beach developed into a successful venue and eight GPs were run there before the organizers decided there was more financial sense in running a round of the domestic CART single-seater championship than F1.

With the demise of Watkins Glen as a GP circuit in 1980, other cities decided that it would be advantageous for them to stage a GP. Following the example of the creation of a successful street circuit at Long Beach, **LAS VEGAS** was the first of the other cities to have a go. The car park adjacent to Caesar's Palace was the chosen site for this featureless, tight and twisting 2.26-mile (3.63km) track that ran between concrete blocks.

Las Vegas survived for just two seasons before the novelty wore off. Meanwhile **DETROIT**, heart of the USA's motor industry, had stepped forward to stage the Detroit GP in 1982. Short straights and endless right-angled corners were the hallmarks of this concrete-lined 2.56-mile (4.12km) track which managed an unbroken seven-year run of GPs through to 1987 before opting to stage CART racing instead.

DALLAS was another circuit to spring up in an attempt to take over the GP. However, the one-off Dallas GP of 1984 was the only time the F1 racers visited this contrived and tedious 2.42-mile (3.89km) circuit in the grounds of Dallas Fair Park.

With the USA again staging only one GP fixture in 1989, yet another circuit managed to put together the right deal to attract the teams. Another 'concrete tunnel' circuit, **PHOENIX**, Arizona, gave a 2.36-mile (3.79km) lap with a familiar recipe of short straights and right-angled bends. Like all the other temporary American circuits, with maybe the exception of Long Beach, Phoenix was not much liked by the drivers, some of whom yearned for the chance to be back at a 'proper' circuit like Watkins Glen. But the power of money and TV means that, for the time being, GP racing in the United States will stay in the streets or the car parks of a big city.

Right: Huge crowds at the Indianapolis Speedbowl watch the progress of the 1988 500-mile race

PHOENIX, USA

The Major Records

The results listed below stretch back right to 1911 in the case of Indianapolis. However, restraints of space mean that Grand Prix results are confined to those of the modern Championship years: 1950 to date. Before then GPs were of varying status and title and any compilation of results would be an involved web, to say the least. The results of Le Mans, Targa Florio and Mille Miglia are here in their entirety as they make interesting reading. Also included are the winners of the F1 World Championships, since 1950, both for drivers and constructors, plus the winners of the comparable titles in the world of sports car racing.

Italian driver Giancarlo Baghetti won the first Championship GP he ever entered, driving the 1.5-litre 'shark nose' F1 Ferrari. He is seen here on his winning way in that race at Reims in 1961

WORLD CHAMPIONSHIP GRAND PRIX RESULTS 1950–1989

1950

BRITISH GP
Silverstone, May 13
202 miles/325km

PLACE	DRIVER	CAR
1	G. Farina	Alfa Romeo
	90.95mph/145.52km/h	
2	L. Fagioli	Alfa Romeo
3	R. Parnell	Alfa Romeo
4	Y. Giraud-Canbantous	Lago-Talbot
5	L. Rosier	Lago-Talbot
6	R. Gerard	ERA

Fastest lap: G. Farina 94.02mph/151.28km/h
Pole position: Farina

MONACO GP
Monte Carlo, May 21
198 miles/318km

PLACE	DRIVER	CAR
1	J. M. Fangio	Alfa Romeo
	61.33mph/98.68km/h	
2	A. Ascari	Maserati
3	L. Chiron	Maserati
4	R. Sommer	Ferrari
5	B. Bira	Maserati
6	R. Gerard	ERA

Fastest lap: J. M. Fangio 64.09mph/103.12km/h
Pole position: J. M. Fangio

INDIANAPOLIS 500
Indianapolis, May 30
500 miles/805km

PLACE	DRIVER	CAR
1	J. Parsons	Wynn's Friction Proof
	124mph/199.52km/h	
2	W. Holland	Blue Crown
3	M. Rose	Howard Keck
4	C. Green	John Zink
5	J. Chitwood/ T. Bettennhausen	Wolfe
6	L. Wallard	

Fastest lap: W. Holland 129mph/207.56km/h
Pole position: W. Faulkner

SWISS GP
Bremgarten, June 4
190 miles/306km

PLACE	DRIVER	CAR
1	G. Farina	Alfa Romeo
	92.76mph/149.25km/h	
2	L. Fagioli	Alfa Romeo
3	L. Rosier	Lago Talbot
4	B. Bira	Maserati
5	F. Bonetto	Maserati
6	E. de Graffenried	Maserati

Fastest lap: G. Farina 100.78mph/162.15km/h
Pole position: J. M. Fangio (Alfa Romeo)

BELGIAN GP
Spa, June 18
307 miles/494km

PLACE	DRIVER	CAR
1	J. M. Fangio	Alfa Romeo
	110.05mph/177.07km/h	
2	L. Fagioli	Alfa Romeo
3	L. Rosier	Lago Talbot
4	G. Farina	Alfa Romeo
5	A. Ascari	Ferrari
6	L. Villoresi	Ferrari

Fastest lap: G. Farina 115.4mph/185.68km/h
Pole position: G. Farina

FRENCH GP
Reims, July 2
311 miles/500km

PLACE	DRIVER	CAR
1	J. M. Fangio	Alfa Romeo
	104.84mph/168.69km/h	
2	L. Fagioli	Alfa Romeo
3	P. Whitehead	Ferrari
4	R. Manzon	Simca-Gordini
5	P. Etancelin/E. Chaboud	Lago-Talbot
6	C. Pozzi/L. Rosier	Lago-Talbot

Fastest lap: J. M. Fangio 112.36mph/180.79km/h
Pole position: J. M. Fangio

ITALIAN GP
Monza, September 3
313 miles/504km

PLACE	DRIVER	CAR
1	G. Farina	Alfa Romeo
	109.63mph/176.39km/h	
2	D. Serafini/A. Ascari	Ferrari
3	L. Fagioli	Alfa Romeo
4	L. Rosier	Lago-Talbot
5	P. Etancelin	Lago-Talbot
6	E. de Graffenried	Maserati

Fastest lap: J. M. Fangio (Alfa Romeo)
117.44mph/186.96km/h
Pole position: J. M. Fangio

1951

SWISS GP
Bremgarten, May 27
190 miles/306km

PLACE	DRIVER	CAR
1	J. M. Fangio	Alfa Romeo
	89.05mph/143.28km/h	
2	P. Taruffi	Ferrari
3	G. Farina	Alfa Romeo
4	C. Sanesi	Alfa Romeo
5	E. De Graffenried	Alfa Romeo
6	A. Ascari	Ferrari

Fastest lap: J. M. Fangio 95.18mph/153.18km/h
Pole position: J. M. Fangio

INDIANAPOLIS 500
Indianapolis, May 30
500 miles/805km

PLACE	DRIVER	CAR
1	L. Wallard	Belanger
	126.24mph/203.12km/h	
2	M. Nazaruk	Robbins
3	J. McGrath/M. Ayulo	Hinkle
4	A. Linden	Leitenberger
5	B. Ball	Blakely
6	H. Banks	Blue Crown

Fastest lap: L. Wallard 133.81mph/215.30km/h
Pole position: D. Nalon (Novi Purelube)

BELGIAN GP
Spa, June 17
316 miles/508km

PLACE	DRIVER	CAR
1	G. Farina	Alfa Romeo
	114.3mph/183.94km/h	
2	A. Ascari	Ferrari
3	L. Villoresi	Ferrari
4	L. Rosier	Lago-Talbot
5	Y. Giraud-Canbantous	Lago-Talbot
6	A. Pilette	Lago-Talbot

Fastest lap: J. M. Fangio (Alfa Romeo)
120.51mph/193.90km/h
Pole position: J. M. Fangio

FRENCH GP
Reims, July 1
374 miles/602km

PLACE	DRIVER	CAR
1	J. M. Fangio/L. Fagioli	Alfa Romeo
	110.97mph/178.55km/h	
2	A. Ascari/F. Gonzalez	Ferrari
3	L. Villoresi	Ferrari
4	R. Parnell	Ferrari
5	G. Farina	Alfa Romeo
6	L. Chiron	Lago-Talbot

Fastest lap: J. M. Fangio 118.29mph/190.33km/h
Pole position: J. M. Fangio

BRITISH GP
Silverstone, July 14
260 miles/418km

PLACE	DRIVER	CAR
1	F. Gonzalez	Ferrari
	96.11mph/154.64km/h	
2	J. M. Fangio	Alfa Romeo
3	L. Villoresi	Ferrari
4	F. Bonetto	Alfa Romeo
5	R. Parnell	BRM
6	C. Sanesi	Alfa Romeo

Fastest lap: G. Farina (Alfa Romeo)
99.99mph/160.88km/h
Pole position: F. Gonzalez

GERMAN GP
Nürburgring, July 29
283 miles/456km

PLACE	DRIVER	CAR
1	A. Ascari	Ferrari
	83.76mph/134.77km/h	
2	J. M. Fangio	Alfa Romeo
3	F. Gonzalez	Ferrari
4	L. Villoresi	Ferrari
5	P. Taruffi	Ferrari
6	R. Fischer	Ferrari

Fastest lap: J. M. Fangio 85.64mph/137.79km/h
Pole position: A. Ascari

ITALIAN GP
Monza, September 16
313 miles/504km

PLACE	DRIVER	CAR
1	A. Ascari	Ferrari
	115.53mph/185.89km/h	
2	F. Gonzalez	Ferrari
3	G. Farina/F. Bonetto	Alfa Romeo
4	L. Villoresi	Ferrari
5	P. Taruffi	Ferrari
6	A. Simon	Simca-Gordini

Fastest lap: G. Farina 121.49mph/195.52km/h
Pole position: J. M. Fangio (Alfa Romeo)

1953

SPANISH GP
Pedralbes, October 28
275 miles/442km

PLACE	DRIVER	CAR
1	J. M. Fangio 98.76mph/158.90km/h	Alfa Romeo
2	F. Gonzalez	Ferrari
3	G. Farina	Alfa Romeo
4	A. Ascari	Ferrari
5	F. Bonetto	Alfa Romeo
6	E. de Graffenried	Alfa Romeo

Fastest lap: J. M. Fangio 105.20mph/169.27km/h
Pole position: A. Ascari

1952

SWISS GP
Bremgarten, May 18
280 miles/451km

PLACE	DRIVER	CAR
1	P. Taruffi 92.78mph/149.38km/h	Ferrari
2	R. Fischer	Ferrari
3	J. Behra	Gordini
4	K. Wharton	Frazer-Nash
5	A. Brown	Cooper-Bristol
6	E. de Graffenried	Masserati-Plate

Fastest lap: P. Taruffi 96.25mph/154.84km/h
Pole position: G. Farina (Ferrari)

INDIANAPOLIS 500
Indianapolis, May 30
500 miles/805km

PLACE	DRIVER	CAR
1	T. Ruttman 128.92mph/207.43km/h	Agajanian
2	J. Rathmann	Grancor-Wynn
3	S. Hanks	Bardahl
4	D. Carter	Belanger
5	A. Cross	Bowes Seal Fast
6	J. Bryan	Peter Schmidt

Fastest lap: W. Vukovich (Fuel Injection) 135.14mph/217.44km/h
Pole position: F. Agabashian (Cummins Diesel)

BELGIAN GP
Spa, June 22
316 miles/508km

PLACE	DRIVER	CAR
1	A. Ascari 103.13mph/165.94km/h	Ferrari
2	G. Farina	Ferrari
3	R. Manzon	Gordini
4	M. Hawthorn	Cooper-Bristol
5	P. Frere	HWM
6	A. Brown	Cooper-Bristol

Fastest lap: A. Ascari 107.44mph/172.87km/h
Pole position: A. Ascari

FRENCH GP
Rouen, July 6
240 miles/387km

PLACE	DRIVER	CAR
1	A. Ascari 80.14mph/128.94km/h	Ferrari
2	G. Farina	Ferrari
3	P. Taruffi	Ferrari
4	R. Manzon	Gordini
5	M. Trintignant	Gordini
6	P. Collins	HWM

Fastest lap: G. Farina 84.57mph/136.03km/h
Pole position: A. Ascari

BRITISH GP
Silverstone, July 19
249 miles/400km

PLACE	DRIVER	CAR
1	A. Ascari 90.92mph/146.29km/h	Ferrari
2	P. Taruffi	Ferrari
3	M. Hawthorn	Cooper-Bristol
4	D. Poore	Connaught
5	E. Thompson	Connaught
6	G. Farina	Ferrari

Fastest lap: A. Ascari 94.08mph/151.37km/h
Pole position: G. Farina

GERMAN GP
Nürburgring, August 3
255 miles/411km

PLACE	DRIVER	CAR
1	A. Ascari 82.20mph/132.26km/h	Ferrari
2	G. Farina	Ferrari
3	R. Fischer	Ferrari
4	P. Taruffi	Ferrari
5	J. Behra	Gordini
6	R. Laurent	Ferrari

Fastest lap: A. Ascari 84.33mph/135.71km/h
Pole position: A. Ascari

DUTCH GP
Zandvoort, August 17
234 miles/377km

PLACE	DRIVER	CAR
1	A. Ascari 81.15mph/130.57km/h	Ferrari
2	G. Farina	Ferrari
3	L. Villoresi	Ferrari
4	M. Hawthorn	Cooper-Bristol
5	R. Manzon	Gordini
6	M. Trintignant	Gordini

Fastest lap: A. Ascari 85.43mph/137.48km/h
Pole position: A. Ascari

ITALIAN GP
Monza, September 7
313 miles/504km

PLACE	DRIVER	CAR
1	A. Ascari 109.80mph/176.67km/h	Ferrari
2	F. Gonzalez	Maserati
3	L. Villoresi	Ferrari
4	G. Farina	Ferrari
5	F. Bonetto	Maserati
6	A. Simon	Ferrari

Fastest lap: A. Ascari and F. Gonzalez 111.76mph/179.86km/h
Pole position: A. Ascari

1953

ARGENTINE GP
Buenos Aires, January 18
236 miles/379km

PLACE	DRIVER	CAR
1	A. Ascari 78.14mph/125.73km/h	Ferrari
2	L. Villoresi	Ferrari
3	F. Gonzalez	Maserati
4	M. Hawthorn	Ferari
5	O. Galvez	Maserati
6	J. Behra	Gordini

Fastest lap: A. Ascari 80.74mph/129.93km/h
Pole position: A. Ascari

INDIANAPOLIS 500
Indianapolis, May 30
500 miles/805km

PLACE	DRIVER	CAR
1	W. Vukovich 128.92mph/207.14km/h	Fuel Injection
2	A. Cross	Springfield Welding
3	S. Hanks/D. Carter	Bardahl
4	F. Agabashian/P. Russo	Grancor-Elgin
5	J. McGrath	Hinkle
6	J. Daywalt	Sumar

Fastest lap: W. Vukovich 135.87mph/218.61km/h
Pole position: W. Vukovich

DUTCH GP
Zandvoort, June 7
234 miles/377km

PLACE	DRIVER	CAR
1	A. Ascari 81.04mph/130.39km/h	Ferrari
2	G. Farina	Ferrari
3	F. Bonetto/F. Gonzalez	Maserati
4	M. Hawthorn	Ferrari
5	E. de Graffenried	Maserati
6	M. Trintignant	Gordini

Fastest lap: L. Villoresi (Ferrari) 83.15mph/133.79km/h
Pole position: A. Ascari

BELGIAN GP
Spa, June 21
316 miles/508km

PLACE	DRIVER	CAR
1	A. Ascari 112.47mph/180.96km/h	Ferrari
2	L. Villoresi	Ferrari
3	O. Marimon	Maserati
4	E. de Graffenried	Maserati
5	M. Trintignant	Gordini
6	M. Hawthorn	Ferrari

Fastest lap: F. Gonzalez (Maserati) 115.27mph/185.47km/h
Pole position: J. M. Fangio (Maserati)

WORLD CHAMPIONSHIP GRAND PRIX RESULTS 1950–1989

1954

FRENCH GP

Reims, July 5
311 miles/500km

PLACE	DRIVER	CAR
1	M. Hawthorn 113.65mph/182.86km/h	Ferrari
2	J. M. Fangio	Maserati
3	F. Gonzalez	Maserati
4	A. Ascari	Ferrari
5	G. Farina	Ferrari
6	L. Villoresi	Ferrari

Fastest lap: J. M. Fangio 115.91mph/186.50km/h
Pole position: A. Ascari

BRITISH GP

Silverstone, July 18
263 miles/424km

1	A. Ascari 92.97mph/149.59km/h	Ferrari
2	J. M. Fangio	Maserati
3	G. Farina	Ferrari
4	F. Gonzalez	Maserati
5	M. Hawthorn	Ferrari
6	F. Bonetto	Maserati

Fastest lap: F. Gonzalez/A. Ascari 95.79mph/154.13km/h
Pole position: A. Ascari

GERMAN GP

Nürburgring, August 2
255 miles/411km

1	G. Farina 83.89mph/134.98km/h	Ferrari
2	J. M. Fangio	Maserati
3	M. Hawthorn	Ferrari
4	F. Bonetto	Maserati
5	E. de Graffenried	Maserati
6	S. Moss	Cooper-Alta

Fastest lap: A. Ascari (Ferrari) 85.62mph/137.76km/h
Pole position: A. Ascari

SWISS GP

Bremgarten, August 23
294 miles/473km

1	A. Ascari 97.17mph/156.35km/h	Ferrari
2	G. Farina	Ferrari
3	M. Hawthorn	Ferrari
4	F. Bonetto/J. M. Fangio	Maserati
5	H. Lang	Maserati
6	L. Villoresi	Ferrari

Fastest lap: A. Ascari 100.96mph/162.44km/h
Pole position: J. M. Fangio

ITALIAN GP

Monza, September 13
313 miles/504km

1	J. M. Fangio 110.69mph/178.10km/h	Maserati
2	G. Farina	Ferrari
3	L. Villoresi	Ferrari
4	M. Hawthorn	Ferrari
5	M. Trintignant	Gordini
6	R. Mieres	Gordini

Fastest lap: J. M. Fangio 113.20mph/182.14km/h
Pole position: A. Ascari (Ferrari)

ARGENTINE GP

Buenos Aires, January 17
211 miles/340km

PLACE	DRIVER	CAR
1	J. M. Fangio 70.13mph/112.84km/h	Maserati
2	G. Farina	Ferrari
3	F. Gonzalez	Ferrari
4	M. Trintignant	Ferrari
5	E. Bayol	Gordini
6	H. Schell	Maserati

Fastest lap: F. Gonzalez 80.76mph/129.95km/h
Pole position: G. Farina

INDIANAPOLIS 500

Indianapolis, May 31
500 miles/805km

1	W. Vukovich 130.84mph/210.52km/h	Fuel injection
2	J. Bryan	Dean Van Lines
3	J. McGrath	Hinkle
4	T. Ruttman/D. Carter	Auto Shippers
5	M. Nazaruk	McNamara
6	F. Agabashian	Merz

Fastest lap: J. McGrath 140.54mph/226.12km/h
Pole position: J. McGrath

BELGIAN GP

Spa, June 20
315 miles/507km

1	J. M. Fangio 115.08mph/185.16km/h	Maserati
2	M. Trintignant	Ferrari
3	S. Moss	Maserati
4	F. Gonzalez/M. Hawthorn	Ferrari
5	A. Pilette	Gordini
6	B. Bira	Maserati

Fastest lap: J. M. Fangio 118.97mph/191.42km/h
Pole position: J. M. Fangio

FRENCH GP

Reims, July 4
315 miles/507km

1	J. M. Fangio 115.97mph/186.64km/h	Mercedes-Benz
2	K. Kling	Mercedes-Benz
3	R. Manzon	Ferrari
4	B. Bira	Maserati
5	L. Villoresi	Maserati
6	J. Behra	Gordini

Fastest lap: H. Herrmann (Mercedes-Benz) 121.46mph/195.43km/h
Pole position: J. M. Fangio

BRITISH GP

Silverstone, July 17
263 miles/424km

PLACE	DRIVER	CAR
1	F. Gonzalez 89.69mph/144.31km/h	Ferrari
2	M. Hawthorn	Ferrari
3	O. Marimon	Maserati
4	J. M. Fangio	Mercedes-Benz
5	M. Trintignant	Ferrari
6	R. Mieres	Maserati

Fastest lap: F. Gonzalez/M. Hawthorn/
O. Marimon/J. M. Fangio/S. Moss (Maserati)/
A. Ascari (Maserati)/J. Behra (Gordini)
95.79mph/154.13km/h
Pole position: J. M. Fangio

GERMAN GP

Nürburgring, August 1
312 miles/502 km

1	J. M. Fangio 82.87mph/133.37km/h	Mercedes-Benz
2	F. Gonzalez/M. Hawthorn	Ferrari
3	M. Trintignant	Ferrari
4	K. Kling	Mercedez-Benz
5	S. Mantovani	Maserati
6	P. Taruffi	Ferrari

Fastest lap: K. Kling 85.75mph/137.97km/h
Pole position: J. M. Fangio

SWISS GP

Bremgarten, August 22
299 miles/480km

1	J. M. Fangio 99.17mph/159.56km/h	Mercedes-Benz
2	F. Gonzalez	Ferrari
3	H. Herrmann	Mercedes-Benz
4	R. Mieres	Maserati
5	S. Mantovani	Maserati
6	K. Wharton	Maserati

Fastest lap: J. M. Fangio 101.97mph/164.90km/h
Pole position: F. Gonzalez

ITALIAN GP

Monza, September 5
313 miles/504km

1	J. M. Fangio 111.98mph/180.17km/h	Mercedes-Benz
2	M. Hawthorn	Ferrari
3	F. Gonzalez/U. Maglioli	Ferrari
4	H. Herrmann	Mercedes-Benz
5	M. Trintignant	Ferrari
6	F. Wacker	Gordini

Fastest lap: F. Gonzalez 116.66mph/187.73km/h
Pole position: J. M. Fangio

SPANISH GP
Pedralbes, October 24
314 miles/505km

PLACE	DRIVER	CAR
1	M. Hawthorn 97.16mph/156.38km/h	Ferrari
2	L. Musso	Maserati
3	J. M. Fangio	Mercedes-Benz
4	R. Mieres	Maserati
5	K. Kling	Mercedes-Benz
6	F. Godia	Maserati

Fastest lap: A. Ascari (Lancia)
100.64mph/161.97km/h
Pole position: A. Ascari

1955

ARGENTINE GP
Buenos Aires, January 16
233 miles/376km

PLACE	DRIVER	CAR
1	J. M. Fangio 77.51mph/124.74km/h	Mercedes-Benz
2	F. Gonzalez/G. Farina/ M. Trintignant	Ferrari
3	G. Farina/U. Maglioli/ M. Trintignant	Ferrari
4	H. Herrmann/K. Kling/ S. Moss	Mercedes-Benz
5	R. Mieres	Maserati
6	H. Schell/J. Behra	Maserati

Fastest lap: J. M. Fangio 80.81mph/130.05km/h
Pole position: F. Gonzalez

MONACO GP
Monte Carlo, May 22
195 miles/315km

1	M. Trintignant 65.81mph/105.91km/h	Ferrari
2	E. Castellotti	Lancia
3	J. Behra/C. Perdisa	Maserati
4	G. Farina	Ferrari
5	L. Villoresi	Lancia
6	L. Chiron	Lancia

Fastest lap: J. M. Fangio (Mercedes-Benz)
68.70mph/110.57km/h
Pole position: J. M. Fangio

INDIANAPOLIS 500
Indianapolis, May 30
500 miles/805km

1	B. Sweikert 128.21mph/206.29km/h	John Zink
2	T. Bettenhausen/ P. Russo	Chapman
3	J. Davies	Bardahl
4	J. Thomson	Schmidt
5	W. Faulkner/B. Homeier	Merz
6	A. Linden	Massaglia

Fastest lap: W. Vukovich (Hopkins)
141.35mph/227.44km/h
Pole position: J. Hoyt (Jim Robins)

BELGIAN GP
Spa, June 5
316 miles/508km

PLACE	DRIVER	CAR
1	J. M. Fangio 118.83mph/191.24km/h	Mercedes-Benz
2	S. Moss	Mercedes-Benz
3	G. Farina	Ferrari
4	P. Frere	Ferrari
5	R. Mieres/J. Behra	Maserati
6	M. Trintignant	Ferrari

Fastest lap: J. M. Fangio 121.21mph/195.05km/h
Pole position: E. Castellotti (Lancia)

DUTCH GP
Zandvoort, June 19
261 miles/419km

1	J. M. Fangio 89.60mph/144.17km/h	Mercedes-Benz
2	S. Moss	Mercedes-Benz
3	L. Musso	Maserati
4	R. Mieres	Maserati
5	E. Castellotti	Ferrari
6	J. Behra	Maserati

Fastest lap: R. Mieres 92.96mph/149.60km/h
Pole position: J. M. Fangio

BRITISH GP
Aintree, July 16
270 miles/434km

1	S. Moss 86.47mph/139.16km/h	Mercedes-Benz
2	J. M. Fangio	Mercedes-Benz
3	K. Kling	Mercedes-Benz
4	P. Taruffi	Mercedes-Benz
5	L. Musso	Maserati
6	M. Hawthorn/ E. Castellotti	Ferrari

Fastest lap: S. Moss 89.70mph/144.36km/h
Pole position: S. Moss

ITALIAN GP
Monza, September 11
311 miles/500 km

1	J. M. Fangio 128.49mph/206.79km/h	Mercedes-Benz
2	P. Taruffi	Mercedes-Benz
3	E. Castellotti	Ferrari
4	J. Behra	Maserati
5	C. Menditeguy	Maserati
6	U. Maglioli	Ferrari

Fastest lap: S. Moss (Mercedes-Benz)
134.03mph/215.70km/h
Pole position: J. M. Fangio

1956

ARGENTINE GP
Buenos Aires, January 22
238 miles/383km

PLACE	DRIVER	CAR
1	L. Musso/J. M. Fangio 79.39mph/127.76km/h	Lancia-Ferrari
2	J. Behra	Maserati
3	M. Hawthorn	Maserati
4	C. Landi/G. Gerini	Maserati
5	O. Gendebien	Lancia-Ferrari
6	A. Uria/O. Gonzalez	Maserati

Fastest lap: J. M. Fangio 83.11mph/133.74km/h
Pole position: J. M. Fangio

MONACO GP
Monte Carlo, May 13
195 miles/315km

1	S. Moss 64.94mph/104.51km/h	Maserati
2	P. Collins/J. M. Fangio	Lancia-Ferrari
3	J. Behra	Maserati
4	J. M. Fangio/ E. Castellotti	Lancia-Ferrari
5	H. da Silva Ramos	Gordini
6	E. Bayol/A. Pilette	Gordini

Fastest lap: J. M. Fangio 67.39mph/108.45km/h
Pole position: J. M. Fangio

INDIANAPOLIS 500
Indianapolis, May 30
500 miles/805km

1	P. Flaherty 128.49mph/206.74km/h	John Zink
2	S. Hanks	Jones & Maley
3	D. Freeland	Bob Estes
4	J. Parsons	Agajanian
5	D. Rathmann	McNamara
6	B. Sweikert	D-A. Lubricant

Fastest lap: P. Russo (Novi Vespa)
144.42mph/232.37km/h
Pole position: P. Flaherty

BELGIAN GP
Spa, June 3
316 miles/508km

1	P. Collins 118.44mph/190.61km/h	Lancia-Ferrari
2	P. Frere	Lancia-Ferrari
3	C. Perdisa/S. Moss	Maserati
4	H. Schell	Vanwall
5	L. Villoresi	Maserati
6	A. Pilette	Lancia-Ferrari

Fastest lap: S. Moss 124.01mph/199.58km/h
Pole position: J. M. Fangio (Lancia-Ferrari)

FRENCH GP
Reims, July 1
315 miles/507km

1	P. Collins 122.29mph/196.80km/h	Lancia-Ferrari
2	E. Castellotti	Lancia-Ferrari
3	J. Behra	Maserati
4	J. M. Fangio	Lancia-Ferrari
5	C. Perdisa/S. Moss	Maserati
6	L. Rosier	Maserati

Fastest lap: J. M. Fangio 127.37mph/204.98km/h
Pole position: J. M. Fangio

WORLD CHAMPIONSHIP GRAND PRIX RESULTS 1950–1989

BRITISH GP
Silverstone, July 14
296 miles/476km

PLACE	DRIVER	CAR
1	J. M. Fangio 98.65mph/158.76km/h	Lancia-Ferrari
2	A. de Portago/P. Collins	Lancia-Ferrari
3	J. Behra	Maserati
4	J. Fairman	Connaught
5	H. Gould	Maserati
6	L. Villoresi	Maserati

Fastest lap: S. Moss (Maserati) 102.10mph/164.32km/h
Pole position: S. Moss

GERMAN GP
Nürburgring, August 5
312 miles/502km

1	J. M. Fangio 85.54mph/137.66km/h	Lancia-Ferrari
2	S. Moss	Maserati
3	J. Behra	Maserati
4	F. Godia	Maserati
5	L. Rosier	Maserati
	Only five finished	

Fastest lap: J. M. Fangio 87.73mph/141.19km/h
Pole position: J. M. Fangio

ITALIAN GP
Monza, September 2
311 miles/500km

1	S. Moss 129.73mph/208.79km/h	Maserati
2	P. Collins/J. M. Fangio	Lancia-Ferrari
3	R. Flockhart	Connaught
4	F. Godia	Maserati
5	J. Fairman	Connaught
6	L. Piotti	Maserati

Fastest lap: S. Moss 135.41mph/217.92km/h
Pole position: J. M. Fangio.

1957

ARGENTINE GP
Buenos Aires, January 13
243 miles/391km

PLACE	DRIVER	CAR
1	J. M. Fangio 80.61mph/129.73km/h	Maserati
2	J. Behra	Maserati
3	C. Menditeguy	Maserati
4	H. Schell	Maserati
5	F. Gonzalez/ A. de Portago	Lancia-Ferrari
6	C. Perdisa/W. von Trips/ P. Collins	Lancia-Ferrari

Fastest lap: S. Moss (Maserati) 83.58mph/134.51km/h
Pole position: S. Moss

MONACO GP
Monte Carlo, May 19
205 miles/330km

PLACE	DRIVER	CAR
1	J. M. Fangio 64.72mph/104.16km/h	Maserati
2	C. A. S. Brooks	Vanwall
3	M. Gregory	Maserati
4	S. Lewis-Evans	Connaught
5	M. Trintignant	Lancia-Ferrari
6	J. Brabham	Cooper-Climax

Fastest lap: J. M. Fangio 66.62mph/107.22km/h
Pole position: J. M. Fangio

INDIANAPOLIS 500
Indianapolis, May 30
500 miles/805km

1	S. Hanks 135.60mph/218.18km/h	Belond Exhaust
2	J. Rathmann	Chiropractic
3	J. Bryan	Dean Van Lines
4	P. Russo	Novi Auto Air
5	A. Linden	McNamara
6	J. Boyd	Bowes Seal Fast

Fastest lap: J. Rathmann 143.43mph/230.77km/h
Pole position: P. O.'Connor (Sumar)

FRENCH GP
Rouen, July 7
313 miles/504km

1	J. M. Fangio 100.02mph/160.96km/h	Maserati
2	L. Musso	Lancia-Ferrari
3	P. Collins	Lancia-Ferrari
4	M. Hawthorn	Lancia-Ferrari
5	J. Behra	Maserati
6	H. Schell	Maserati

Fastest lap: L. Musso 102.87mph/165.55km/h
Pole position: J. M. Fangio

BRITISH GP
Aintree, July 20
270 miles/434km

1	C. A. S. Brooks/S. Moss 86.79mph/139.68km/h	Vanwall
2	L. Musso	Lancia-Ferrari
3	M. Hawthorn	Lancia-Ferrari
4	M. Trintignant/P. Collins	Lancia-Ferrari
5	R. Salvadori	Cooper-Climax
6	F. R. Gerard	Cooper-Bristol

Fastest lap: S. Moss 90.60mph/145.81km/h
Pole position: S. Moss

GERMAN GP
Nürburgring, August 4
312 miles/502km

1	J. M. Fangio 88.82mph/142.95km/h	Maserati
2	M. Hawthorn	Lancia-Ferrari
3	P. Collins	Lancia-Ferrari
4	L. Musso	Lancia-Ferrari
5	S. Moss	Vanwall
6	J. Behra	Maserati

Fastest lap: J. M. Fangio 91.54mph/147.32km/h
Pole position: J. M. Fangio

PESCARA GP
Pescara, August 18
286 miles/460km

PLACE	DRIVER	CAR
1	S. Moss 95.70mph/154.00km/h	Vanwall
2	J. M. Fangio	Maserati
3	H. Schell	Maserati
4	M. Gregory	Maserati
5	S. Lewis-Evans	Vanwall
6	G. Scarlatti	Maserati

Fastest lap: S. Moss 97.88mph/157.50km/h
Pole position: J. M. Fangio

ITALIAN GP
Monza, September 8
311 miles/500km

1	S. Moss 120.27mph/193.56km/h	Vanwall
2	J. M. Fangio	Maserati
3	W. von Trips	Lancia-Ferrari
4	M. Gregory	Maserati
5	G. Scarlatti/H. Schell	Maserati
6	M. Hawthorn	Lancia-Ferrari

Fastest lap: C. A. S. Brooks (Vanwall) 124.03mph/199.61km/h
Pole position: S. Lewis-Evans (Vanwall)

1958

ARGENTINE GP
Buenos Aires, January 19
194 miles/313km

PLACE	DRIVER	CAR
1	S. Moss 83.61mph/134.56km/h	Cooper-Climax
2	L. Musso	Ferrari
3	M. Hawthorn	Ferrari
4	J. M. Fangio	Maserati
5	J. Behra	Maserati
6	H. Schell	Maserati

Fastest lap: J. M. Fangio 85.96mph/138.34km/h
Pole position: J. M. Fangio

MONACO GP
Monte Carlo, May 18
195 miles/315km

1	M. Trintignant 67.99mph/109.41km/h	Cooper-Climax
2	L. Musso	Ferrari
3	P. Collins	Ferrari
4	J. Brabham	Cooper-Climax
5	H. Schell	BRM
6	C. Allison	Lotus-Climax

Fastest lap: M. Hawthorn (Ferrari) 69.93mph/112.55km/h
Pole position: C. A. S. Brooks (Vanwall)

1959

DUTCH GP
Zandvoort, May 25
195 miles/315km

PLACE	DRIVER	CAR
1	S. Moss 93.95mph/151.16km/h	Vanwall
2	H. Schell	BRM
3	J. Behra	BRM
4	R. Salvadori	Cooper-Climax
5	M. Hawthorn	Ferrari
6	C. Allison	Lotus-Climax

Fastest lap: S. Moss 96.10mph/154.66km/h
Pole position: S. Lewis-Evans (Vanwall)

INDIANAPOLIS 500
Indianapolis, May 30
500 miles/805km

PLACE	DRIVER	CAR
1	J. Bryan 133.79mph/215.27km/h	Belond Exhaust
2	G. Amick	Demler
3	J. Boyd	Bowes Seal Fast
4	T. Bettenhausen	Jones & Maley
5	J. Rathmann	Leader Card
6	J. Reece	John Zink

Fastest lap: T. Bettenhausen
144.30mph/232.18km/h
Pole position: D. Rathmann (McNamara)

BELGIAN GP
Spa, June 15
210 miles/338km

PLACE	DRIVER	CAR
1	C. A. S. Brooks 129.92mph/209.09km/h	Vanwall
2	M. Hawthorn	Ferrari
3	S. Lewis-Evans	Vanwall
4	C. Allison	Lotus-Climax
5	H. Schell	BRM
6	O. Gendebien	Ferrari

Fastest lap: M. Hawthorn 132.36mph/213.01km/h
Pole position: M. Hawthorn

FRENCH GP
Reims, July 6
258 miles/415km

PLACE	DRIVER	CAR
1	M. Hawthorn 125.45mph/201.90km/h	Ferrari
2	S. Moss	Vanwall
3	W. von Trips	Ferrari
4	J. M. Fangio	Maserati
5	P. Collins	Ferrari
6	J. Brabham	Cooper-Climax

Fastest lap: M. Hawthorn 128.16mph/206.25km/h
Pole position: M. Hawthorn

BRITISH GP
Silverstone, July 19
220 miles/353km

PLACE	DRIVER	CAR
1	P. Collins 102.05mph/164.23km/h	Ferrari
2	M. Hawthorn	Ferrari
3	R. Salvadori	Cooper-Climax
4	S. Lewis-Evans	Vanwall
5	H. Schell	BRM
6	J. Brabham	Cooper-Climax

Fastest lap: M. Hawthorn 104.53mph/168.23km/h
Pole position: S. Moss (Vanwall)

GERMAN GP
Nürburgring, August 3
213 miles/342km

PLACE	DRIVER	CAR
1	C. A. S. Brooks 90.31mph/145.34km/h	Vanwall
2	R. Salvadori	Cooper-Climax
3	M. Trintignant	Cooper-Climax
4	W. von Trips	Ferrari
5	B. McLaren	Cooper-Climax
6	E. Barth	Porsche

Fastest lap: S. Moss (Vanwall)
92.91mph/149.50km/h
Pole position: M. Hawthorn (Ferrari)

PORTUGUESE GP
Oporto, August 24
230 miles/370km

PLACE	DRIVER	CAR
1	S. Moss 105.03mph/169.03km/h	Vanwall
2	M. Hawthorn	Ferrari
3	S. Lewis-Evans	Vanwall
4	J. Behra	BRM
5	W. von Trips	Ferrari
6	H. Schell	BRM

Fastest lap: M. Hawthorn 110.75mph/178.20km/h
Pole position: S. Moss

ITALIAN GP
Monza, September 7
250 miles/402km

PLACE	DRIVER	CAR
1	C. A. S. Brooks 121.22mph/195.05km/h	Vanwall
2	M. Hawthorn	Ferrari
3	P. Hill	Ferrari
4	M. Gregory/C. Shelby	Maserati
5	R. Salvadori	Cooper-Climax
6	G. Hill	Lotus-Climax

Fastest lap: P. Hill 125.00mph/201.17km/h
Pole position: S. Moss (Vanwall)

MOROCCAN GP
Casablanca, October 19
251 miles/403km

PLACE	DRIVER	CAR
1	S. Moss 116.46mph/187.43km/h	Vanwall
2	M. Hawthorn	Ferrari
3	P. Hill	Ferrari
4	J. Bonnier	BRM
5	H. Schell	BRM
6	M. Gregory	Maserati

Fastest lap: S. Moss 119.59mph/192.46km/h
Pole position: M. Hawthorn

MONACO GP
Monte Carlo, May 10
195 miles/315km

PLACE	DRIVER	CAR
1	J. Brabham 66.71mph/107.36km/h	Cooper-Climax
2	C. A. S. Brooks	Ferrari
3	M. Trintignant	Cooper-Climax
4	P. Hill	Ferrari
5	B. McLaren	Cooper-Climax
6	R. Salvadori	Cooper-Maserati

Fastest lap: J. Brabham 70.07mph/112.77km/h
Pole position: S. Moss (Cooper-Climax)

INDIANAPOLIS 500
Indianapolis, May 30
500 miles/805km

PLACE	DRIVER	CAR
1	R. Ward 135.86mph/218.60km/h	Leader Card
2	J. Rathmann	Simoniz
3	J. Thomson	Racing Associates
4	T. Bettenhausen	Hoover M.E.
5	P. Goldsmith	Demler
6	J. Boyd	Bowes Seal Fast

Fastest lap: J. Thomson 145.42mph/233.98km/h
Pole position: J. Thomson

DUTCH GP
Zandvoort, May 31
195 miles/315km

PLACE	DRIVER	CAR
1	J. Bonnier 93.46mph/150.41km/h	BRM
2	J. Brabham	Cooper-Climax
3	M. Gregory	Cooper-Climax
4	I. Ireland	Lotus-Climax
5	J. Behra	Ferrari
6	P. Hill	Ferrari

Fastest lap: S. Moss (Cooper-Climax)
96.99mph/156.09km/h
Pole position: J. Bonnier

FRENCH GP
Reims, July 5
258 miles/415km

PLACE	DRIVER	CAR
1	C. A. S. Brooks 127.43mph/205.05km/h	Ferrari
2	P. Hill	Ferrari
3	J. Brabham	Cooper-Climax
4	O. Gendebien	Ferrari
5	B. McLaren	Cooper-Climax
6	R. Flockhart	BRM

Fastest lap: S. Moss (BRM)
130.05mph/209.29km/h
Pole position: C. A. S. Brooks

WORLD CHAMPIONSHIP GRAND PRIX RESULTS 1950–1989

BRITISH GP
Aintree, July 18
225 miles/362km

PLACE	DRIVER	CAR
1	J. Brabham 89.88mph/144.65km/h	Cooper-Climax
2	S. Moss	BRM
3	B. McLaren	Cooper-Climax
4	H. Schell	BRM
5	M. Trintignant	Cooper-Climax
6	R. Salvadori	Aston Martin

Fastest lap: S. Moss/B. McLaren 92.31mph/148.56km/h
Pole position: J. Brabham

GERMAN GP
Avus, August 2
309 miles/498km

PLACE	DRIVER	CAR
1	C. A. S. Brooks 146.67mph/236.04km/h	Ferrari
2	D. Gurney	Ferrari
3	P. Hill	Ferrari
4	M. Trintignant	Cooper-Climax
5	J. Bonnier	BRM
6	I. Burgess	Cooper-Maserati

Fastest lap: C. A. S. Brooks 149.14mph/239.97km/h
Pole position: (Heat 1) J. Brabham (Cooper-Climax); (Heat 2) C. A. S. Brooks

PORTUGUESE GP
Monsanto, August 23
210 miles/338km

PLACE	DRIVER	CAR
1	S. Moss 95.32mph/153.40km/h	Cooper-Climax
2	M. Gregory	Cooper-Climax
3	D. Gurney	Ferrari
4	M. Trintignant	Cooper-Climax
5	H. Schell	BRM
6	R. Salvadori	Aston Martin

Fastest lap: S. Moss 97.30mph/156.58km/h
Pole position: S. Moss

ITALIAN GP
Monza, September 13
257 miles/414km

PLACE	DRIVER	CAR
1	S. Moss 124.38mph/200.18km/h	Cooper-Climax
2	P. Hill	Ferrari
3	J. Brabham	Cooper-Climax
4	D. Gurney	Ferrari
5	C. Allison	Ferrari
6	O. Gendebien	Ferrari

Fastest lap: P. Hill 128.11mph/206.14km/h
Pole position: S. Moss

UNITED STATES GP
Sebring, December 12
218 miles/352km

PLACE	DRIVER	CAR
1	B. McLaren 98.83mph/159.06km/h	Cooper-Climax
2	M. Trintignant	Cooper-Climax
3	C. A. S. Brooks	Ferrari
4	J. Brabham	Cooper-Climax
5	I. Ireland	Lotus-Climax
6	W. von Trips	Ferrari

Fastest lap: M. Trintignant 101.19mph/162.85km/h
Pole position: S. Moss (Cooper-Climax)

1960

ARGENTINE GP
Buenos Aires, February 7
194 miles/313km

PLACE	DRIVER	CAR
1	B. McLaren 82.77mph/133.18km/h	Cooper-Climax
2	C. Allison	Ferrari
3	M. Trintignant/S. Moss	Cooper-Climax
4	C. Menditeguy	Cooper-Maserati
5	W. von Trips	Ferrari
6	I. Ireland	Lotus-Climax

Fastest lap: S. Moss 88.48mph/142.36km/h
Pole position: S. Moss

MONACO GP
Monte Carlo, May 29
195 miles/315km

1	S. Moss 67.48mph/108.60km/h	Lotus-Climax
2	B. McLaren	Cooper-Climax
3	P. Hill	Ferrari
4	C. A. S. Brooks	Cooper-Climax
5	J. Bonnier	BRM
6	R. Ginther	Ferrari

Fastest lap: B. McLaren 73.13mph/117.69km/h
Pole position: S. Moss

INDIANAPOLIS 500
Indianapolis, May 30
500 miles/805km

1	J. Rathmann 138.77mph/223.28km/h	Ken Paul
2	R. Ward	Leader Card
3	P. Goldsmith	Demler
4	D. Branson	Bob Estes
5	J. Thomson	Adams Quarter-Horse
6	E. Johnson	Jim Robbins

Fastest lap: J. Rathmann 146.13mph/235.12km/h
Pole position: E. Sachs (Dean Van Lines)

DUTCH GP
Zandvoort, June 6
195 miles/315km

PLACE	DRIVER	CAR
1	J. Brabham 96.27mph/154.90km/h	Cooper-Climax
2	I. Ireland	Lotus-Climax
3	G. Hill	BRM
4	S. Moss	Lotus-Climax
5	W. von Trips	Ferrari
6	R. Ginther	Ferrari

Fastest lap: S. Moss 99.99mph/160.90km/h
Pole position: S. Moss

BELGIAN GP
Spa, June 19
315 miles/507km

1	J. Brabham 133.63mph/215.02km/h	Cooper-Climax
2	B. McLaren	Cooper-Climax
3	O. Gendebien	Cooper-Climax
4	P. Hill	Ferrari
5	J. Clark	Lotus-Climax
6	L. Bianchi	Cooper-Climax

Fastest lap: J. Brabham/P. Hill/I. Ireland (Lotus-Climax) 136.01mph/218.89km/h
Pole position: J. Brabham

FRENCH GP
Reims, July 3
258 miles/415km

1	J. Brabham 131.19mph/212.69km/h	Cooper-Climax
2	O. Gendebien	Cooper-Climax
3	B. McLaren	Cooper-Climax
4	H. Taylor	Cooper-Climax
5	J. Clark	Lotus-Climax
6	R. Flockhart	Lotus-Climax

Fastest lap: J. Brabham 135.06mph/217.32km/h
Pole position: J. Brabham

BRITISH GP
Silverstone, July 16
225 miles/362km

1	J. Brabham 108.69mph/174.90km/h	Cooper-Climax
2	J. Surtees	Lotus-Climax
3	I. Ireland	Lotus-Climax
4	B. McLaren	Cooper-Climax
5	C. A. S. Brooks	Cooper-Climax
6	W. von Trips	Ferrari

Fastest lap: G. Hill (BRM) 111.62mph/179.60km/h
Pole position: J. Brabham

PORTUGUESE GP
Oporto, August 14
253 miles/407km

1	J. Brabham 109.27mph/175.82km/h	Cooper-Climax
2	B. McLaren	Cooper-Climax
3	J. Clark	Lotus-Climax
4	W. von Trips	Ferrari
5	C. A. S. Brooks	Cooper-Climax
6	I. Ireland	Lotus-Climax

Fastest lap: J. Surtees (Lotus-Climax) 112.31mph/180.70km/h
Pole position: J. Surtees

ITALIAN GP
Monza, September 4
311 miles/500km

PLACE	DRIVER	CAR
1	P. Hill 132.06mph/212.51km/h	Ferrari
2	R. Ginther	Ferrari
3	W. Mairesse	Ferrari
4	G. Cabianca	Cooper-Ferrari
5	W. von Trips	Ferrari
6	H. Herrmann	Porsche

Fastest lap: P. Hill 136.73mph/220.00km/h
Pole position: P. Hill

UNITED STATES GP
Riverside, November 20
246 miles/395km

PLACE	DRIVER	CAR
1	S. Moss 99.00mph/159.31km/h	Lotus-Climax
2	I. Ireland	Lotus-Climax
3	B. McLaren	Cooper-Climax
4	J. Brabham	Cooper-Climax
5	J. Bonnier	BRM
6	P. Hill	Cooper-Climax

Fastest lap: J. Brabham 101.38mph/163.15km/h
Pole position: S. Moss

1961

MONACO GP
Monte Carlo, May 14
195 miles/315km

PLACE	DRIVER	CAR
1	S. Moss 70.70mph/113.76km/h	Lotus-Climax
2	R. Ginther	Ferrari
3	P. Hill	Ferrari
4	W. von Trips	Ferrari
5	D. Gurney	Porsche
6	B. McLaren	Cooper-Climax

Fastest lap: R. Ginther/S. Moss 72.05mph/115.93km/h
Pole position: S. Moss

DUTCH GP
Zandvoort, May 22
195 miles/315km

PLACE	DRIVER	CAR
1	W. von Trips 96.21mph/154.80km/h	Ferrari
2	P. Hill	Ferrari
3	J. Clark	Lotus-Climax
4	S. Moss	Lotus-Climax
5	R. Ginther	Ferrari
6	J. Brabham	Cooper-Climax

Fastest lap: J. Clark 98.21mph/158.03km/h
Pole position: P. Hill

BELGIAN GP
Spa, June 18
263 miles/424km

PLACE	DRIVER	CAR
1	P. Hill 128.15mph/206.20km/h	Ferrari
2	W. von Trips	Ferrari
3	R. Ginther	Ferrari
4	O. Gendebien	Ferrari
5	J. Surtees	Cooper-Climax
6	D. Gurney	Porsche

Fastest lap: R. Ginther 131.53mph/211.60km/h
Pole position: P. Hill

FRENCH GP
Reims, July 2
268 miles/432km

PLACE	DRIVER	CAR
1	G. Baghetti 119.85mph/192.82km/h	Ferrari
2	D. Gurney	Porsche
3	J. Clark	Lotus-Climax
4	I. Ireland	Lotus-Climax
5	B. McLaren	Cooper-Climax
6	G. Hill	BRM-Climax

Fastest lap: P. Hill 126.25mph/203.18km/h
Pole position: P. Hill

BRITISH GP
Aintree, July 15
225 miles/362km

PLACE	DRIVER	CAR
1	W. von Trips 83.91mph/135.02km/h	Ferrari
2	P. Hill	Ferrari
3	R. Ginther	Ferrari
4	J. Brabham	Cooper-Climax
5	J. Bonnier	Porsche
6	R. Salvadori	Cooper-Climax

Fastest lap: C. A. S. Brooks (BRM-Climax) 91.68mph/147.54km/h
Pole position: P. Hill

GERMAN GP
Nürburgring, August 6
212 miles/341km

PLACE	DRIVER	CAR
1	S. Moss 92.30mph/148.54km/h	Lotus-Climax
2	W. von Trips	Ferrari
3	P. Hill	Ferrari
4	J. Clark	Lotus-Climax
5	J. Surtees	Cooper-Climax
6	B. McLaren	Cooper-Climax

Fastest lap: P. Hill 94.88mph/152.69km/h
Pole position: P. Hill

ITALIAN GP
Monza, September 10
267 miles/430km

PLACE	DRIVER	CAR
1	P. Hill 130.11mph/209.36km/h	Ferrari
2	D. Gurney	Porsche
3	B. McLaren	Cooper-Climax
4	J. Lewis	Cooper-Climax
5	C. A. S. Brooks	BRM-Climax
6	R. Salvadori	Cooper-Climax

Fastest lap: G. Baghetti (Ferrari) 132.83mph/213.74km/h
Pole position: W. von Trips (Ferrari)

UNITED STATES GP
Watkins Glen, October 8
230 miles/370km

PLACE	DRIVER	CAR
1	I. Ireland 103.17mph/166.03km/h	Lotus-Climax
2	D. Gurney	Porsche
3	C. A. S. Brooks	BRM-Climax
4	B. McLaren	Cooper-Climax
5	G. Hill	BRM-Climax
6	J. Bonnier	Porsche

Fastest lap: S. Moss (Lotus-Climax) 105.80mph/170.23km/h
Pole position: J. Brabham (Cooper-Climax)

1962

DUTCH GP
Zandvoort, May 20
208 miles/335km

PLACE	DRIVER	CAR
1	G. Hill 95.44mph/153.57km/h	BRM
2	T. Taylor	Lotus-Climax
3	P. Hill	Ferrari
4	G. Baghetti	Ferrari
5	A. Maggs	Cooper-Climax
6	C. G. de Beaufort	Porsche

Fastest lap: B. McLaren (Cooper-Climax) 99.36mph/159.88km/h
Pole position: J. Surtees (Lola-Climax)

MONACO GP
Monte Carlo, June 3
195 miles/315km

PLACE	DRIVER	CAR
1	B. McLaren 70.46pmh/113.37km/h	Cooper-Climax
2	P. Hill	Ferrari
3	L. Bandini	Ferrari
4	J. Surtees	Lola-Climax
5	J. Bonnier	Porsche
6	G. Hill	BRM

Fastest lap: J. Clark (Lotus-Climax) 73.67mph/118.54km/h
Pole position: J. Clark

WORLD CHAMPIONSHIP GRAND PRIX RESULTS 1950–1989

BELGIAN GP
Spa, June 17
280 miles/451km

PLACE	DRIVER	CAR
1	J. Clark 131.90mph/212.24km/h	Lotus-Climax
2	G. Hill	BRM
3	P. Hill	Ferrari
4	R. Rodriguez	Ferrari
5	J. Surtees	Lola-Climax
6	J. Brabham	Lotus-Climax

Fastest lap: J. Clark 133.98mph/215.57km/h
Pole position: G. Hill

FRENCH GP
Rouen, July 8
220 miles/353km

PLACE	DRIVER	CAR
1	D. Gurney 101.89mph/163.94km/h	Porsche
2	A. Maggs	Cooper-Climax
3	R. Ginther	BRM
4	B. McLaren	Cooper-Climax
5	J. Surtees	Lola-Climax
6	C. G. de Beaufort	Porsche

Fastest lap: G. Hill (BRM) 106.90mph/172.01km/h
Pole position: J. Clark (Lotus-Climax)

BRITISH GP
Aintree, July 21
225 miles/362km

PLACE	DRIVER	CAR
1	J. Clark 92.25mph/148.44km/h	Lotus-Climax
2	J. Surtees	Lola-Climax
3	B. McLaren	Cooper-Climax
4	G. Hill	BRM
5	J. Brabham	Lotus-Climax
6	A. Maggs	Cooper-Climax

Fastest lap: J. Clark 93.91mph/151.10km/h
Pole position: J. Clark

GERMAN GP
Nürburgring, August 5
212 miles/341km

PLACE	DRIVER	CAR
1	G. Hill 80.35mph/129.30km/h	BRM
2	J. Surtees	Lola-Climax
3	D. Gurney	Porsche
4	J. Clark	Lotus-Climax
5	B. McLaren	Cooper-Climax
6	R. Rodriguez	Ferrari

Fastest lap: G. Hill 83.30mph/134.03km/h
Pole position: D. Gurney

ITALIAN GP
Monza, September 16
307 miles/494km

PLACE	DRIVER	CAR
1	G. Hill 123.62mph/198.91km/h	BRM
2	R. Ginther	BRM
3	B. McLaren	Cooper-Climax
4	W. Mairesse	Ferrari
5	G. Baghetti	Ferrari
6	J. Bonnier	Porsche

Fastest lap: G. Hill 125.73mph/202.32km/h
Pole position: J. Clark (Lotus-Climax)

UNITED STATES GP
Watkins Glen, October 7
230 miles/370km

PLACE	DRIVER	CAR
1	J. Clark 108.48mph/174.58km/h	Lotus-Climax
2	G. Hill	BRM
3	B. McLaren	Cooper-Climax
4	J. Brabham	Brabham-Climax
5	D. Gurney	Porsche
6	M. Gregory	Lotus-BRM

Fastest lap: J. Clark 110.40mph/177.64km/h
Pole position: J. Clark

SOUTH AFRICAN GP
East London, December 29
200 miles/321km

PLACE	DRIVER	CAR
1	G. Hill 93.57mph/150.55km/h	BRM
2	B. McLaren	Cooper-Climax
3	A. Maggs	Cooper-Climax
4	J. Brabham	Brabham-Climax
5	I. Ireland	Lotus-Climax
6	N. Lederle	Lotus-Climax

Fastest lap: J. Clark (Lotus-Climax) 96.35mph/155.03km/h
Pole position: J. Clark

1963

MONACO GP
Monte Carlo, May 26
195 miles/315km

PLACE	DRIVER	CAR
1	G. Hill 72.42mph/116.56km/h	BRM
2	R. Ginther	BRM
3	B. McLaren	Cooper-Climax
4	J. Surtees	Ferrari
5	A. Maggs	Cooper-Climax
6	T. Taylor	Lotus-Climax

Fastest lap: J. Surtees 74.45mph/119.81km/h
Pole position: J. Clark (Lotus-Climax)

BELGIAN GP
Spa, June 9
280 miles/451km

PLACE	DRIVER	CAR
1	J. Clark 114.10mph/183.63km/h	Lotus-Climax
2	B. McLaren	Cooper-Climax
3	D. Gurney	Brabham-Climax
4	R. Ginther	BRM
5	J. Bonnier	Cooper-Climax
6	C. G. de Beaufort	Porsche

Fastest lap: J. Clark 132.47mph/213.19km/h
Pole position: G. Hill (BRM)

DUTCH GP
Zandvoort, June 23
208 miles/335km

PLACE	DRIVER	CAR
1	J. Clark 97.53mph/156.96km/h	Lotus-Climax
2	D. Gurney	Brabham-Climax
3	J. Surtees	Ferrari
4	I. Ireland	BRP-BRM
5	R. Ginther	BRM
6	L. Scarfiotti	Ferrari

Fastest lap: J. Clark 100.10mph/161.10km/h
Pole position: J. Clark

FRENCH GP
Reims, June 30
273 miles/440km

PLACE	DRIVER	CAR
1	J. Clark 125.31mph/210.67km/h	Lotus-Climax
2	A. Maggs	Cooper-Climax
3	G. Hill	BRM
4	J. Brabham	Brabham-Climax
5	D. Gurney	Brabham-Climax
6	J. Siffert	Lotus-BRM

Fastest lap: J. Clark 131.15mph/211.06km/h
Pole position: J. Clark

BRITISH GP
Silverstone, July 20
240 miles/387km

PLACE	DRIVER	CAR
1	J. Clark 107.35mph/172.75km/h	Lotus-Climax
2	J. Surtees	Ferrari
3	G. Hill	BRM
4	R. Ginther	BRM
5	L. Bandini	BRM
6	J. Hall	Lotus-BRM

Fastest lap: J. Surtees 109.76mph/176.65km/h
Pole position: J. Clark

GERMAN GP
Nürburgring, August 4
213 miles/342km

PLACE	DRIVER	CAR
1	J. Surtees 95.83mph/154.22km/h	Ferrari
2	J. Clark	Lotus-Climax
3	R. Ginther	BRM
4	G. Mitter	Porsche
5	J. Hall	Lotus-BRM
6	J. Bonnier	Cooper-Climax

Fastest lap: J. Surtees 96.82mph/155.82km/h
Pole position: J. Clark

ITALIAN GP
Monza, September 8
307 miles/494km

PLACE	DRIVER	CAR
1	J. Clark 127.74mph/205.58km/h	Lotus-Climax
2	R. Ginther	BRM
3	B. McLaren	Cooper-Climax
4	I. Ireland	BRP-BRM
5	J. Brabham	Brabham-Climax
6	A. Maggs	Cooper-Climax

Fastest lap: J. Clark 130.05mph/209.28km/h
Pole position: J. Surtees (Ferrari)

UNITED STATES GP
Watkins Glen, October 6
253 miles/407km

PLACE	DRIVER	CAR
1	G. Hill	BRM
	108.92mph/175.29km/h	
2	R. Ginther	BRM
3	J. Clark	Lotus-Climax
4	J. Brabham	Brabham-Climax
5	L. Bandini	Ferrari
6	C. G. de Beaufort	Porsche

Fastest lap: J. Clark 111.14mph/178.83km/h
Pole position: G. Hill

MEXICAN GP
Mexico City, October 27
202 miles/325km

PLACE	DRIVER	CAR
1	J. Clark	Lotus-Climax
	93.30mph/150.15km/h	
2	J. Brabham	Brabham-Climax
3	R. Ginther	BRM
4	G. Hill	BRM
5	J. Bonnier	Cooper-Climax
6	D. Gurney	Brabham-Climax

Fastest lap: J. Clark 94.71mph/152.42km/h
Pole position: J. Clark

1964

MONACO GP
Monte Carlo, May 10
195 miles/315km

PLACE	DRIVER	CAR
1	G. Hill	BRM
	72.64mph/116.88km/h	
2	R. Ginther	BRM
3	P. Arundell	Lotus-Climax
4	J. Clark	Lotus-Climax
5	J. Bonnier	Cooper-Climax
6	M. Hailwood	Lotus-BRM

Fastest lap: G. Hill 74.92mph/120.55km/h
Pole position: J. Clark

DUTCH GP
Zandvoort, May 24
208 miles/335km

PLACE	DRIVER	CAR
1	J. Clark	Lotus-Climax
	98.02mph/157.71km/h	
2	J. Surtees	Ferrari
3	P. Arundell	Lotus-Climax
4	G. Hill	BRM
5	C. Amon	Lotus-BRM
6	R. Anderson	Brabham-Climax

Fastest lap: J. Clark 101.07mph/162.62km/h
Pole position: D. Gurney (Brabham-Climax)

BELGIAN GP
Spa, June 14
280 miles/451km

PLACE	DRIVER	CAR
1	J. Clark	Lotus-Climax
	132.79mph/213.68km/h	
2	B. McLaren	Cooper-Climax
3	J. Brabham	Brabham-Climax
4	R. Ginther	BRM
5	G. Hill	BRM
6	D. Gurney	Brabham-Climax

Fastest lap: D. Gurney 137.61mph/221.42km/h
Pole position: D. Gurney

FRENCH GP
Rouen, June 28
232 miles/373km

PLACE	DRIVER	CAR
1	D. Gurney	Brabham-Climax
	108.77mph/175.01km/h	
2	G. Hill	BRM
3	J. Brabham	Brabham-Climax
4	P. Arundell	Lotus-Climax
5	R. Ginther	BRM
6	B. McLaren	Cooper-Climax

Fastest lap: J. Brabham 111.37mph/179.20km/h
Pole position: J. Clark (Lotus-Climax)

BRITISH GP
Brands Hatch, July 11
212 miles/ 341km

PLACE	DRIVER	CAR
1	J. Clark	Lotus-Climax
	94.14mph/151.47km/h	
2	G. Hill	BRM
3	J. Surtees	Ferrari
4	J. Brabham	Brabham-Climax
5	L. Bandini	Ferrari
6	P. Hill	Cooper-Climax

Fastest lap: J. Clark 96.56mph/155.36km/h
Pole position: J. Clark

GERMAN GP
Nürburgring, August 2
213 miles/342km

PLACE	DRIVER	CAR
1	J. Surtees	Ferrari
	96.58mph/155.40km/h	
2	G. Hill	BRM
3	L. Bandini	Ferrari
4	J. Siffert	Brabham-BRM
5	M. Trintignant	BRM
6	A. Maggs	BRM

Fastest lap: J. Surtees 98.31mph/158.20km/h
Pole position: J. Surtees

AUSTRIAN GP
Zeltweg, August 23
209 miles/336km

PLACE	DRIVER	CAR
1	L. Bandini	Ferrari
	99.20mph/159.62km/h	
2	R. Ginther	BRM
3	R. Anderson	Brabham-Climax
4	A. Maggs	BRM
5	I. Ireland	BRP-BRM
6	J. Bonnier	Brabham-Climax

Fastest lap: D. Gurney (Brabham-Climax)
101.57mph/163.46km/h
Pole position: G. Hill (BRM)

ITALIAN GP
Monza, September 6
279 miles/449km

PLACE	DRIVER	CAR
1	J. Surtees	Ferrari
	127.78mph/205.60km/h	
2	B. McLaren	Cooper-Climax
3	L. Bandini	Ferrari
4	R. Ginther	BRM
5	I. Ireland	BRP-BRM
6	M. Spence	Lotus-Climax

Fastest lap: J. Surtees 130.19mph/209.51km/h
Pole position: J. Surtees

UNITED STATES GP
Watkins Glen, October 4
253 miles/407km

PLACE	DRIVER	CAR
1	G. Hill	BRM
	111.10mph/178.77km/h	
2	J. Surtees	Ferrari
3	J. Siffert	Brabham-BRM
4	R. Ginther	BRM
5	W. Hansgen	Lotus-Climax
6	T. Taylor	BRP-BRM

Fastest lap: J. Clark (Lotus-Climax)
113.89mph/183.25km/h
Pole position: J. Clark

MEXICAN GP
Mexico City, October 25
202 miles/325km

	DRIVER	CAR
1	D. Gurney	Brabham-Climax
	93.32mph/150.16km/h	
2	J. Surtees	Ferrari
3	L. Bandini	Ferrari
4	M. Spence	Lotus-Climax
5	J. Clark	Lotus-Climax
6	P. Rodriguez	Ferrari

Fastest lap: J. Clark 94.49mph/152.07km/h
Pole position: J. Clark

1965

SOUTH AFRICAN GP
East London, Jan 1
207 miles/333km

PLACE	DRIVER	CAR
1	J. Clark	Lotus-Climax
	97.97mph/157.63km/h	
2	J. Surtees	Ferrari
3	G. Hill	BRM
4	M. Spence	Lotus-Climax
5	B. McLaren	Cooper-Climax
6	J. Stewart	BRM

Fastest lap: J. Clark 100.10mph/161.06km/h
Pole position: J. Clark

WORLD CHAMPIONSHIP GRAND PRIX RESULTS 1950–1989

1966

MONACO GP
Monte Carlo, May 30
195 miles/315km

PLACE	DRIVER	CAR
1	G. Hill 74.34mph/119.60km/h	BRM
2	L. Bandini	Ferrari
3	J. Stewart	BRM
4	J. Surtees	Ferrari
5	B. McLaren	Cooper-Climax
6	J. Siffert	Brabham-BRM

Fastest lap: G. Hill 76.72mph/123.44km/h
Pole position: G. Hill

BELGIAN GP
Spa, June 13
280 miles/451km

PLACE	DRIVER	CAR
1	J. Clark 117.16mph/188.51km/h	Lotus-Climax
2	J. Stewart	BRM
3	B. McLaren	Cooper-Climax
4	J. Brabham	Brabhma-Climax
5	G. Hill	BRM
6	R. Ginther	Honda

Fastest lap: J. Clark 124.72mph/200.67km/h
Pole position: G. Hill

FRENCH GP
Clermont-Ferrand, June 27
200 miles/321km

PLACE	DRIVER	CAR
1	J. Clark 89.22mph/143.56km/h	Lotus-Climax
2	J. Stewart	BRM
3	J. Surtees	Ferrari
4	D. Hulme	Brabham-Climax
5	G. Hill	BRM
6	J. Siffert	Brabham-BRM

Fastest lap: J. Clark 90.59mph/145.79km/h
Pole position: J. Clark

BRITISH GP
Silverstone, July 10
234 miles/377km

PLACE	DRIVER	CAR
1	J. Clark 112.02mph/180.25km/h	Lotus-Climax
2	G. Hill	BRM
3	J. Surtees	Ferrari
4	M. Spence	Lotus-Climax
5	J. Stewart	BRM
6	D. Gurney	Brabham-Climax

Fastest lap: G. Hill 114.29mph/183.90km/h
Pole position: J. Clark

DUTCH GP
Zandvoort, July 18
208 miles/335km

PLACE	DRIVER	CAR
1	J. Clark 100.87mph/162.30km/h	Lotus-Climax
2	J. Stewart	BRM
3	D. Gurney	Brabham-Climax
4	G. Hill	BRM
5	D. Hulme	Brabham-Climax
6	R. Ginther	Honda

Fastest lap: J. Clark 103.53mph/166.58km/h
Pole position: G. Hill

GERMAN GP
Nürburgring, August 1
213 miles/342km

PLACE	DRIVER	CAR
1	J. Clark 99.76mph/160.54km/h	Lotus-Climax
2	G. Hill	BRM
3	D. Gurney	Brabham-Climax
4	J. Rindt	Cooper-Climax
5	J. Brabham	Brabham-Climax
6	L. Bandini	Ferrari

Fastest lap: J. Clark 101.22mph/162.87km/h
Pole position: J. Clark

ITALIAN GP
Monza, September 12
272 miles/437km

PLACE	DRIVER	CAR
1	J. Stewart 130.46mph/209.92km/h	BRM
2	G. Hill	BRM
3	D. Gurney	Brabham-Climax
4	L. Bandini	Ferrari
5	B. McLaren	Cooper-Climax
6	R. Attwood	Lotus-Climax

Fastest lap: J. Clark (Lotus-Climax) 133.43mph/ 214.70km/h
Pole position: J. Clark

UNITED STATES GP
Watkins Glen, October 3
253 miles/407km

PLACE	DRIVER	CAR
1	G. Hill 107.98mph/173.74km/h	BRM
2	D. Gurney	Brabham-Climax
3	J. Brabham	Brabham-Climax
4	L. Bandini	Ferrari
5	P. Rodriguez	Ferrari
6	J. Rindt	Cooper-Climax

Fastest lap: G. Hill 115.16mph/185.30km/h
Pole position: G. Hill

MEXICAN GP
Mexico City, October 24
202 miles/325km

PLACE	DRIVER	CAR
1	R. Ginther 94.26mph/151.66km/h	Honda
2	D. Gurney	Brabham-Climax
3	M. Spence	Lotus-Climax
4	J. Siffert	Brabham-BRM
5	R. Bucknum	Honda
6	R. Attwood	Lotus-BRM

Fastest lap: D. Gurney 96.55mph/155.39km/h
Pole position: J. Clark (Lotus-Climax)

MONACO GP
Monte Carlo, May 22
195 miles/315km

PLACE	DRIVER	CAR
1	J. Stewart 76.52mph/123.14km/h	BRM
2	L. Bandini	Ferrari
3	G. Hill	BRM
4	B. Bondurant	BRM

(Only four finished)
Fastest lap: L. Bandini 78.34mph/126.08km/h
Pole position: J. Clark (Lotus-Climax)

BELGIAN GP
Spa, June 12
245 miles/394km

PLACE	DRIVER	CAR
1	J. Surtees 113.93mph/183.36km/h	Ferrari
2	J. Rindt	Cooper-Maserati
3	L. Bandini	Ferrari
4	J. Brabham	Brabham-Repco
5	R. Ginther	Cooper-Maserati

(Only five finished)
Fastest lap: J. Surtees 121.92mph/196.21km/h
Pole position: J. Surtees

FRENCH GP
Reims, July 3
248 miles/398km

PLACE	DRIVER	CAR
1	J. Brabham 136.90mph/220.32km/h	Brabham-Repco
2	M. Parkes	Ferrari
3	D. Hulme	Brabham-Repco
4	J. Rindt	Cooper-Maserati
5	D. Gurney	Eagle-Climax
6	J. Taylor	Brabham-BRM

Fastest lap: L. Bandini (Ferrari) 141.44mph/227.62km/h
Pole position: L. Bandini

BRITISH GP
Brands Hatch, July 16
212 miles/341km

PLACE	DRIVER	CAR
1	J. Brabham 95.48mph/153.66km/h	Brabham-Repco
2	D. Hulme	Brabham-Repco
3	G. Hill	BRM
4	J. Clark	Lotus-Climax
5	J. Rindt	Cooper-Maserati
6	B. McLaren	McLaren-Serenissima

Fastest lap: J. Brabham 98.35mph/158.28km/h
Pole position: J. Brabham

DUTCH GP
Zandvoort, July 24
234 miles/377km

PLACE	DRIVER	CAR
1	J. Brabham 100.11mph/161.11km/h	Brabham-Repco
2	G. Hill	BRM
3	J. Clark	Lotus-Climax
4	J. Stewart	BRM
5	M. Spence	Lotus-BRM
6	L. Bandini	Ferrari

Fastest lap: D. Hulme (Brabham-Repco) 103.53mph/166.61km/h
Pole position: J. Brabham

1967

GERMAN GP
Nürburgring, August 7
213 miles/342km

PLACE	DRIVER	CAR
1	J. Brabham 86.75mph/139.61km/h	Brabham-Repco
2	J. Surtees	Cooper-Maserati
3	J. Rindt	Cooper-Maserati
4	G. Hill	BRM
5	J. Stewart	BRM
6	L. Bandini	Ferrari

Fastest lap: J. Surtees 96.45mph/155.23km/h
Pole position: J. Clark (Lotus-Climax)

ITALIAN GP
Monza, September 4
243 miles/391km

PLACE	DRIVER	CAR
1	L. Scarfiotti 135.92mph/218.75km/h	Ferrari
2	M. Parkes	Ferrari
3	D. Hulme	Brabham-Repco
4	J. Rindt	Cooper-Maserati
5	M. Spence	Lotus-BRM
6	R. Anderson	Brabham-Climax

Fastest lap: L. Scarfiotti 139.20mph/224.03km/h
Pole position: M. Parkes

UNITED STATES GP
Watkins Glen, October 2
248 miles/398km

PLACE	DRIVER	CAR
1	J. Clark 114.94mph/184.98km/h	Lotus-BRM
2	J. Rindt	Cooper-Maserati
3	J. Surtees	Cooper-Maserati
4	J. Siffert	Cooper-Maserati
5	B. McLaren	McLaren-Ford
6	P. Arundell	Lotus-Climax

Fastest lap: J. Surtees 118.85mph/191.26km/h
Pole position: J. Brabham (Brabham-Repco)

MEXICAN GP
Mexico City, October 23
202 miles/325km

PLACE	DRIVER	CAR
1	J. Surtees 95.72mph/154.04km/h	Cooper-Maserati
2	J. Brabham	Brabham-Repco
3	D. Hulme	Brabham-Repco
4	R. Ginther	Honda
5	D. Gurney	Eagle-Climax
6	J. Bonnier	Cooper-Maserati

Fastest lap: R. Ginther 98.33mph/158.24km/h
Pole position: J. Surtees

SOUTH AFRICAN GP
Kyalami, January 2
204 miles/328km

PLACE	DRIVER	CAR
1	P. Rodriguez 97.09mph/156.26km/h	Cooper-Maserati
2	J. Love	Cooper-Climax
3	J. Surtees	Honda
4	D. Hulme	Brabham-Repco
5	R. Anderson	Brabham-Climax
6	J. Brabham	Brabham-Repco

Fastest lap: D. Hulme 101.87mph/163.95km/h
Pole position: J. Brabham

MONACO GP
Monte Carlo, May 7
195 miles/315km

PLACE	DRIVER	CAR
1	D. Hulme 75.90mph/122.14km/h	Brabham-Repco
2	G. Hill	Lotus-BRM
3	C. Amon	Ferrari
4	B. McLaren	McLaren-BRM
5	P. Rodriguez	Cooper-Maserati
6	M. Spence	BRM

Fastest lap: J. Clark (Lotus-Climax) 78.61mph/126.50km/h
Pole position: J. Brabham (Brabham-Repco)

DUTCH GP
Zandvoort, June 4
234 miles/377km

PLACE	DRIVER	CAR
1	J. Clark 104.44mph/168.09km/h	Lotus-Ford
2	J. Brabham	Brabham-Repco
3	D. Hulme	Brabham-Repco
4	C. Amon	Ferrari
5	M. Parkes	Ferrari
6	L. Scarfiotti	Ferrari

Fastest lap: J. Clark 106.49mph/171.39km/h
Pole position: G. Hill (Lotus-Ford)

BELGIAN GP
Spa, June 18
245 miles/394km

PLACE	DRIVER	CAR
1	D. Gurney 145.99mph/234.95km/h	Eagle-Weslake
2	J. Stewart	BRM
3	C. Amon	Ferrari
4	J. Rindt	Cooper-Maserati
5	M. Spence	BRM
6	J. Clark	Lotus-Ford

Fastest lap: D. Gurney 148.85mph/239.55km/h
Pole position: J. Clark

FRENCH GP
Le Mans, July 2
220 miles/355km

PLACE	DRIVER	CAR
1	J. Brabham 98.90mph/159.17km/h	Brabham-Repco
2	D. Hulme	Brabham-Repco
3	J. Stewart	BRM
4	J. Siffert	Cooper-Maserati
5	C. Irwin	BRM
6	P. Rodriguez	Cooper-Maserati

Fastest lap: G. Hill (Lotus-Ford) 102.29mph/164.64km/h
Pole position: G. Hill

BRITISH GP
Silverstone, July 15
234 miles/377km

PLACE	DRIVER	CAR
1	J. Clark 117.64mph/189.33km/h	Lotus-Ford
2	D. Hulme	Brabham-Repco
3	C. Amon	Ferrari
4	J. Brabham	Brabham-Repco
5	P. Rodriguez	Cooper-Maserati
6	J. Surtees	Honda

Fastest lap: D. Hulme 121.12mph/194.92km/h
Pole position: J. Clark

GERMAN GP
Nürburgring, August 6
213 miles/342km

PLACE	DRIVER	CAR
1	D. Hulme 101.41mph/163.20km/h	Brabham-Repco
2	J. Brabham	Brabham-Repco
3	C. Amon	Ferrari
4	J. Surtees	Honda
5	J. Bonnier	Cooper-Maserati
6	G. Ligier	Brabham-Repco

Fastest lap: D. Gurney (Eagle-Weslake) 103.17mph/166.04km/h
Pole position: J. Clark (Lotus-Ford)

CANADIAN GP
Mosport, August 27
221 miles/356km

PLACE	DRIVER	CAR
1	J. Brabham 82.65mph/133.01km/h	Brabham-Repco
2	D. Hulme	Brabham-Repco
3	D. Gurney	Eagle-Weslake
4	G. Hill	Lotus-Ford
5	M. Spence	BRM
6	C. Amon	Ferrari

Fastest lap: J. Clark (Lotus-Ford) 106.54mph/171.47km/h
Pole position: J. Clark

ITALIAN GP
Monza, September 10
243 miles/391km

PLACE	DRIVER	CAR
1	J. Surtees 140.50mph/226.12km/h	Honda
2	J. Brabham	Brabham-Repco
3	J. Clark	Lotus-Ford
4	J. Rindt	Cooper-Maserati
5	M. Spence	BRM
6	J. Ickx	Cooper-Maserati

Fastest lap: J. Clark 145.34mph/233.90km/h
Pole position: J. Clark

UNITED STATES GP
Watkins Glen, October 1
248 miles/398km

PLACE	DRIVER	CAR
1	J. Clark 120.95mph/194.66km/h	Lotus-Ford
2	G. Hill	Lotus-Ford
3	D. Hulme	Brabham-Repco
4	J. Siffert	Cooper-Maserati
5	J. Brabham	Brabham-Repco
6	J. Bonnier	Cooper-Maserati

Fastest lap: G. Hill 125.46mph/201.90km/h
Pole position: G. Hill

WORLD CHAMPIONSHIP GRAND PRIX RESULTS 1950–1989

MEXICAN GP
Mexico City, October 22
202 miles/325km

PLACE	DRIVER	CAR
1	J. Clark 101.42mph/163.22km/h	Lotus-Ford
2	J. Brabham	Brabham-Repco
3	D. Hulme	Brabham-Repco
4	J. Surtees	Honda
5	M. Spence	BRM
6	P. Rodriguez	Cooper-Maserati

Fastest lap: J. Clark 103.44mph/166.47km/h
Pole position: J. Clark

1968

SOUTH AFRICAN GP
Kyalami, January 1
204 miles/328km

PLACE	DRIVER	CAR
1	J. Clark 107.42mph/172.89km/h	Lotus-Ford
2	G. Hill	Lotus-Ford
3	J. Rindt	Brabham-Repco
4	C. Amon	Ferrari
5	D. Hulme	McLaren-BRM
6	J. P. Beltoise	Matra-Ford

Fastest lap: J. Clark 109.68mph/176.51km/h
Pole position: J. Clark

SPANISH GP
Jarama, May 12
190 miles/306km

PLACE	DRIVER	CAR
1	G. Hill 84.40mph/135.84km/h	Lotus-Ford
2	D. Hulme	McLaren-Ford
3	B. Redman	Cooper-BRM
4	L. Scarfiotti	Cooper-BRM
5	J. P. Beltoise	Matra-Ford

(Only five finished)
Fastest lap: J. P. Beltoise 86.24mph/138.80km/h
Pole position: C. Amon (Ferrari)

MONACO GP
Monte Carlo, May 26
156 miles/252km

PLACE	DRIVER	CAR
1	G. Hill 77.82mph/125.24km/h	Lotus-Ford
2	R. Attwood	BRM
3	L. Bianchi	Cooper-BRM
4	L. Scarfiotti	Cooper-BRM
5	D. Hulme	McLaren-Ford

(Only five finished)
Fastest lap: R. Attwood 79.85mph/128.51km/h
Pole position: G. Hill

BELGIAN GP
Spa, June 9
245 miles/394km

PLACE	DRIVER	CAR
1	B. McLaren 147.14mph/236.80km/h	McLaren-Ford
2	P. Rodriguez	BRM
3	J. Ickx	Ferrari
4	J. Stewart	Matra-Ford
5	J. Oliver	Lotus-Ford
6	L. Bianchi	Cooper-BRM

Fastest lap: J. Surtees (Honda)
149.84mph/241.14km/h
Pole position: C. Amon (Ferrari)

DUTCH GP
Zandvoort, June 23
234 miles/377km

1	J. Stewart 84.66mph/136.25km/h	Matra-Ford
2	J. P. Beltoise	Matra
3	P. Rodriguez	BRM
4	J. Ickx	Ferrari
5	S. Moser	Brabham-Repco
6	C. Amon	Ferrari

Fastest lap: J. P. Beltoise 88.56mph/142.52km/h
Pole position: C. Amon

FRENCH GP
Rouen, July 7
244 miles/393km

1	J. Ickx 100.45mph/161.66km/h	Ferrari
2	J. Surtees	Honda
3	J. Stewart	Matra-Ford
4	V. Elford	Cooper-BRM
5	D. Hulme	McLaren-Ford
6	P. Courage	BRM

Fastest lap: P. Rodriguez (BRM)
111.29mph/179.10km/h
Pole position: J. Rindt (Brabham-Repco)

BRITISH GP
Brands Hatch, July 20
212 miles/341km

1	J. Siffert 104.83mph/168.70km/h	Lotus-Ford
2	C. Amon	Ferrari
3	J. Ickx	Ferrari
4	D. Hulme	McLaren-Ford
5	J. Surtees	Honda
6	J. Stewart	Matra-Ford

Fastest lap: J. Siffert 106.35mph/171.16km/h
Pole position: G. Hill (Lotus-Ford)

GERMAN GP
Nürburgring, August 4
199 miles/320km

PLACE	DRIVER	CAR
1	J. Stewart 85.71mph/137.94km/h	Matra-Ford
2	G. Hill	Lotus-Ford
3	J. Rindt	Brabham-Repco
4	J. Ickx	Ferrari
5	J. Brabham	Brabham-Repco
6	P. Rodriguez	BRM

Fastest lap: J. Stewart 88.68mph/142.72km/h
Pole position: J. Ickx

ITALIAN GP
Monza, September 8
243 miles/391km

1	D. Hulme 145.41mph/234.02km/h	McLaren-Ford
2	J. Servoz-Gavin	Matra-Ford
3	J. Ickx	Ferrari
4	P. Courage	BRM
5	J. P. Beltoise	Matra
6	J. Bonnier	McLaren-BRM

Fastest lap: J. Oliver (Lotus-Ford)
148.70mph/239.31km/h
Pole position: J. Surtees (Honda)

CANADIAN GP
St Jovite, September 22
239 miles/384km

1	D. Hulme 97.22mph/156.47km/h	McLaren-Ford
2	B. McLaren	McLaren-Ford
3	P. Rodriguez	BRM
4	G. Hill	Lotus-Ford
5	V. Elford	Cooper-BRM
6	J. Stewart	Matra-Ford

Fastest lap: J. Siffert (Lotus-Ford)
100.31mph/161.44km/h
Pole position: J. Rindt (Brabham-Repco)

UNITED STATES GP
Watkins Glen, October 6
248 miles/398km

1	J. Stewart 124.90mph/200.99km/h	Matra-Ford
2	G. Hill	Lotus-Ford
3	J. Surtees	Honda
4	D. Gurney	McLaren-Ford
5	J. Siffert	Lotus-Ford
6	B. McLaren	McLaren-Ford

Fastest lap: J. Stewart 126.96mph/204.31km/h
Pole position: M. Andretti (Lotus-Ford)

MEXICAN GP
Mexico City, November 3
202 miles/325km

1	G. Hill 103.80mph/167.05km/h	Lotus-Ford
2	B. McLaren	McLaren-Ford
3	J. Oliver	Lotus-Ford
4	P. Rodriguez	BRM
5	J. Bonnier	Honda
6	J. Siffert	Lotus-Ford

Fastest lap: J. Siffert 107.31mph/172.70km/h
Pole position: J. Siffert

1969

SOUTH AFRICAN GP
Kyalami, March 1
204 miles/328km

PLACE	DRIVER	CAR
1	J. Stewart 110.62mph/178.03km/h	Matra-Ford
2	G. Hill	Lotus-Ford
3	D. Hulme	McLaren-Ford
4	J. Siffert	Lotus-Ford
5	B. McLaren	McLaren-Ford
6	J. P. Beltoise	Matra-Ford

Fastest lap: J. Stewart 112.50mph/181.05km/h
Pole position: J. Brabham (Brabham-Ford)

SPANISH GP
Montjuich, May 4
212 miles/341km

PLACE	DRIVER	CAR
1	J. Stewart 92.91mph/149.52km/h	Matra-Ford
2	B. McLaren	McLaren-Ford
3	J. P. Beltoise	Matra-Ford
4	D. Hulme	McLaren-Ford
5	J. Surtees	BRM
6	J. Ickx	Brabham-Ford

Fastest lap: J. Rindt (Lotus-Ford) 96.02mph/154.54km/h
Pole position: J. Rindt

MONACO GP
Monte Carlo, May 18
156 miles/252km

PLACE	DRIVER	CAR
1	G. Hill 80.18mph/129.04km/h	Lotus-Ford
2	P. Courage	Brabham-Ford
3	J. Siffert	Lotus-Ford
4	R. Attwood	Lotus-Ford
5	B. McLaren	McLaren-Ford
6	D. Hulme	McLaren-Ford

Fastest lap: J. Stewart (Matra-Ford) 82.67mph/133.04km/h
Pole position: J. Stewart

DUTCH GP
Zandvoort, June 21
234 miles/377km

PLACE	DRIVER	CAR
1	J. Stewart 111.04mph/178.71km/h	Matra-Ford
2	J. Siffert	Lotus-Ford
3	C. Amon	Ferrari
4	D. Hulme	McLaren-Ford
5	J. Ickx	Brabham-Ford
6	J. Brabham	Brabham-Ford

Fastest lap: J. Stewart 113.09mph/182.00km/h
Pole position: J. Rindt (Lotus-Ford)

FRENCH GP
Clermont-Ferrand, July 6
190 miles/306km

PLACE	DRIVER	CAR
1	J. Stewart 97.71mph/157.25km/h	Matra-Ford
2	J. P. Beltoise	Matra-Ford
3	J. Ickx	Brabham-Ford
4	B. McLaren	McLaren-Ford
5	V. Elford	McLaren-Ford
6	G. Hill	Lotus-Ford

Fastest lap: J. Stewart 98.62mph/158.72km/h
Pole position: J. Stewart

BRITISH GP
Silverstone, July 19
246 miles/395km

PLACE	DRIVER	CAR
1	J. Stewart 127.25mph/204.79km/h	Matra-Ford
2	J. Ickx	Brabham-Ford
3	B. McLaren	McLaren-Ford
4	J. Rindt	Lotus-Ford
5	P. Courage	Brabham-Ford
6	V. Elford	McLaren-Ford

Fastest lap: J. Stewart 129.61mph/208.58km/h
Pole position: J. Rindt

GERMAN GP
Nürburgring, August 3
199 miles/320km

PLACE	DRIVER	CAR
1	J. Ickx 108.43mph/174.50km/h	Brabham-Ford
2	J. Stewart	Matra-Ford
3	B. McLaren	McLaren-Ford
4	G. Hill	Lotus-Ford
5	J. Siffert	Lotus-Ford
6	J. P. Beltoise	Matra-Ford

Fastest lap: J. Ickx 110.13mph/177.24km/h
Pole position: J. Ickx

ITALIAN GP
Monza, September 7
243 miles/391km

PLACE	DRIVER	CAR
1	J. Stewart 146.97mph/236.52km/h	Matra-Ford
2	J. Rindt	Lotus-Ford
3	J. P. Beltoise	Matra-Ford
4	B. McLaren	McLaren-Ford
5	P. Courage	Brabham-Ford
6	P. Rodriguez	Ferrari

Fastest lap: J. P. Beltoise 150.97mph/242.96km/h
Pole position: J. Rindt

CANADIAN GP
Mosport, September 20
221 miles/356km

PLACE	DRIVER	CAR
1	J. Ickx 111.18mph/178.93km/h	Brabham-Ford
2	J. Brabham	Brabham-Ford
3	J. Rindt	Lotus-Ford
4	J. P. Beltoise	Matra-Ford
5	B. McLaren	McLaren-Ford
6	J. Servoz-Gavin	Matra-Ford

Fastest lap: J. Ickx 114.78mph/184.67km/h
Pole position: J. Ickx

UNITED STATES GP
Watkins Glen, October 5
248 miles/398km

PLACE	DRIVER	CAR
1	J. Rindt 126.36mph/203.36km/h	Lotus-Ford
2	P. Courage	Brabham-Ford
3	J. Surtees	BRM
4	J. Brabham	Brabham-Ford
5	P. Rodriguez	Ferrari
6	S. Moser	Brabham-Ford

Fastest lap: J. Rindt 128.69mph/207.11km/h
Pole position: J. Rindt

MEXICAN GP
Mexico City, October 19
202 miles/325km

PLACE	DRIVER	CAR
1	D. Hulme 106.15mph/170.83km/h	McLaren-Ford
2	J. Ickx	Brabham-Ford
3	J. Brabham	Brabham-Ford
4	J. Stewart	Matra-Ford
5	J. P. Beltoise	Matra-Ford
6	J. Oliver	BRM

Fastest lap: J. Ickx 108.54mph/174.67km/h
Pole position: J. Brabham

1970

SOUTH AFRICAN GP
Kyalami, March 7
204 miles/328km

PLACE	DRIVER	CAR
1	J. Brabham 111.70mph/179.76km/h	Brabham-Ford
2	D. Hulme	McLaren-Ford
3	J. Stewart	March-Ford
4	J. P. Beltoise	Matra-Simca
5	J. Miles	Lotus-Ford
6	G. Hill	Lotus-Ford

Fastest lap: J. Surtees (McLaren-Ford)/ J. Brabham 113.61mph/182.84km/h
Pole position: J. Stewart

SPANISH GP
Jarama, April 19
190 miles/306km

PLACE	DRIVER	CAR
1	J. Stewart 87.22mph/140.36km/h	March-Ford
2	B. McLaren	McLaren-Ford
3	M. Andretti	March-Ford
4	G. Hill	Lotus-Ford
5	J. Servoz-Gavin	March-Ford

(Only five finished)
Fastest lap: J. Brabham (Brabham-Ford) 90.33mph/145.38km/h
Pole position: J. Brabham

MONACO GP
Monte Carlo, May 10
156 miles/252km

PLACE	DRIVER	CAR
1	J. Rindt 81.85mph/131.72km/h	Lotus-Ford
2	J. Brabham	Brabham-Ford
3	H. Pescarolo	Matra-Simca
4	D. Hulme	McLaren-Ford
5	G. Hill	Lotus-Ford
6	P. Rodriguez	BRM

Fastest lap: J. Rindt 84.56mph/136.08km/h
Pole position: J. Stewart (March-Ford)

WORLD CHAMPIONSHIP GRAND PRIX RESULTS 1950–1989

1971

BELGIAN GP
Spa, June 7
245 miles/394km

PLACE	DRIVER	CAR
1	P. Rodriguez 149.94mph/241.31km/h	BRM
2	C. Amon	March-Ford
3	J. P. Beltoise	Matra-Simca
4	I. Giunti	Ferrari
5	R. Stommelen	Brabham-Ford
6	H. Pescarolo	Matra-Simca

Fastest lap: C. Amon 152.08mph/244.74km/h
Pole position: J. Stewart (March-Ford)

DUTCH GP
Zandvoort, June 21
208 miles/335km

PLACE	DRIVER	CAR
1	J. Rindt 112.95mph/181.78km/h	Lotus-Ford
2	J. Stewart	March-Ford
3	J. Ickx	Ferrari
4	C. Regazzoni	Ferrari
5	J. P. Beltoise	Matra-Simca
6	J. Surtees	McLaren-Ford

Fastest lap: J. Ickx 118.38mph/190.52km/h
Pole position: J. Rindt

FRENCH GP
Clermont-Ferrand, July 5
190 miles/306km

PLACE	DRIVER	CAR
1	J. Rindt 98.42mph/158.39km/h	Lotus-Ford
2	C. Amon	March-Ford
3	J. Brabham	Brabham-Ford
4	D. Hulme	McLaren-Ford
5	H. Pescarolo	Matra-Simca
6	D. Gurney	McLaren-Ford

Fastest lap: J. Brabham 99.69mph/160.43km/h
Pole position: J. Ickx (Ferrari)

BRITISH GP
Brands Hatch, July 18
212 miles/341km

PLACE	DRIVER	CAR
1	J. Rindt 108.69mph/174.91km/h	Lotus-Ford
2	J. Brabham	Brabham-Ford
3	D. Hulme	McLaren-Ford
4	C. Regazzoni	Ferrari
5	C. Amon	March-Ford
6	G. Hill	Lotus-Ford

Fastest lap: J. Brabham 111.06mph/178.73km/h
Pole position: J. Rindt

GERMAN GP
Hockenheim, August 2
211 miles/340km

PLACE	DRIVER	CAR
1	J. Rindt 124.07mph/199.67km/h	Lotus-Ford
2	J. Ickx	Ferrari
3	D. Hulme	McLaren-Ford
4	E. Fittipaldi	Lotus-Ford
5	R. Stommelen	Brabham-Ford
6	H. Pescarolo	Matra-Simca

Fastest lap: J. Ickx 126.03mph/202.83km/h
Pole position: J. Ickx

AUSTRIAN GP
Osterreichring, August 16
220 miles/355km

PLACE	DRIVER	CAR
1	J. Ickx 129.27mph/208.04km/h	Ferrari
2	C. Regazzoni	Ferrari
3	R. Stommelen	Brabham-Ford
4	P. Rodriguez	BRM
5	J. Oliver	BRM
6	J. P. Beltoise	Matra-Simca

Fastest lap: J. Ickx/C. Regazzoni 131.70mph/211.95km/h
Pole position: J. Rindt (Lotus-Ford)

ITALIAN GP
Monza, September 6
243 miles/391km

PLACE	DRIVER	CAR
1	C. Regazzoni 147.08mph/236.70km/h	Ferrari
2	J. Stewart	March-Ford
3	J. P. Beltoise	Matra-Simca
4	D. Hulme	McLaren-Ford
5	R. Stommelen	Brabham-Ford
6	F. Cevert	March-Ford

Fastest lap: C. Regazzoni 150.97mph/242.96km/h
Pole position: J. Ickx (Ferrari)

CANADIAN GP
St Jovite, September 20
239 miles/384km

PLACE	DRIVER	CAR
1	J. Ickx 101.27mph/162.97km/h	Ferrari
2	C. Regazzoni	Ferrari
3	C. Amon	March-Ford
4	P. Rodriguez	BRM
5	J. Surtees	Surtees-Ford
6	P. Gethin	McLaren-Ford

Fastest lap: C. Regazzoni 103.47mph/166.51km/h
Pole position: J. Stewart (Tyrrell-Ford)

UNITED STATES GP
Watkins Glen, October 4
248 miles/398km

PLACE	DRIVER	CAR
1	E. Fittipaldi 126.79mph/204.05km/h	Lotus-Ford
2	P. Rodriguez	BRM
3	R. Wisell	Lotus-Ford
4	J. Ickx	Ferrari
5	C. Amon	March-Ford
6	D. Bell	Surtees-Ford

Fastest lap: J. Ickx 131.97mph/212.39km/h
Pole position: J. Ickx

MEXICAN GP
Mexico City, October 18
202 miles/325km

PLACE	DRIVER	CAR
1	J. Ickx 106.78mph/171.85km/h	Ferrari
2	C. Regazzoni	Ferrari
3	D. Hulme	McLaren-Ford
4	C. Amon	March-Ford
5	J. P. Beltoise	Matra-Simca
6	P. Rodriguez	BRM

Fastest lap: J. Ickx 108.47mph/174.57km/h
Pole position: C. Regazzoni

SOUTH AFRICAN GP
Kyalami, March 6
201 miles/324km

PLACE	DRIVER	CAR
1	M. Andretti 112.35mph/180.80km/h	Ferrari
2	J. Stewart	Tyrell-Ford
3	C. Regazzoni	Ferrari
4	R. Wisell	Lotus-Ford
5	C. Amon	Matra-Simca
6	D. Hulme	McLaren-Ford

Fastest lap: M. Andretti 114.33mph/183.99km/h
Pole position: J. Stewart

SPANISH GP
Montjuich, April 18
177 miles/284km

PLACE	DRIVER	CAR
1	J. Stewart 97.19mph/156.41km/h	Tyrrell-Ford
2	J. Ickx	Ferrari
3	C. Amon	Matra-Simca
4	P. Rodriguez	BRM
5	D. Hulme	McLaren-Ford
6	J. P. Beltoise	Matra-Simca

Fastest lap: J. Ickx 99.64mph/160.36km/h
Pole position: J. Ickx

MONACO GP
Monte Carlo, May 23
156 miles/252km

PLACE	DRIVER	CAR
1	J. Stewart 83.49mph/134.36km/h	Tyrrell-Ford
2	R. Peterson	March-Ford
3	J. Ickx	Ferrari
4	D. Hulme	McLaren-Ford
5	E. Fittipaldi	Lotus-Ford
6	R. Stommelen	Surtees-Ford

Fastest lap: J. Stewart 85.59mph/137.74km/h
Pole position: J. Stewart

DUTCH GP
Zandvoort, June 20
182 miles/294km

PLACE	DRIVER	CAR
1	J. Ickx 94.06mph/151.38km/h	Ferrari
2	P. Rodriguez	BRM
3	C. Regazzoni	Ferrari
4	R. Peterson	March-Ford
5	J. Surtees	Surtees-Ford
6	J. Siffert	BRM

Fastest lap: J. Ickx 98.78mph/158.98km/h
Pole position: J. Ickx

FRENCH GP
Paul Ricard, July 4
199 miles/320km

PLACE	DRIVER	CAR
1	J. Stewart 111.66mph/179.70km/h	Tyrrell-Ford
2	F. Cevert	Tyrrell-Ford
3	E. Fittipaldi	Lotus-Ford
4	J. Siffert	BRM
5	C. Amon	Matra-Simca
6	R. Wisell	Lotus-Ford

Fastest lap: J. Stewart 113.92mph/183.33km/h
Pole position: J. Stewart

BRITISH GP
Silverstone, July 17
199 miles/320km

PLACE	DRIVER	CAR
1	J. Stewart 130.48mph/209.99km/h	Tyrrell-Ford
2	R. Peterson	March-Ford
3	E. Fittipaldi	Lotus-Ford
4	H. Pescarolo	March-Ford
5	R. Stommelen	Surtees-Ford
6	J. Surtees	Surtees-Ford

Fastest lap: J. Stewart 131.88mph/212.24km/h
Pole position: C. Regazzoni (Ferrari)

GERMAN GP
Nürburgring, August 1
170 miles/247km

PLACE	DRIVER	CAR
1	J. Stewart 114.45mph/184.19km/h	Tyrrell-Ford
2	F. Cevert	Tyrrell-Ford
3	C. Regazzoni	Ferrari
4	M. Andretti	Ferrari
5	R. Peterson	March-Ford
6	T. Schenken	Brabham-Ford

Fastest lap: F. Cevert 116.07mph/186.79km/h
Pole position: J. Stewart

AUSTRIAN GP
Osterreichring, August 15
198 miles/318km

PLACE	DRIVER	CAR
1	J. Siffert 131.64mph/211.86km/h	BRM
2	E. Fittipaldi	Lotus-Ford
3	T. Schenken	Brabham-Ford
4	R. Wisell	Lotus-Ford
5	G. Hill	Brabham-Ford
6	H. Pescarolo	March-Ford

Fastest lap: J. Siffert 134.28mph/216.10km/h
Pole position: J. Siffert

ITALIAN GP
Monza, September 5
197 miles/317km

PLACE	DRIVER	CAR
1	P. Gethin 150.75mph/242.62km/h	BRM
2	R. Peterson	March-Ford
3	F. Cevert	Tyrrell-Ford
4	M. Hailwood	Surtees-Ford
5	H. Ganley	BRM
6	C. Amon	Matra-Simca

Fastest lap: H. Pescarolo (March-Ford) 153.49mph/247.02km/h
Pole position: C. Amon

CANADIAN GP
Mosport, September 19
157 miles/253km

PLACE	DRIVER	CAR
1	J. Stewart 81.95mph/131.88km/h	Tyrrell-Ford
2	R. Peterson	March-Ford
3	M. Donohue	McLaren-Ford
4	D. Hulme	McLaren-Ford
5	R. Wisell	Lotus-Ford
6	F. Cevert	Tyrrell-Ford

Fastest lap: D. Hulme 85.52mph/137.64km/h
Pole position: J. Stewart

UNITED STATES GP
Watkins Glen, October 3
199 miles/320km

PLACE	DRIVER	CAR
1	F. Cevert 115.10mph/185.24km/h	Tyrrell-Ford
2	J. Siffert	BRM
3	R. Peterson	March-Ford
4	H. Ganley	BRM
5	J. Stewart	Tyrrell-Ford
6	C. Regazzoni	Ferrari

Fastest lap: J. Ickx (Ferrari) 117.50mph/189.09km/h
Pole position: J. Stewart

1972

ARGENTINE GP
Buenos Aires, January 23
197 miles/317km

PLACE	DRIVER	CAR
1	J. Stewart 100.42mph/161.61km/h	Tyrrell-Ford
2	D. Hulme	McLaren-Ford
3	J. Ickx	Ferrari
4	C. Regazzoni	Ferrari
5	T. Schenken	Surtees-Ford
6	R. Peterson	March-Ford

Fastest lap: J. Stewart 101.58mph/163.48km/h
Pole position: C. Reutemann (Brabham-Ford)

SOUTH AFRICAN GP
Kyalami, March 4
201 miles/324km

PLACE	DRIVER	CAR
1	D. Hulme 114.23mph/183.83km/h	McLaren-Ford
2	E. Fittipaldi	Lotus-Ford
3	P. Revson	McLaren-Ford
4	M. Andretti	Ferrari
5	R. Peterson	March-Ford
6	G. Hill	Brabham-Ford

Fastest lap: M. Hailwood (Surtees-Ford) 116.35mph/187.25km/h
Pole position: J. Stewart (Tyrrell-Ford)

SPANISH GP
Jarama, May 1
190 miles/306km

PLACE	DRIVER	CAR
1	E. Fittipaldi 92.35mph/148.63km/h	Lotus-Ford
2	J. Ickx	Ferrari
3	C. Regazzoni	Ferrari
4	A. de Adamich	Surtees-Ford
5	P. Revson	McLaren-Ford
6	C. Pace	March-Ford

Fastest lap: J. Ickx 94.00mph/151.28km/h
Pole position: J. Ickx

MONACO GP
Monte Carlo, May 14
156 miles/252km

PLACE	DRIVER	CAR
1	J. P. Beltoise 63.85mph/102.76km/h	BRM
2	J. Ickx	Ferrari
3	E. Fittipaldi	Lotus-Ford
4	J. Stewart	Tyrrell-Ford
5	B. Redman	McLaren-Ford
6	C. Amon	Matra-Simca

Fastest lap: J. P. Beltoise 70.35mph/113.22km/h
Pole position: E. Fittipaldi

BELGIAN GP
Nivelles, June 4
197 miles/317km

PLACE	DRIVER	CAR
1	E. Fittipaldi 113.35mph/182.42km/h	Lotus-Ford
2	F. Cevert	Tyrrell-Ford
3	D. Hulme	McLaren-Ford
4	M. Hailwood	Surtees-Ford
5	C. Pace	March-Ford
6	C. Amon	Matra-Simca

Fastest lap: C. Amon 115.51mph/185.89km/h
Pole position: E. Fittipaldi

FRENCH GP
Clermont-Ferrand, July 2
190 miles/306km

PLACE	DRIVER	CAR
1	J. Stewart 101.57mph/163.45km/h	Tyrrell-Ford
2	E. Fittipaldi	Lotus-Ford
3	C. Amon	Matra-Simca
4	F. Cevert	Tyrrell-Ford
5	R. Peterson	March-Ford
6	M. Hailwood	Surtees-Ford

Fastest lap: C. Amon 103.61mph/166.75km/h
Pole position: D. Hulme (McLaren-Ford)

BRITISH GP
Brands Hatch, July 15
201 miles/324km

PLACE	DRIVER	CAR
1	E. Fittipaldi 112.06mph/180.34km/h	Lotus-Ford
2	J. Stewart	Tyrrell-Ford
3	P. Revson	McLaren-Ford
4	C. Amon	Matra-Simca
5	D. Hulme	McLaren-Ford
6	A. Merzario	Ferrari

Fastest lap: J. Stewart 113.57mph/182.78km/h
Pole position: J. Ickx (Ferrari)

GERMAN GP
Nürburgring, July 30
199 miles/320km

PLACE	DRIVER	CAR
1	J. Ickx 116.62mph/187.68km/h	Ferrari
2	C. Regazzoni	Ferrari
3	R. Peterson	March-Ford
4	H. Ganley	BRM
5	B. Redman	McLaren-Ford
6	G. Hill	Brabham-Ford

Fastest lap: J. Ickx 117.81mph/189.59km/h
Pole position: J. Ickx

WORLD CHAMPIONSHIP GRAND PRIX RESULTS 1950–1989

1973

AUSTRIAN GP
Osterreichring, August 13
198 miles/318km

PLACE	DRIVER	CAR
1	E. Fittipaldi 133.30mph/214.52km/h	Lotus-Ford
2	D. Hulme	McLaren-Ford
3	P. Revson	McLaren-Ford
4	M. Hailwood	Surtees-Ford
5	C. Amon	Matra-Simca
6	H. Ganley	BRM

Fastest lap: D. Hulme 134.48mph/216.43km/h
Pole position: E. Fittipaldi

ITALIAN GP
Monza, September 10
197 miles/317km

PLACE	DRIVER	CAR
1	E. Fittipaldi 131.61mph/211.81km/h	Lotus-Ford
2	M. Hailwood	Surtees-Ford
3	D. Hulme	McLaren-Ford
4	P. Revson	McLaren-Ford
5	G. Hill	Brabham-Ford
6	P. Gethin	BRM

Fastest lap: J. Ickx (Ferrari) 134.15mph/215.89km/h
Pole position: J. Ickx

CANADIAN GP
Mosport, September 24
197 miles/317km

PLACE	DRIVER	CAR
1	J. Stewart 114.27mph/183.90km/h	Tyrrell-Ford
2	P. Revson	McLaren-Ford
3	D. Hulme	McLaren-Ford
4	C. Reutemann	Brabham-Ford
5	C. Regazzoni	Ferrari
6	C. Amon	Matra-Simca

Fastest lap: J. Stewart 117.57mph/189.17km/h
Pole position: P. Revson

UNITED STATES GP
Watkins Glen, October 8
199 miles/320km

PLACE	DRIVER	CAR
1	J. Stewart 117.49mph/189.09km/h	Tyrrell-Ford
2	F. Cevert	Tyrrell-Ford
3	D. Hulme	McLaren-Ford
4	R. Peterson	March-Ford
5	J. Ickx	Ferrari
6	M. Andretti	Ferrari

Fastest lap: J. Stewart 119.61mph/192.50km/h
Pole position: D. Hulme

ARGENTINE GP
Buenos Aires, January 28
200 miles/321km

PLACE	DRIVER	CAR
1	E. Fittipaldi 102.95mph/165.69km/h	Lotus-Ford
2	F. Cevert	Tyrrell-Ford
3	J. Stewart	Tyrrell-Ford
4	J. Ickx	Ferrari
5	D. Hulme	McLaren-Ford
6	W. Fittipaldi	Brabham-Ford

Fastest lap: E. Fittipaldi 105.08mph/169.11km/h
Pole position: C. Regazzoni (BRM)

BRAZILIAN GP
Interlagos, February 11
198 miles/318km

PLACE	DRIVER	CAR
1	E. Fittipaldi 114.22mph/183.82km/h	Lotus-Ford
2	J. Stewart	Tyrrell-Ford
3	D. Hulme	McLaren-Ford
4	A. Merzario	Ferrari
5	J. Ickx	Ferrari
6	C. Regazzoni	BRM

Fastest lap: E. Fittipaldi/D. Hulme 114.88mph/184.88km/h
Pole position: R. Peterson (Lotus-Ford)

SOUTH AFRICAN GP
Kyalami, March 3
201 miles/324km

PLACE	DRIVER	CAR
1	J. Stewart 117.14mph/188.53km/h	Tyrrell-Ford
2	P. Revson	McLaren-Ford
3	E. Fittipaldi	Lotus-Ford
4	A. Merzario	Ferrari
5	D. Hulme	McLaren-Ford
6	G. Follmer	Shadow-Ford

Fastest lap: E. Fittipaldi 119.07mph/191.63km/h
Pole position: D. Hulme

SPANISH GP
Montjuich, April 29
177 miles/284km

PLACE	DRIVER	CAR
1	E. Fittipaldi 97.86mph/157.49km/h	Lotus-Ford
2	F. Cevert	Tyrrell-Ford
3	G. Follmer	Shadow-Ford
4	P. Revson	McLaren-Ford
5	J. P. Beltoise	BRM
6	D. Hulme	McLaren-Ford

Fastest lap: R. Peterson (Lotus-Ford) 101.19mph/162.84km/h
Pole position: R. Peterson

BELGIAN GP
Zolder, May 20
184 miles/295km

PLACE	DRIVER	CAR
1	J. Stewart 107.74mph/173.38km/h	Tyrrell-Ford
2	F. Cevert	Tyrrell-Ford
3	E. Fittipaldi	Lotus-Ford
4	A. de Adamich	Brabham-Ford
5	N. Lauda	BRM
6	C. Amon	Tecno

Fastest lap: F. Cevert 110.51mph/177.85km/h
Pole position: R. Peterson (Lotus-Ford)

MONACO GP
Monte Carlo, June 3
159 miles/256km

PLACE	DRIVER	CAR
1	J. Stewart 80.96mph/130.30km/h	Tyrrell-Ford
2	E. Fittipaldi	Lotus-Ford
3	R. Peterson	Lotus-Ford
4	F. Cevert	Tyrrell-Ford
5	P. Revson	McLaren-Ford
6	D. Hulme	McLaren-Ford

Fastest lap: E. Fittipaldi 83.23mph/133.95km/h
Pole position: J. Stewart

SWEDISH GP
Anderstorp, June 17
200 miles/321km

PLACE	DRIVER	CAR
1	D. Hulme 102.63mph/165.17km/h	McLaren-Ford
2	R. Peterson	Lotus-Ford
3	F. Cevert	Tyrrell-Ford
4	C. Reutemann	Brabham-Ford
5	J. Stewart	Tyrrell-Ford
6	J. Ickx	Ferrari

Fastest lap: D. Hulme 104.33mph/167.91km/h
Pole position: R. Peterson

FRENCH GP
Paul Ricard, July 1
195 miles/315km

PLACE	DRIVER	CAR
1	R. Peterson 115.12mph/185.26km/h	Lotus-Ford
2	F. Cevert	Tyrrell-Ford
3	C. Reutemann	Brabham-Ford
4	J. Stewart	Tyrrell-Ford
5	J. Ickx	Ferrari
6	J. Hunt	March-Ford

Fastest lap: D. Hulme (McLaren-Ford) 117.10mph/188.45km/h
Pole position: J. Stewart

BRITISH GP
Silverstone, July 14
196 miles/316km

PLACE	DRIVER	CAR
1	P. Revson 131.75mph/212.03km/h	McLaren-Ford
2	R. Peterson	Lotus-Ford
3	D. Hulme	McLaren-Ford
4	J. Hunt	March-Ford
5	F. Cevert	Tyrrell-Ford
6	C. Reutemann	Brabham-Ford

Fastest lap: J. Hunt 134.06mph/215.75km/h
Pole position: R. Peterson

DUTCH GP
Zandvoort, July 29
189 miles/304km

PLACE	DRIVER	CAR
1	J. Stewart 114.35mph/184.03km/h	Tyrrell-Ford
2	F. Cevert	Tyrrell-Ford
3	J. Hunt	March-Ford
4	P. Revson	McLaren-Ford
5	J. P. Beltoise	BRM
6	G. van Lennep	Williams-Ford

Fastest lap: R. Peterson (Lotus-Ford) 117.71mph/189.44km/h
Pole position: R. Peterson

GERMAN GP
Nürburgring, August 5
199 miles/320km

PLACE	DRIVER	CAR
1	J. Stewart 116.79mph/187.96km/h	Tyrrell-Ford
2	F. Cevert	Tyrrell-Ford
3	J. Ickx	McLaren-Ford
4	C. Pace	Surtees-Ford
5	W. Fittipaldi	Brabham-Ford
6	E. Fittipaldi	Lotus-Ford

Fastest lap: C. Pace 118.41mph/190.56km/h
Pole position: J. Stewart

AUSTRIAN GP
Osterreichring, August 19
198 miles/318km

PLACE	DRIVER	CAR
1	R. Peterson 133.99mph/215.64km/h	Lotus-Ford
2	J. Stewart	Tyrrell-Ford
3	C. Pace	Surtees-Ford
4	C. Reutemann	Brabham-Ford
5	J. P. Beltoise	BRM
6	C. Regazzoni	BRM

Fastest lap: C. Pace 135.91mph/218.72km/h
Pole position: E. Fittipaldi (Lotus-Ford)

ITALIAN GP
Monza, September 9
197 miles/317km

PLACE	DRIVER	CAR
1	R. Peterson 132.63mph/213.45km/h	Lotus-Ford
2	E. Fittipaldi	Lotus-Ford
3	P. Revson	McLaren-Ford
4	J. Stewart	Tyrrell-Ford
5	F. Cevert	Tyrrell-Ford
6	C. Reutemann	Brabham-Ford

Fastest lap: J. Stewart 135.55mph/218.15km/h
Pole position: R. Peterson

CANADIAN GP
Mosport, September 23
197 miles/317km

PLACE	DRIVER	CAR
1	P. Revson 99.13mph/159.53km/h	McLaren-Ford
2	E. Fittipaldi	Lotus-Ford
3	J. Oliver	Shadow-Ford
4	J. P. Beltoise	BRM
5	J. Stewart	Tyrrell-Ford
6	H. Ganley	Williams-Ford

Fastest lap: E. Fittipaldi 117.26mph/188.71km/h
Pole position: R. Peterson (Lotus-Ford)

UNITED STATES GP
Watkins Glen, October 7
199 miles/320km

PLACE	DRIVER	CAR
1	R. Peterson 118.06mph/189.99km/h	Lotus-Ford
2	J. Hunt	March-Ford
3	C. Reutemann	Brabham-Ford
4	D. Hulme	McLaren-Ford
5	P. Revson	McLaren-Ford
6	E. Fittipaldi	Lotus-Ford

Fastest lap: J. Hunt 119.60mph/192.47km/h
Pole position: R. Peterson

1974

ARGENTINE GP
Buenos Aires, January 13
197 miles/317km

PLACE	DRIVER	CAR
1	D. Hulme 116.72mph/187.85km/h	McLaren-Ford
2	N. Lauda	Ferrari
3	C. Regazzoni	Ferrari
4	M. Hailwood	McLaren-Ford
5	J. P. Beltoise	BRM
6	P. Depailler	Tyrrell-Ford

Fastest lap: C. Regazzoni 119.09mph/191.66km/h
Pole position: R. Peterson (Lotus-Ford)

BRAZILIAN GP
Interlagos, January 27
158 miles/255km

PLACE	DRIVER	CAR
1	E. Fittipaldi 112.23mph/180.62km/h	McLaren-Ford
2	C. Regazzoni	Ferrari
3	J. Ickx	Lotus-Ford
4	C. Pace	Surtees-Ford
5	M. Hailwood	McLaren-Ford
6	R. Peterson	Lotus-Ford

Fastest lap: C. Regazzoni 114.10mph/183.63km/h
Pole position: E. Fittipaldi

SOUTH AFRICAN GP
Kyalami, March 30
199 miles/320km

PLACE	DRIVER	CAR
1	C. Reutemann 116.23mph/187.05km/h	Brabham-Ford
2	J. P. Beltoise	BRM
3	M. Hailwood	McLaren-Ford
4	P. Depailler	Tyrrell-Ford
5	H. Stuck	March Ford
6	A. Merzario	Williams-Ford

Fastest lap: C. Reutemann 117.46mph/189.03km/h
Pole position: N. Lauda (Ferrari)

SPANISH GP
Jarama, April 28
178 miles/286km

PLACE	DRIVER	CAR
1	N. Lauda 88.48mph/142.40km/h	Ferrari
2	C. Regazzoni	Ferrari
3	E. Fittipaldi	McLaren-Ford
4	H. Stuck	March-Ford
5	J. Scheckter	Tyrrell-Ford
6	D. Hulme	McLaren-Ford

Fastest lap: N. Lauda 94.21mph/151.62km/h
Pole position: N. Lauda

BELGIAN GP
Nivelles, May 12
197 miles/317km

PLACE	DRIVER	CAR
1	E. Fittipaldi 113.10mph/182.02km/h	McLaren-Ford
2	N. Lauda	Ferrari
3	J. Scheckter	Tyrrell-Ford
4	C. Regazzoni	Ferrari
5	J. P. Beltoise	BRM
6	D. Hulme	McLaren-Ford

Fastest lap: D. Hulme 116.82mph/188.00km/h
Pole position: C. Regazzoni

MONACO GP
Monte Carlo, May 26
159 miles/256km

PLACE	DRIVER	CAR
1	R. Peterson 80.74mph/129.94km/h	Lotus-Ford
2	J. Scheckter	Tyrrell-Ford
3	J. P. Jarier	Shadow-Ford
4	C. Regazzoni	Ferrari
5	E. Fittipaldi	McLaren-Ford
6	J. Watson	Brabham-Ford

Fastest lap: R. Peterson 83.42mph/134.25km/h
Pole position: N. Lauda (Ferrari)

SWEDISH GP
Anderstorp, June 9
200 miles/321km

PLACE	DRIVER	CAR
1	J. Scheckter 101.11mph/162.72km/h	Tyrrell-Ford
2	P. Depailler	Tyrrell-Ford
3	J. Hunt	Hesketh-Ford
4	E. Fittipaldi	McLaren-Ford
5	J. P. Jarier	Shadow-Ford
6	G. Hill	Lola-Ford

Fastest lap: P. Depailler 103.00mph/165.76km/h
Pole position: P. Depailler

DUTCH GP
Zandvoort, June 23
197 miles/317km

PLACE	DRIVER	CAR
1	N. Lauda 114.72mph/184.63km/h	Ferrari
2	C. Regazzoni	Ferrari
3	E. Fittipaldi	McLaren-Ford
4	M. Hailwood	McLaren-Ford
5	J. Scheckter	Tyrrell-Ford
6	P. Depailler	Tyrrell-Ford

Fastest lap: R. Peterson (Lotus-Ford) 116.08mph/186.81km/h
Pole position: N. Lauda

WORLD CHAMPIONSHIP GRAND PRIX RESULTS 1950–1989

FRENCH GP
Dijon, July 7
163 miles/263km

PLACE	DRIVER	CAR
1	R. Peterson 119.75mph/192.72km/h	Lotus-Ford
2	N. Lauda	Ferrari
3	C. Regazzoni	Ferrari
4	J. Scheckter	Tyrrell-Ford
5	J. Ickx	Lotus-Ford
6	D. Hulme	McLaren-Ford

Fastest lap: J. Scheckter 122.62mph/197.34km/h
Pole position: N. Lauda

BRITISH GP
Brands Hatch, July 20
199 miles/320km

1	J. Scheckter 115.74mph/186.26km/h	Tyrrell-Ford
2	E. Fittipaldi	McLaren-Ford
3	J. Ickx	Lotus-Ford
4	C. Regazzoni	Ferrari
5	N. Lauda	Ferrari
6	C. Reutemann	Brabham-Ford

Fastest lap: N. Lauda 117.63mph/189.31km/h
Pole position: N. Lauda

GERMAN GP
Nürburgring, August 4
199 miles/320km

1	C. Regazzoni 117.33mph/188.83km/h	Ferrari
2	J. Scheckter	Tyrrell-Ford
3	C. Reutemann	Brabham-Ford
4	R. Peterson	Lotus-Ford
5	J. Ickx	Lotus-Ford
6	T. Pryce	Shadow-Ford

Fastest lap: J. Scheckter 118.49mph/190.69km/h
Pole position: N. Lauda (Ferrari)

AUSTRIAN GP
Osterreichring, August 18
198 miles/318km

1	C. Reutemann 134.09mph/215.80km/h	Brabham-Ford
2	D. Hulme	McLaren-Ford
3	J. Hunt	Hesketh-Ford
4	J. Watson	Brabham-Ford
5	C. Regazzoni	Ferrari
6	V. Brambilla	March-Ford

Fastest lap: C. Regazzoni 136.01mph/218.88km/h
Pole position: N. Lauda (Ferrari)

ITALIAN GP
Monza, September 8
187 miles/301km

1	R. Peterson 135.10mph/217.42km/h	Lotus-Ford
2	E. Fittipaldi	McLaren-Ford
3	J. Scheckter	Tyrrell-Ford
4	A. Merzario	Williams-Ford
5	C. Pace	Brabham-Ford
6	D. Hulme	McLaren-Ford

Fastest lap: C. Pace 137.26mph/220.89km/h
Pole position: N. Lauda (Ferrari)

CANADIAN GP
Mosport, September 22
197 miles/317km

PLACE	DRIVER	CAR
1	E. Fittipaldi 117.52mph/189.13km/h	McLaren-Ford
2	C. Regazzoni	Ferrari
3	R. Peterson	Lotus-Ford
4	J. Hunt	Hesketh-Ford
5	P. Depailler	Tyrrell-Ford
6	D. Hulme	McLaren-Ford

Fastest lap: N. Lauda (Ferrari) 120.18mph/192.41km/h
Pole position: E. Fittipaldi

UNITED STATES GP
Watkins Glen, October 6
199 miles/320km

1	C. Reutemann 119.12mph/191.71km/h	Brabham-Ford
2	C. Pace	Brabham-Ford
3	J. Hunt	Hesketh-Ford
4	E. Fittipaldi	McLaren-Ford
5	J. Watson	Brabham-Ford
6	P. Depailler	Tyrrell-Ford

Fastest lap: C. Pace 120.84mph/194.47km/h
Pole position: C. Reutemann

1975

ARGENTINE GP
Buenos Aires, January 12
197 miles/317km

PLACE	DRIVER	CAR
1	E. Fittipaldi 118.60mph/190.86km/h	McLaren-Ford
2	J. Hunt	Hesketh-Ford
3	C. Reutemann	Brabham-Ford
4	C. Regazzoni	Ferrari
5	P. Depailler	Tyrrell-Ford
6	N. Lauda	Ferrari

Fastest lap: J. Hunt 120.37mph/193.72km/h
Pole position: J. P. Jarier (Shadow-Ford)

BRAZILIAN GP
Interlagos, January 26
198 miles/318km

1	C. Pace 113.39mph/182.49km/h	Brabham-Ford
2	E. Fittipaldi	McLaren-Ford
3	J. Mass	McLaren-Ford
4	C. Regazzoni	Ferrari
5	N. Lauda	Ferrari
6	J. Hunt	Hesketh-Ford

Fastest lap: J. P. Jarier (Shadow-Ford) 115.50mph/185.88km/h
Pole position: J. P. Jarier

SOUTH AFRICAN GP
Kyalami, March 1
199 miles/320km

PLACE	DRIVER	CAR
1	J. Scheckter 115.55mph/185.96km/h	Tyrrell-Ford
2	C. Reutemann	Brabham-Ford
3	P. Depailler	Tyrrell-Ford
4	C. Pace	Brabham-Ford
5	N. Lauda	Ferrari
6	J. Mass	McLaren-Ford

Fastest lap: C. Pace 118.92mph/191.38km/h
Pole position: C. Pace

SPANISH GP
Montjuich, April 27
68 miles/110km

1	J. Mass 95.54mph/153.76km/h	McLaren-Ford
2	J. Ickx	Lotus-Ford
3	C. Reutemann	Brabham-Ford
4	J. P. Jarier	Shadow-Ford
5	V. Brambilla	March-Ford
6	L. Lombardi	March-Ford

Fastest lap: M. Andretti (Parnelli-Ford) 99.64mph/160.36km/h
Pole position: N. Lauda (Ferrari)

MONACO GP
Monte Carlo, May 11
153 miles/246km

1	N. Lauda 75.53mph/121.55km/h	Ferrari
2	E. Fittipaldi	McLaren-Ford
3	C. Pace	Brabham-Ford
4	R. Peterson	Lotus-Ford
5	P. Depailler	Tyrrell-Ford
6	J. Mass	McLaren-Ford

Fastest lap: P. Depailler 82.70mph/133.09km/h
Pole position: N. Lauda

BELGIAN GP
Zolder, May 25
185 miles/298km

1	N. Lauda 107.05mph/172.29km/h	Ferrari
2	J. Scheckter	Tyrrell-Ford
3	C. Reutemann	Brabham-Ford
4	P. Depailler	Tyrrell-Ford
5	C. Regazzoni	Ferrari
6	T. Pryce	Shadow-Ford

Fastest lap: C. Regazzoni 109.89mph/176.85km/h
Pole position: N. Lauda

SWEDISH GP
Anderstorp, June 8
200 miles/321km

1	N. Lauda 100.45mph/161.66km/h	Ferrari
2	C. Reutemann	Brabham-Ford
3	C. Regazzoni	Ferrari
4	M. Andretti	Parnelli-Ford
5	M. Donohue	Penske-Ford
6	A. Brise	Hill-Ford

Fastest lap: N. Lauda 101.83mph/163.88km/h
Pole position: V. Brambilla (March-Ford)

DUTCH GP
Zandvoort, June 22
197 miles/317km

PLACE	DRIVER	CAR
1	J. Hunt 110.48mph/177.80km/h	Hesketh-Ford
2	N. Lauda	Ferrari
3	C. Regazzoni	Ferrari
4	C. Reutemann	Brabham-Ford
5	C. Pace	Brabham-Ford
6	T. Pryce	Shadow-Ford

Fastest lap: N. Lauda 115.93mph/186.58km/h
Pole position: N. Lauda

FRENCH GP
Paul Ricard, July 6
195 miles/315km

PLACE	DRIVER	CAR
1	N. Lauda 116.60mph/187.65km/h	Ferrari
2	J. Hunt	Hesketh-Ford
3	J. Mass	McLaren-Ford
4	E. Fittipaldi	McLaren-Ford
5	M. Andretti	Parnelli-Ford
6	P. Depailler	Tyrrell-Ford

Fastest lap: J. Mass 117.51mph/189.11km/h
Pole position: N. Lauda

BRITISH GP
Silverstone, July 19
164 miles/264km

PLACE	DRIVER	CAR
1	E. Fittipaldi 120.02mph/193.15km/h	McLaren-Ford
2	C. Pace	Brabham/Ford
3	J. Scheckter	Tyrrell-Ford
4	J. Hunt	Hesketh-Ford
5	M. Donohue	March-Ford
6	V. Brambilla	March-Ford

Fastest lap: C. Regazzoni (Ferrari)
130.47mph/209.97km/h
Pole position: T. Pryce (Shadow-Ford)

GERMAN GP
Nürburgring, August 3
199 miles/320km

PLACE	DRIVER	CAR
1	C. Reutemann 117.73mph/189.47km/h	Brabham-Ford
2	J. Laffite	Williams-Ford
3	N. Lauda	Ferrari
4	T. Pryce	Shadow-Ford
5	A. Jones	Hill-Ford
6	G. van Lennep	Ensign-Ford

Fastest lap: C. Regazzoni (Ferrari)
119.79mph/192.79km/h
Pole position: N. Lauda

AUSTRIAN GP
Osterreichring, August 17
107 miles/171km

PLACE	DRIVER	CAR
1	V. Brambilla 110.29mph/177.50km/h	March-Ford
2	J. Hunt	Hesketh-Ford
3	T. Pryce	Shadow-Ford
4	J. Mass	McLaren-Ford
5	R. Peterson	Lotus-Ford
6	N. Lauda	Ferrari

Fastest lap: V. Brambilla 116.09mph/186.83km/h
Pole position: N. Lauda

ITALIAN GP
Monza, September 7
187 miles/301km

PLACE	DRIVER	CAR
1	C. Regazzoni 135.48mph/218.03km/h	Ferrari
2	E. Fittipaldi	McLaren-Ford
3	N. Lauda	Ferrari
4	C. Reutemann	Brabham-Ford
5	J. Hunt	Hesketh-Ford
6	T. Pryce	Shadow-Ford

Fastest lap: C. Regazzoni 138.88mph/223.50km/h
Pole position: N. Lauda

UNITED STATES GP
Watkins Glen, October 5
199 miles/320km

PLACE	DRIVER	CAR
1	N. Lauda 116.10mph/186.84km/h	Ferrari
2	E. Fittipaldi	McLaren-Ford
3	J. Mass	McLaren-Ford
4	J. Hunt	Hesketh-Ford
5	R. Peterson	Lotus-Ford
6	J. Scheckter	Tyrrell-Ford

Fastest lap: E. Fittipaldi 117.60mph/189.27km/h
Pole position: N. Lauda

1976

BRAZILIAN GP
Interlagos, January 25
198 miles/318km

PLACE	DRIVER	CAR
1	N. Lauda 112.76mph/181.47km/h	Ferrari
2	P. Depailler	Tyrrell-Ford
3	T. Pryce	Shadow-Ford
4	H. Stuck	March-Ford
5	J. Scheckter	Tyrrell-Ford
6	J. Mass	McLaren-Ford

Fastest lap: J. P. Jarier (Shadow-Ford)
114.83mph/184.80km/h
Pole position: J. Hunt (McLaren-Ford)

SOUTH AFRICAN GP
Kyalami, March 6
199 miles/320km

PLACE	DRIVER	CAR
1	N. Lauda 116.65mph/187.74km/h	Ferrari
2	J. Hunt	McLaren-Ford
3	J. Mass	McLaren-Ford
4	J. Scheckter	Tyrrell-Ford
5	J. Watson	Penske-Ford
6	M. Andretti	Parnelli-Ford

Fastest lap: N. Lauda 117.74mph/189.49km/h
Pole position: J. Hunt

UNITED STATES GP (WEST)
Long Beach, March 28
162 miles/260km

PLACE	DRIVER	CAR
1	C. Regazzoni 85.57mph/137.72km/h	Ferrari
2	N. Lauda	Ferrari
3	P. Depailler	Tyrrell-Ford
4	J. Laffite	Ligier-Matra
5	J. Mass	McLaren-Ford
6	E. Fittipaldi	Fittipaldi-Ford

Fastest lap: C. Regazzoni 87.53mph/140.87km/h
Pole position: C. Regazzoni

SPANISH GP
Jarama, May 2
159 miles/256km

PLACE	DRIVER	CAR
1	J. Hunt 93.01mph/149.69km/h	McLaren-Ford
2	N. Lauda	Ferrari
3	G. Nilsson	Lotus-Ford
4	C. Reutemann	Brabham-Alfa Romeo
5	C. Amon	Ensign-Ford
6	C. Pace	Brabham-Alfa Romeo

Fastest lap: J. Mass (McLaren-Ford)
94.10mph/151.43km/h
Pole position: J. Hunt

BELGIAN GP
Zolder, May 16
185 miles/298km

PLACE	DRIVER	CAR
1	N. Lauda 108.10mph/173.98km/h	Ferrari
2	C. Regazzoni	Ferrari
3	J. Laffite	Ligier-Matra
4	J. Scheckter	Tyrrell-Ford
5	A. Jones	Surtees-Ford
6	J. Mass	McLaren-Ford

Fastest lap: N. Lauda 110.88mph/178.45km/h
Pole position: N. Lauda

MONACO GP
Monte Carlo, May 30
160 miles/258km

PLACE	DRIVER	CAR
1	N. Lauda 80.35mph/129.32km/h	Ferrari
2	J. Scheckter	Tyrrell-Ford
3	P. Depailler	Tyrrell-Ford
4	H. Stuck	March-Ford
5	J. Mass	McLaren-Ford
6	E. Fittipaldi	Fittipaldi-Ford

Fastest lap: C. Regazzoni (Ferrari)
82.06mph/132.07km/h
Pole position: N. Lauda

WORLD CHAMPIONSHIP GRAND PRIX RESULTS 1950–1989

SWEDISH GP
Anderstorp, June 13
180 miles/289km

PLACE	DRIVER	CAR
1	J. Scheckter 100.90mph/162.38km/h	Tyrrell-Ford
2	P. Depailler	Tyrrell-Ford
3	N. Lauda	Ferrari
4	J. Laffite	Ligier-Matra
5	J. Hunt	McLaren-Ford
6	C. Regazzoni	Ferrari

Fastest lap: M. Andretti (Lotus-Ford) 102.13mph/164.37km/h
Pole position: J. Scheckter

FRENCH GP
Paul Ricard, July 4
195 miles/315km

1	J. Hunt 115.84mph/186.42km/h	McLaren-Ford
2	P. Depailler	Tyrrell-Ford
3	J. Watson	Penske-Ford
4	C. Pace	Brabham-Alfa Romeo
5	M. Andretti	Lotus-Ford
6	J. Scheckter	Tyrrell-Ford

Fastest lap: N. Lauda (Ferrari) 117.09mph/188.43km/h
Pole position: N. Lauda

BRITISH GP
Brands Hatch, July 18
199 miles/320km

1	N. Lauda 114.23mph/183.84km/h	Ferrari
2	J. Scheckter	Tyrrell-Ford
3	J. Watson	Penske-Ford
4	T. Pryce	Shadow-Ford
5	A. Jones	Surtees-Ford
6	E. Fittipaldi	Fittipaldi-Ford

Fastest lap: N. Lauda 117.74mph/189.49km/h
Pole position: N. Lauda

GERMAN GP
Nürburgring, August 1
199 miles/320km

1	J. Hunt 117.18mph/188.59km/h	McLaren-Ford
2	J. Scheckter	Tyrrell-Ford
3	J. Mass	McLaren-Ford
4	C. Pace	Brabham-Alfa Romeo
5	G. Nilsson	Lotus-Ford
6	R. Stommelen	Brabham-Alfa Romeo

Fastest lap: J. Scheckter 118.57mph/190.82km/h
Pole position: J. Hunt

AUSTRIAN GP
Osterreichring, August 15
198 miles/318km

PLACE	DRIVER	CAR
1	J. Watson 132.00mph/212.43km/h	Penske-Ford
2	J. Laffite	Ligier-Matra
3	G. Nilsson	Lotus-Ford
4	J. Hunt	McLaren-Ford
5	M. Andretti	Lotus-Ford
6	R. Peterson	March-Ford

Fastest lap: J. Hunt 137.83mph/221.81km/h
Pole position: J. Hunt

DUTCH GP
Zandvoort, August 29
197 miles/317km

1	J. Hunt 112.68mph/181.34km/h	McLaren-Ford
2	C. Regazzoni	Ferrari
3	M. Andretti	Lotus-Ford
4	T. Pryce	Shadow-Ford
5	J. Scheckter	Tyrrell-Ford
6	V. Brambilla	March-Ford

Fastest lap: C. Regazzoni 114.46mph/184.21km/h
Pole position: R. Peterson (March-Ford)

ITALIAN GP
Monza, September 12
187 miles/301km

1	R. Peterson 124.12mph/199.75km/h	March-Ford
2	C. Regazzoni	Ferrari
3	J. Laffite	Ligier-Matra
4	N. Lauda	Ferrari
5	J. Scheckter	Tyrrell-Ford
6	P. Depailler	Tyrrell-Ford

Fastest lap: R. Peterson 128.08mph/206.12km/h
Pole position: J. Laffite

CANADIAN GP
Mosport, October 3
197 miles/317km

1	J. Hunt 117.84mph/189.65km/h	McLaren-Ford
2	P. Depailler	Tyrrell-Ford
3	M. Andretti	Lotus-Ford
4	J. Scheckter	Tyrrell-Ford
5	J. Mass	McLaren-Ford
6	C. Regazzoni	Ferrari

Fastest lap: P. Depailler 119.92mph/193.00km/h
Pole position: J. Hunt

UNITED STATES GP
Watkins Glen, October 10
199 miles/320km

1	J. Hunt 116.43mph/187.37km/h	McLaren-Ford
2	J. Scheckter	Tyrrell-Ford
3	N. Lauda	Ferrari
4	J. Mass	McLaren-Ford
5	H. Stuck	March-Ford
6	J. Watson	Penske-Ford

Fastest lap: J. Hunt 118.20mph/190.22km/h
Pole position: J. Hunt

JAPANESE GP
Fuji, October 24
198 miles/318km

PLACE	DRIVER	CAR
1	M. Andretti 114.09mph/183.62km/h	Lotus-Ford
2	P. Depailler	Tyrrell-Ford
3	J. Hunt	McLaren-Ford
4	A. Jones	Surtees-Ford
5	C. Regazzoni	Ferrari
6	G. Nilsson	Lotus-Ford

Fastest lap: M. Hasemi (Kojima-Ford) 124.64mph/200.59km/h
Pole position: M. Andretti

1977

ARGENTINE GP
Buenos Aires, January 9
197 miles/317km

PLACE	DRIVER	CAR
1	J. Scheckter 117.71mph/189.44km/h	Wolf-Ford
2	C. Pace	Brabham-Alfa Romeo
3	C. Reutemann	Ferrari
4	E. Fittipaldi	Fittipaldi-Ford
5	M. Andretti	Lotus-Ford
6	C. Regazzoni	Ensign-Ford

Fastest lap: J. Hunt (McLaren-Ford) 120.21mph/193.46km/h
Pole position: J. Hunt

BRAZILIAN GP
Interlagos, January 23
198 miles/318km

1	C. Reutemann 112.92mph/181.73km/h	Ferrari
2	J. Hunt	McLaren-Ford
3	N. Lauda	Ferrari
4	E. Fittipaldi	Fittipaldi-Ford
5	G. Nilsson	Lotus-Ford
6	R. Zorzi	Shadow-Ford

Fastest lap: J. Hunt 115.22mph/185.43km/h
Pole position: J. Hunt

SOUTH AFRICAN GP
Kyalami, March 5
199 miles/320km

1	N. Lauda 116.59mph/187.64km/h	Ferrari
2	J. Scheckter	Wolf-Ford
3	P. Depailler	Tyrrell-Ford
4	J. Hunt	McLaren-Ford
5	J. Mass	McLaren-Ford
6	J. Watson	Brabham-Alfa Romeo

Fastest lap: J. Watson 118.26mph/190.32km/h
Pole position: J. Hunt

UNITED STATES GP (WEST)
Long Beach, April 3
162 miles/260km

PLACE	DRIVER	CAR
1	M. Andretti 86.89mph/139.84km/h	Lotus-Ford
2	N. Lauda	Ferrari
3	J. Scheckter	Wolf-Ford
4	P. Depailler	Tyrrell-Ford
5	E. Fittipaldi	Fittipaldi-Ford
6	J. P. Jarier	Penske-Ford

Fastest lap: N. Lauda 87.88mph/141.42km/h
Pole position: N. Lauda

SPANISH GP
Jarama, May 8
159 miles/256km

PLACE	DRIVER	CAR
1	M. Andretti 92.53mph/148.92km/h	Lotus-Ford
2	C. Reutemann	Ferrari
3	J. Scheckter	Wolf-Ford
4	J. Mass	McLaren-Ford
5	G. Nilsson	Lotus-Ford
6	H. Stuck	Brabham-Alfa Romeo

Fastest lap: J. Laffite (Ligier-Matra) 94.24mph/151.66km/h
Pole position: M. Andretti

MONACO GP
Monte Carlo, May 22
156 miles/252km

PLACE	DRIVER	CAR
1	J. Scheckter 79.61mph/128.12km/h	Wolf-Ford
2	N. Lauda	Ferrari
3	C. Reutemann	Ferrari
4	J. Mass	McLaren-Ford
5	M. Andretti	Lotus-Ford
6	A. Jones	Shadow-Ford

Fastest lap: J. Scheckter 81.35mph/130.92km/h
Pole position: J. Watson (Brabham-Alfa Romeo)

BELGIAN GP
Zolder, June 5
185 miles/298km

PLACE	DRIVER	CAR
1	G. Nilsson 96.64mph/155.53km/h	Lotus-Ford
2	N. Lauda	Ferrari
3	R. Peterson	Tyrrell-Ford
4	V. Brambilla	Surtees-Ford
5	A. Jones	Shadow-Ford
6	H. Stuck	Brabham-Alfa Romeo

Fastest lap: G. Nilsson 109.13mph/175.63km/h
Pole position: M. Andretti (Lotus-Ford)

SWEDISH GP
Anderstorp, June 19
180 miles/289km

PLACE	DRIVER	CAR
1	J. Laffite 100.87mph/162.34km/h	Ligier-Matra
2	J. Mass	McLaren-Ford
3	C. Reutemann	Ferrari
4	P. Depailler	Tyrrell-Ford
5	J. Watson	Brabham-Alfa Romeo
6	M. Andretti	Lotus-Ford

Fastest lap: M. Andretti 102.59mph/165.11km/h
Pole position: M. Andretti

FRENCH GP
Dijon, July 3
189 miles/304km

PLACE	DRIVER	CAR
1	M. Andretti 113.71mph/183.01km/h	Lotus-Ford
2	J. Watson	Brabham-Alfa Romeo
3	J. Hunt	McLaren-Ford
4	G. Nilsson	Lotus-Ford
5	N. Lauda	Ferrari
6	C. Reutemann	Ferrari

Fastest lap: M. Andretti 115.26mph/185.49km/h
Pole position: M. Andretti

BRITISH GP
Silverstone, July 16
199 miles/320km

PLACE	DRIVER	CAR
1	J. Hunt 130.35mph/209.79km/h	McLaren-Ford
2	N. Lauda	Ferrari
3	G. Nilsson	Lotus-Ford
4	J. Mass	McLaren-Ford
5	H. Stuck	Brabham-Alfa Romeo
6	J. Laffite	Ligier-Matra

Fastest lap: J. Hunt 132.60mph/213.40km/h
Pole position: J. Hunt

GERMAN GP
Hockenheim, July 31
198 miles/318km

PLACE	DRIVER	CAR
1	N. Lauda 129.57mph/208.53km/h	Ferrari
2	J. Scheckter	Wolf-Ford
3	H. Stuck	Brabham-Alfa Romeo
4	C. Reutemann	Ferrari
5	V. Brambilla	Surtees-Ford
6	P. Tambay	Ensign-Ford

Fastest lap: N. Lauda 130.93mph/210.71km/h
Pole position: J. Scheckter

AUSTRIAN GP
Osterreichring, August 14
199 miles/320km

PLACE	DRIVER	CAR
1	A. Jones 122.99mph/197.93km/h	Shadow-Ford
2	N. Lauda	Ferrari
3	H. Stuck	Brabham-Alfa Romeo
4	C. Reutemann	Ferrari
5	R. Peterson	Tyrrell-Ford
6	J. Mass	McLaren-Ford

Fastest lap: J. Watson (Brabham-Alfa Romeo) 131.66mph/211.89km/h
Pole position: N. Lauda

DUTCH GP
Zandvoort, August 28
197 miles/317km

	DRIVER	CAR
1	N. Lauda 116.12mph/186.87km/h	Ferrari
2	J. Laffite	Ligier-Matra
3	J. Scheckter	Wolf-Ford
4	E. Fittipaldi	Fittipaldi-Ford
5	P. Tambay	Ensign-Ford
6	C. Reutemann	Ferrari

Fastest lap: N. Lauda 118.18mph/190.19km/h
Pole position: M. Andretti (Lotus-Ford)

ITALIAN GP
Monza, September 11
187 miles/301km

	DRIVER	CAR
1	M. Andretti 128.01mph/206.02km/h	Lotus-Ford
2	N. Lauda	Ferrari
3	A. Jones	Shadow-Ford
4	J. Mass	McLaren-Ford
5	C. Regazzoni	Ensign-Ford
6	R. Peterson	Tyrrell-Ford

Fastest lap: M. Andretti 130.92mph/210.70km/h
Pole position: J. Hunt (McLaren-Ford)

UNITED STATES GP
Watkins Glen, October 2
199 miles/320km

	DRIVER	CAR
1	J. Hunt 100.98mph/162.51km/h	McLaren-Ford
2	M. Andretti	Lotus-Ford
3	J. Scheckter	Wolf-Ford
4	N. Lauda	Ferrari
5	C. Regazzoni	Ensign-Ford
6	C. Reutemann	Ferrari

Fastest lap: R. Peterson (Tyrrell-Ford) 108.69mph/174.92km/h
Pole position: J. Hunt

WORLD CHAMPIONSHIP GRAND PRIX RESULTS 1950–1989

CANADIAN GP
Mosport, October 9
197 miles/317km

PLACE	DRIVER	CAR
1	J. Scheckter 118.03mph/189.95km/h	Wolf-Ford
2	P. Depailler	Tyrrell-Ford
3	J. Mass	McLaren-Ford
4	A. Jones	Shadow-Ford
5	P. Tambay	Ensign-Ford
6	V. Brambilla	Surtees-Ford

Fastest lap: M. Andretti (Lotus-Ford)
120.77mph/194.36km/h
Pole position: M. Andretti

JAPANESE GP
Fuji, October 23
198 miles/318km

1	J. Hunt 129.15mph/207.84km/h	McLaren-Ford
2	C. Reutemann	Ferrari
3	P. Depailler	Tyrrell-Ford
4	A. Jones	Shadow-Ford
5	J. Laffite	Ligier-Matra
6	R. Patrese	Shadow-Ford

Fastest lap: J. Scheckter (Wolf-Ford)
131.24mph/211.20km/h
Pole position: M. Andretti (Lotus-Ford)

1978

ARGENTINE GP
Buenos Aires, January 15
197 miles/317km

PLACE	DRIVER	CAR
1	M. Andretti 119.19mph/191.82km/h	Lotus-Ford
2	N. Lauda	Brabham-Alfa Romeo
3	P. Depailler	Tyrrell-Ford
4	J. Hunt	McLaren-Ford
5	R. Peterson	Lotus-Ford
6	P. Tambay	McLaren-Ford

Fastest lap: G. Villeneuve (Ferrari)
121.63mph/195.75km/h
Pole position: M. Andretti

BRAZILIAN GP
Rio de Janeiro, January 29
197 miles/317km

1	C. Reutemann 107.43mph/172.89km/h	Ferrari
2	E. Fittipaldi	Fittipaldi-Ford
3	N. Lauda	Brabham-Alfa Romeo
4	M. Andretti	Lotus-Ford
5	C. Regazzoni	Shadow-Ford
6	D. Pironi	Tyrrell-Ford

Fastest lap: C. Reutemann
109.19mph/175.72km/h
Pole position: R. Peterson (Lotus-Ford)

SOUTH AFRICAN GP
Kyalami, March 4
199 miles/320km

PLACE	DRIVER	CAR
1	R. Peterson 116.70mph/187.81km/h	Lotus-Ford
2	P. Depailler	Tyrrell-Ford
3	J. Watson	Brabham-Alfa Romeo
4	A. Jones	Williams-Ford
5	J. Laffite	Ligier-Matra
6	D. Pironi	Tyrrell-Ford

Fastest lap: M. Andretti (Lotus-Ford)
119.08mph/191.64km/h
Pole position: N. Lauda (Brabham-Alfa Romeo)

UNITED STATES GP (WEST)
Long Beach, April 2
163 miles/263km

1	C. Reutemann 87.10mph/140.17km/h	Ferrari
2	M. Andretti	Lotus-Ford
3	P. Depailler	Tyrrell-Ford
4	R. Peterson	Lotus-Ford
5	J. Laffite	Ligier-Matra
6	R. Patrese	Arrows-Ford

Fastest lap: A. Jones (Williams-Ford)
88.45mph/142.35km/h
Pole position: C. Reutemann

MONACO GP
Monte Carlo, May 7
154 miles/248km

1	P. Depailler 80.36mph/129.33km/h	Tyrrell-Ford
2	N. Lauda	Brabham-Alfa Romeo
3	J. Scheckter	Wolf-Ford
4	J. Watson	Brabham-Alfa Romeo
5	D. Pironi	Tyrrell-Ford
6	R. Patrese	Arrows-Ford

Fastest lap: N. Lauda 83.57mph/134.50km/h
Pole position: C. Reutemann (Ferrari)

BELGIAN GP
Zolder, May 21
185 miles/298km

1	M. Andretti 111.38mph/179.24km/h	Lotus-Ford
2	R. Peterson	Lotus-Ford
3	C. Reutemann	Ferrari
4	G. Villeneuve	Ferrari
5	J. Laffite	Ligier-Matra
6	D. Pironi	Tyrrell-Ford

Fastest lap: R. Peterson 114.69mph/184.57km/h
Pole position: M. Andretti

SPANISH GP
Jarama, June 4
159 miles/256km

PLACE	DRIVER	CAR
1	M. Andretti 93.52mph/150.51km/h	Lotus-Ford
2	R. Peterson	Lotus-Ford
3	J. Laffite	Ligier-Matra
4	J. Scheckter	Wolf-Ford
5	J. Watson	Brabham-Alfa Romeo
6	J. Hunt	McLaren-Ford

Fastest lap: M. Andretti 95.12mph/153.08km/h
Pole position: M. Andretti

SWEDISH GP
Anderstorp, June 17
175 miles/282km

1	N. Lauda 104.15mph/167.61km/h	Brabham-Alfa Romeo
2	R. Patrese	Arrows-Ford
3	R. Peterson	Lotus-Ford
4	P. Tambay	McLaren-Ford
5	C. Regazzoni	Shadow-Ford
6	E. Fittipaldi	Fittipaldi-Ford

Fastest lap: N. Lauda 106.29mph/171.06km/h
Pole position: M. Andretti (Lotus-Ford)

FRENCH GP
Paul Ricard, July 2
195 miles/315km

1	M. Andretti 118.31mph/190.41km/h	Lotus-Ford
2	R. Peterson	Lotus-Ford
3	J. Hunt	McLaren-Ford
4	J. Watson	Brabham-Alfa Romeo
5	A. Jones	Williams-Ford
6	J. Scheckter	Wolf-Ford

Fastest lap: C. Reutemann (Ferrari)
119.72mph/192.67km/h
Pole position: J. Watson

BRITISH GP
Brands Hatch, July 16
199 miles/320km

1	C. Reutemann 116.61mph/187.66km/h	Ferrari
2	N. Lauda	Brabham-Alfa Romeo
3	J. Watson	Brabham-Alfa Romeo
4	P. Depailler	Tyrrell-Ford
5	H. Stuck	Shadow-Ford
6	P. Tambay	McLaren-Ford

Fastest lap: N. Lauda 119.71mph/192.65km/h
Pole position: R. Peterson (Lotus-Ford)

GERMAN GP
Hockenheim, July 30
190 miles/306km

PLACE	DRIVER	CAR
1	M. Andretti 129.41mph/208.26km/h	Lotus-Ford
2	J. Scheckter	Wolf-Ford
3	J. Laffite	Ligier-Matra
4	E. Fittipaldi	Fittipaldi-Ford
5	D. Pironi	Tyrrell-Ford
6	H. Rebaque	Lotus-Ford

Fastest lap: R. Peterson (Lotus-Ford) 131.35mph/211.39km/h
Pole position: M. Andretti

AUSTRIAN GP
Osterreichring, August 13
199 miles/320km

PLACE	DRIVER	CAR
1	R. Peterson 118.03mph/189.95km/h	Lotus-Ford
2	P. Depailler	Tyrrell-Ford
3	G. Villeneuve	Ferrari
4	E. Fittipaldi	Fittipaldi-Ford
5	J. Laffite	Ligier-Matra
6	V. Brambilla	Surtees-Ford

Fastest lap: R. Peterson 128.91mph/207.45km/h
Pole position: R. Peterson

DUTCH GP
Zandvoort, August 27
197 miles/317km

PLACE	DRIVER	CAR
1	M. Andretti 116.91mph/188.16km/h	Lotus-Ford
2	R. Peterson	Lotus-Ford
3	N. Lauda	Brabham Alfa Romeo
4	J. Watson	Brabham-Alfa Romeo
5	E. Fittipaldi	Fittipaldi-Ford
6	G. Villeneuve	Ferrari

Fastest lap: N. Lauda 118.81mph/191.20km/h
Pole position: M. Andretti

ITALIAN GP
Monza, September 10
144 miles/232km

PLACE	DRIVER	CAR
1	N. Lauda 128.95mph/207.52km/h	Brabham-Alfa Romeo
2	J. Watson	Brabham-Alfa Romeo
3	C. Reutemann	Ferrari
4	J. Laffite	Ligier-Matra
5	P. Tambay	McLaren-Ford
6	M. Andretti	Lotus-Ford

Fastest lap: M. Andretti 132.08mph/212.56km/h
Pole position: M. Andretti

UNITED STATES GP
Watkins Glen, October 1
199 miles/320km

PLACE	DRIVER	CAR
1	C. Reutemann 118.59mph/190.85km/h	Ferrari
2	A. Jones	Williams-Ford
3	J. Scheckter	Wolf-Ford
4	J. P. Jabouille	Renault
5	E. Fittipaldi	Fittipaldi-Ford
6	P. Tambay	McLaren-Ford

Fastest lap: J. P. Jarier (Lotus-Ford) 122.12mph/196.53km/h
Pole position: M. Andretti (Lotus-Ford)

CANADIAN GP
Montreal, October 8
196 miles/316km

PLACE	DRIVER	CAR
1	G. Villeneuve 99.67mph/160.40km/h	Ferrari
2	J. Scheckter	Wolf-Ford
3	C. Reutemann	Ferrari
4	R. Patrese	Arrows-Ford
5	P. Depailler	Tyrrell-Ford
6	D. Daly	Ensign-Ford

Fastest lap: A. Jones (Williams-Ford) 102.64mph/165.18km/h
Pole position: J. P. Jarier (Lotus-Ford)

1979

ARGENTINE GP
Buenos Aires, January 21
197 miles/317km

PLACE	DRIVER	CAR
1	J. Laffite 122.78mph/197.59km/h	Ligier-Ford
2	C. Reutemann	Lotus-Ford
3	J. Watson	McLaren-Ford
4	P. Depailler	Ligier-Ford
5	M. Andretti	Lotus-Ford
6	E. Fittipaldi	Fittipaldi-Ford

Fastest lap: J. Laffite 124.88mph/200.97km/h
Pole position: J. Laffite

BRAZILIAN GP
Interlagos, February 4
196 miles/316km

PLACE	DRIVER	CAR
1	J. Laffite 117.23mph/188.67km/h	Ligier-Ford
2	P. Depailler	Ligier-Ford
3	C. Reutemann	Lotus-Ford
4	D. Pironi	Tyrrell-Ford
5	G. Villeneuve	Ferrari
6	J. Scheckter	Ferrari

Fastest lap: J. Laffite 118.40mph/190.55km/h
Pole position: J. Laffite

SOUTH AFRICAN GP
Kyalami, March 3
199 miles/320km

PLACE	DRIVER	CAR
1	G. Villeneuve 117.19mph/188.60km/h	Ferrari
2	J. Scheckter	Ferrari
3	J. P. Jarier	Tyrrell-Ford
4	M. Andretti	Lotus-Ford
5	C. Reutemann	Lotus-Ford
6	N. Lauda	Brabham-Alfa Romeo

Fastest lap: G. Villeneuve 123.38mph/198.54km/h
Pole position: J. P. Jabouille (Renault)

UNITED STATES GP (WEST)
Long Beach, April 8
163 miles/263km

PLACE	DRIVER	CAR
1	G. Villeneuve 87.81mph/141.31km/h	Ferrari
2	J. Scheckter	Ferrari
3	A. Jones	Williams-Ford
4	M. Andretti	Lotus-Ford
5	P. Depailler	Ligier-Ford
6	J. P. Jarier	Tyrrell-Ford

Fastest lap: G. Villeneuve 89.65mph/144.28km/h
Pole position: G. Villeneuve

SPANISH GP
Jarama, April 29
159 miles/256km

PLACE	DRIVER	CAR
1	P. Depailler 95.97mph/154.45km/h	Ligier-Ford
2	C. Reutemann	Lotus-Ford
3	M. Andretti	Lotus-Ford
4	J. Scheckter	Ferrari
5	J. P. Jarier	Tyrrell-Ford
6	D. Pironi	Tyrrell-Ford

Fastest lap: G. Villeneuve (Ferrari) 99.70mph/160.45km/h
Pole position: J. Laffite (Ligier-Ford)

BELGIAN GP
Zolder, May 13
185 miles/298km

PLACE	DRIVER	CAR
1	J. Scheckter 111.24mph/179.02km/h	Ferrari
2	J. Laffite	Ligier-Ford
3	D. Pironi	Tyrrell-Ford
4	C. Reutemann	Lotus-Ford
5	R. Patrese	Arrows-Ford
6	J. Watson	McLaren-Ford

Fastest lap: J. Scheckter 115.72mph/186.23km/h
Pole position: J. Laffite

MONACO GP
Monte Carlo, May 27
156 miles/252km

PLACE	DRIVER	CAR
1	J. Scheckter 81.34mph/130.90km/h	Ferrari
2	C. Regazzoni	Williams-Ford
3	C. Reutemann	Lotus-Ford
4	J. Watson	McLaren-Ford
5	P. Depailler	Ligier-Ford
6	J. Mass	Arrows-Ford

Fastest lap: P. Depailler 83.41mph/134.24km/h
Pole position: J. Scheckter

WORLD CHAMPIONSHIP GRAND PRIX RESULTS 1950–1989

1980

FRENCH GP
Dijon, July 1
189 miles/304km

PLACE	DRIVER	CAR
1	J. P. Jabouille 118.88mph/191.32km/h	Renault
2	G. Villeneuve	Ferrari
3	R. Arnoux	Renault
4	A. Jones	Williams-Ford
5	J. P. Jarier	Tyrrell-Ford
6	C. Regazzoni	Williams-Ford

Fastest lap: R. Arnoux 122.91mph/197.80km/h
Pole position: J. P. Jabouille

BRITISH GP
Silverstone, July 14
199 miles/320km

PLACE	DRIVER	CAR
1	C. Regazzoni 138.80mph/223.37km/h	Williams-Ford
2	R. Arnoux	Renault
3	J. P. Jarier	Tyrrell-Ford
4	J. Watson	McLaren-Ford
5	J. Scheckter	Ferrari
6	J. Ickx	Ligier-Ford

Fastest lap: C. Regazzoni 141.87mph/228.31km/h
Pole position: A. Jones (Williams-Ford)

GERMAN GP
Hockenheim, July 29
190 miles/306km

PLACE	DRIVER	CAR
1	A. Jones 134.27mph/216.09km/h	Williams-Ford
2	C. Regazzoni	Williams-Ford
3	J. Laffite	Ligier-Ford
4	J. Scheckter	Ferrari
5	J. Watson	McLaren-Ford
6	J. Mass	Arrows-Ford

Fastest lap: G. Villeneuve (Ferrari) 135.71mph/218.40km/h
Pole position: J. P. Jabouille (Renault)

AUSTRIAN GP
Osterreichring, August 12
199 miles/320km

PLACE	DRIVER	CAR
1	A. Jones 136.52mph/219.71km/h	Williams-Ford
2	G. Villeneuve	Ferrari
3	J. Laffite	Ligier-Ford
4	J. Scheckter	Ferrari
5	C. Regazzoni	Williams-Ford
6	R. Arnoux	Renault

Fastest lap: R. Arnoux 139.08mph/223.82km/h
Pole position: R. Arnoux

DUTCH GP
Zandvoort, August 26
197 miles/317km

PLACE	DRIVER	CAR
1	A. Jones 116.62mph/187.67km/h	Williams-Ford
2	J. Scheckter	Ferrari
3	J. Laffite	Ligier-Ford
4	N. Piquet	Brabham-Alfa Romeo
5	J. Ickx	Ligier-Ford
6	J. Mass	Arrows-Ford

Fastest lap: G. Villeneuve (Ferrari) 119.00mph/191.52km/h
Pole position: R. Arnoux (Renault)

ITALIAN GP
Monza, September 9
180 miles/289km

PLACE	DRIVER	CAR
1	J. Scheckter 131.85mph/212.19km/h	Ferrari
2	G. Villeneuve	Ferrari
3	C. Regazzoni	Williams-Ford
4	N. Lauda	Brabham-Alfa Romeo
5	M. Andretti	Lotus-Ford
6	J. P. Jarier	Tyrrell-Ford

Fastest lap: C. Regazzoni 135.71mph/218.41km/h
Pole position: J. P. Jabouille (Renault)

CANADIAN GP
Montreal, September 30
197 miles/317km

PLACE	DRIVER	CAR
1	A. Jones 105.59mph/169.93km/h	Williams-Ford
2	G. Villeneuve	Ferrari
3	C. Regazzoni	Williams-Ford
4	J. Scheckter	Ferrari
5	D. Pironi	Tyrrell-Ford
6	J. Watson	McLaren-Ford

Fastest lap: A. Jones 108.08mph/173.94km/h
Pole position: A. Jones

UNITED STATES GP
Watkins Glen, October 7
199 miles/320km

PLACE	DRIVER	CAR
1	G. Villeneuve 106.46mph/171.33km/h	Ferrari
2	R. Arnoux	Renault
3	D. Pironi	Tyrrell-Ford
4	E. de Angelis	Shadow-Ford
5	H. Stuck	ATS-Ford
6	J. Watson	McLaren-Ford

Fastest lap: N. Piquet (Brabham-Ford) 121.51mph/195.55km/h
Pole position: A. Jones (Williams-Ford)

ARGENTINE GP
Buenos Aires, January 13
197 miles/317km

PLACE	DRIVER	CAR
1	A. Jones 113.99mph/183.44km/h	Williams-Ford
2	N. Piquet	Brabham-Ford
3	K. Rosberg	Fittipaldi-Ford
4	D. Daly	Tyrrell-Ford
5	B. Giacomelli	Alfa Romeo
6	A. Prost	McLaren-Ford

Fastest lap: A. Jones 120.87mph/194.53km/h
Pole position: A. Jones

BRAZILIAN GP
Interlagos, January 27
196 miles/316km

PLACE	DRIVER	CAR
1	R. Arnoux 117.40mph/188.93km/h	Renault
2	E. de Angelis	Lotus-Ford
3	A. Jones	Williams-Ford
4	D. Pironi	Ligier-Ford
5	A. Prost	McLaren-Ford
6	R. Patrese	Arrows-Ford

Fastest lap: R. Arnoux 119.57mph/192.42km/h
Pole position: J. P. Jabouille (Renault)

SOUTH AFRICAN GP
Kyalami, March 1
199 miles/320km

PLACE	DRIVER	CAR
1	R. Arnoux 123.19mph/198.25km/h	Renault
2	J. Laffite	Ligier-Ford
3	D. Pironi	Ligier-Ford
4	N. Piquet	Brabham-Ford
5	C. Reutemann	Williams-Ford
6	J. Mass	Arrows-Ford

Fastest lap: R. Arnoux 125.50mph/201.97km/h
Pole position: J. P. Jabouille (Renault)

UNITED STATES GP (WEST)
Long Beach, March 30
163 miles/263km

PLACE	DRIVER	CAR
1	N. Piquet 88.45mph/142.35km/h	Brabham-Ford
2	R. Patrese	Arrows-Ford
3	E. Fittipaldi	Fittipaldi-Ford
4	J. Watson	McLaren-Ford
5	J. Scheckter	Ferrari
6	D. Pironi	Ligier-Ford

Fastest lap: N. Piquet 91.10mph/146.61km/h
Pole position: N. Piquet

BELGIAN GP
Zolder, May 4
191 miles/307km

PLACE	DRIVER	CAR
1	D. Pironi 115.82mph/186.40km/h	Ligier-Ford
2	A. Jones	Williams-Ford
3	C. Reutemann	Williams-Ford
4	R. Arnoux	Renault
5	J. P. Jarier	Tyrrell-Ford
6	G. Villeneuve	Ferrari

Fastest lap: J. Laffite (Ligier-Ford) 117.88mph/189.70km/h
Pole position: A. Jones

1981

MONACO GP
Monte Carlo, May 18
156 miles/252km

PLACE	DRIVER	CAR
1	C. Reutemann 81.20mph/130.68km/h	Williams-Ford
2	J. Laffite	Ligier-Ford
3	N. Piquet	Brabham-Ford
4	J. Mass	Arrows-Ford
5	G. Villeneuve	Ferrari
6	E. Fittipaldi	Fittipaldi-Ford

Fastest lap: R. Patrese (Arrows-Ford) 86.09mph/138.55km/h
Pole position: D. Pironi (Ligier-Ford)

FRENCH GP
Paul Ricard, June 29
195 miles/315km

PLACE	DRIVER	CAR
1	A. Jones 126.15mph/203.02km/h	Williams-Ford
2	D. Pironi	Ligier-Ford
3	J. Laffite	Ligier-Ford
4	N. Piquet	Brabham-Ford
5	R. Arnoux	Renault
6	C. Reutemann	Williams-Ford

Fastest lap: A. Jones: 128.11mph/206.17km/h
Pole position: J. Laffite

BRITISH GP
Brands Hatch, July 13
199 miles/320km

PLACE	DRIVER	CAR
1	A. Jones 125.69mph/202.28km/h	Williams-Ford
2	N. Piquet	Brabham-Ford
3	C. Reutemann	Williams-Ford
4	D. Daly	Tyrrell-Ford
5	J. P. Jarier	Tyrrell-Ford
6	A. Prost	McLaren-Ford

Fastest lap: D. Pironi (Ligier-Ford) 130.02mph/209.24km/h
Pole position: D. Pironi

GERMAN GP
Hockenheim, August 10
190 miles/306km

PLACE	DRIVER	CAR
1	J. Laffite 137.22mph/220.83km/h	Ligier-Ford
2	C. Reutemann	Williams-Ford
3	A. Jones	Williams-Ford
4	N. Piquet	Brabham-Ford
5	B. Giacomelli	Alfa Romeo
6	G. Villeneuve	Ferrari

Fastest lap: A. Jones 139.96mph/225.25km/h
Pole position: A. Jones

AUSTRIAN GP
Osterreichring, August 17
199 miles/320km

PLACE	DRIVER	CAR
1	J. P. Jabouille 138.69mph/223.20km/h	Renault
2	A. Jones	Williams-Ford
3	C. Reutemann	Williams-Ford
4	J. Laffite	Ligier-Ford
5	N. Piquet	Brabham-Ford
6	E. de Angelis	Lotus-Ford

Fastest lap: R. Arnoux (Renault) 143.66mph/231.20km/h
Pole position: R. Arnoux

DUTCH GP
Zandvoort, August 31
190 miles/306km

PLACE	DRIVER	CAR
1	N. Piquet 116.19mph/186.98km/h	Brabham-Ford
2	R. Arnoux	Renault
3	J. Laffite	Ligier-Ford
4	C. Reutemann	Williams-Ford
5	J. P. Jarier	Tyrrell-Ford
6	A. Prost	McLaren-Ford

Fastest lap: R. Arnoux 119.87mph/192.91km/h
Pole position: R. Arnoux

ITALIAN GP
Imola, September 14
186 miles/300km

PLACE	DRIVER	CAR
1	N. Piquet 113.98mph/183.44km/h	Brabham-Ford
2	A. Jones	Williams-Ford
3	C. Reutemann	Williams-Ford
4	E. de Angelis	Lotus-Ford
5	K. Rosberg	Fittipaldi-Ford
6	D. Pironi	Ligier-Ford

Fastest lap: A. Jones 116.40mph/187.33km/h
Pole position: R. Arnoux (Renault)

CANADIAN GP
Montreal, September 28
192 miles/309km

PLACE	DRIVER	CAR
1	A. Jones 110.00mph/177.03km/h	Williams-Ford
2	C. Reutemann	Williams-Ford
3	D. Pironi	Ligier-Ford
4	J. Watson	McLaren-Ford
5	G. Villeneuve	Ferrari
6	H. Rebaque	Brabham-Ford

Fastest lap: D. Pironi 111.13mph/178.85km/h
Pole position: N. Piquet (Brabham-Ford)

UNITED STATES GP
Watkins Glen, October 5
199 miles/320km

PLACE	DRIVER	CAR
1	A. Jones 126.37mph/203.37km/h	Williams-Ford
2	C. Reutemann	Williams-Ford
3	D. Pironi	Ligier-Ford
4	E. de Angelis	Lotus-Ford
5	J. Laffite	Ligier-Ford
6	M. Andretti	Lotus-Ford

Fastest lap: A. Jones 129.24mph/207.99km/h
Pole position: B. Giacomelli (Alfa Romeo)

UNITED STATES GP (WEST)
Long Beach, March 15
163 miles/263km

PLACE	DRIVER	CAR
1	A. Jones 87.60mph/140.98km/h	Williams-Ford
2	C. Reutemann	Williams-Ford
3	N. Piquet	Brabham-Ford
4	M. Andretti	Alfa Romeo
5	E. Cheever	Tyrrell-Ford
6	P. Tambay	Theodore-Ford

Fastest lap: A. Jones 89.89mph/144.66km/h
Pole position: R. Patrese (Arrows-Ford)

BRAZILIAN GP
Rio de Janeiro, March 29
194 miles/313km

PLACE	DRIVER	CAR
1	C. Reutemann 96.60mph/155.45km/h	Williams-Ford
2	A. Jones	Williams-Ford
3	R. Patrese	Arrows-Ford
4	M. Surer	Ensign-Ford
5	E. de Angelis	Lotus-Ford
6	J. Laffite	Talbot-Matra

Fastest lap: M. Surer 98.46mph/158.45km/h
Pole position: N. Piquet (Brabham-Ford)

ARGENTINE GP
Buenos Aires, April 12
196 miles/316km

PLACE	DRIVER	CAR
1	N. Piquet 124.67mph/200.63km/h	Brabham-Ford
2	C. Reutemann	Williams-Ford
3	A. Prost	Renault
4	A. Jones	Williams-Ford
5	R. Arnoux	Renault
6	E. de Angelis	Lotus-Ford

Fastest lap: N. Piquet 126.81mph/204.07km/h
Pole position: N. Piquet

SAN MARINO GP
Imola, May 3
188 miles/302km

PLACE	DRIVER	CAR
1	N. Piquet 101.21mph/162.87km/h	Brabham
2	R. Patrese	Arrows-Ford
3	C. Reutemann	Williams-Ford
4	H. Rebaque	Brabham-Ford
5	D. Pironi	Ferrari
6	A. de Cesaris	McLaren-Ford

Fastest lap: G. Villeneuve (Ferrari) 104.33mph/167.90km/h
Pole position: G. Villeneuve

BELGIAN GP
Zolder, May 17
143 miles/230km

PLACE	DRIVER	CAR
1	C. Reutemann 112.13mph/180.45km/h	Williams-Ford
2	J. Laffite	Talbot-Matra
3	N. Mansell	Lotus-Ford
4	G. Villeneuve	Ferrari
5	E. de Angelis	Lotus-Ford
6	E. Cheever	Tyrrell-Ford

Fastest lap: C. Reutemann 114.45mph/184.19km/h
Pole position: C. Reutemann

WORLD CHAMPIONSHIP GRAND PRIX RESULTS 1950–1989

MONACO GP
Monte Carlo, May 31
157 miles/253km

PLACE	DRIVER	CAR
1	G. Villeneuve 82.04mph/132.03km/h	Ferrari
2	A. Jones	Williams-Ford
3	J. Laffite	Talbot-Matra
4	D. Pironi	Ferrari
5	E. Cheever	Tyrrell-Ford
6	M. Surer	Ensign-Ford

Fastest lap: A. Jones 84.70mph/136.31km/h
Pole position: N. Piquet (Brabham-Ford)

SPANISH GP
Jarama, June 21
165 miles/265km

PLACE	DRIVER	CAR
1	G. Villeneuve 92.65mph/149.10km/h	Ferrari
2	J. Laffite	Talbot-Matra
3	J. Watson	McLaren-Ford
4	C. Reutemann	Williams-Ford
5	E. de Angelis	Lotus-Ford
6	N. Mansell	Lotus-Ford

Fastest lap: A. Jones (Williams-Ford)
95.21mph/153.22km/h
Pole position: J. Laffite

FRENCH GP
Dijon, July 5
189 miles/304km

PLACE	DRIVER	CAR
1	A. Prost 118.31mph/190.39km/h	Renault
2	J. Watson	McLaren-Ford
3	N. Piquet	Brabham-Ford
4	R. Arnoux	Renault
5	D. Pironi	Ferrari
6	E. de Angelis	Lotus-Ford

Fastest lap: A. Prost 122.95mph/197.86km/h
Pole position: R. Arnoux

BRITISH GP
Silverstone, July 18
199 miles/320km

PLACE	DRIVER	CAR
1	J. Watson 137.65mph/221.51km/h	McLaren-Ford
2	C. Reutemann	Williams-Ford
3	J. Laffite	Talbot-Matra
4	E. Cheever	Tyrrell-Ford
5	H. Rebaque	Brabham-Ford
6	S. Borgudd	ATS-Ford

Fastest lap: R. Arnoux (Renault)
140.62mph/226.29km/h
Pole position: R. Arnoux

GERMAN GP
Hockenheim, August 2
190 miles/306km

PLACE	DRIVER	CAR
1	N. Piquet 132.54mph/213.29km/h	Brabham-Ford
2	A. Prost	Renault
3	J. Laffite	Talbot-Matra
4	H. Rebaque	Brabham-Ford
5	E. Cheever	Tyrrell-Ford
6	J. Watson	McLaren-Ford

Fastest lap: A. Jones (Williams-Ford)
135.07mph/217.37km/h
Pole position: A. Prost

AUSTRIAN GP
Osterreichring, August 16
196 miles/316km

PLACE	DRIVER	CAR
1	J. Laffite 134.03mph/215.70km/h	Talbot-Matra
2	R. Arnoux	Renault
3	N. Piquet	Brabham-Ford
4	A. Jones	Williams-Ford
5	C. Reutemann	Williams-Ford
6	J. Watson	McLaren-Ford

Fastest lap: J. Laffite 136.17mph/219.14km/h
Pole position: R. Arnoux

DUTCH GP
Zandvoort, August 30
190 miles/306km

PLACE	DRIVER	CAR
1	A. Prost 113.72mph/183.00km/h	Renault
2	N. Piquet	Brabham-Ford
3	A. Jones	Williams-Ford
4	H. Rebaque	Brabham-Ford
5	E. de Angelis	Lotus-Ford
6	E. Salazar	Ensign-Ford

Fastest lap: A. Jones 116.24mph/187.06km/h
Pole position: A. Prost

ITALIAN GP
Monza, September 13
188 miles/302km

PLACE	DRIVER	CAR
1	A. Prost 129.87mph/209.00km/h	Renault
2	A. Jones	Williams-Ford
3	C. Reutemann	Williams-Ford
4	E. de Angelis	Lotus-Ford
5	D. Pironi	Ferrari
6	N. Piquet	Brabham-Ford

Fastest lap: C. Reutemann
133.04mph/214.09km/h
Pole position: R. Arnoux (Renault)

CANADIAN GP
Montreal, September 27
173 miles/278km

PLACE	DRIVER	CAR
1	J. Laffite 85.31mph/137.29km/h	Talbot-Matra
2	J. Watson	McLaren-Ford
3	G. Villeneuve	Ferrari
4	B. Giacomelli	Alfa Romeo
5	N. Piquet	Brabham-Ford
6	E. de Angelis	Lotus-Ford

Fastest lap: J. Watson 90.12mph/145.02km/h
Pole position: N. Piquet

LAS VEGAS GP
Las Vegas, October 17
170 miles/273km

PLACE	DRIVER	CAR
1	A. Jones 97.90mph/157.55km/h	Williams-Ford
2	A. Prost	Renault
3	B. Giacomelli	Alfa Romeo
4	N. Mansell	Lotus-Ford
5	N. Piquet	Brabham-Ford
6	J. Laffite	Talbot-Matra

Fastest lap: D. Pironi (Ferrari)
101.87mph/163.93km/h
Pole position: C. Reutemann (Williams-Ford)

1982

SOUTH AFRICAN GP
Kyalami, January 23
197 miles/317km

PLACE	DRIVER	CAR
1	A. Prost 127.82mph/205.70km/h	Renault
2	C. Reutemann	Williams-Ford
3	R. Arnoux	Renault
4	N. Lauda	McLaren-Ford
5	K. Rosberg	Williams-Ford
6	J. Watson	McLaren-Ford

Fastest lap: A. Prost 134.46mph/216.39km/h
Pole position: R. Arnoux

BRAZILIAN GP
Rio de Janeiro, March 21
197 miles/317km

PLACE	DRIVER	CAR
1	N. Piquet* 113.72mph/183.00km/h	Brabham-Ford
2	K. Rosberg*	Williams-Ford
3	A. Prost	Renault
4	J. Watson	McLaren-Ford
5	N. Mansell	Lotus-Ford
6	M. Alboreto	Tyrrell-Ford

* Disqualified
Fastest lap: N. Piquet (Brabham-Ford)
116.52mph/187.52km/h
Pole position: A. Prost

UNITED STATES GP (WEST)
Long Beach, April 4
160 miles/258km

PLACE	DRIVER	CAR
1	N. Lauda 81.40mph/131.00km/h	McLaren-Ford
2	K. Rosberg	Williams-Ford
3	G. Villeneuve*	Ferrari
4	R. Patrese	Brabham-Ford
5	M. Alboreto	Tyrrell-Ford
6	E. de Angelis	Lotus-Ford

* Disqualified
Fastest lap: N. Lauda 84.42mph/135.86km/h
Pole position: A. de Cesaris (Alfa Romeo)

SAN MARINO GP
Imola, April 25
188 miles/302km

PLACE	DRIVER	CAR
1	D. Pironi	Ferrari
	117.30mph/187.77km/h	
2	G. Villeneuve	Ferrari
3	M. Alboreto	Tyrrell-Ford
4	J. P. Jarier	Osella-Ford
5	E. Salazar	ATS-Ford

(Only five finished)
Fastest lap: D. Pironi 118.64mph/190.92km/h
Pole position: R. Arnoux (Renault)

BELGIAN GP
Zolder, May 9
185 miles/298km

	DRIVER	CAR
1	J. Watson	McLaren-Ford
	116.88mph/188.09km/h	
2	K. Rosberg	Williams-Ford
3	N. Lauda*	McLaren-Ford
4	E. Cheever	Talbot-Matra
5	E. de Angelis	Lotus-Ford
6	N. Piquet	Brabham-BMW

* Disqualified
Fastest lap: J. Watson 119.55mph/192.39km/h
Pole position: A. Prost (Renault)

MONACO GP
Monte Carlo, May 23
157 miles/253km

	DRIVER	CAR
1	R. Patrese	Brabham-Ford
	82.21mph/132.30km/h	
2	D. Pironi	Ferrari
3	A. de Cesaris	Alfa Romeo
4	N. Mansell	Lotus-Ford
5	E. de Angelis	Lotus-Ford
6	D. Daly	Williams-Ford

Fastest lap: R. Patrese 85.79mph/139.67km/h
Pole position: R. Arnoux (Renault)

DETROIT GP
Detroit, June 6
194 miles/313km

	DRIVER	CAR
1	J. Watson	McLaren-Ford
	78.20mph/125.85km/h	
2	E. Cheever	Talbot-Matra
3	D. Pironi	Ferrari
4	K. Rosberg	Williams-Ford
5	D. Daly	Williams-Ford
6	J. Laffite	Talbot-Matra

Fastest lap: A. Prost (Renault)
81.28mph/130.80km/h
Pole position: A. Prost

CANADIAN GP
Montreal, June 13
192 miles/309km

PLACE	DRIVER	CAR
1	N. Piquet	Brabham-BMW
	107.94mph/173.70km/h	
2	R. Patrese	Brabham-Ford
3	J. Watson	McLaren-Ford
4	E. de Angelis	Lotus-Ford
5	M. Surer	Arrows-Ford
6	A. de Cesaris	Alfa Romeo

Fastest lap: D. Pironi (Ferrari)
111.70mph/179.75km/h
Pole position: D. Pironi

DUTCH GP
Zandvoort, July 3
190 miles/306km

	DRIVER	CAR
1	D. Pironi	Ferrari
	116.39mph/187.30km/h	
2	N. Piquet	Brabham-BMW
3	K. Rosberg	Williams-Ford
4	N. Lauda	McLaren-Ford
5	D. Daly	Williams-Ford
6	M. Baldi	Arrows-Ford

Fastest lap: D. Warwick (Toleman-Hart)
119.23mph/191.87km/h
Pole position: R. Arnoux (Renault)

BRITISH GP
Brands Hatch, July 18
199 miles/320km

	DRIVER	CAR
1	N. Lauda	McLaren-Ford
	124.71mph/200.69km/h	
2	D. Pironi	Ferrari
3	P. Tambay	Ferrari
4	E. de Angelis	Lotus-Ford
5	D. Daly	Williams-Ford
6	A. Prost	Renault

Fastest lap: B. Henton (Tyrrell-Ford)
128.85mph/207.35km/h
Pole position: K. Rosberg (Williams-Ford)

FRENCH GP
Paul Ricard, July 25
188 miles/302km

	DRIVER	CAR
1	R. Arnoux	Renault
	125.03mph/201.20km/h	
2	A. Prost	Renault
3	D. Pironi	Ferrari
4	P. Tambay	Ferrari
5	K. Rosberg	Williams-Ford
6	M. Alboreto	Tyrrell-Ford

Fastest lap: R. Patrese (Brabham-BMW)
129.88mph/209.01km/h
Pole position: R. Arnoux

GERMAN GP
Hockenheim, August 8
190 miles/306km

	DRIVER	CAR
1	P. Tambay	Ferrari
	130.43mph/209.90km/h	
2	R. Arnoux	Renault
3	K. Rosberg	Williams-Ford
4	M. Alboreto	Tyrrell-Ford
5	B. Giacomelli	Alfa Romeo
6	M. Surer	Arrows-Ford

Fastest lap: N. Piquet (Brabham-BMW)
133.34mph/214.58km/h
Pole position: D. Pironi (Ferrari) did not start

AUSTRIAN GP
Osterreichring, August 15
196 miles/316km

	DRIVER	CAR
1	E. de Angelis	Lotus-Ford
	138.01mph/222.10km/h	
2	K. Rosberg	Williams-Ford
3	J. Laffite	Talbot-Matra
4	P. Tambay	Ferrari
5	N. Lauda	McLaren-Ford
6	M. Baldi	Arrows-Ford

Fastest lap: N. Piquet (Brabham-BMW)
141.88mph/228.32km/h
Pole position: N. Piquet

SWISS GP
Dijon, August 29
189 miles/304km

	DRIVER	CAR
1	K. Rosberg	Williams-Ford
	122.29mph/196.80km/h	
2	A. Prost	Renault
3	N. Lauda	McLaren-Ford
4	N. Piquet	Brabham-BMW
5	R. Patrese	Brabham-BMW
6	E. de Angelis	Lotus-Ford

Fastest lap: A. Prost 125.98mph/202.74km/h
Pole position: A. Prost

ITALIAN GP
Monza, September 12
188 miles/302km

	DRIVER	CAR
1	R. Arnoux	Renault
	136.40mph/219.50km/h	
2	P. Tambay	Ferrari
3	M. Andretti	Ferrari
4	J. Watson	McLaren-Ford
5	M. Alboreto	Tyrrell-Ford
6	E. Cheever	Talbot-Matra

Fastest lap: R. Arnoux 138.59mph/223.03km/h
Pole position: M. Andretti

LAS VEGAS GP
Las Vegas, September 25
170 miles/273km

	DRIVER	CAR
1	M. Alboreto	Tyrrell-Ford
	100.10mph/161.09km/h	
2	J. Watson	McLaren-Ford
3	E. Cheever	Talbot-Matra
4	A. Prost	Renault
5	K. Rosberg	Williams-Ford
6	D. Daly	Williams-Ford

Fastest lap: M. Alboreto 102.52mph/164.99km/h
Pole position: A. Prost

WORLD CHAMPIONSHIP GRAND PRIX RESULTS 1950–1989

1983

BRAZILIAN GP
Rio de Janeiro, March 13
197 miles/317km

PLACE	DRIVER	CAR
1	N. Piquet 108.93mph/175.30km/h	Brabham-BMW
2	K. Rosberg*	Williams-Ford
3	N. Lauda	McLaren-Ford
4	J. Laffite	Williams-Ford
5	P. Tambay	Ferrari
6	M. Surer	Arrows-Ford

* Disqualified
Fastest lap: N. Piquet 112.74mph/181.43km/h
Pole position: K. Rosberg

UNITED STATES GP (WEST)
Long Beach, March 27
153 miles/246km

PLACE	DRIVER	CAR
1	J. Watson 80.65mph/129.79km/h	McLaren-Ford
2	N. Lauda	McLaren-Ford
3	R. Arnoux	Ferrari
4	J. Laffite	Williams-Ford
5	M. Surer	Arrows-Ford
6	J. Cecotto	Theodore-Ford

Fastest lap: N. Lauda 82.94mph/133.48km/h
Pole position: P. Tambay (Ferrari)

FRENCH GP
Paul Ricard, April 17
195 miles/315km

PLACE	DRIVER	CAR
1	A. Prost 124.20mph/199.87km/h	Renault
2	N. Piquet	Brabham-BMW
3	E. Cheever	Renault
4	P. Tambay	Ferrari
5	K. Rosberg	Williams-Ford
6	J. Laffite	Williams-Ford

Fastest lap: A. Prost 126.57mph/203.67km/h
Pole position: A. Prost

SAN MARINO GP
Imola, May 1
188 miles/302km

PLACE	DRIVER	CAR
1	P. Tambay 115.26mph/185.48km/h	Ferrari
2	A. Prost	Renault
3	R. Arnoux	Ferrari
4	K. Rosberg	Williams-Ford
5	J. Watson	McLaren-Ford
6	M. Surer	Arrows-Ford

Fastest lap: R. Patrese (Brabham-BMW) 119.39mph/192.13km/h
Pole position: R. Arnoux

MONACO GP
Monte Carlo, May 15
156 miles/252km

PLACE	DRIVER	CAR
1	K. Rosberg 80.52mph/129.59km/h	Williams-Ford
2	N. Piquet	Brabham-BMW
3	A. Prost	Renault
4	P. Tambay	Ferrari
5	D. Sullivan	Tyrrell-Ford
6	M. Baldi	Alfa Romeo

Fastest lap: N. Piquet 84.89mph/136.61km/h
Pole position: A. Prost

BELGIAN GP
Spa, May 22
172 miles/276km

PLACE	DRIVER	CAR
1	A. Prost 119.14mph/191.73km/h	Renault
2	P. Tambay	Ferrari
3	E. Cheever	Renault
4	N. Piquet	Brabham-BMW
5	K. Rosberg	Williams-Ford
6	J. Laffite	Williams-Ford

Fastest lap: A. de Cesaris (Alfa Romeo) 121.93mph/196.22km/h
Pole position: A. Prost

DETROIT GP
Detroit, June 5
154 miles/248km

PLACE	DRIVER	CAR
1	M. Alboreto 81.04mph/130.41km/h	Tyrrell-Ford
2	K. Rosberg	Williams-Ford
3	J. Watson	McLaren-Ford
4	N. Piquet	Brabham-BMW
5	J. Laffite	Williams-Ford
6	N. Mansell	Lotus-Ford

Fastest lap: J. Watson 83.60mph/134.53km/h
Pole position: R. Arnoux (Ferrari)

CANADIAN GP
Montreal, June 12
192 miles/309km

PLACE	DRIVER	CAR
1	R. Arnoux 106.05mph/170.66km/h	Ferrari
2	E. Cheever	Renault
3	P. Tambay	Ferrari
4	K. Rosberg	Williams-Ford
5	A. Prost	Renault
6	J. Watson	McLaren-Ford

Fastest lap: P. Tambay 108.59mph/174.75km/h
Pole position: R. Arnoux

BRITISH GP
Silverstone, July 16
196 miles/316km

PLACE	DRIVER	CAR
1	A. Prost 139.22mph/224.05km/h	Renault
2	N. Piquet	Brabham-BMW
3	P. Tambay	Ferrari
4	N. Mansell	Lotus-Renault
5	R. Arnoux	Ferrari
6	N. Lauda	McLaren-Ford

Fastest lap: A. Prost 142.24mph/228.90km/h
Pole position: R. Arnoux

GERMAN GP
Hockenheim, August 7
190 miles/306km

PLACE	DRIVER	CAR
1	R. Arnoux 130.82mph/210.52km/h	Ferrari
2	A. de Cesaris	Alfa Romeo
3	R. Patrese	Brabham-BMW
4	A. Prost	Renault
5	N. Lauda	McLaren-Ford
6	J. Watson	McLaren-Ford

Fastest lap: R. Arnoux 133.45mph/214.76km/h
Pole position: P. Tambay (Ferrari)

AUSTRIAN GP
Osterreichring, August 14
196 miles/316km

PLACE	DRIVER	CAR
1	A. Prost 138.88mph/223.49km/h	Renault
2	R. Arnoux	Ferrari
3	N. Piquet	Brabham-BMW
4	E. Cheever	Renault
5	N. Mansell	Lotus-Renault
6	N. Lauda	McLaren-Ford

Fastest lap: A. Prost 141.47mph/227.66km/h
Pole position: P. Tambay (Ferrari)

DUTCH GP
Zandvoort, August 28
190 miles/306km

1	R. Arnoux 115.64mph.186.10km/h	Ferrari
2	P. Tambay	Ferrari
3	J. Watson	McLaren-Ford
4	D. Warwick	Toleman-Hart
5	M. Baldi	Alfa Romeo
6	M. Alboreto	Tyrrell-Ford

Fastest lap: R. Arnoux 119.10mph/191.67km/h
Pole position: N. Piquet (Brabham-BMW)

ITALIAN GP
Monza, September 11
187 miles/301km

1	N. Piquet 135.19mph/217.55km/h	Brabham-BMW
2	R. Arnoux	Ferrari
3	E. Cheever	Renault
4	P. Tambay	Ferrari
5	E. de Angelis	Lotus-Renault
6	D. Warwick	Toleman-Hart

Fastest lap: N. Piquet 137.40mph/221.11km/h
Pole position: R. Patrese (Brabham-BMW)

EUROPEAN GP
Brands Hatch, September 25
199 miles/320km

1	N. Piquet 123.17mph/198.21km/h	Brabham-BMW
2	A. Prost	Renault
3	N. Mansell	Lotus-Renault
4	A. de Cesaris	Alfa Romeo
5	D. Warwick	Toleman-Hart
6	B. Giacomelli	Toleman-Hart

Fastest lap: N. Mansell 126.57mph/203.68km/h
Pole position: E. de Angelis (Lotus-Renault)

SOUTH AFRICAN GP
Kyalami, October 16
196 miles/316km

1	R. Patrese 126.11mph/202.94km/h	Brabham-BMW
2	A. de Cesaris	Alfa Romeo
3	N. Piquet	Brabham-BMW
4	D. Warwick	Toleman-Hart
5	K. Rosberg	Williams-Honda
6	E. Cheever	Renault

Fastest lap: N. Piquet 131.25mph/211.22km/h
Pole position: P. Tambay (Ferrari)

1984

BRAZILIAN GP
Rio de Janeiro, March 25
191 miles/307km

PLACE	DRIVER	CAR
1	A. Prost	McLaren-Porsche
	111.55mph/179.51km/h	
2	K. Rosberg	Williams-Honda
3	E. de Angelis	Lotus-Renault
4	E. Cheever	Alfa Romeo
5	M. Brundle*	Tyrrell-Ford
6	P. Tambay	Renault

* Disqualified
Fastest lap: A. Prost 116.63mph/187.69km/h
Pole position: E. de Angelis

SOUTH AFRICAN GP
Kyalami, April 7
191 miles/307km

PLACE	DRIVER	CAR
1	N. Lauda	McLaren-Porsche
	128.38mph/206.59km/h	
2	A. Prost	McLaren-Porsche
3	D. Warwick	Renault
4	R. Patrese	Alfa Romeo
5	A. de Cesaris	Ligier-Renault
6	A. Senna	Toleman-Hart

Fastest lap: P. Tambay (Renault)
133.28mph/214.49km/h
Pole position: N. Piquet (Brabham-BMW)

BELGIAN GP
Zolder, April 29
185 miles/298km

PLACE	DRIVER	CAR
1	M. Alboreto	Ferrari
	115.23mph/185.43km/h	
2	D. Warwick	Renault
3	R. Arnoux	Ferrari
4	K. Rosberg	Williams-Honda
5	E. de Angelis	Lotus-Renault
6	S. Bellof	Tyrrell-Ford

Fastest lap: R. Arnoux 120.24mph/193.50km/h
Pole position: M. Alboreto

SAN MARINO GP
Imola, May 6
188 miles/302km

PLACE	DRIVER	CAR
1	A. Prost	McLaren-Porsche
	116.36mph/187.25km/h	
2	R. Arnoux	Ferrari
3	E. de Angelis	Lotus-Renault
4	D. Warwick	Renault
5	S. Bellof	Tyrrell-Ford
6	T. Boutsen	Arrows-Ford

Fastest lap: N. Piquet (Brabham-BMW)
120.87mph/194.52km/h
Pole position: N. Piquet

FRENCH GP
Dijon, May 20
191 miles/307km

PLACE	DRIVER	CAR
1	N. Lauda	McLaren-Porsche
	125.54mph/202.02km/h	
2	P. Tambay	Renault
3	N. Mansell	Lotus-Renault
4	R. Arnoux	Ferrari
5	E. de Angelis	Lotus-Renault
6	K. Rosberg	Williams-Honda

Fastest lap: A. Prost (McLaren-Porsche)
133.25mph/214.43km/h
Pole position: P. Tambay

MONACO GP
Monte Carlo, June 3
64 miles/103km

PLACE	DRIVER	CAR
1	A. Prost	McLaren-Porsche
	62.62mph/100.78km/h	
2	A. Senna	Toleman-Hart
3	S. Bellof	Tyrrell-Ford
4	R. Arnoux	Ferrari
5	K. Rosberg	Williams-Honda
6	E. de Angelis	Lotus-Renault

Shortened race; half points
Fastest lap: A. Senna 64.80mph/104.28km/h
Pole position: A. Prost

CANADIAN GP
Montreal, June 17
192 miles/309km

PLACE	DRIVER	CAR
1	N. Piquet	Brabham-BMW
	108.18mph/174.09km/h	
2	N. Lauda	McLaren-Porsche
3	A. Prost	McLaren-Porsche
4	E. de Angelis	Lotus-Renault
5	R. Arnoux	Ferrari
6	N. Mansell	Lotus-Renault

Fastest lap: N. Piquet 111.14mph/178.86km/h
Pole position: N. Piquet

DETROIT GP
Detroit, June 24
157 miles/253km

PLACE	DRIVER	CAR
1	N. Piquet	Brabham-BMW
	81.68mph/131.45km/h	
2	M. Brundle*	Tyrrell-Ford
3	E. de Angelis	Lotus-Renault
4	T. Fabi	Brabham-BMW
5	A. Prost	McLaren-Porsche
6	J. Laffite	Williams-Honda

* Disqualified
Fastest lap: D. Warwick (Renault)
84.73mph/136.36km/h
Pole position: N. Piquet

DALLAS GP
Fir Park, July 8
162 miles/260km

PLACE	DRIVER	CAR
1	K. Rosberg	Williams-Honda
	80.30mph/129.22km/h	
2	R. Arnoux	Ferrari
3	E. de Angelis	Lotus-Renault
4	J. Laffite	Williams-Honda
5	P. Ghinzani	Osella-Alfa
6	N. Mansell	Lotus-Renault

Fastest lap: N. Lauda (McLaren-Porsche)
82.83mph/133.30km/h
Pole position: N. Mansell

BRITISH GP
Brands Hatch, July 22
186 miles/300km

PLACE	DRIVER	CAR
1	N. Lauda	McLaren-Porsche
	124.41mph/200.21km/h	
2	D. Warwick	Renault
3	A. Senna	Toleman-Hart
4	E. de Angelis	Lotus-Renault
5	M. Alboreto	Ferrari
6	R. Arnoux	Ferrari

Fastest lap: N. Lauda 128.52mph/206.83km/h
Pole position: N. Piquet (Brabham-BMW)

GERMAN GP
Hockenheim, August 5
186 miles/300km

PLACE	DRIVER	CAR
1	A. Prost	McLaren-Porsche
	131.61mph/211.80km/h	
2	N. Lauda	McLaren-Porsche
3	D. Warwick	Renault
4	N. Mansell	Lotus-Renault
5	P. Tambay	Renault
6	R. Arnoux	Ferrari

Fastest lap: A. Prost 133.92mph/215.52km/h
Pole position: A. Prost

AUSTRIAN GP
Osterreichring, August 19
188 miles/302km

PLACE	DRIVER	CAR
1	N. Lauda	McLaren-Porsche
	139.12mph/223.88km/h	
2	N. Piquet	Brabham-BMW
3	M. Alboreto	Ferrari
4	T. Fabi	Brabham-BMW
5	T. Boutsen	Arrows-BMW
6	M. Surer	Arrows-BMW

Fastest lap: N. Lauda 143.11mph/230.31km/h
Pole position: N. Piquet

DUTCH GP
Zandvoort, August 26
188 miles/302km

PLACE	DRIVER	CAR
1	A. Prost	McLaren-Porsche
	115.61mph/186.05km/h	
2	N. Lauda	McLaren-Porsche
3	N. Mansell	Lotus-Renault
4	E. de Angelis	Lotus-Renault
5	T. Fabi	Brabham-BMW
6	P. Tambay	Renault

Fastest lap: R. Arnoux (Ferrari)
119.70mph/192.63km/h
Pole position: A. Prost

WORLD CHAMPIONSHIP GRAND PRIX RESULTS 1950–1989

ITALIAN GP
Monza, September 9
184 miles/295km

PLACE	DRIVER	CAR
1	N. Lauda 137.02mph/220.51km/h	McLaren-Porsche
2	M. Alboreto	Ferrari
3	R. Patrese	Alfa Romeo
4	S. Johansson	Toleman-Hart
5	J. Gartner	Osella-Alfa
6	G. Berger	ATS-BMW

Fastest lap: N. Lauda 141.16mph/227.17km/h
Pole position: N. Piquet (Brabham-BMW)

EUROPEAN GP
Nürburgring, October 7
189 miles/304km

1	A. Prost 119.15mph/191.75km/h	McLaren-Porsche
2	M. Alboreto	Ferrari
3	N. Piquet	Brabham-BMW
4	N. Lauda	McLaren-Porsche
5	R. Arnoux	Ferrari
6	R. Patrese	Alfa Romeo

Fastest lap: N. Piquet 122.20mph/196.66km/h
Pole position: N. Piquet

PORTUGUESE GP
Estoril, October 21
186 miles/300km

1	A. Prost 112.19mph/180.54km/h	McLaren-Porsche
2	N. Lauda	McLaren-Porsche
3	A. Senna	Toleman-Hart
4	M. Alboreto	Ferrari
5	E. de Angelis	Lotus-Renault
6	N. Piquet	Brabham-BMW

Fastest lap: N. Lauda 117.25mph/188.68km/h
Pole position: N. Piquet

1985

BRAZILIAN GP
Rio de Janeiro, April 7
191 miles/307km

PLACE	DRIVER	CAR
1	A. Prost 112.80mph/181.53km/h	McLaren-TAG
2	M. Alboreto	Ferrari
3	E. de Angelis	Lotus-Renault
4	R. Arnoux	Ferrari
5	P. Tambay	Renault
6	J. Laffite	Ligier-Renault

Fastest lap: A. Prost 116.38mph/187.29km/h
Pole position: M. Alboreto

PORTUGUESE GP
Estoril, April 21
181 miles/291km

PLACE	DRIVER	CAR
1	A. Senna 90.20mph/145.16km/h	Lotus-Renault
2	M. Alboreto	Ferrari
3	P. Tambay	Renault
4	E. de Angelis	Lotus-Renault
5	N. Mansell	Williams-Honda
6	S. Bellof	Tyrrell-Ford

Fastest lap: A. Senna 93.46mph/150.40km/h
Pole position: A. Senna

SAN MARINO GP
Imola, May 5
188 miles/302km

1	E. de Angelis 119.18mph/191.80km/h	Lotus-Renault
2	T. Boutsen	Arrows-BMW
3	P. Tambay	Renault
4	N. Lauda	McLaren-TAG
5	N. Mansell	Williams-Honda
6	S. Johansson	Ferrari

Fastest lap: M. Alboreto (Ferrari) 123.95mph/199.47km/h
Pole position: A. Senna (Lotus-Renault)

MONACO GP
Monte Carlo, May 19
161 miles/258km

1	A. Prost 86.02mph/138.43km/h	McLaren-TAG
2	M. Alboreto	Ferrari
3	E. de Angelis	Lotus-Renault
4	A. de Cesaris	Ligier-Renault
5	D. Warwick	Renault
6	J. Laffite	Ligier-Renault

Fastest lap: M. Alboreto 89.66mph/144.28km/h
Pole position: A. Senna (Lotus-Renault)

CANADIAN GP
Montreal, June 17
192 miles/309km

1	M. Alboreto 108.55mph/174.69km/h	Ferrari
2	S. Johansson	Ferrari
3	A. Prost	McLaren-TAG
4	K. Rosberg	Williams-Honda
5	E. de Angelis	Lotus-Renault
6	N. Mansell	Williams-Honda

Fastest lap: A. Senna (Lotus-Renault) 112.82mph/181.55km/h
Pole position: E. de Angelis

DETROIT GP
Detroit, June 23
161 miles/258km

1	K. Rosberg 81.71mph/131.49km/h	Williams-Honda
2	S. Johansson	Ferrari
3	M. Alboreto	Ferrari
4	S. Bellof	Tyrrell-Ford
5	E. de Angelis	Lotus-Renault
6	N. Piquet	Brabham-BMW

Fastest lap: A. Senna (Lotus-Renault) 85.21mph/137.13km/h
Pole position: A. Senna

FRENCH GP
Paul Ricard, July 7
191 miles/307km

1	N. Piquet 125.10mph/201.32km/h	Brabham-BMW
2	K. Rosberg	Williams-Honda
3	A. Prost	McLaren-TAG
4	S. Johansson	Ferrari
5	E. de Angelis	Lotus-Renault
6	P. Tambay	Renault

Fastest lap: K. Rosberg 130.08mph/209.34km/h
Pole position: K. Rosberg

BRITISH GP
Silverstone, July 21
191 miles/307km

1	A. Prost 146.28mph/235.40km/h	McLaren-TAG
2	M. Alboreto	Ferrari
3	J. Laffite	Ligier-Renault
4	N. Piquet	Brabham-BMW
5	D. Warwick	Renault
6	M. Surer	Brabham-BMW

Fastest lap: A. Prost 151.04mph/243.07km/h
Pole position: K. Rosberg (Williams-Honda)

GERMAN GP
Nürburgring, August 4
187 miles/301km

1	M. Alboreto 118.78mph/191.15km/h	Ferrari
2	A. Prost	McLaren-TAG
3	J. Laffite	Ligier-Renault
4	T. Boutsen	Arrows-BMW
5	N. Lauda	McLaren-TAG
6	N. Mansell	Williams-Honda

Fastest lap: N. Lauda 122.70mph/197.46km/h
Pole position: T. Fabi (Toleman-Hart)

AUSTRIAN GP
Osterreichring, August 18
193 miles/311km

1	A. Prost 143.62mph/231.13km/h	McLaren-TAG
2	A. Senna	Lotus-Renault
3	M. Alboreto	Ferrari
4	S. Johansson	Ferrari
5	E. de Angelis	Lotus-Renault
6	M. Surer	Brabham-BMW

Fastest lap: A. Prost 148.95mph/239.70km/h
Pole position: A. Prost

DUTCH GP
Zandvoort, August 25
185 miles/298km

PLACE	DRIVER	CAR
1	N.Lauda 119.99mph/193.09km/h	McLaren-TAG
2	A. Prost	McLaren-TAG
3	A. Senna	Lotus-Renault
4	M. Alboreto	Ferrari
5	E. de Angelis	Lotus-Renault
6	N. Mansell	Williams-Honda

Fastest lap: A. Prost 124.27mph/199.99km/h
Pole position: N. Piquet (Brabham-BMW)

ITALIAN GP
Monza, September 8
184 miles/295km

PLACE	DRIVER	CAR
1	A. Prost 141.41mph/227.57km/h	McLaren-TAG
2	N. Piquet	Brabham-BMW
3	A. Senna	Lotus-Renault
4	M. Surer	Brabham-BMW
5	S. Johansson	Ferrari
6	E. de Angelis	Lotus-Renault

Fastest lap: N. Mansell (Williams-Honda)
146.97mph/236.51km/h
Pole position: A. Senna

BELGIAN GP
Spa, September 15
186 miles/300km

PLACE	DRIVER	CAR
1	A. Senna 117.95mph/189.81km/h	Lotus-Renault
2	N. Mansell	Williams-Honda
3	A. Prost	McLaren-TAG
4	K. Rosberg	Williams-Honda
5	N. Piquet	Brabham-BMW
6	D. Warwick	Renault

Fastest lap: A. Prost 127.54mph/205.24km/h
Pole position: A. Prost

EUROPEAN GP
Brands Hatch, October 6
196 miles/316km

PLACE	DRIVER	CAR
1	N. Mansell 126.54mph/203.63km/h	Williams-Honda
2	A. Senna	Lotus-Renault
3	K. Rosberg	Williams-Honda
4	A. Prost	McLaren-TAG
5	E. de Angelis	Lotus-Renault
6	T. Boutsen	Arrows-BMW

Fastest lap: J. Laffite (Ligier-Renault)
131.57mph/211.73km/h
Pole position: A. Senna

SOUTH AFRICAN GP
Kyalami, October 19
191 miles/307km

PLACE	DRIVER	CAR
1	N. Mansell 129.85mph/208.96km/h	Williams-Honda
2	K. Rosberg	Williams-Honda
3	A. Prost	McLaren-TAG
4	S. Johansson	Ferrari
5	G. Berger	Arrows-BMW
6	T. Boutsen	Arrows-BMW

Fastest lap: K. Rosberg 134.72mph/216.80km/h
Pole position: N. Mansell

AUSTRALIAN GP
Adelaide, November 3
193 miles/311km

PLACE	DRIVER	CAR
1	K. Rosberg 95.71mph/154.03km/h	Williams-Honda
2	J. Laffite	Ligier-Renault
3	P. Streiff	Ligier-Renault
4	I. Capelli	Tyrrell-Renault
5	S. Johansson	Ferrari
6	G. Berger	Arrows-BMW

Fastest lap: K. Rosberg 100.90mph/162.38km/h
Pole position: A. Senna (Lotus-Renault)

1986

BRAZILIAN GP
Rio de Janeiro, March 23
191 miles/307km

PLACE	DRIVER	CAR
1	N. Piquet 114.94mph/184.97km/h	Williams-Honda
2	A. Senna	Lotus-Renault
3	J. Laffite	Ligier-Renault
4	R. Arnoux	Ligier-Renault
5	M. Brundle	Tyrrell-Renault
6	G. Berger	Benetton-BMW

Fastest lap: N. Piquet 120.39mph/193.74km/h
Pole position: A. Senna

SPANISH GP
Jerez, April 13
189 miles/304km

PLACE	DRIVER	CAR
1	A. Senna 104.07mph/167.48km/h	Lotus-Renault
2	N. Mansell	Williams-Honda
3	A. Prost	McLaren-TAG
4	K. Rosberg	McLaren-TAG
5	T. Fabi	Benetton-BMW
6	G. Berger	Benetton-BMW

Fastest lap: N. Mansell 108.23mph/174.17km/h
Pole position: A. Senna

SAN MARINO GP
Imola, April 27
188 miles/302km

PLACE	DRIVER	CAR
1	A. Prost 121.92mph/196.20km/h	McLaren-TAG
2	N. Piquet	Williams-Honda
3	G. Berger	Benetton-BMW
4	S. Johansson	Ferrari
5	K. Rosberg	McLaren-TAG
6	R. Patrese	Brabham-BMW

Fastest lap: N. Piquet 123.95mph/199.47km/h
Pole position: A. Senna (Lotus-Renault)

MONACO GP
Monte Carlo, May 11
162 miles/260km

PLACE	DRIVER	CAR
1	A. Prost 83.66mph/134.56km/h	McLaren-TAG
2	K. Rosberg	McLaren-TAG
3	A. Senna	Lotus-Renault
4	N. Mansell	Williams-Honda
5	R. Arnoux	Ligier-Renault
6	J. Laffite	Ligier-Renault

Fastest lap: A. Prost 85.96mph/138.34km/h
Pole position: A. Prost

BELGIAN GP
Spa, May 25
186 miles/300km

PLACE	DRIVER	CAR
1	N. Mansell 126.48mph/206.75km/h	Williams-Honda
2	A. Senna	Lotus-Renault
3	S. Johansson	Ferrari
4	M. Alboreto	Ferrari
5	J. Laffite	Ligier-Renault
6	A. Prost	McLaren-TAG

Fastest lap: A. Prost 130.15mph/209.44km/h
Pole position: N. Piquet (Williams-Honda)

CANADIAN GP
Montreal, June 15
190 miles/306km

PLACE	DRIVER	CAR
1	N. Mansell 111.39mph/179.26km/h	Williams-Honda
2	A. Prost	McLaren-TAG
3	N. Piquet	Williams-Honda
4	K. Rosberg	McLaren-TAG
5	A. Senna	Lotus-Renault
6	R. Arnoux	Ligier-Renault

Fastest lap: N. Piquet 116.13mph/186.88km/h
Pole position: N. Mansell

DETROIT GP
Detroit, June 22
158 miles/255km

PLACE	DRIVER	CAR
1	A. Senna 84.97mph/136.75km/h	Lotus-Renault
2	J. Laffite	Ligier-Renault
3	A. Prost	McLaren-TAG
4	M. Alboreto	Ferrari
5	N. Mansell	Williams-Honda
6	R. Patrese	Brabham-BMW

Fastest lap: N. Piquet (Williams-Honda)
88.90mph/143.07km/h
Pole position: A. Senna

FRENCH GP
Paul Ricard, July 6
191 miles/307km

PLACE	DRIVER	CAR
1	N. Mansell 117.54mph/189.15km/h	Williams-Honda
2	A. Prost	McLaren-TAG
3	N. Piquet	Williams-Honda
4	K. Rosberg	McLaren-TAG
5	R. Arnoux	Ligier-Renault
6	J. Laffite	Ligier-Renault

Fastest lap: N. Mansell 122.57mph/197.25km/h
Pole position: A. Senna (Lotus-Renault)

WORLD CHAMPIONSHIP GRAND PRIX RESULTS 1950–1989

1987

BRITISH GP
Brands Hatch, July 13
196 miles/316km

PLACE	DRIVER	CAR
1	N. Mansell 129.78mph/208.85km/h	Williams-Honda
2	N. Piquet	Williams-Honda
3	A. Prost	McLaren-TAG
4	R. Arnoux	Ligier-Renault
5	M. Brundle	Tyrrell-Renault
6	P. Streiff	Tyrrell-Renault

Fastest lap: N. Mansell 135.22mph/217.60km/h
Pole position: N. Piquet

GERMAN GP
Hockenheim, July 27
187 miles/301km

1	N. Piquet 136.54mph/219.72km/h	Williams-Honda
2	A. Senna	Lotus-Renault
3	N. Mansell	Williams-Honda
4	R. Arnoux	Ligier-Renault
5	K. Rosberg	McLaren-TAG
6	A. Prost	McLaren-TAG

Fastest lap: G. Berger (Benetton-BMW)
143.46mph/230.86km/h
Pole position: K. Rosberg

HUNGARIAN GP
Budapest, August 10
190 miles/306km

1	N. Piquet 94.33mph//151.81km/h	Williams-Honda
2	A. Senna	Lotus-Renault
3	N. Mansell	Williams-Honda
4	S. Johansson	Ferrari
5	J. Dumfries	Lotus-Renault
6	M. Brundle	Tyrrell-Renault

Fastest lap: N. Piquet 98.67mph/158.79km/h
Pole position: A. Senna

AUSTRIAN GP
Osterreichring, August 17
192 miles/309km

1	A. Prost 141.56mph/227.80km/h	McLaren-TAG
2	M. Alboreto	Ferrari
3	S. Johansson	Ferrari
4	A. Jones	Lola-Ford
5	P. Tambay	Lola-Ford
6	C. Danner	Arrows-BMW

Fastest lap: G. Berger (Benetton-BMW)
148.46mph/238.90km/h
Pole position: T. Fabi (Benetton-BMW)

ITALIAN GP
Monza, September 7
184 miles/295km

PLACE	DRIVER	CAR
1	N. Piquet 141.90mph/228.35km/h	Williams-Honda
2	N. Mansell	Williams-Honda
3	S. Johansson	Ferrari
4	K. Rosberg	McLaren-TAG
5	G. Berger	Benetton-BMW
6	A. Jones	Lola-Ford

Fastest lap: T. Fabi (Benetton-BMW)
147.27mph/236.99km/h
Pole position: T. Fabi

PORTUGUESE GP
Estoril, September 21
189 miles/304km

1	N. Mansell 116.60mph/187.64km/h	Williams-Honda
2	A. Prost	McLaren-TAG
3	N. Piquet	Williams-Honda
4	A. Senna	Lotus-Renault
5	M. Alboreto	Ferrari
6	S. Johansson	Ferrari

Fastest lap: N. Mansell 120.22mph/193.43km/h
Pole position: A. Senna

MEXICAN GP
Mexico City, October 12
187 miles/301km

1	G. Berger 120.14mph/193.34km/h	Benetton-BMW
2	A. Prost	McLaren-TAG
3	A. Senna	Lotus-Renault
4	N. Piquet	Williams-Honda
5	N. Mansell	Williams-Honda
6	P. Alliot	Ligier-Renault

Fastest lap: N. Piquet 124.60mph/200.50km/h
Pole position: A. Senna

AUSTRALIAN GP
Adelaide, October 26
193 miles/311km

1	A. Prost 101.63mph/163.55km/h	McLaren-TAG
2	N. Piquet	Williams-Honda
3	S. Johansson	Ferrari
4	M. Brundle	Tyrrell-Renault
5	P. Streiff	Tyrrell-Renault
6	J. Dumfries	Lotus-Renault

Fastest lap: N. Piquet 104.60mph/168.34km/h
Pole position: N. Mansell

BRAZILIAN GP
Rio de Janeiro, April 12
191 miles/307km

PLACE	DRIVER	CAR
1	A. Prost 114.70mph/184.59km/h	McLaren-TAG
2	N. Piquet	Williams-Honda
3	S. Johansson	McLaren-TAG
4	G. Berger	Ferrari
5	T. Boutsen	Benetton-Ford
6	N. Mansell	Williams-Honda

Fastest lap: N. Piquet 119.90mph/192.96km/h
Pole position: N. Mansell

SAN MARINO GP
Imola, May 3
185 miles/298km

1	N. Mansell 121.29mph/195.20km/h	Williams-Honda
2	A. Senna	Lotus-Honda
3	M. Alboreto	Ferrari
4	S. Johansson	McLaren-TAG
5	M. Brundle	Zakspeed
6	S. Nakajima	Lotus-Honda

Fastest lap: T. Fabi (Benetton-Ford)
126.33mph/203.30km/h
Pole position: A. Senna

BELGIAN GP
Spa, May 17
185 miles/298km

1	A. Prost 127.80mph/205.68km/h	McLaren-TAG
2	S. Johansson	McLaren-TAG
3	A. de Cesaris	Brabham-BMW
4	E. Cheever	Arrows-Megatron
5	S. Nakajima	Lotus-Honda
6	R. Arnoux	Ligier-Megatron

Fastest lap: A. Prost 132.51mph/213.60km/h
Pole position: N. Mansell (Williams-Honda)

MONACO GP
Monte Carlo, May 31
161 miles/258km

1	A. Senna 82.08mph/132.10km/h	Lotus-Honda
2	N. Piquet	Williams-Honda
3	M. Alboreto	Ferrari
4	G. Berger	Ferrari
5	J. Palmer	Tyrrell-Cosworth
6	I. Capelli	March-Cosworth

Fastest lap: A. Senna 84.90mph/136.64km/h
Pole position: N. Mansell (Williams-Honda)

UNITED STATES GP
Detroit, June 21
158 miles/255km

1	A. Senna 85.70mph/137.92km/h	Lotus-Honda
2	N. Piquet	Williams-Honda
3	A. Prost	McLaren-TAG
4	G. Berger	Ferrari
5	N. Mansell	Williams-Honda
6	E. Cheever	Arrows-Megatron

Fastest lap: A. Senna 89.58mph/144.17km/h
Pole position: N. Mansell

FRENCH GP
Paul Ricard, July 5
190 miles/306km

PLACE	DRIVER	CAR
1	N. Mansell 117.17mph/188.56km/h	Williams-Honda
2	N. Piquet	Williams-Honda
3	A. Prost	McLaren-TAG
4	A. Senna	Lotus-Honda
5	T. Fabi	Benetton-Ford
6	P. Streiff	Tyrrell-Cosworth

Fastest lap: N. Piquet 122.64mph/197.37km/h
Pole position: N. Mansell

BRITISH GP
Silverstone, July 12
193 miles/311km

PLACE	DRIVER	CAR
1	N. Mansell 146.21mph/253.30km/h	Williams-Honda
2	N. Piquet	Williams-Honda
3	A. Senna	Lotus-Honda
4	S. Nakajima	Lotus-Honda
5	D. Warwick	Arrows-Megatron
6	T. Fabi	Benetton-Ford

Fastest lap: N. Mansell 153.06mph/246.33km/h
Pole position: N. Piquet

GERMAN GP
Hockenheim, July 26
185 miles/298km

PLACE	DRIVER	CAR
1	N. Piquet 136.95mph/220.39km/h	Williams-Honda
2	S. Johansson	McLaren-TAG
3	A. Senna	Lotus-Honda
4	P. Streiff	Tyrrell-Cosworth
5	J. Palmer	Tyrrell-Cosworth
6	P. Alliot	Lola-Cosworth

Fastest lap: N. Mansell (Williams-Honda) 143.83mph/231.46km/h
Pole position: N. Mansell

HUNGARIAN GP
Budapest, August 9
190 miles/306km

PLACE	DRIVER	CAR
1	N. Piquet 95.22mph/153.24km/h	Williams-Honda
2	A. Senna	Lotus-Honda
3	A. Prost	McLaren-TAG
4	T. Boutsen	Benetton-Ford
5	R. Patrese	Brabham-BMW
6	D. Warwick	Arrows-Megatron

Fastest lap: N. Piquet 99.60mph/160.30km/h
Pole position: N. Mansell (Williams-Honda)

AUSTRIAN GP
Osterreichring, August 16
192 miles/309km

PLACE	DRIVER	CAR
1	N. Mansell 146.28mph/235.42km/h	Williams-Honda
2	N. Piquet	Williams-Honda
3	T. Fabi	Benetton-Ford
4	T. Boutsen	Benetton-Ford
5	A. Senna	Lotus-Honda
6	A. Prost	McLaren-TAG

Fastest lap: N. Mansell 150.50mph/242.21km/h
Pole position: N. Piquet

ITALIAN GP
Monza, September 6
180 miles/289km

PLACE	DRIVER	CAR
1	N. Piquet 144.55mph/232.64km/h	Williams-Honda
2	A. Senna	Lotus-Honda
3	N. Mansell	Williams-Honda
4	G. Berger	Ferrari
5	T. Boutsen	Benetton-Ford
6	S. Johansson	McLaren-TAG

Fastest lap: A. Senna 149.48mph/240.56km/h
Pole position: N. Piquet

PORTUGUESE GP
Estoril, September 20
189 miles/304km

PLACE	DRIVER	CAR
1	A. Prost 116.96mph/188.22km/h	McLaren-TAG
2	G. Berger	Ferrari
3	N. Piquet	Williams-Honda
4	T. Fabi	Benetton-Ford
5	S. Johansson	McLaren-TAG
6	E. Cheever	Arrows-Megatron

Fastest lap: G. Berger 122.74mph/197.53km/h
Pole position: G. Berger

SPANISH GP
Jerez, September 27
189 miles/304km

PLACE	DRIVER	CAR
1	N. Mansell 103.67mph/166.85km/h	Williams-Honda
2	A. Prost	McLaren-TAG
3	S. Johansson	McLaren-TAG
4	N. Piquet	Williams-Honda
5	A. Senna	Lotus-Honda
6	P. Alliot	Lola-Cosworth

Fastest lap: G. Berger (Ferrari) 108.47mph/174.57km/h
Pole position: N. Piquet

MEXICAN GP
Mexico City, October 18
173 miles/278km

PLACE	DRIVER	CAR
1	N. Mansell 120.18mph/193.41km/h	Williams-Honda
2	N. Piquet	Williams-Honda
3	R. Patrese	Brabham-BMW
4	E. Cheever	Arrows-Megatron
5	T. Fabi	Benetton-Ford
6	P. Alliot	Lola-Cosworth

Fastest lap: N. Piquet 124.97mph/201.13km/h
Pole position: N. Mansell

JAPANESE GP
Suzuka, November 1
186 miles/300km

PLACE	DRIVER	CAR
1	G. Berger 119.83mph/192.85km/h	Ferrari
2	A. Senna	Lotus-Honda
3	S. Johansson	McLaren-TAG
4	M. Alboreto	Ferrari
5	T. Boutsen	Benetton-Ford
6	S. Nakajima	Lotus-Honda

Fastest lap: A. Prost (McLaren-TAG) 126.21mph/203.12km/h
Pole position: G. Berger

AUSTRALIAN GP
Adelaide, November 15
192 miles/309km

PLACE	DRIVER	CAR
1	G. Berger 102.30mph/164.63km/h	Ferrari
2	M. Alboreto	Ferrari
3	T. Boutsen	Benetton-Ford
4	J. Palmer	Tyrrell-Cosworth
5	Y. Dalmas	Lola-Cosworth
6	R. Moreno	AGS-Cosworth

(Senna disqualified from 2nd)
Fastest lap: G. Berger 105.12mph/169.18km/h
Pole position: G. Berger

1988

BRAZILIAN GP
Rio de Janeiro, April 3
187 miles/301km

PLACE	DRIVER	CAR
1	A. Prost 117.09mph/188.44km/h	McLaren-Honda
2	G. Berger	Ferrari
3	N. Piquet	Lotus-Honda
4	D. Warwick	Arrows-Megatron
5	M. Alboreto	Ferrari
6	S. Nakajima	Lotus-Honda

Fastest lap: G. Berger 121.09mph/194.83km/h
Pole position: A. Senna (McLaren-Honda)

SAN MARINO GP
Imola, May 1
189 miles/304km

PLACE	DRIVER	CAR
1	A. Senna 122.30mph/196.78km/h	McLaren-Honda
2	A. Prost	McLaren-Honda
3	N. Piquet	Lotus-Honda
4	T. Boutsen	Benetton-Ford
5	G. Berger	Ferrari
6	A. Nannini	Benetton-Ford

Fastest lap: A. Prost 122.40mph/196.94km/h
Pole position: A. Senna

MONACO GP
Monte Carlo, May 15
161 miles/258km

PLACE	DRIVER	CAR
1	A. Prost 82.52mph/132.80km/h	McLaren-Honda
2	G. Berger	Ferrari
3	M. Alboreto	Ferrari
4	D. Warwick	Arrows-Megatron
5	J. Palmer	Tyrrell-Cosworth
6	R. Patrese	Williams-Judd

Fastest lap: A. Senna (McLaren-Honda) 85.26mph/137.18km/h
Pole position: A. Senna

WORLD CHAMPIONSHIP GRAND PRIX RESULTS 1950–1989

MEXICAN GP
Mexico City, May 29
180 miles/289km

PLACE	DRIVER	CAR
1	A. Prost 123.08mph/198.04km/h	McLaren-Honda
2	A. Senna	McLaren-Honda
3	G. Berger	Ferrari
4	M. Alboreto	Ferrari
5	D. Warwick	Arrows-Megatron
6	E. Cheever	Arrows-Megatron

Fastest lap: A. Prost 125.80mph/202.41km/h
Pole position: A. Senna

CANADIAN GP
Montreal, June 12
189 miles/304km

1	A. Senna 113.19mph/182.12km/h	McLaren-Honda
2	A. Prost	McLaren-Honda
3	T. Boutsen	Benetton-Ford
4	N. Piquet	Lotus-Honda
5	I. Capelli	March-Judd
6	J. Palmer	Tyrrell-Cosworth

Fastest lap: A. Senna 115.60mph/186.00km/h
Pole position: A. Senna

UNITED STATES GP
Detroit, June 19
157 miles/253km

1	A. Senna 82.22mph/132.29km/h	McLaren-Honda
2	A. Prost	McLaren-Honda
3	T. Boutsen	Benetton-Ford
4	A. de Cesaris	Rial-Cosworth
5	J. Palmer	Tyrrell-Cosworth
6	P. Martini	Minardi-Cosworth

Fastest lap: A. Prost 85.84mph/138.12km/h
Pole position: A. Senna

FRENCH GP
Paul Ricard, July 3
186 miles/300km

1	A. Prost 116.50mph/187.44km/h	McLaren-Honda
2	A. Senna	McLaren-Honda
3	M. Alboreto	Ferrari
4	G. Berger	Ferrari
5	N. Piquet	Lotus-Honda
6	A. Nannini	Benetton-Ford

Fastest lap: A. Prost 118.90mph/191.31km/h
Pole position: A. Prost

BRITISH GP
Silverstone, July 10
193 miles/311km

1	A. Senna 124.14mph/199.74km/h	McLaren-Honda
2	N. Mansell	Williams-Judd
3	A. Nannini	Benetton-Ford
4	M. Gugelmin	March-Judd
5	N. Piquet	Lotus-Honda
6	D.Warwick	Arrows-Megatron

Fastest lap: N. Mansell 128.30mph/206.43km/h
Pole position: G. Berger (Ferrari)

GERMAN GP
Hockenheim, July 24
186 miles/300km

PLACE	DRIVER	CAR
1	A. Senna 120.71mph/194.22km/h	McLaren-Honda
2	A. Prost	McLaren-Honda
3	G. Berger	Ferrari
4	M. Alboreto	Ferrari
5	I. Capelli	March-Judd
6	T. Boutsen	Benetton-Ford

Fastest lap: A. Nannini (Benetton-Ford) 124.30mph/200.00km/h
Pole position: A. Senna

HUNGARIAN GP
Hungaroring, Budapest, August 7
190 miles/306km

1	A. Senna 96.56mph/155.30km/h	McLaren-Honda
2	A. Prost	McLaren-Honda
3	T. Boutsen	Benetton-Ford
4	G. Berger	Ferrari
5	M. Gugelmin	March-Judd
6	R. Patrese	Williams-Judd

Fastest lap: A. Prost 99.06mph/159.39km/h
Pole position: A. Senna

BELGIAN GP
Spa, August, 28
185 miles/298km

1	A. Senna 126.42mph/203.41km/h	McLaren-Honda
2	A. Prost	McLaren-Honda
3	T. Boutsen*	Benetton-Ford
4	A. Nannini*	Benetton-Ford
5	I. Capelli	March-Judd
6	N. Piquet	Lotus-Honda

* Disqualified
Fastest lap: G. Berger (Ferrari) 128.54mph/206.82km/h
Pole position: A. Senna

ITALIAN GP
Monza, September 11
184 miles/295km

1	G. Berger 141.96mph/228.42km/h	Ferrari
2	M. Alboreto	Ferrari
3	E. Cheever	Arrows-Megatron
4	D. Warwick	Arrows-Megatron
5	I. Capelli	March-Judd
6	T. Boutsen	Benetton-Ford

Fastest lap: M. Alboreto 145.63mph/234.31km/h
Pole position: A. Senna (McLaren-Honda)

PORTUGUESE GP
Estoril, September 25
189 miles/304km

PLACE	DRIVER	CAR
1	A. Prost 116.15mph/186.88km/h	McLaren-Honda
2	I. Capelli	March-Judd
3	T. Boutsen	Benetton-Ford
4	D. Warwick	Arrows-Megatron
5	M. Alboreto	Ferrari
6	A. Senna	McLaren-Honda

Fastest lap: G. Berger (Ferrari) 118.65mph/190.91km/h
Pole position: A. Prost

SPANISH GP
Jerez, October 2
189 miles/304km

1	A. Prost 104.07mph/167.45km/h	McLaren-Honda
2	N. Mansell	Williams-Judd
3	A. Nannini	Benetton-Ford
4	A. Senna	McLaren-Honda
5	R. Patrese	Williams-Judd
6	G. Berger	Ferrari

Fastest lap: A. Prost 107.35mph/172.72km/h
Pole position: A. Senna

JAPANESE GP
Suzuka, October 30
186 miles/300km

1	A. Senna 119.16mph/191.72km/h	McLaren-Honda
2	A. Prost	McLaren-Honda
3	T. Boutsen	Benetton-Ford
4	G. Berger	Ferrari
5	A. Nannini	Benetton-Ford
6	R. Patrese	Williams-Judd

Fastest lap: A. Senna 123.19mph/198.21km/h
Pole position: A. Senna

AUSTRALIAN GP
Adelaide, November 13
192 miles/309km

1	A. Prost 102.07mph/164.23km/h	McLaren-Honda
2	A. Senna	McLaren-Honda
3	N. Piquet	Lotus-Honda
4	R. Patrese	Williams-Judd
5	T. Boutsen	Benetton-Ford
6	I. Capelli	March-Judd

Fastest lap: A. Prost 104.12mph/167.52km/h
Pole position: A. Senna

1989

BRAZILIAN GP
Rio de Janeiro, March 3
191 miles/307km

PLACE	DRIVER	CAR
1	N. Mansell 115.52mph/186km/h	Ferrari
2	A. Prost	McLaren-Honda
3	M. Gugelmin	March-Judd
4	J. Herbert	Benetton-Ford
5	D. Warwick	Arrows-Cosworth
6	A. Nannini	Benneton-Ford

Fastest lap: R. Patrese (Williams) 121.58mph/195.78km/h
Pole position: A. Senna

SAN MARINO GP
Imola, April 23
188 miles/302km

PLACE	DRIVER	CAR
1	A. Senna 125.48mph/201.93km/h	McLaren-Honda
2	A. Prost	McLaren-Honda
3	A. Nannini	Benetton-Ford
4	T. Boutsen	Williams-Renault
5	D. Warwick	Arrows-Cosworth
6	J. Palmer	Tyrrell-Cosworth

Fastest lap: A. Prost 126.79mph/209km/h
Pole position: A. Senna

MONACO GP
Monte Carlo, May 7
161 miles/258km

PLACE	DRIVER	CAR
1	A. Senna 84.13mph/135.40km/h	McLaren-Honda
2	A. Prost	McLaren-Honda
3	S. Modena	Brabham-Judd
4	A. Caffi	Dallara-Cosworth
5	M. Alboreto	Tyrrell-Renault
6	M. Brundle	Brabham-Judd

Fastest lap: A. Prost 87.06mph/140.12km/h
Pole position: A. Senna

MEXICAN GP
Mexico City, May 28
189 miles/304km

PLACE	DRIVER	CAR
1	A. Senna 119.19mph/191.94km/h	McLaren-Honda
2	R. Patrese	Williams-Renault
3	M. Alboreto	Tyrrell-Cosworth
4	A. Nannini	Benetton-Ford
5	A. Prost	McLaren-Honda
6	G. Tarquini	AGS-Cosworth

Fastest lap: N. Mansell (Ferrari) 125.80mph/202.46km/h
Pole position: A. Senna

UNITED STATES GP
Phoenix, June 4
177 miles/284km

PLACE	DRIVER	CAR
1	A. Prost 87.37mph/140.57km/h	McLaren-Honda
2	R. Patrese	Williams-Renault
3	E. Cheever	Arrows-Cosworth
4	C. Danner	Rial-Cosworth
5	J. Herbert	Benetton-Ford
6	T. Boutsen	Williams-Renault

Fastest lap: A. Senna (McLaren) 90.41mph/145.47km/h
Pole position: A. Senna

CANADIAN GP
Montreal, June 14
188 miles/302km

PLACE	DRIVER	CAR
1	T. Boutsen 92.96mph/149.70km/h	Williams-Renault
2	R. Patrese	Williams-Renault
3	A. de Cesaris	Dallara-Cosworth
4	N. Piquet	Lotus-Judd
5	R. Arnoux	Ligier-Cosworth
6	A. Caffi	Dallara-Cosworth

Fastest lap: J. Palmer (Tyrrell) 106.76mph/171.92km/h
Pole position: A. Prost

FRENCH GP
Paul Ricard, July 9
189 miles/304km

PLACE	DRIVER	CAR
1	A. Prost 115.4mph/185.8km/h	McLaren-Honda
2	N. Mansell	Ferrari
3	R. Patrese	Williams-Renault
4	J. Alesi	Tyrrell-Cosworth
5	S. Johansson	Onyx-Cosworth
6	O. Grouillard	Ligier-Cosworth

Fastest lap: M. Gugelmin (Leyton House) 118.24mph/190.41km/h
Pole position: A. Prost

BRITISH GP
Silverstone, July 16
190 miles/306km

PLACE	DRIVER	CAR
1	A. Prost 143.69mph/231.20km/h	McLaren-Honda
2	N. Mansell	Ferrari
3	A. Nannini	Benetton-Ford
4	N. Piquet	Lotus-Judd
5	P. Martini	Minardi-Cosworth
6	L. Sala	Minardi-Cosworth

Fastest lap: N. Mansell 148.46mph/238.88km/h
Pole position: A. Senna

GERMAN GP
Hockenheim, July 30
190 miles/305km

PLACE	DRIVER	CAR
1	A. Senna 139.45mph/224.56km/h	McLaren-Honda
2	A. Prost	McLaren-Honda
3	N. Mansell	Ferrari
4	R. Patrese	Williams-Renault
5	N. Piquet	Lotus-Judd
6	D. Warwick	Arrows-Cosworth

Fastest lap: A. Senna 143.5mph/231.1km/h
Pole position: A. Senna

HUNGARIAN GP
Hungaroring, Budapest, August 13   190 miles/306km

PLACE	DRIVER	CAR
1	N. Mansell 103.82mph/172.86km/h	Ferrari
2	A. Senna	McLaren-Honda
3	T. Boutsen	Williams-Renault
4	A. Prost	McLaren-Honda
5	E. Cheever	Arrows-Cosworth
6	N. Piquet	Lotus-Judd

Fastest lap: N. Mansell 107.34mph/172.86km/h
Pole position: R. Patrese (Williams)

BELGIAN GP
Spa, August 27
185 miles/298km

PLACE	DRIVER	CAR
1	A. Senna 112.75mph/181.57km/h	McLaren-Honda
2	A. Prost	McLaren-Honda
3	N. Mansell	Ferrari
4	T. Boutsen	Williams-Renault
5	A. Nannini	Benetton-Ford
6	D. Warwick	Arrows-Cosworth

Fastest lap: A. Prost 117.92mph/189.89km/h
Pole position: A. Senna

ITALIAN GP
Monza, September 10
184 miles/295km

PLACE	DRIVER	CAR
1	A. Prost 144.14mph/232.11km/h	McLaren-Honda
2	G. Berger	Ferrari
3	T. Boutsen	Williams-Renault
4	R. Patrese	Williams-Renault
5	J. Alesi	Tyrrell-Cosworth
6	M. Brundle	Brabham-Judd

Fastest lap: A. Prost (McLaren) 147.16mph/236.98km/h
Pole position: A. Senna (McLaren)

PORTUGUESE GP
Estoril, September 24
191 miles/308km

PLACE	DRIVER	CAR
1	G. Berger 118.87mph/191.41km/h	Ferrari
2	A. Prost	McLaren-Honda
3	S. Johansson	Onyx-Cosworth
4	A. Nannini	Benetton-Ford
5	P. Martini	Minardi-Cosworth
6	J. Palmer	Tyrrell-Cosworth

Fastest lap: G. Berger 123.12mph/198.26km/h
Pole position: A. Senna (McLaren)

SPANISH GP
Jerez, October 1
189 miles/304km

PLACE	DRIVER	CAR
1	A. Senna 106.49mph/171.37km/h	McLaren-Honda
2	G. Berger	Ferrari
3	A. Prost	McLaren-Honda
4	J. Alesi	Tyrrell-Cosworth
5	R. Patrese	Williams-Renault
6	P. Alliot	Lola-Lamborghini

Fastest lap: A. Senna 109.99mph/177.02km/h
Pole position: A. Senna

WORLD CHAMPIONSHIP GRAND PRIX RESULTS 1950–1989

JAPANESE GP
Suzuka, October 22
186 miles/300km

PLACE	DRIVER	CAR
1	A. Nannini 121.75mph/195.93km/h	Benetton-Ford
2	R. Patrese	Williams-Renault
3	T. Boutsen	Williams-Renault
4	N. Piquet	Lotus-Judd
5	M. Brundle	Brabham-Judd
6	D. Warwick	Arrows-Cosworth

Fastest lap: A. Prost (McLaren)
126.64mph/203.77km/h
Pole position: A. Senna

AUSTRALIAN GP
Adelaide, November 5
192 miles/309km

PLACE	DRIVER	CAR
1	T. Boutsen 82.02mph/131.98km/h	Williams-Renault
2	A. Nannini	Benetton-Ford
3	R. Patrese	Williams-Renault
4	S. Nakajima	Lotus-Judd
5	E. Pirro	Benetton-Ford
6	P. Martini	Leyton House-Cosworth

Fastest lap: S. Nakajima 85.87mph/138.18km/h
Pole position: A. Senna (McLaren)

FORMULA 1 CONSTRUCTORS' CHAMPIONSHIP WINNERS

YEAR	CONSTRUCTORS
1958	Vanwall
1959	Cooper-Climax
1960	Cooper-Climax
1961	Ferrari
1962	BRM
1963	Lotus-Climax
1964	Ferrari
1965	Lotus-Climax
1966	Brabham-Repco
1967	Brabham-Repco
1968	Lotus-Ford
1969	Matra-Ford
1970	Lotus-Ford
1971	Tyrrell-Ford
1972	Lotus-Ford
1973	Lotus-Ford
1974	McLaren-Ford
1975	Ferrari
1976	Ferrari
1977	Ferrari
1978	Lotus-Ford
1979	Ferrari
1980	Williams-Ford
1981	Williams-Ford
1982	Ferrari
1983	Ferrari
1984	McLaren-TAG
1985	McLaren-TAG
1986	Williams-Honda
1987	Williams-Honda
1988	McLaren-Honda
1989	McLaren-Honda

WORLD DRIVERS' CHAMPIONSHIP WINNER AND RUNNER-UP

YEAR	DRIVER	WINS	CAR	SECOND PLACE
1950	Farina	3	Alfa Romeo	Fangio
1951	Fangio	3	Alfa Romeo	Ascari
1952	Ascari	6	Ferrari	Farina
1953	Ascari	5	Ferrari	Fangio
1954	Fangio	6	Maserati/ Mercedes-Benz	Gonzales
1955	Fangio	4	Mercedes	Moss
1956	Fangio	3	Ferrari	Moss
1957	Fangio	4	Maserati	Moss
1958	Hawthorn	1	Ferrari	Moss
1959	Brabham	2	Cooper	Brooks
1960	Brabham	5	Cooper	McLaren
1961	Hill	2	Ferrari	von Trips
1962	Hill	4	BRM	Clark
1963	Clark	7	Lotus	Hill
1964	Surtees	2	Ferrari	Hill
1965	Clark	6	Lotus	Hill
1966	Brabham	4	Brabham	Surtees
1967	Hulme	2	Brabham	Brabham
1968	Hill	3	Lotus	Stewart
1969	Stewart	6	Matra	Ickx
1970	Rindt	5	Lotus	Ickx
1971	Stewart	6	Tyrrell	Peterson
1972	Fittipaldi	5	Lotus	Stewart
1973	Stewart	5	Tyrrell	Fittipaldi
1974	Fittipaldi	3	McLaren	Reggazoni
1975	Lauda	5	Ferrari	Fittipaldi
1976	Hunt	6	McLaren	Lauda
1977	Lauda	3	Ferrari	Scheckter
1978	Andretti	6	Lotus	Peterson
1979	Scheckter	3	Ferrari	Villeneuve
1980	Jones	5	Williams	Piquet
1981	Piquet	3	Brabham	Reutemann
1982	Rosberg	1	Williams	Watson
1983	Piquet	3	Brabham	Prost
1984	Lauda	5	McLaren	Prost
1985	Prost	5	McLaren	Alboreto
1986	Prost	4	McLaren	Mansell
1987	Piquet	3	Williams	Mansell
1988	Senna	8	McLaren	Prost
1989	Prost	4	McLaren	Senna

Alain Prost in his McLaren on his way to winning the 1989 French GP at Paul Ricard, one of four wins in his third Championship-winning season

LE MANS 24 HOURS RESULTS 1923–1989

1923

PLACE	DRIVERS	CAR
1	Lagache/Leonard	Chenard & Walcker
2	Bachmann/Dauvergne	Chenard & Walcker
3	de Tornaco/Gros	Bignan

Winning average 57.21mph/92.04km/h

1924

PLACE	DRIVERS	CAR
1	Duff/Clement	Bentley
2	Stoffel/Brisson	La Lorraine
3	de Courcelles/Rossignol	La Lorraine

Winning average 53.78mph/86.53km/h

1925

PLACE	DRIVERS	CAR
1	de Courcelles/Rossignol	La Lorraine
2	Chassagne/Davis	Sunbeam
3	Stalter/Brisson	La Lorraine

Winning average 57.84mph/93.06km/h

1926

PLACE	DRIVERS	CAR
1	Bloch/Rossignol	La Lorraine
2	de Courcelles/Mongin	La Lorraine
3	Stalter/Brisson	La Lorraine

Winning average 66.08mph/106.33km/h

1927

PLACE	DRIVERS	CAR
1	Benjafield/Davis	Bentley
2	de Victor/Hasley	Salmson
3	Desveaux/Vallon	SCAP

Winning average 61.35mph/98.72km/h

1928

PLACE	DRIVERS	CAR
1	Barnato/Rubin	Bentley
2	Brisson/Bloch	Stutz
3	Stoffel/Rossignol	Chrysler

Winning average 69.11mph/111.20km/h

1929

PLACE	DRIVERS	CAR
1	Barnato/Birkin	Bentley
2	Dunfee/Kidston	Bentley
3	Benjafield/d'Erlanger	Bentley

Winning average 73.63mph/118.47km/h

1930

PLACE	DRIVERS	CAR
1	Barnato/Kidston	Bentley
2	Clement/Watney	Bentley
3	Lewis/Eaton	Talbot

Winning average 75.88mph/122.08km/h

1931

PLACE	DRIVERS	CAR
1	Howe/Birkin	Alfa Romeo
2	Ivanowski/Stoffel	Mercedes-Benz
3	Rose-Richards/ Saunders-Davis	Talbot

Winning average 78.13mph/125.71km/h

1932

PLACE	DRIVERS	CAR
1	Sommer/Chinetti	Alfa Romeo
2	Cortese/Guidotti	Alfa Romeo
3	Lewis/Rose-Richards	Talbot

Winning average 76.48mph/123.06km/h

1933

PLACE	DRIVERS	CAR
1	Sommer/Nuvolari	Alfa Romeo
2	Chinetti/Varent	Alfa Romeo
3	Lewis/Rose-Richards	Talbot

Winning average 81.40mph/130.97km/h

1934

PLACE	DRIVERS	CAR
1	Chinetti/Etancelin	Alfa Romeo
2	Sebilleau/Delaroche	Riley
3	Dixon/Paul	Riley

Winning average 74.74mph/120.26km/h

1935

PLACE	DRIVERS	CAR
1	Hindmarsh/Fontes	Lagonda
2	Helde/Stoffel	Alfa Romeo
3	Martin/Brackenbury	Aston Martin

Winning average 77.85mph/125.26km/h

1936

Not held

1937

PLACE	DRIVERS	CAR
1	Wimille/Benoist	Bugatti
2	Paul/Mongin	Delahaye
3	Dreyfus/Stoffel	Delahaye

Winning average 85.13mph/136.97km/h

1938

PLACE	DRIVERS	CAR
1	Chaboud/Tremoulet	Delahaye
2	Seraud/ Giraud-Cabantous	Delahaye
3	Prenant/Morel	Lago-Talbot

Winning average 82.36mph/132.51km/h

1939

PLACE	DRIVERS	CAR
1	Wimille/Veyron	Bugatti
2	Gerard/Monneret	Delage
3	Dobson/Brackenbury	Lagonda

Winning average 86.86mph/139.75km/h

1940–1948

Not held

1949

PLACE	DRIVERS	CAR
1	Chinetti/Lord Selsdon	Ferrari
2	Louveau/Joyer	Delage
3	Culpan/Aldington	Frazer-Nash

Winning average 82.28mph/132.40km/h

1950

PLACE	DRIVERS	CAR
1	Rosier/Rosier	Lago-Talbot
2	Meyrat/Mairesse	Lago-Talbot
3	Allard/Cole	Allard

Winning average 89.71mph/144.35km/h

1951

PLACE	DRIVERS	CAR
1	Whitehead/Walker	Jaguar
2	Meyrat/Mairesse	Lago-Talbot
3	Macklin/Thompson	Aston Martin

Winning average 93.50mph/150.43km/h

1952

PLACE	DRIVERS	CAR
1	Lang/Riess	Mercedes-Benz
2	Helfrich/Niedermayr	Mercedes-Benz
3	Johnson/Wisdom	Nash-Healey

Winning average 96.67mph/155.54km/h

1953

PLACE	DRIVERS	CAR
1	Rolt/Hamilton	Jaguar
2	Moss/Walker	Jaguar
3	Walters/Fitch	Cunningham

Winning average 105.82mph/170.30km/h

1954

PLACE	DRIVERS	CAR
1	Gonzalez/Trintignant	Ferrari
2	Rolt/Hamilton	Jaguar
3	Spear/Johnson	Cunningham

Winning average 105.13mph/169.19km/h

1955

PLACE	DRIVERS	CAR
1	Hawthorn/Bueb	Jaguar
2	Collins/Frere	Aston Martin
3	Claes/Swaters	Jaguar

Winning average 107.05mph/172.28km/h

1956

PLACE	DRIVERS	CAR
1	Flockhart/Sanderson	Jaguar
2	Moss/Collins	Aston Martin
3	Gendebien/Trintignant	Ferrari

Winning average 104.47mph/168.08km/h

1957

PLACE	DRIVERS	CAR
1	Flockhart/Bueb	Jaguar
2	Sanderson/Lawrence	Jaguar
3	Lucas/'Jean Marie'	Jaguar

Winning average 113.83mph/183.18km/h

1958

PLACE	DRIVERS	CAR
1	Hill/Gendebien	Ferrari
2	Whitehead/Whitehead	Aston Martin
3	Herrmann/Behra	Porsche

Winning average 106.18mph/170.88km/h

1959

PLACE	DRIVERS	CAR
1	Salvadori/Shelby	Aston Martin
2	Trintignant/Frere	Aston Martin
3	'Buerlys'/'Elde'	Ferrari

Winning average 112.55mph/181.13km/h

LE MANS 24 HOURS RESULTS 1923–1989

1960

PLACE	DRIVERS	CAR
1	Gendebien/Frere	Ferrari
2	Pilette/Rodriguez	Ferrari
3	Clark/Salvadori	Aston Martin

Winning average 109.17mph/175.69km/h

1961

1	Gendebien/Hill	Ferrari
2	Mairesse/Parkes	Ferrari
3	Guichet/Noblet	Ferrari

Winning average 115.88mph/186.48km/h

1962

PLACE	DRIVERS	CAR
1	Gendebien/Hill	Ferrari
2	Guichet/Noblet	Ferrari
3	'Beurlys'/'Elde'	Ferrari

Winning average 115.22mph/185.42km/h

1963

1	Bandini/Scarfiotti	Ferrari
2	'Buerlys'/Langlois	Ferrari
3	Parkes/Maglioli	Ferrari

Winning average 118.08mph/190.02km/h

1964

PLACE	DRIVERS	CAR
1	Guichet/Vaccarella	Ferrari
2	Hill/Bonnier	Ferrari
3	Surtees/Bandini	Ferrari

Winning average 121.54mph/195.59km/h

1965

1	Gregory/Rindt	Ferrari
2	Dumay/Gosselin	Ferrari
3	Mairesse/'Beurlys'	Ferrari

Winning average 121.07mph/194.83km/h

1966

1	McLaren/Amon	Ford
2	Miles/Hulme	Ford
3	Bucknum/Hutcherson	Ford

Winning average 125.37mph/201.75km/h

1967

1	Foyt/Gurney	Ford
2	Scarfiotti/Parkes	Ferrari
3	Mairesse/'Beurlys'	Ferrari

Winning average 135.46mph/217.99km/h

1968

1	Rodriguez/Bianchi	Ford
2	Steinemann/Spoerry	Porsche
3	Stommelen/Neerpasch	Porsche

Winning average 115.27mph/185.50km/h

1969

1	Ickx/Oliver	Ford
2	Herrmann/Larrousse	Porsche
3	Hobbs/Hailwood	Ford

Winning average 129.38mph/208.20km/h

1970

1	Herrmann/Attwood	Porsche
2	Larrousse/Hauhsen	Porsche
3	Lins/Marko	Porsche

Winning average 119.28mph/191.95km/h

1971

1	van Lennep/Marko	Porsche
2	Attwood/Muller	Porsche
3	Posey/Adamowicz	Ferrari

Winning average 138.13mph/222.25km/h

1972

1	Hill/Pescarolo	Matra-Simca
2	Cevert/Ganley	Matra-Simca
3	Jost/Weber/Casoni	Porsche

Winning average 121.45mph/195.41km/h

1973

1	Pescarolo/Larrousse	Matra-Simca
2	Merzario/Pace	Ferrari
3	Jaussaud/Jabouille	Matra-Simca

Winning average 125.67mph/202.20km/h

The Jaguars keep close company during the round of the 1989 World Sports Car Championship at Dijon

1974

PLACE	DRIVERS	CAR
1	Pescarolo/Larrousse	Matra-Simca
2	Muller/van Lennep	Porsche
3	Jabouille/Migault	Matra-Simca

Winning average 119.27mph/191.91km/h

1975

PLACE	DRIVERS	CAR
1	Bell/Ickx	Gulf-Cosworth
2	Lafosse/Chasseuil	Ligier-Cosworth
3	Schuppan/Jaussaud	Gulf-Cosworth

Winning average 118.98mph/191.44km/h

1976

PLACE	DRIVERS	CAR
1	Ickx/van Lennep	Porsche
2	Lafosse/Migault	Mirage-Cosworth
3	de Cadenet/Craft	Lola-Porsche

Winning average 123.49mph/198.70km/h

1977

PLACE	DRIVERS	CAR
1	Ickx/Barth/Haywood	Porsche
2	Schuppan/Jarier	Mirage-Cosworth
3	Ballot-Lena/Gregg	Porsche

Winning average 120.95mph/194.61km/h

1978

PLACE	DRIVERS	CAR
1	Pironi/Jaussaud	Renalt-Alpine
2	Wollek/Ickx/Barth	Porsche
3	Joest/Gregg/Haywood	Porsche

Winning average 130.60mph/210.19km/h

1979

PLACE	DRIVERS	CAR
1	Whittington/Ludwig/ Whittington	Porsche
2	Stommelen/Barbour/ Newman	Porsche
3	Ferrier/Servanin/ Trisconi	Porsche

Winning average 108.10mph/173.93km/h

1980

PLACE	DRIVERS	CAR
1	Rondeau/Jaussaud	Rondeau-Cosworth
2	Ickx/Joest/Leclere	Porsche
3	Spice/Martin/Martin	Rondeau-Cosworth

Winning average 119.23mph/191.84km/h

1981

PLACE	DRIVERS	CAR
1	Ickx/Bell	Porsche
2	Haran/Schlesser/Streiff	Rondeau-Cosworth
3	Spice/Migault	Rondeau-Cosworth

Winning average 124.94mph/201.06km/h

1982

PLACE	DRIVERS	CAR
1	Ickx/Bell	Porsche
2	Mass/Schuppan	Porsche
3	Haywood/Hobert/Barth	Porsche

Winning average 126.85mph/204.13km/h

1983

PLACE	DRIVERS	CAR
1	Schuppan/Haywood/ Holbert	Porsche
2	Ickx/Bell	Porsche
3	Andretti Snr/Alliot/ Andretti Jnr	Porsche

Winning average 130.70mph/210.33km/h

1984

PLACE	DRIVERS	CAR
1	Ludwig/Pescarolo	Porsche
2	Henn/Paul Jnr/Rondeau	Porsche
3	Hobbs/Streiff/ van der Merwe	Porsche

Winning average 126.88mph/204.18km/h

1985

PLACE	DRIVERS	CAR
1	Ludwig/Barilla/Winter	Porsche
2	Palmer/Lloyd/Weaver	Porsche
3	Bell/Stuck	Porsche

Winning average 131.75mph/212.02km/h

1986

PLACE	DRIVERS	CAR
1	Stuck/Bell/Holbert	Porsche
2	Larrauri/Gouhier/Pareja	Porsche
3	Follmer/Morton/Miller	Porsche

Winning average 128.75mph/207.20km/h

1987

PLACE	DRIVERS	CAR
1	Bell/Stuck/Holbert	Porsche
2	Lassig/Yver/de Dryver	Porsche
3	Raphanel/Regout/ Courage	Porsche

Winning average 124.06mph/199.66km/h

1988

PLACE	DRIVERS	CAR
1	Lammers/Dumfries/ Wallace	Jaguar
2	Stuck/Bell/Ludwig	Porsche
3	Winter/Jelinski/Dickens	Porsche

Winning average 137.75mph/221.67km/h

1989

PLACE	DRIVERS	CAR
1	Mass/Reuter/Dickens	Sauber Mercedes
2	Baldi/Acheson/ Brancatelli	Sauber Mercedes
3	Stuck/Wolleck	Porsche

Winning average 136.70mph/219.99km/h

WORLD SPORTS CAR DRIVERS' CHAMPIONSHIP WINNERS

YEAR	DRIVER
1981	Bob Garretson (USA)
1982	Jacky Ickx (Belgium)
1983	Jacky Ickx (Belgium)
1984	Stefan Bellof (W Germany)
1985	Derek Bell (GB)
1986	Derek Bell (GB)
1987	Raul Boesel (Brazil)
1988	Martin Brundle (GB)
1989	Jean-Louis Schlesser (France)

WORLD SPORTS CAR MANUFACTURERS' CHAMPIONSHIP WINNERS

YEAR	MANUFACTURERS
1953	Ferrari
1954	Ferrari
1955	Mercedes-Benz
1956	Ferrari
1957	Ferrari
1958	Ferrari
1959	Aston Martin
1960	Ferrari
1961	Ferrari
1962	–
1963	–
1964	–
1965	–
1966	–
1967	–
1968	Ford
1969	Porsche
1970	Prosche
1971	Porsche
1972	Ferrari
1973	Matra-Simca
1974	Matra-Simca
1975	Alfa Romeo
1976	Porsche
1977	Porsche
1978	Porsche
1979	Porsche
1980	Lancia
1981	Porsche
1982	Porsche
1983	Porsche
1984	Porsche
1985	Rothmans-Porsche
1986	Brun Motorsport
1987	Silk Cut Jaguar
1988	Silk Cut Jaguar
1989	Sauber Mercedes

MILLE MIGLIA RESULTS 1927–1957

1927

PLACE	DRIVERS	CAR
1	Minoia/Morandi	OM
2	Danieli/Balestrero	OM
3	Danieli/Rosa	OM

Winning average 47.99mph/77.22km/h

1928

PLACE	DRIVERS	CAR
1	Campari/Ramponi	Alfa Romeo
2	Mazotti/Rosa	OM
3	Strazza/Varallo	Lancia

Winning average 52.27mph/84.10km/h

1929

PLACE	DRIVERS	CAR
1	Campari/Ramponi	Alfa Romeo
2	Morandi/Rosa	OM
3	Varzi/Colombo	Alfa Romeo

Winning average 55.73mph/89.67km/h

1930

PLACE	DRIVERS	CAR
1	Nuvolari/Guidotti	Alfa Romeo
2	Varzi/Canavesi	Alfa Romeo
3	Campari/Marinoni	Alfa Romeo

Winning average 62.42mph/100.43km/h

1931

PLACE	DRIVERS	CAR
1	Caracciola/Sebastian	Mercedes Benz
2	Campari/Marinoni	Alfa Romeo
3	Morandi/Rosa	OM

Winning average 62.85mph/101.13km/h

1932

PLACE	DRIVERS	CAR
1	Borzacchini/Bignami	Alfa Romeo
2	Brivio/Trossi	Alfa Romeo
3	Scarfiotti/d'Ippolito	Alfa Romeo

Winning average 68.28mph/109.86km/h

1933

PLACE	DRIVERS	CAR
1	Nuvolari/Compagnoni	Alfa Romeo
2	Castelbarco/Cortese	Alfa Romeo
3	Taruffi/Pellegrini	Alfa Romeo

Winning average 67.46mph/108.54km/h

1934

PLACE	DRIVERS	CAR
1	Varzi/Bignami	Alfa Romeo
2	Nuvolari/Siena	Alfa Romeo
3	Chiron/Rosa	Alfa Romeo

Winning average 71.03mph/114.29km/h

1935

PLACE	DRIVERS	CAR
1	Pintacuda/della Stufa	Alfa Romeo
2	Tadini/Chiari	Alfa Romeo
3	Battaglia/Tuffanelli	Alfa Romeo

Winning average 71.30mph/114.72km/h

1936

PLACE	DRIVERS	CAR
1	Brivio/Ongaro	Alfa Romeo
2	Farina/Meazza	Alfa Romeo
3	Pintacuda/Stefani	Alfa Romeo

Winning average 75.57mph/121.59km/h

1937

PLACE	DRIVERS	CAR
1	Pintacuda/Mambelli	Alfa Romeo
2	Farina/Meazza	Alfa Romeo
3	Schell/Carriere	Delahaye

Winning average 71.30mph/114.72km/h

1938

PLACE	DRIVERS	CAR
1	Biondetti/Stefani	Alfa Romeo
2	Pintacuda/Mambelli	Alfa Romeo
3	Dusio/Boninsegni	Alfa Romeo

Winning average 84.13mph/135.37km/h

1939

PLACE	DRIVERS	CAR
1	Boratto/Sanesi	Alfa Romeo
2	Biondetti/Monzani	Alfa Romeo
3	Pintacuda/Mambelli	Alfa Romeo

Winning average 87.86mph/141.37km/h

1940

PLACE	DRIVERS	CAR
1	von Hanstein/Baumer	BMW
2	Farina/Mambelli	Alfa Romeo
3	Brudes/Rosese	BMW

Winning average 103.60mph/166.69km/h

1941–1946

Not held

1947

PLACE	DRIVERS	CAR
1	Biondetti/Romano	Alfa Romeo
2	Nuvolari/Carena	Cisitalia
3	Bernabei/Pacini	Cisitalia

Winning average 68.63mph/110.43km/h

1948

PLACE	DRIVERS	CAR
1	Biondetti/Navone	Ferrari
2	Compirato/Dumas	Fiat
3	Apruzzi/Apruzzi	Fiat

Winning average 75.16mph/120.93km/h

1949

PLACE	DRIVERS	CAR
1	Biondetti/Salani	Ferrari
2	Bonetto/Carpani	Ferrari
3	Rol/Richiero	Alfa Romeo

Winning average 81.53mph/131.18km/h

1950

PLACE	DRIVERS	CAR
1	Marzotto/Crosara	Ferrari
2	Serafini/Salani	Ferrari
3	Fangio/Zanardi	Alfa Romeo

Winning average 76.79mph/123.56km/h

1951

PLACE	DRIVERS	CAR
1	Villoresi/Cassani	Ferrari
2	Bracco/Maglioli	Lancia
3	Scotti/Ruspaggiari	Ferrari

Winning average 75.52mph/121.51km/h

1952

PLACE	DRIVERS	CAR
1	Bracco/Rolfo	Ferrari
2	Kling/Klenk	Mercedes-Benz
3	Fagioli/Borghi	Lancia

Winning average 79.90mph/128.56km/h

1953

PLACE	DRIVERS	CAR
1	Marzotto/Crosara	Ferrari
2	Fangio/Sala	Alfa Romeo
3	Bonetto/Peruzzi	Lancia

Winning average 88.45mph/142.32km/h

1954

PLACE	DRIVERS	CAR
1	Ascari	Lancia
2	Marzotto	Ferrari
3	Musso/Zocca	Maserati

Winning average 86.77mph/139.61km/h

1955

PLACE	DRIVERS	CAR
1	Moss/Jenkinson	Mercedes-Benz
2	Fangio	Mercedes-Benz
3	Maglioli	Ferrari

Winning average 97.96mph/157.62km/h

1956

PLACE	DRIVERS	CAR
1	Castellotti	Ferrari
2	Collins/Klementaski	Ferrari
3	Musso	Ferrari

Winning average 85.40mph/137.41km/h

1957

PLACE	DRIVERS	CAR
1	Taruffi	Ferrari
2	von Trips	Ferrari
3	Gendebien/Wascher	Ferrari

Winning average 94.84mph/152.60km/h

TARGA FLORIO RESULTS 1906–1973

1906

PLACE	DRIVER	CAR
1	A. Cagno	Itala
2	E. Graziana	Itala
3	P. Bablot	Berliet

Winning average 29.18mph/46.95km/h

1907

PLACE	DRIVER	CAR
1	F. Nazzaro	Fiat
2	V. Lancia	Fiat
3	M. Fabry	Itala

Winning average 33.50mph/53.90km/h

1908

PLACE	DRIVER	CAR
1	V. Trucco	Isotta-Fraschini
2	V. Lancia	Fiat
3	M. Ceirano	SPA

Winning average 35.46mph/57.06km/h

1909

PLACE	DRIVER	CAR
1	R. Ciuppa	SPA
2	V. Florio	Fiat
3	G. Airoldi	Lancia

Winning average 33.79mph/54.37km/h

1910

PLACE	DRIVER	CAR
1	F. Cariolato	Franco
2	L. de Prosperis	Sigma

Winning average 29.38mph/47.27km/h

1911

PLACE	DRIVER	CAR
1	E. Ceirano	SCAT
2	M. Cortese	Lancia
3	B. Soldatenkoff	Mercedes

Winning average 29.08mph/46.79km/h

1912

PLACE	DRIVER	CAR
1	C. Snipe	SCAT
2	Garetto	Lancia
3	G. Giordano	Fiat

Winning average 27.62mph/44.44km/h

1913

PLACE	DRIVER	CAR
1	F. Nazarro	Nazarro
2	G. Marsaglia	Aquila-Italiana
3	A. Mariani	De Vecchi

Winning average 33.78mph/54.35km/h

1914

PLACE	DRIVER	CAR
1	E. Ceirano	SCAT
2	A. Mariani	De Vecchi
3	L. Lopez	Fiat

Winning average 36.08mph/58.05km/h

1915–1918

Not held

1919

PLACE	DRIVER	CAR
1	A. Boillot	Peugeot
2	A. Moriendo	Itala
3	D. Gamboni	Diatto

Winning average 34.19mph/55.01km/h

1920

PLACE	DRIVER	CAR
1	G. Meregalli	Nazarro
2	E. Ferrari	Alfa Romeo
3	L. Lopez	Darracq

Winning average 31.74mph/51.07km/h

1921

PLACE	DRIVER	CAR
1	G. Masetti	Fiat
2	M. Sailer	Mercedes
3	G. Campari	Alfa Romeo

Winning average 36.19mph/58.23km/h

1922

PLACE	DRIVER	CAR
1	G. Masetti	Mercedes
2	J. Goux	Ballot
3	G. Foresti	Ballot

Winning average 39.66mph/63.81km/h

1923

PLACE	DRIVER	CAR
1	U. Sivocci	Alfa Romeo
2	A. Ascari	Alfa Romeo
3	F. Minoia	Steyr

Winning average 36.77mph/59.16km/h

1924

PLACE	DRIVER	CAR
1	C. Werner	Mercedes
2	G. Masetti	Alfa Romeo
3	P. Bordino	Fiat

Winning average 41.02mph/66.00km/h

1925

PLACE	DRIVER	CAR
1	B. Constantini	Bugatti
2	L. Wagner	Peugeot
3	A. Boillot	Peugeot

Winning average 44.50mph/71.60km/h

1926

PLACE	DRIVER	CAR
1	B. Constantini	Bugatti
2	F. Minoia	Bugatti
3	J. Goux	Bugatti

Winning average 45.68mph/73.50km/h

1927

PLACE	DRIVER	CAR
1	E. Materassi	Bugatti
2	B. Conelli	Bugatti
3	A. Maserati	Maserati

Winning average 44.61mph/71.78km/h

1928

PLACE	DRIVER	CAR
1	A. Divo	Bugatti
2	G. Campari	Alfa Romeo
3	C. Conelli	Bugatti

Winning average 45.65mph/73.45km/h

1929

PLACE	DRIVER	CAR
1	A. Divo	Bugatti
2	F. Minoia	Bugatti
3	G. Brilli-Peri	Alfa Romeo

Winning average 46.21mph/74.35km/h

1930

PLACE	DRIVER	CAR
1	A. Varzi	Alfa Romeo
2	L. Chiron	Bugatti
3	C. Conelli	Bugatti

Winning average 48.48mph/78.00km/h

1931

PLACE	DRIVER	CAR
1	T. Nuvolari	Alfa Romeo
2	B. Borzacchini	Alfa Romeo
3	A. Varzi	Bugatti

Winning average 40.29mph/64.83km/h

1932

PLACE	DRIVER	CAR
1	T. Nuvolari	Alfa Romeo
2	B. Borzacchini	Alfa Romeo
3	L. Chiron/A. Varzi	Bugatti

Winning average 49.27mph/79.28km/h

1933

PLACE	DRIVER	CAR
1	A. Brivio	Alfa Romeo
2	R. Balestrero	Alfa Romeo
3	G. Carraroli	Alfa Romeo

Winning average 47.56mph/76.52km/h

1934

PLACE	DRIVER	CAR
1	A. Varzi	Alfa Romeo
2	N. Barbieri	Alfa Romeo
3	G. Magistri	Alfa Romeo

Winning average 43.01mph/69.20km/h

1935

PLACE	DRIVER	CAR
1	A. Brivio	Alfa Romeo
2	L. Chiron	Alfa Romeo
3	N. Barbieri	Maserati

Winning average 49.18mph/79.13km/h

1936

PLACE	DRIVER	CAR
1	G. Magistri	Lancia
2	S. di Pietro	Lancia
3	'Gladio'	Lancia

Winning average 41.69mph/67.08km/h

1937

PLACE	DRIVER	CAR
1	F. Severi	Maserati
2	G. Lurani	Maserati
3	E. Bianco	Maserati

Winning average 41.58mph/66.92km/h

1938

PLACE	DRIVER	CAR
1	G. Rocco	Maserati
2	G. Ralph	Maserati
3	L. Villoresi	Maserati

Winning average 44.13mph/71.02km/h

TARGA FLORIO RESULTS 1906–1973

1939

PLACE	DRIVERS	CAR
1	L. Villoresi	Maserati
2	P. Taruffi	Maserati
3	N. Barbieri	Maserati

Winning average 52.68mph/84.78km/h

1940

PLACE	DRIVERS	CAR
1	L. Villoresi	Maserati
2	F. Cortese	Maserati
3	G. Rocco	Maserati

Winning average 54.94mph/88.41km/h

1941–1947

Not held

1948

PLACE	DRIVERS	CAR
1	C. Biondetti/ I. Troubetskoy	Ferrari
2	P. Taruffi/M. Rabia	Cisitalia
3	Macchieraldo/M. Savio	Cisitalia

Winning average 55.50mph/89.30km/h

1949

PLACE	DRIVERS	CAR
1	C. Biondetti/P. Benedetti	Ferrari
2	F. Rol/A. Richiero	Alfa Romeo
3	G. Rocco/R. Prete	AMP

Winning average 51.29mph/82.53km/h

1950

PLACE	DRIVERS	CAR
1	F. Bornigia/M. Bornigia	Alfa Romeo
2	I. Bernabei/N. Pacini	Ferrari
3	S. LaMotta/R. Altiero	Ferrari

Winning average 53.87mph/86.68km/h

1951

PLACE	DRIVERS	CAR
1	F. Cortese	Frazer Nash
2	F. Cornacchia/G. Bracco	Ferrari
3	I. Bernabei/N. Pacini	Maserati

Winning average 45.57mph/73.32km/h

1952

PLACE	DRIVERS	CAR
1	F. Bonetto	Lancia
2	L. Valenzano	Lancia
3	E. Anselmi	Lancia

Winning average 49.70mph/79.97km/h

1953

PLACE	DRIVERS	CAR
1	U. Maglioli	Lancia
2	E. Giletti	Maserati
3	S. Mantovani/ J. M. Fangio	Maserati

Winning average 50.10mph/80.61km/h

1954

PLACE	DRIVERS	CAR
1	P. Taruffi	Lancia
2	L. Musso	Maserati
3	R. Prioli	Lancia

Winning average 55.85mph/89.96km/h

1955

PLACE	DRIVERS	CAR
1	S. Moss/P. Collins	Mercedes-Benz
2	J. M. Fangio/K. Kling	Mercedes-Benz
3	E. Castellotti/R. Manzon	Ferrari

Winning average 59.60mph/95.90km/h

1956

PLACE	DRIVERS	CAR
1	U. Maglioli/ H. von Hanstein	Porsche
2	P. Taruffi	Maserati
3	O. Gendebien/ H. Herrmann	Ferrari

Winning average 56.37mph/90.70km/h

1957

Not held

1958

PLACE	DRIVERS	CAR
1	L. Musso/O. Gendebien	Ferrari
2	J. Behra/G. Scarlatti	Porsche
3	W. von Trips/ M. Hawthorn	Ferrari

Winning average 58.91mph/94.79km/h

1959

PLACE	DRIVERS	CAR
1	E. Barth/W. Seidel	Porsche
2	E. Mahle/H. Linge/ P. Strahle	Porsche
3	A. Pucci/H. von Hanstein	Porsche

Winning average 56.74mph/91.29km/h

INDIANAPOLIS 500 WINNERS 1911–1989

1911

PLACE	DRIVER	CAR
1	R. Harroun/C. Patschke	Marmon
2	R. Mulford	Lozier
3	D. Bruce-Brown	Fiat

Winning average 74.59mph/120.02km/h

1912

PLACE	DRIVER	CAR
1	J. Dawson/D.Herr	National
2	E. Teztlaff/C. Bragg	Fiat
3	H. Hughes	Mercer

Winning average 78.72mph/126.66km/h

1913

PLACE	DRIVER	CAR
1	J. Goux	Peugeot
2	S. Wishart/R. de Palma	Mercer
3	C. Merz/E. Cooper	Stutz

Winning average 75.93mph/122.17km/h

1914

PLACE	DRIVER	CAR
1	R. Thomas	Delage
2	A. Duray	Peugeot
3	A. Guyot	Delage

Winning average 82.47mph/132.69km/h

1915

PLACE	DRIVER	CAR
1	R. de Palma	Mercedes
2	D. Resta	Peugeot
3	G. Anderson	Stutz

Winning average 89.84mph/144.55km/h

1916

PLACE	DRIVER	CAR
1	D. Resta	Peugeot
2	W. d'Alene	Duesenberg
3	R. Mulford	Peugeot

Winning average 84.00mph/135.16km/h

1917–1918

Not held

1919

PLACE	DRIVER	CAR
1	H. Wilcox	Peugeot
2	E. Hearne	Durant-Stutz
3	J. Goux	Peugeot

Winning average 88.05mph/141.67km/h

1920

PLACE	DRIVER	CAR
1	G. Chevrolet	Monroe-Frontenac
2	R. Thomas	Ballot
3	T. Milton	Duesenberg

Winning average 88.62mph/142.59km/h

1921

PLACE	DRIVER	CAR
1	T. Milton	Frontenac
2	R. Sarles	Duesenberg
3	P. Ford/J. Ellingboe	Frontenac

Winning average 89.62mph/144.20km/h

1922

PLACE	DRIVER	CAR
1	J. Murphy	Duesenberg-Miller
2	H. C. Hartz	Duesenberg
3	E. Hearne	Ballot

Winning average 94.48mph/152.02km/h

1923

PLACE	DRIVER	CAR
1	T. Milton/H. Wilcox	Miller
2	H. C. Hartz	Miller
3	J. Murphy	Miller

Winning average 90.95mph/146.34km/h

1960

PLACE	DRIVERS	CAR
1	J. Bonnier/H. Herrmann	Porsche
2	W. von Trips/P. Hill	Ferrari
3	O. Gendebien/ H. Herrmann	Porsche

Winning average 59.24mph/95.32km/h

1961

PLACE	DRIVERS	CAR
1	W. von Trips/ O. Gendebien	Ferrari
2	D. Gurney/J. Bonnier	Porsche
3	E. Barth/H. Herrmann	Porsche

Winning average 64.27mph/103.41km/h

1962

PLACE	DRIVERS	CAR
1	W. Mairesse/ P. Rodriguez/ O. Gendebien	Ferrari
2	G. Baghetti/L. Bandini	Ferrari
3	N. Vaccarella/J. Bonnier	Porsche

Winning average 63.47mph/102.12km/h

1963

PLACE	DRIVERS	CAR
1	J. Bonnier/C. M. Abate	Porsche
2	L. Bandini/L. Scarfiotti/ W. Mairesse	Ferrari
3	H. Linge/E. Barth	Porsche

Winning average 64.57mph/103.89km/h

1964

PLACE	DRIVERS	CAR
1	C. Davis/A. Pucci	Porsche
2	H. Linge/G. Balzarini	Porsche
3	R. Bussinello/N. Todaro	Alfa Romeo

Winning average 62.28mph/100.21km/h

1965

PLACE	DRIVERS	CAR
1	N. Vaccrella/L. Bandini	Ferrari
2	C. Davis/G. Mitter	Porsche
3	U. Maglioli/H. Linge	Porsche

Winning average 63.70mph/102.49km/h

1966

PLACE	DRIVERS	CAR
1	W. Mairesse/H. Muller	Porsche
2	G. Baghetti/J. Guichet	Ferrari
3	A. Pucci/V. Arena	Porsche

Winning average 61.47mph/98.91km/h

1967

PLACE	DRIVERS	CAR
1	P. Hawkins/ R. Stommelen	Porsche
2	L. Cella/G. Biscaldi	Porsche
3	J. Neerpasch/V. Elford	Porsche

Winning average 67.61mph/108.78km/h

1968

PLACE	DRIVERS	CAR
1	V. Elford/U. Maglioli	Porsche
2	N. Galli/I. Giunti	Alfa Romeo
3	M. Casoni/L. Bianchi	Alfa Romeo

Winning average 69.04mph/111.09km/h

1969

PLACE	DRIVERS	CAR
1	G. Mitter/U.Schutz	Porsche
2	V. Elford/U. Maglioli	Porsche
3	H. Herrmann/ R. Stommelen	Porsche

Winning average 72.99mph/117.44km/h

1970

PLACE	DRIVERS	CAR
1	J. Siffert/B. Redman	Porsche
2	P. Rodriguez/L. Kinnunen	Porsche
3	N. Vaccarella/I. Giunti	Ferrari

Winning average 74.66mph/120.15km/h

1971

PLACE	DRIVERS	CAR
1	N. Vaccarella/ T. Hezemans	Alfa Romeo
2	A. de Adamich/ G. van Lennep	Alfa Romeo
3	J. Bonnier/R. Attwood	Lola

Winning average 74.61mph/120.06km/h

1972

PLACE	DRIVERS	CAR
1	A. Merzario/S. Munari	Ferrari
2	H. Marko/N. Galli	Alfa Romeo
3	T. Hezemans/ A. de Adamich	Alfa Romeo

Winning average 76.15mph/122.54km/h

1973

PLACE	DRIVERS	CAR
1	H. Muller/G. van Lennep	Porsche
2	S. Munari/J. C. Andruet	Lancia
3	L. Kinnunen/C. Haldi	Porsche

Winning average 71.27mph/114.69km/h

1924

PLACE	DRIVER	CAR
1	L. Corum/J. Boyer	Duesenberg
2	E. Cooper	Studebaker-Miller
3	J. Murphy	Miller

Winning average 98.23mph/158.05km/h

1925

PLACE	DRIVER	CAR
1	P. de Paolo/N. K. Batten	Duesenberg
2	D. N. Lewis/B. Hill	Miller
3	P. Shafer/W. Morton	Duesenberg

Winning average 101.13mph/162.72km/h

1926

PLACE	DRIVER	CAR
1	F. Lockhart	Miller
2	H. C. Hartz	Miller
3	C. Woodbury	Miller

Winning average 95.91mph/154.32km/h

1927

PLACE	DRIVER	CAR
1	G. Souders	Duesenberg
2	E. Devore/Z. Myers	Miller
3	A. Gulotta/P. de Paolo	Miller

Winning average 97.54mph/156.95km/h

1928

PLACE	DRIVER	CAR
1	L. Meyer	Miller
2	L. Moore/L. Schneider	Miller
3	G. Souders	Miller

Winning average 99.48mph/160.06km/h

1929

PLACE	DRIVER	CAR
1	R. Keech	Miller
2	L. Meyer	Miller
3	J. Gleason/F. Triplett	Duesenberg

Winning average 97.59mph/157.01km/h

1930

PLACE	DRIVER	CAR
1	W. Arnold	Miller
2	W. Cantion	Miller
3	L. Schneider	Miller

Winning average 100.45mph/161.62km/h

1931

PLACE	DRIVER	CAR
1	L. Schneider	Miller
2	F. Frame	Duesenberg
3	R. Hepburn/R. Kreis	Miller

Winning average 96.63mph/155.48km/h

1932

PLACE	DRIVER	CAR
1	F. Frame	Miller
2	W. Wilcox	Miller
3	C. Bergere	Studebaker

Winning average 104.14mph/167.56km/h

1933

PLACE	DRIVER	CAR
1	L. Meyer	Miller
2	W. Shaw	Miller
3	L. Moore	Miller

Winning average 104.16mph/167.59km/h

1934

PLACE	DRIVER	CAR
1	B. Cummings	Miller
2	M. Rose	Miller
3	L. Moore	Miller

Winning average 104.86mph/168.43km/h

1935

PLACE	DRIVER	CAR
1	K. Petillo	Miller
2	W. Shaw	Miller
3	B. Cummings	Miller

Winning average 106.24mph/170.94km/h

INDIANAPOLIS 500 WINNERS 1911–1989

1936

PLACE	DRIVER	CAR
1	L. Meyer	Miller
2	T. Horn	Miller
3	D. Mackenzie/K. Petillo	Miller

Winning average 109.07mph/175.49km/h

1937

PLACE	DRIVER	CAR
1	W. Shaw	Gilmore-Offenhauser
2	R. Hepburn	Miller
3	T. Horn	Miller

Winning average 113.58mph/182.75km/h

1938

PLACE	DRIVER	CAR
1	F. Roberts	Miller
2	W. Shaw	Offenhauser
3	C. Miller	Offenhauser

Winning average 117.20mph/188.57km/h

1939

PLACE	DRIVER	CAR
1	W. Shaw	Maserati
2	J. Snyder	Thorne-Sparks
3	C. Bergere	Offenhauser

Winning average 115.04mph/185.07km/h

1940

PLACE	DRIVER	CAR
1	W. Shaw	Maserati
2	R. Mays	Bowes Seal Fast
3	M. Rose	Miller

Winning average 114.82mph/183.86km/h

1941

PLACE	DRIVER	CAR
1	F. Davis/M. Rose	Nock-Out Hose Clamp
2	R. Mays	Bowes Seal Fast
3	T. Horn	Thorne-Sparks

Winning average 115.12mph/185.23km/h

1942–1945

Not held

1946

PLACE	DRIVER	CAR
1	G. Robson	Thorne-Sparks
2	J. Jackson	Offenhauser
3	T. Horn	Maserati

Winning average 114.82mph/184.75km/h

1947

PLACE	DRIVER	CAR
1	M. Rose	Blue Crown
2	W. Holland	Blue Crown
3	T. Horn	Maserati

Winning average 116.34mph/187.19km/h

1948

PLACE	DRIVER	CAR
1	M. Rose	Blue Crown
2	W. Holland	Blue Crown
3	D. Nalon	Novi

Winning average 119.81mph/192.77km/h

1949

PLACE	DRIVER	CAR
1	W. Holland	Blue Crown
2	J. Parson	Kurtis-Kraft
3	G. Conner	Blue Crown

Winning average 121.33mph/195.22km/h

1950

PLACE	DRIVER	CAR
1	J. Parsons	Wynn's Friction Proof
2	W. Holland	Blue Crown
3	M. Rose	Howard Keck

Winning average 124.00mph/199.52km/h

1951

PLACE	DRIVER	CAR
1	L. Wallard	Belanger
2	M. Nazaruk	Robbins
3	J. McGrath/M. Ayulo	Hinkle

Winning average 126.24mph/203.12km/h

1952

PLACE	DRIVER	CAR
1	T. Ruttman	Agajanian
2	J. Rathmann	Grancor-Wynn
3	S. Hanks	Bardahl

Winning average 128.92mph/207.43km/h

1953

PLACE	DRIVER	CAR
1	W. Vokovich	Fuel Injection
2	A. Cross	Springfield Welding
3	S. Hanks/D. Carter	Bardahl

Winning average 128.74mph/207.14km/h

1954

PLACE	DRIVER	CAR
1	W. Vukovich	Fuel Injection
2	J. Bryan	Dean Van Lines
3	J. McGrath	Hinkle

Winning average 130.84mph/210.52km/h

1955

PLACE	DRIVER	CAR
1	B. Sweikert	John Zink
2	T. Bettenhausen/ P. Russo	Chapman
3	J. Davies	Bardahl

Winning average 128.21mph/206.29km/h

1956

PLACE	DRIVER	CAR
1	P. Flaherty	John Zink
2	S. Hanks	Jones & Maley
3	D. Freeland	Bob Estes

Winning average 128.49mph/206.74km/h

1957

PLACE	DRIVER	CAR
1	S. Hanks	Belond Exhaust
2	J. Rathmann	Chiropractic
3	J. Bryan	Dean Van Lines

Winning average 135.60mph/218.18km/h

1958

PLACE	DRIVER	CAR
1	J. Bryan	Belond Exhaust
2	G. Amick	Demler
3	J. Boyd	Bowes Seal Fast

Winning average 133.79mph/215.27km/h

1959

PLACE	DRIVER	CAR
1	R. Ward	Leader Caro
2	J. Rathmann	Simoniz
3	J. Thomson	Racing Associates

Winning average 135.86mph/218.60km/h

1960

PLACE	DRIVER	CAR
1	J. Rathmann	Ken Paul
2	R. Ward	Leader Card
3	P. Goldsmith	Demler

Winning average 138.77mph/223.28km/h

1961

PLACE	DRIVER	CAR
1	A. J. Foyt	Bowes Seal Fast
2	E. Sachs	Dean Van Lines
3	R. Ward	Del Webb Sun City

Winning average 139.13mph/223.86km/h

1962

PLACE	DRIVER	CAR
1	R. Ward	Leader Card
2	L. Sutton	Leader Card
3	E. Sachs	Dean Autolite

Winning average 140.29mph/225.73km/h

1963

PLACE	DRIVER	CAR
1	A. P. Jones	Agajanian
2	J. Clark	Lotus
3	A. J. Foyt	Thompson

Winning average 143.14mph/230.31km/h

1964

PLACE	DRIVER	CAR
1	A. J. Foyt	Sheraton
2	R. Ward	Kaiser
3	L. Ruby	Forbes

Winning average 147.35mph/237.09km/h

1965

PLACE	DRIVER	CAR
1	J. Clark	Lotus
2	A. P. Jones	Lotus
3	M. Andretti	Brawner

Winning average 150.69mph/242.46km/h

1966

PLACE	DRIVER	CAR
1	G. Hill	Lola
2	J. Clark	Lotus
3	J. McElreath	Brabham

Winning average 144.33mph/232.24km/h

1967

PLACE	DRIVER	CAR
1	A. J. Foyt	Coyote
2	A. Unser	Lola
3	J. Leonard	Coyote

Winning average 151.21mph/243.30km/h

1968

PLACE	DRIVER	CAR
1	R. Unser	Rislone
2	D. Gurney	Eagle
3	M. Kenyon	Gerhardt

Winning average 152.88mph/245.98km/h

1969

PLACE	DRIVER	CAR
1	M. Andretti	Hawk
2	D. Gurney	Eagle
3	R. Unser	Lola

Winning average 156.86mph/252.40km/h

1970

PLACE	DRIVER	CAR
1	A. Unser	Johnny Lightning
2	M. Donohue	Lola
3	D. Gurney	Eagle

Winning average 155.70mph/250.60km/h

1971

PLACE	DRIVER	CAR
1	A. Unser	Colt
2	P. Revson	McLaren
3	A. J. Foyt	Coyote

Winning average 157.73mph/253.79km/h

1972

PLACE	DRIVER	CAR
1	M. Donohue	McLaren
2	A. Unser	Parnelli
3	J. Leonard	Parnelli

Winning average 162.96mph/262.20km/h

1973

PLACE	DRIVER	CAR
1	G. Johncock	Eagle
2	W. Vukovich	Eagle
3	R. McCluskey	McLaren

Winning average 159.04mph/255.90km/h

1974

PLACE	DRIVER	CAR
1	J. Rutherford	McLaren
2	B. Unser	Eagle
3	W. Vukovich	Eagle

Winning average 158.59mph/255.17km/h

1975

PLACE	DRIVER	CAR
1	R. Unser	Eagle
2	J. Rutherford	McLaren
3	A. J. Foyt	Coyote

Winning average 149.21mph/240.08km/h

1976

PLACE	DRIVER	CAR
1	J. Rutherford	McLaren
2	A. J. Foyt	Coyote
3	G. Johncock	Wildcat

Winning average 148.73mph/238.28km/h

1977

PLACE	DRIVER	CAR
1	A. J. Foyt	Coyote
2	T. Sneva	McLaren
3	A. Unser	Parnelli

Winning average 161.33mph/259.58km/h

1978

PLACE	DRIVER	CAR
1	A. Unser	Lola
2	T. Sneva	Penske
3	G. Johncock	Wildcat

Winning average 161.36mph/259.63km/h

1979

PLACE	DRIVER	CAR
1	R. Mears	Penske
2	A. J. Foyt	Parnelli
3	M. Moseley	Eagle

Winning average 158.90mph/255.64km/h

1980

PLACE	DRIVER	CAR
1	J. Rutherford	Chaparral
2	T. Sneva	McLaren
3	G. Bettenhausen	Wildcat

Winning average 142.86mph/229.86km/h

1981

PLACE	DRIVER	CAR
1	R. Unser	Penske
2	M. Andretti	Wildcat
3	V. Schuppan	McLaren

Winning average 139.08mph/222.78km/h

1982

PLACE	DRIVER	CAR
1	G. Johncock	Wildcat
2	R. Mears	Penske
3	P. Carter	March

Winning average 162.02mph/260.69km/h

1983

PLACE	DRIVER	CAR
1	T. Sneva	March
2	A. Unser	Penske
3	R. Mears	Penske

Winning average 162.11mph/260.83km/h

1984

PLACE	DRIVER	CAR
1	R. Mears	March
2	R. Guerrero	March
3	A. Unser	March

Winning average 163.61mph/263.25km/h

1985

PLACE	DRIVER	CAR
1	D. Sullivan	March
2	M. Andretti	Lola
3	R. Guerrero	March

Winning average 152.98mph/246.14km/h

1986

PLACE	DRIVER	CAR
1	B. Rahal	March
2	K. Cogan	March
3	R. Mears	March

Winning average 170.72mph/274.69km/h

1987

PLACE	DRIVER	CAR
1	A. Unser	March
2	R. Guerrero	March
3	F. Barbazza	March

Winning average 162.16mph/260.92km/h

1988

PLACE	DRIVER	CAR
1	R. Mears	Penske
2	E. Fittipaldi	March
3	A. Unser	Penske

Winning average 144.81mph/233.00km/h

1989

PLACE	DRIVER	CAR
1	E. Fittipaldi	Penske
2	A. Unser Jnr	Lola
3	R. Boesel	Lola

Winning average 167.58mph/268.12km/h

USAC INDY CAR NATIONAL CHAMPIONS

YEAR	DRIVER
1950	Henry Banks
1951	Tony Bettenhausen
1952	Chuck Stevenson
1953	Sam Hanks
1954	Jimmy Bryan
1955	Bob Sweikert
1956	Jimmy Bryan
1957	Jimmy Bryan
1958	Tony Bettenhausen
1959	Rodger Ward
1960	A. J. Foyt
1961	A. J. Foyt
1962	Rodger Ward
1963	A. J. Foyt
1964	A. J. Foyt
1965	Mario Andretti
1966	Mario Andretti
1967	A. J. Foyt
1968	Bobby Unser
1969	Mario Andretti
1970	Al Unser
1971	Joe Leonard
1972	Joe Leonard
1973	Roger McCluskey
1974	Bobby Unser
1975	A. J. Foyt
1976	Gordon Johncock
1977	Tom Sneva
1978	Tom Sneva
1979	A. J. Foyt

CART CHAMPIONS

YEAR	DRIVER
1979	Rick Mears
1980	Johnny Rutherford
1981	Rick Mears
1982	Rick Mears
1983	Al Unser Snr
1984	Mario Andretti
1985	Al Unser Snr
1986	Bobby Rahal
1987	Bobby Rahal
1988	Danny Sullivan
1989	Emerson Fittipaldi

Index

Figures in **bold type** refer to a main entry;
figures in *italic type* refer to an illustration.

Picture Credits

Action Plus: 146, 151. All Action: 144/5, 193, 244, 246. Allsport: 22/3, 43, 48/9, 56, 60/1, 71, 86/7, 90, 92, 93, 142, 143, 146, 148, 157, 163, 165, 166, 168, 169, 173, 174, 176, 178, 190/1, 193, 200/1, 244, 246. D. Burnett: 76, 96/7, 115, 124/5, 162, 184/5, 186/7. Classic Motoring Years: 8, 14/5, 16/7, 26, 27, 31, 39, 62, 63, 64, 65, 66/7, 68, 74, 88, 98, 100, 100/1, 104/5, 105, 112/3, 128, 130, 138/9, 140, 141, 147, 148, 149, 150, 152, 153, 154, 155, 157, 158, 160, 161, 163, 164, 167, 170, 171, 172, 176, 177, 179, 180, 194. Colorsport: 24/5, 50/1, 54/5, 68, 70, 129, 132/3, 205. Mary Evans Picture Library: 6/7. Fotosports: 2, 159. Chris Harvey: 88/9, 91, 94, 95, 134. Hulton Deutsch Collection: 158, 167, 179. London Art Technical: 19, 20, 28/9, 29, 30, 33, 34/5, 36/7, 38, 40/1, 44, 45, 52, 57, 68, 75, 80, 81, 83, 84/5, 91, 107, 111, 114/5, 116/7, 120/1, 123, 126/7, 135, 136/7, 142, 154, 156, 196/7, 206/7. Cyril Posthumus: 174, 175. Nigel Snowdon: 43, 47, 50/1, 58/9, 72/3, 77, 78/9, 131, 180, 181, 188, 191, 198/9, 202/3. Sporting Pictures (UK) Ltd: 182, 183. Quadrant Picture Library: 12, 102, 108/9, 110, 112, 139.

Artwork Credits

Grand Prix Circuit artwork supplied by Autosport, 60 Waldegrave Road, Teddington, Middlesex.